AF352635

Christopher Bruell

SUNY series in the Thought and Legacy of Leo Strauss

―――――――

Kenneth Hart Green, editor

Christopher Bruell

Essays of Five Decades on Philosophy and Philosophers

Edited by

ERIC BUZZETTI and DEVIN STAUFFER

Introduction by

JAMES W. GUEST II

EU GPSR Authorised Representative:
Logos Europe, 9 rue Nicolas Poussin, 17000, La Rochelle, France
contact@logoseurope.eu

For information, contact State University of New York Press, Albany, NY
www.sunypress.edu

Library of Congress Cataloging-in-Publication Data

Names: Bruell, Christopher, 1942–2024 author. | Buzzetti, Eric, 1969– , editor. | Stauffer, Devin, 1970– , editor.
Title: Christopher Bruell : essays of five decades on philosophy and philosophers / edited by Eric Buzzetti and Devin Stauffer.
Description: Albany : State University of New York Press, [2025] | Includes bibliographical references and index.
Identifiers: LCCN 2025012562 | ISBN 9798855804119 (hardcover : alk. paper) | ISBN 9798855804133 (ebook)
Subjects: LCSH: Political science—Philosophy | Philosophy, Ancient | Strauss, Leo | Bruell, Christopher, 1942–2024
Classification: LCC JC73 .B78 2025 | DDC 320.01—dc23/eng/20250430
LC record available at https://lccn.loc.gov/2025012562

Contents

Part VI. An Undelivered Lecture

Editors' Preface

Christopher Bruell was one of the few great thinkers of our time, but he remains largely unknown. He taught political philosophy in the Department of Political Science at Boston College for forty years, retiring as Professor Emeritus in 2010. Prior to his career at Boston College, he received his MA and PhD from the University of Chicago for work done under the supervision of Leo Strauss. He passed away on November 6, 2024. Because he was one of Strauss's finest students, it is appropriate for the SUNY series on the thought and legacy of Strauss to include a collection of his essays.

Anyone who had the good fortune to attend Bruell's graduate seminars at Boston College can attest to the brilliance of his mind and the depth of his thinking. His seminars focused primarily on the works of the great classical political philosophers, though he would occasionally devote a seminar to a modern thinker, such as Machiavelli or Spinoza, or a classical poet, such as Homer or Aristophanes. His teaching was a model of rigor and philosophic seriousness. He interpreted texts with a penetration and insight none of us had witnessed before, and his students were transformed by the experience of studying with him. Bruell led us to see not only the enduring relevance of classical political philosophy, but the unrivaled power of the exploration by the classics of questions of fundamental human importance: What is justice? What are the possibilities and limits of politics? What is the best way of life? In the course of time, Bruell's teaching became the stuff of legend in a small but distinguished circle of scholars of political philosophy. Many of his students have become noted scholars who teach at leading colleges and universities.

The present collection includes almost all the essays, lectures, and book chapters Bruell published during a scholarly career that spanned more than four decades.[1] Five of these writings focus on Strauss himself. But the scope of the collection extends well beyond Bruell's work on Strauss. The essays take up a wide range of topics, including liberal education, the problem of relativism, the American Founding, the nature of citizenship, and the question of happiness. Above all, the collection focuses on the recovery of classical political philosophy and includes several pathbreaking essays on Thucydides, Plato, Xenophon, and Aristotle. These essays are a peak of classical scholarship. Although his work has never received the attention it deserves, Bruell was one of the great modern interpreters of classical political philosophy. The essays collected here are more immediately accessible than his two books—*On the Socratic Education* (1999) and *Aristotle as Teacher* (2014)—which are quite challenging, each in its own way. It is our hope that the present volume will serve as an introduction to Bruell's thought and make more people aware of his remarkable work. The essay by James Guest, included here at Bruell's request, will help in both regards.

A short preface is not the place to attempt an extensive comparison of Bruell's thought with that of Strauss. But a few words may help to orient those who would like to make the comparison for themselves. Bruell's work would not have been possible without the pioneering efforts of his great teacher. But in his studies of classical political philosophy, Bruell approached the classical texts in his own way, focusing above all on discovering and following the central thread of the argument of each work. In his extraordinary book on Plato, *On the Socratic Education*, Bruell treats, among many other dialogues, some that were also treated in writing by Strauss (*Minos, Euthydemus, Euthyphro, Apology of Socrates,* and *Crito*). Those who compare Bruell's interpretations with Strauss's will find similarities of substance as well as method, but a close comparison will also reveal notable differences. In addition to forging his own path, Bruell extended Strauss's legacy in a necessary direction. Strauss often said that philosophy is the quest for wisdom about the whole, and that

---

1. Three papers have not been republished here: "Introduction," in *Xenophon, Memorabilia,* translated and annotated by Amy L. Bonnette, Cornell University Press, 1994, pp. vii–xxii; "Foreword" to Leo Strauss *Xenophon's Socratic Discourse* and to Leo Strauss *Xenophon's Socrates,* St. Augustine's Press, 2004, pp. ix–xviii and x–xviii; and "Thucydides and Perikles," *The St. John's Review,* Vol. XXXII, No. 3, Summer 1981, pp. 24–29. The decision not to republish these three papers was made by Bruell. A bibliography of his works (both published and unpublished) is included at the end of James Guest's introduction.

political philosophy is therefore a mere part of philosophy as such. By and large, however, Strauss himself limited his own scholarship to political philosophy. The recovery of classical political philosophy, which required the detailed study of many modern thinkers alongside the ancient ones, was the central task of his life's work. Strauss thereby laid the foundation for a return to philosophy in the full and original sense of the word. Bruell, by contrast, after a career spent teaching the great works of political philosophy, spent the last two and a half decades of his life studying Aristotle's natural philosophy and some of its leading modern alternatives. Although most of the essays included in this collection have previously appeared in print, the volume contains a recent lecture, never before published, in which Bruell develops a set of "Theses" bearing on the proper understanding of Aristotle's natural science.[2] That lecture is the culmination of Bruell's magisterial effort to grasp and articulate Aristotle's thought on nature, an effort that includes an exploration of the basis of any genuine science of nature. Written by a man who himself deserves to be called a philosopher, that lecture alone, to say nothing of the other essays in the collection, should make this volume of special importance to those interested in what it means to live a philosophic life and what is required for the restoration of genuine philosophy.

Eric Buzzetti, Concordia University (Montréal)
Devin Stauffer, University of Texas at Austin
December 30, 2024

---

2. See chapter 18. Another lecture included in this volume that has not been previously published is "What Xenophon Learned from Socrates about Philosophy and the Philosophic Life" (chapter 17). The essay "Death in the Perspective of Philosophy" (chapter 15) was published before in a German translation and appears here for the first time in the English original.

Acknowledgments

Chapter 1 was published as "Liberal Education and Education for Citizenship," in *The Recovery of American Education: Reclaiming a Vision*, ed. Stephen M. Krason, University Press of America, 1991, pp. 75–86.

Chapter 2 was published as "On Reading Plato Today," in *Political Philosophy and the Human Soul*, eds. Thomas Pangle and Michael Palmer, Rowman & Littlefield, 1995, pp. 95–108. The original lecture that became the published essay was delivered at Kenyon College in November 1991.

Chapter 3 was published as "Plato and Relativism," in *Enlightening Revolutions*, ed. Svetozar Minkov, Lexington Books, 2006, pp. 309–18. The original lecture that became the published essay was delivered at Middlebury College on October 1, 2001.

Chapter 4 was published as "Thucydides' View of Athenian Imperialism," in *American Political Science Review*, Vol. LXVIII, No. 1, March 1974, pp. 11–17.

Chapter 5 was published as "Socratic Politics and Self-knowledge: An Interpretation of Plato's *Charmides*," in *Interpretation, A Journal of Political Philosophy*, Vol. 6/3, October 1977, pp. 141–203.

Chapter 6 was published as "On the Original Meaning of Political Philosophy: An Interpretation of Plato's *Lovers*," in *The Roots of Political Philosophy*, ed. Thomas Pangle, Cornell University Press, 1987, pp. 91–110. An earlier version of the essay was given as a lecture at St. John's College, Annapolis, on October 17, 1980.

Chapter 7 was published as "Strauss on Xenophon's Socrates," in *The Political Science Reviewer*, Vol. XIV, Fall 1984, pp. 262–318.

Chapter 8 was published as "A Return to Classical Political Philosophy and the Understanding of the American Founding," in *Leo Strauss: Political Philosopher and Jewish Thinker*, eds. Kenneth L. Deutsch and Walter N.

Nicgorski, Rowman & Littlefield, 1993, pp. 325–38. The original paper that became the published essay was given at a conference on Classical Theory and Practice and the American Founding, John M. Olin Center for Inquiry into the Theory and Practice of Democracy, the University of Chicago, June 16–18, 1988.

Chapter 9 was published as "True Esotericism," in *Gladly to Learn and Gladly to Teach: Essays in Honor of Ernest L. Fortin A. A.*, eds. Michael P. Foley and Douglas Kries, Lexington Books, 2002, pp. 271–76. The original paper that became the published essay was given at a conference on Ernest Fortin and the Revival of Christian Political Philosophy, Boston College, October 25, 1997.

Chapter 10 was published as "On the Place of the Treatment of Classical Philosophy in the Plan of the Work as a Whole," in *Klesis, Revue Philosophique*, Vol. 19, 2011, pp. 85–91. The original paper that became the published essay was given at a conference on Leo Strauss's *Natural Right and History*, Michigan State University, April 20, 2001.

Chapter 11 was published as "The Question of Nature and the Thought of Leo Strauss," in *Klesis, Revue Philosophique*, Vol. 19, 2011, pp. 92–101. The original paper that became the published essay was given at a conference on Living Issues in the Thought of Leo Strauss, Carl Friedrich von Siemens Foundation, Munich, June 18, 2002.

Chapter 12 was published as "Xenophon," in *History of Political Philosophy*, 3rd edition, eds. Leo Strauss and Joseph Cropsey, University of Chicago Press, 1987, pp. 90–117. A lecture based on the published essay was delivered in the series "Politische Philosophie" at the Carl Friedrich von Siemens Foundation, Munich, July 11, 1988. The essay itself was republished, in slightly enlarged and revised form, in German translation as *Xenophons Politische Philosophie* (Munich: Carl Friedrich von Siemens Foundation, 1990; 2nd printing 1994). It is volume 48 in the series "Themen."

Chapter 13 was published as "On Plato's Political Philosophy," in *The Review of Politics*, Vol. 56, No. 2, Spring 1994, pp. 261–82. The original lecture that became the published essay was delivered in the series "Politische Philosophie" at the Carl Friedrich von Siemens Foundation, Munich, July 3, 1995. A version of the lecture was also given at St. John's College, Santa Fe, on February 18, 1994.

Chapter 14 was published as "Aristotle on Theory and Practice," in *Political Philosophy Cross-Examined*, eds. Thomas L. Pangle and J. Harvey Lomax, Palgrave Macmillan, 2013, pp. 17–28. Reproduced with permission of the Licensor through PLSclear. The original lecture that became the published essay was delivered at the École des Hautes Études en Sciences Sociales, Paris, April 2006. The lecture was titled "Aristotle on Theory and Practice: Part One." Christopher Bruell chose not to publish "Aristotle on Theory and Practice: Part Two," a different lecture delivered at the same venue on the same occasion.

Chapter 15 was published in German translation as "Der Tod aus der Sicht der Philosophie" in *Der Tod im Leben*, eds. Friedrich Wilhelm Graf and Heinrich Meier, Piper Verlag, 2004, pp. 201–20. The original lecture that became the published German essay was delivered at the Carl Friedrich von Siemens Foundation, Munich, July 17, 2003. It was the keynote lecture in the series "Der Tod im Leben."

Chapter 16 was published as "Happiness in the Perspective of Philosophy," in *Recovering Reason*, ed. Timothy Burns, Lexington Books, 2010, pp. 147–59. It was also published in German translation as "Das Glück aus der Sicht der Philosophie," in *Über das Glück*, ed. Heinrich Meier, Piper Verlag, 2008, 2nd edition 2010, pp. 253–71. The original lecture that became the published German essay was delivered at the Carl Friedrich von Siemens Foundation, Munich, July 12, 2007. It was the keynote lecture in the series "Über das Glück."

Chapter 17 was the E. L. Wiegand Visiting Lecture, St. John's College, Santa Fe, New Mexico, and Thomas Aquinas College, Santa Paula, California, November 10 and 17, 2000.

Chapter 18 was prepared for delivery at the Carl Friedrich von Siemens Foundation, Munich, October 18, 2021, but could not be given.

~

We wish to thank the editors and copyright holders of the above-mentioned works for their permission to republish.

We also thank Michael P. Foley, Douglas Kries, and Heinrich Meier for information regarding the various lectures. Above all, our deepest gratitude is to Marjorie Bruell for taking on the task of typing the entire manuscript.

A Note on the Manuscript

We reproduce here the previously published essays of Christopher Bruell as they appeared in the originals. This means that we have not edited the essays in any way except for correcting a few clerical errors (we supply missing italics, for example, and we correct typographical errors, though we preserve unusual spellings and punctuation). Nor have we removed or sought to harmonize minor formatting variations among the essays. On p. 235 we did introduce one change. The phrase "follows immediately the confrontation [in Chapter XII]" was changed to "follows immediately the confrontation [in Chapter XI]." The error in the original publication of the passage is clear, though not easy to spot.

The entire manuscript was typed by Marjorie Bruell and reviewed by Christopher Bruell before his death. Minor clerical changes were made by Christopher Bruell himself and have not been noted. In essays 4 and 5, he transliterated words and phrases that originally appeared in Greek. He also chose the order in which the essays are presented, the headings of the six parts, and the title of the collection.

Introduction

Socratic Educations:
On the Writings of Christopher Bruell

James W. Guest II

Are We Open to Education?

The titles of the only two books published by Christopher Bruell are revealing: *On the Socratic Education* (1999) and *Aristotle as Teacher* (2014). Bruell has made a concentrated effort to understand the *education* that may be available to us in the works of the classical political philosophers and the way their authors, as *teachers*, have approached their task. His oeuvre is marked above all by the clarity and depth of insight it evinces in uncovering, posing, and pursuing elementary questions: What are we seeking from a genuine education? What are the qualities of heart and mind required of those who would seek it? What obstacles stand in the way of genuine education, whether specific to our contemporary situation or persistent through the ages? What are the motivations and responsibilities of teachers, above all the greatest teachers who through their lives and work have helped to shape our world? In reading Bruell's work as a whole, we find an introduction to Socratic education that proceeds through three main stages: (1) a specific contemporary effort to recover the original starting point from which a genuinely Socratic education may begin; (2) an articulation of classical political philosophy, with special attention to how Socrates attempted to "turn" or educate others; and (3) an articulation of philosophic activity proper, understood as the pursuit of a philosophic science fully informed by Socrates' human wisdom.[1] After some preliminary remarks and cautions, it is this path that we will seek to explore with Bruell's writings as our guide.

Bruell's total volume of published work consists of his two books, fewer than two dozen essays, and some book reviews, produced during roughly four decades of teaching at Boston College (fall 1969 to fall 2008, retiring in 2010). The work displays a concentrated focus on classical political philosophy, broadly understood: two essays on Thucydides (TVAI, *TP*), two on Xenophon (XEN, *XHS*), five pieces (SPSK, OMPP, OPPP, ORPT, PR) and a book (*SE*) on Plato, and one essay (ATP) and a book (*AAT*) on Aristotle. Six pieces, generally related to classical political philosophy, explore the thought of Leo Strauss (SOXS, UAF, TE, ONRH, *FXS*, QNLS), with whom Bruell studied at the University of Chicago. This compact but demanding body of published work is rounded out by three papers that trace specific themes through different works, a very brief piece on liberalism, and a handful of book reviews (LEEC, DPP, HPP; TC; *RBG, AL, GPAI, CPW*).[2]

In his approach to texts, Bruell maintains that methodological issues must be regarded as secondary to the task of uncovering the elementary questions posed by the texts under consideration (SOXS 203), which in turn requires careful attention to the action or drama within the works (SPSK 128). To this end, his writings attend to the reticence of the "genuine philosophers" (*SE* 11.6, 144) and contain distilled, almost aphoristic, insights into how their difficult writings may be more profitably read. Two observations from *Aristotle as Teacher* are illustrative:

> [T]o understand, to appropriate a thought, if only to be in a position to judge for ourselves of its validity, is not merely to hear or read some expression of it. We must, rather, repeat the thought on our own. And therefore the adequate expression of it, which may have to be difficult or puzzling for just this

---

1. Bruell most tightly ties the term "Socratic education" to the section on education in Xenophon's *Memorabilia* IV. *On the Socratic Education* ties it more generally to an understanding of Socrates' education of others and of himself across a series of shorter Platonic dialogues. Bruell's look at contemporary obstacles and philosophic science in light of that understanding of Socratic education leads to my title: Socratic educations.

2. See the bibliography for my abbreviations of the titles. When citing an essay not included in this volume, I will italicize the abbreviation for the reader's convenience.

reason, will be designed to elicit such a repetition from us. (*AAT* 2)

The thoughts conveyed by a written work are not limited to those expressly stated in it. They include those to which an attentive reader of it may be led. A writer who is a master both of understanding and of expression will have anticipated those thoughts, and he may even have provided deliberate pointers to them. In that case, we readers may hope, by paying due regard to such pointers, to discern the direction of the path that he has already traversed and even to move some of the way along it. (*AAT* 83; see also 27)

Bruell's writing too evinces this sort of reserve. To give only one example: after observing Socrates' general aversion to reliance on claims about the gods or divine care for human beings, Bruell stresses that "we are concerned not merely with Socrates' views, but with how he established or proved those views" (SOXS 213; similarly, XEN2 409–10). Repeating the thought ourselves requires moving from some grasp of *the what* (the conclusion as stated or suggested) to *the why* (the reasons that adequately support the conclusion). Later, near one of the peaks of the same essay, Bruell writes: "A speaker or writer who understands his task to be the casting of seeds does not feel obliged, perhaps not even entitled, to elaborate his thought fully . . . ; he does or must content himself with letting the hints which he has planted, or their juxtaposition or order, lead the listener or reader to that elaboration on his own" (SOXS 240). Bruell recognizes Plato, Xenophon, Aristotle, and Strauss after them as writers of this sort.[3] In this light, perhaps the best way to show one's appreciation for Bruell's work would be to consider and test his suggestions, grapple with the questions he leaves unanswered, or complete the thoughts only partially articulated, by returning to the primary texts themselves. Many of those who studied with him—I am not among these—have written remarkable studies by doing just that. Yet anyone who has wrestled with

---

3. For Bruell's attention to the reserve characteristic of philosophic writers, see, for example, *AAT* 21 as well as 11, 26, 36, 38–39; SOXS 239, 253–54; *XHS* 299; XEN 320–21; *FXS* xiii–xiv; TVAI 93–94; OMPP 192–93, *SE* 11.6, 144). For something close to a self-characterization in this respect, but one in which he counsels us to read the primary texts for ourselves, see XEN2 412.

Bruell's own peculiar manner of writing might find evidence there too that "the most precise speech is not necessarily the most readily graspable" (*AAT* 2). Bruell himself is among the seed planters, and his body of work warrants an appreciation of its own.

One hastens to acknowledge that Bruell often appears to be tracing Strauss' footsteps. His writings do not explore every path cut by Strauss, but those he follows are better cleared on account of it. The education we are seeking to understand requires us to ask the question Strauss made central: What is the right way of life, the just or best way? In a late essay on "The Question of Nature and the Thought of Leo Strauss," Bruell raises sharp questions that forestall an easy acceptance of Strauss' claim that the philosophic life itself is somehow the answer.[4] Bruell focuses here too not merely on the answer as such but on the adequacy of one's path to it: "if philosophy itself, that is, the philosophic life, is to be regarded by us as the answer to the question of the right way of life, its claim to this effect must have been established by an inquiry that is, in principle, prior to our engaging in that life, or to our engaging in it from this point of view." Without this preparatory inquiry, it is hard to see how the "necessary inner freedom vis à vis philosophy's own most proper subject matter is otherwise to be won" (QNLS 289–90). He thus distinguishes (1) an inquiry establishing the desirability of philosophizing from (2) the activity of philosophizing proper. This distinction, it seems to me, roughly corresponds to the two books Bruell wrote: *On the Socratic Education* establishes the desirability of philosophizing by chiefly examining "the obstacle standing in the way of a genuine education" and the deepest purposes of Socrates' "turning speeches" or refutative activity (*SE* 14.1, 190); *Aristotle as Teacher* then supplies a demanding introduction to the character and subject matter of philosophizing proper or the presuppositions and limits of philosophic science. In my view, Bruell's most distinctive contribution to Strauss' recovery of classical political philosophy is his suggestion that Socratic education requires the former inquiry as preparation for the latter: political philosophy is preparatory for an adequately self-aware philosophic science.

Even if we are eager to pursue such an education and believe ourselves open to it, there are subtle and pervasive obstacles that stand in

---

4. E.g., Leo Strauss, *What Is Political Philosophy*, "On Classical Political Philosophy," 91: "the highest subject of political philosophy is the philosophic life: philosophy—not as a teaching or as a body of knowledge, but as a way of life—offers, as it were, the solution to the problem that keeps political life in motion."

the way of our attaining it. Our "openness" to education is thematic in Bruell's work. Each of our lives is ordinarily lived under the influence of one or more comprehensive outlooks. Even the most promising among us become, through disposition or nurture, more powerfully attached to certain convictions associated with those outlooks than to the quest for truth. Any quality human life is, for example, "never free from concern for the noble and the just," and consequently "we are dependent on the *belief* that we know what nobility and justice are" (*TP* 29, Bruell's emphasis; TVAI 94). Those beliefs are primarily, if not entirely, formed and inculcated, whether directly or indirectly, by the familial, political, or religious communities to which we belong. But what if the critical examination of just these attachments is *the* condition of a life well lived? (*SE* Preface) If so, one's very attachment to these beliefs would constitute an obstacle to the critical inquiry required to begin to convert mere opinions to knowledge.

> There are, it seems, certain opinions which are so precious to us that we wish to, and come to, regard them as knowledge, or perhaps divinations of the truth . . . , where we do not employ the awareness of the difference between knowing and opining which seems, otherwise, to be available to us. In those cases, apparently, we are not simply open to the truth or the question of our openness to the truth may be raised. It would be wrong however to conclude that this is because the truth is of no concern to us there: there could be no temptation to conceal what is of no concern to us. (SPSK 156)

The best interpreters of Plato know that reading the dialogues seriously means putting them to the test. Bruell takes a further step and wonders whether the dialogues are not also putting us to the test: do we, their readers, have the qualities of heart and mind required for a genuine education? (*SE* 3.1) If becoming aware of and questioning our attachments is an uphill battle even for the best of us, "openness" to genuine philosophic inquiry and to truth may be the result rather than a condition of the education we are seeking (TVAI 94; ORPT 68; contrast the contemporary, spurious form of openness in UAF 266–67). Genuinely philosophic writings, when read with the proper care, presumably supply the guidance we need to uncover and investigate typical assumptions. But there is another set of obstacles specific to our own time, all the more formidable (not to say more important) insofar as they work together to obstruct access to the older approach or approaches. In this and other ways, it becomes clear that apart from the specific subject matter of any given text, apart from the investigation of the character and content of what virtue or philosophy or the good life is, Bruell must focus on the character of readers and the contemporary assumptions they bring to the text. Whether or not we acknowledge them, our attachments color the kinds of questions we ask and limit the bounds of our inquiries. We must ask then whether the starting point from which Socrates began, the beliefs and concerns he could expect to encounter among promising students, are those with which we can begin today. The emergence of Biblical religion, the success of modern science and technology, the wide adoption of liberal democracy and even wider adoption of commercial economic orders, the critique and collapse of modern Enlightenment as a political and civilizational project: deep reflection on these more or less obvious differences between ancient and modern times is required as a condition of an adequate understanding of classical political philosophy.

This brief look at the question of our openness suggests that the direction of Bruell's thought about Socratic education can be summarized this way: the obstacles specific to our time require a recovery of political philosophy; and the education supplied by political philosophy in turn prepares the activity of philosophic science. To elaborate: (1) For those capable of genuine education, there is a specific effort required today to overcome obstacles unique to our own time before Socratic education can be recovered or understood on its own terms. Even if the questions of the classical political philosophers are the fundamental ones for human beings as such, Bruell acknowledges there have been historical developments, unforeseen by the ancient writers, that have obstructed our view of their approach to those questions (if not obscuring some questions altogether). (2) Having begun to come to grips with these obstacles and recovering to that extent an awareness of the classical (original) starting point, political philosophy first comes to sight as the education that Socrates provided to others. Bruell presents Socrates' exhortations and refutative activity as intended in part to bring about, in distinct stages, a turning around of the soul in good natures. (3) Philosophic science (philosophic activity proper or inquiry into nature), as distinct from political philosophy, subsequently emerges as the education that Socrates himself pursued and supplied to some few others or prepared them to acquire. Importantly, Bruell observes that Socrates' turn from his early investigation of natural science to his post-Delphic dialectical activity is not as complete or final as it is often thought to be. Socrates' dialectical activity, apart from its protreptic or "turning" function, has some bearing on the possibility and limits of philosophic science. Yet this philosophic science is distinct from pre-Socratic natural science insofar as it is both informed and limited by Socrates' human wisdom. Plato and Xenophon have left traces of Socrates' path for others to follow. But, as the Straussian metaphor has it, we must first find our way up from the cave beneath the cave to access that original path; then we must, aided by these guides, come to see the cave as a cave; and only then are we prepared to attempt to see the world and our place in it in whatever light is available to us. It is the elaboration of philosophic science in addition to the specific contemporary protreptics and engagement with the perennial questions of political philosophy, it seems to me, that distinguishes Bruell's work most from other notable students of Strauss, and perhaps to some extent even from Strauss himself. The familiar refrain that political philosophy is the core of the philosophic life need not mean political philosophy is the whole of the philosophic life.[5]

These three stages are not entirely distinct, and there are several reasons to be cautious in articulating them. With a view to the second stage in particular, there is a huge gulf between the above view and just about anything one finds in the Socratic scholarship of the last several centuries. Leo Strauss almost single-handedly saw to it that the literary character of Plato and Xenophon's dialogues can no longer be thoughtlessly dismissed. Bruell deepens the critique of developmentalist views of Plato, according to which apparent changes in the character and content of one dialogue compared with another reflect a change in Plato's own thought. Plato himself, of course, offers no indication that his understanding underwent a "progress" during the composition of the dialogues. What Plato does display is an interest in including enough details concerning time and place such that we are able to arrange many (if not all) dialogues in temporal sequences and relations. The clear temporal sequence of at least seven dialogues spanning *Theaetetus* through *Phaedo* contains works widely held to be from Plato's so-called early, middle, and late periods. If there were serious changes in his thought such that its presentation in one dialogue is, in the final analysis, incompatible with that of another, why would Plato go out of his way to link them so tightly and unmistakably together, or to display in them a Socrates wholly untroubled by any supposed dissonance? Now apart from the wider temporal sequence

---

5. The overall view sketched above is perhaps best introduced by ORPT, XEN, and XEN2.

of Platonic dialogues there are some dialogues which contain further temporal layers. The most complicated of these (*Phaedo, Parmenides*, and *Symposium*) have a "frame" that occurs at "present" time in direct dialogue, and a report (or report of a report) of a past conversation of Socrates. In each of these cases, we find accounts of Socrates' early life, accounts that bear on what is known as the Socratic Turn. This is the only change or progress in Socrates' thought to which Plato (or Xenophon) draws our attention (*CPW* 624 lower right; SOXS 225–26). But therein lies a difficulty. We can crudely put these passages together to produce an account like this: as a youth, Socrates took up and subsequently abandoned as hopeless both materialist natural science and teleological explanations of the whole; he proposed his own theory of separate Ideas, but, still a young man, he was thoroughly refuted by the great Parmenides (c. 450); Socrates then turned to the human things with particular attention to eros, under the tutelage, he claims, of the priestess Diotima (c. 440); and Socrates ultimately arrived at his eponymous form of inquiry and notorious refutative activity, making his public debut against Protagoras (c. 433, noting that Bruell thinks the private conversations with Alcibiades precede the gathering at Callias' house: *SE* 4.9).—Under very different dramatic circumstances, the *Apology of Socrates* provides a marvelously different account of the origin and aims of his refutative activity.—Yet the kind of youth Socrates reports himself as having been bears little resemblance to the young men he is shown to seek out as interlocutors. The paths down which he takes these noble youths differ markedly from his own first steps. Socrates turned from a certain sort of natural science to political philosophy; but he pursues, above all, politically ambitious youths. Where or how far he leads them is one part of the puzzle.—The Eleatics Simmias and Cebes, or the mathematicians Theaetetus and Young Socrates, may be exceptions of a sort; but the closest parallels to Socrates as a youth may be the unnamed boys in the *Lovers* who silently audit Socrates' conversation.—So just how is "the education he acquired himself" related to the education he "supplied to some others"? Or, as Bruell (also) offers, how is it that the education he provided also "prepared them to acquire" the education he himself acquired? (XEN 318; see also OMPP 191–93) Plato and Xenophon open the door to this dark room a crack, and Bruell gives it a push that lets some more light in.

A second reason for caution is that Plato and Xenophon have distinct ways of presenting the Socratic life. For our purposes, allow me to assert that Plato appeals to and makes moving use of the noble, the bold, the erotic, the mythic, the divine; Xenophon appeals to the moderate, the useful, the practical, and yet he is not without his own charms (see *XHS* 297–98). While both writers are ironic in the sense that they speak to more than one audience, the striking differences in approach hinder any attempt to map one picture of Socratic education cleanly onto the other. What sort of corrections, if any, need be made to the emphasis on nobility in Plato and on usefulness in Xenophon? How much more complicated is this problem if there are many paths, rather than one, through the stages of Socratic education? I am compelled to rely here on what Bruell says about Socrates as if there is, as I believe, no fundamental difference between Plato's and Xenophon's genuine understanding of Socrates, but I will make no attempt to prove this (see *FXS* xvii).

Third, Bruell has developed and perfected what one might call an art of prosaic unquotability. Bruell's writing is refreshingly free of idiosyncratic coinages, poetic playfulness, ostentatious cleverness. His writings sharply articulate fundamental questions, whether they begin with clear formulations of the problems and trace alternative solutions or work their way from the surface to the heart of a matter in more elliptical or guarded ways. Though Bruell seems less interested in serving up tasty *bons mots*, those with austere palates will find much to savor. To take one example, in "Happiness in the Perspective of Philosophy" Bruell matter-of-factly sums up his argument by stating that he "has attempted to establish such a link between the classical teaching on happiness and the classical moral teaching as amounts to the dependence of the former on the latter" (HPP 396–97). Anticipating that someone might find this conclusion "true but trivial," he offers the laconic response that this would be "a judgment with which I would not agree"; thereupon, he draws out a single "non-trivial" implication of his argument as to whether we can rightly call the philosophic life that breaks with that teaching a happy one. His other essays typically lack this kind of explicit direction; various important questions or indications of incompleteness are simply left standing. We have to think through the matters on our own in light of brief pointers (e.g., SOXS 243; OMPP 195; ATP 362). Unpacking seemingly dry remarks, carefully reviewing citations, noticing an occasional arch provocation, and rereading with a view to questions explicitly left open is a large part of reading his work well. Bruell allows the argument of texts to unfold without announcing his own judgments at every stage, and perhaps occasionally obscuring them. Consider that one of his most groundbreaking studies is an account of Strauss' account of Xenophon's account of Socrates' conversation with

Critobulous about a conversation Socrates had with Ischomachus decades earlier—absent a first-person pronoun, attributing specific claims therein to Bruell himself is, to say the least, hazardous. And Bruell's first-person remarks are exceedingly rare. While the contexts of the claims I quote are of obvious importance, I cannot even begin to do justice to each context here.[6] One who attempts to survey demanding works written with extreme economy and nuance is bound to pay a price.

Contemporary Obstacles

Stepping back and speaking broadly, what kind of education do the greatest classical texts claim to provide? What are some few of us hoping to get out of reading books like these? Such works aim at "the formation of the best possible human being," or at leading "those capable of it to the discovery of truth, of those truths most important to human beings as such" (LEEC 51). The activity of Plato's Socrates, for example, first appears as a search for the knowledge we need to guide our lives, a search for the best way of life and the correct understanding of the world (*Protagoras* 361c–d; *Republic* 505a–e); Socrates begins from the good-natured assumption that the love of justice is an expression of our desire for our truest good (*Republic* 336e, 344e–345a, 352d). For his part, Thucydides claims that he has written the comprehensive and eternal truth of human or political life (I 20.3, 22.4). Today, some few readers might be eager to learn these things. Most others, however, approach works and claims of this kind with a "widely felt . . . though less widely acknowledged" objection (PR 79). The danger of an objection we merely feel, Bruell observes, is that we do not seek to test it. Without such testing, we cannot know, should the objection prove correct, that we ought not waste our time reading authors that have nothing of any importance to teach us; and, should it be incorrect, the presence of an unacknowledged and uninvestigated doubt robs us of the chance to read these works with sufficient seriousness. On the other hand, if we are not inclined toward contemporary doubts and we solicit the guidance of the ancients undaunted, it is nevertheless an

---

6. Consider that the preface to *On the Socratic Education* explicitly calls attention to the deliberate order of the exposition: the book has numbered paragraphs, several specific internal cross references, and an explicit warning to readers who might be tempted to jump to the heart of things in section III (*SE* viii).

intellectual flaw not to investigate the grounds of contemporary objections (PR 79–81). Further, even if we are inclined to believe that the questions addressed by Plato remain the fundamental questions confronting human beings everywhere and always, "developments not foreseen by him may have affected our awareness of the fundamental questions and hence our capacity to recognize and to comprehend his treatment of them" (ORPT 66; see also *SE* 14.1 190).[7] Bruell argues that since this is indeed our situation, it is necessary that we supplement our reading of Plato with attention to the special features of our own time.

The main historical developments will be familiar to readers of Strauss. In the ancient world, politics took its bearings by the omnipresent political struggle between freedom and empire. The deepest human longings concerning justice and injustice were given probing expression by the political philosophers without being permitted to influence ordinary politics too directly. Thucydides' *History* "[p]roperly used," for example, teaches us how human freedom is constrained by severe necessity in a manner that soberly educates our attachment to justice without breaking it. Similarly, while Aristotle's *Politics* attracts those who wish to know how they might "increase vastly the amount of virtue in the world," it nevertheless provides a "gentle but thorough and relentless account of the difficulties preventing the fulfillment" of that wish (LEEC 62). Sober moderation is the practical aim and effect of classical political philosophy. The Biblical religions, however, "brought more fully to light than ever before certain fundamental human longings and demands." They succeeded in "transforming political life root and branch" in ways the modern philosophers subsequently set out to resist or undo. According to a potent charge found in both Machiavelli and Rousseau, for example, political life was harmed by the pious cruelty Christian political orders used in attempts to implement the newly elevated standards; or, to the extent those standards were understood to be simply other-worldly, care for this-worldly political life waned in light of them, weakening citizens

---

7. To be clear, (1) certain obstacles specific to our time that prevent us from beginning a Socratic education are theoretically distinct from (2) other obstacles which prevent our completing that education under any circumstances even if, in our time, these two sources of obstruction work in concert. Similarly, (1) the earned openness to Socratic education is distinct from (2) the openness in which Socratic education results. I am inclined to say, then, that the kind of ground-clearing that belongs to the first stage is a species of political thought distinct from political philosophy proper.

and statesmen (QNLS 285–86). The Enlightenment thinkers, who were particularly concerned with how Biblical religion had augmented the fear of death, politicized philosophy in an attempt to remedy what they took to be the unprecedented political problems that emerged. Theory had to be engaged in a practical attempt to guide human beings back to what these modern philosophers took to be the sphere of our natural concerns (ONRH 282–83; also DPP 372–73, 375–76). In this protracted battle against Scholastic Aristotelity and other enemies, modern theory was remarkably effective. By Rousseau's time, "philosophy had destroyed the credibility of religion for much of educated Europe" (QNLS 285). Yet this enterprise resulted in a politics stripped of its former pretention to completeness. The new, limited goals lacked the highness and nobility of the older vision. On this and other grounds, doubts arose whether the victory of the Enlightenment project was deserved, escalating to a crisis of reason or of philosophy as such. (See also ATP 351–52 and ONRH in general.)

Bruell outlines the consequences of these developments along similarly familiar lines. The permissiveness of modern liberalism, for example, is more than once contrasted with the authoritative guidance that ancient regimes claimed to supply. The stance of modern liberalism implies that the natural concerns of human beings do not reach beyond the goods that we can procure for ourselves, goods such as the prevention of violent death or the attainment of "recognition." Modern liberalism, in its alleged openness to all opinions about how we should live as are compatible with public peace, puts its stamp on us regarding the order of human concerns and reveals its judgment in its silence regarding those opinions that, even today, flourish in non-liberal regimes and remain politically relevant in our own. (See *SE* 11.14, ORPT 76–78, QNLS 286–88, XEN 320–21 and ATP 351 for details on the shift effected by modern liberalism.) Bruell also takes up the influence of modern science, generally held to be "the only unquestioned authority of our age" (OMPP 179). The classical natural right teaching seems to depend on a teleological view of the universe or of man, but that view seems to have been destroyed by non-teleological modern natural science (ONRH 277–79, summarizing Strauss; ORPT 70–71). The subsequent attempt to model the study of human things on that powerfully transformative modern natural science gave rise to the allegedly "value-free" social sciences (OMPP 179, 195–96). Here too any pretension to knowledge of the right way of life is disavowed. The pitiable rump of political philosophy that has yet to bend the knee in modern political science departments sometimes highlights the shortcomings of methodological political science, yet it rarely even dreams of remedying them. Consequently, our time is characterized above all by omnipresent relativism, "the absence of a norm or standard of universal validity by which to guide our lives both individually and collectively" (QNLS 288); and also by historicism, the view that "all doctrines are tied fundamentally to a particular time and place," that "there can be no universal purposes or timeless truths" (UAF 256). In its most radical form, historicism wholly rejects philosophy "in the full sense of the term" on the grounds that philosophy presupposes the idea of nature, and nature has become "radically questionable" (QNLS 292; ONRH 279). The old Platonic assumption that knowledge is a good and necessary thing is "an assumption that we today *can* no longer make and *do* no longer make" (PR 81, Bruell's emphasis).[8] With respect to various fundamental matters, therefore, "a change *has* taken place in us" (HPP 393, my emphasis). Shaped by these developments, whether or not we ourselves are familiar with this centuries-long conversation (HPP 386), we do not come to the ancient texts with the set of concerns before us that their authors could or would have taken for granted. In these straits, Bruell contends that we can "work our way toward an emancipation from the intervening influences" of various kinds "*only* by *returning* to the most elementary questions" that are addressed in the ancient texts, returning "to the *true* beginning" (*GPAI* 169, my emphasis). The most elementary questions must be rediscovered.

The papers Bruell originally delivered to undergraduate audiences provide some examples of available paths to the elementary questions (e.g., ORPT and PR; and, from a different angle, OMPP). I offer three observations on Bruell's approach to contemporary obstacles with a view to our topic. First, the treatments of relativism (the academic locus of the so-called culture wars at the time of publication) contain the only remarks in his work that one might be tempted to describe as polemical. Relativism is "accepted with equanimity or even welcomed only by the most complacent or thoughtless among our contemporaries"; the way of life such contemporaries are

---

8. Bruell adds to this last remark: "not to say that we have rejected it entirely." Consideration of the grounds supporting this qualification is crucial to his examination of the cogency of the position. Compare the principle of the approach to the Athenians in *TP* 27: "we are obliged to accept their experience as authoritative with respect to the human good only if it is a genuine experience, that is, only if it is based on a clear view of themselves and of the object of their longing."

defending is "almost completely devoid of what makes a life most worth living"; liberal relativism frees us not from judgments about the good and the just, but only from "the inquiry and reflection on which any reasonable judgment is based"; neutral language about "value" and "commitment" is no more than a "cowardly" way to "hide from ourselves" the importance of such judgments; even a simple reflection on the inadequacy of the assertion that reasonable judgments of good and bad are impossible should lead anyone with even "a modicum of self-understanding" to turn to Plato with "mind and heart open and eager to learn" (see QNLS 288, *SE* Preface, ORPT 67 and 68). These rare barbs, it seems to me, serve a pedagogical purpose beyond the expression of Bruell's judgment. Readers already seeking to learn from classical texts are exhorted to press on against the climate of ideologically closed opinion; others unreflectively disposed to contemporary views may be provoked to wonder how Bruell might justify these spirited remarks and thereby come to appreciate something unexpected; unpromising individuals dogmatically committed to prevailing orthodoxy will be put off altogether and spared their time. More importantly, polemical language brings our moral concerns and attachments to the fore in ways studiously detached critical argumentation does not. This, we will see, plays a significant role in Socratic education.

Second, if intervening doctrines have produced in us the changes described, then getting clear on these matters is a necessary step toward self-knowledge. In leading readers back to the "true beginning," Bruell identifies ways in which we lack self-awareness by holding, sometimes simultaneously, unacknowledged hopes and fuzzy doubts. He discerns strong incentives to remain in that quasi-contented state, going so far as to suggest that we conceal from ourselves the character or implications of deeply held beliefs and concerns. The insistence that opinions about the good, noble, and just are sufficiently held by choice, for example, "serves only to blind one" to the necessity of an attempt to convert opinions about those subjects to knowledge (PR 86). Consider too how we speak about happiness. Bruell offers a sketch of the transformation from Aristotle's austere account of happiness as the highest good, inextricably bound up with ethical virtue or morality, to the break with that view effected by Hobbes, and through the subsequent attempts to re-elevate and re-ground happiness made by Rousseau and Nietzsche. Individuals have never ceased using the word "happiness," of course, but in the wake of these changes we now easily apply the word to objects that are much lower than those for which it had previously been reserved.[9] Bruell's critical observation is psychological rather than linguistic: "we conceal from ourselves," by the new usage, "the fact that we have lowered our sights from a high and demanding—but perhaps sufficient—goal to the many lesser goals that we now pursue under this banner, goals that cannot possibly satisfy any human being worthy of the name." By retention of the high term, "we conceal from ourselves the insufficiency of these successor goals and therewith the deepest cause of our dissatisfaction with ourselves and with life" (HPP 393). If life in the cave is characterized by an inadequate view of the good, noble, or just, life in the cave beneath the cave is characterized by a situation in which we continue semi-consciously to care about these matters while at the same time doubting that our hopes can be satisfied. The consequence for education remains front and center: by concealing our dissatisfaction, "we do away in advance with any effort to remove it" (HPP 393; see also PR 86; ORPT 77–78; SPSK 156). And yet, the psychological phenomenon of concealing from oneself one's hopes implies that self-awareness with respect to them is capable of being recovered. Bruell's essays in this vein thus work to draw our attention to our superficial and confused attachments to "success" or "happiness" or "diversity" so as to demonstrate *ad hominem* the incompleteness of the break.

Third, if Bruell has succeeded in drawing out our attachments and in cultivating self-awareness at least in that respect, he does so with a view to sharpening the contrast between our times and ancient ones, thereby making possible the recovery of what he frequently refers to as the fundamental question. Attempting to draw out a precise articulation of this question in these contexts is as good an example as any of Bruell's prosaic unquotability. A critical thread of "On Reading Plato Today" might be summarized as follows. In seeking a certain understanding of the world, the philosopher "seeks to discover the permanent and intelligible causes of all things, together with the natural articulation of those causes or their intrinsic relation to one another" (ORPT 71). The classical approach to this task may seem to have been superseded by the modern scientific approach. Yet we sense, at least dimly, that "the question or questions" asked by modern science differ from "*the* question" addressed by philosophy which "emerged directly from nonphilosophic or prephilosophic life

---

9. Bruell opens HPP with a glance at a passage from Stendhal's *The Charterhouse of Parma* that is remarkably illustrative of how our usage has changed (HPP 383–84).

as Plato and his contemporaries experienced it" (ORPT 71, my emphasis). In keeping with the historical sketch above, the fundamental character of that question has been obscured by the attempt of modern liberal universalism (e.g., the doctrine of universal human rights) to calm the conflicts spurred above all by religious diversity. Many of our present champions of diversity and group identity can attack liberal universalism itself so blithely only or precisely because they have, whether they know it or not, wholly accepted the premise underlying this universalism: no claim to truth in religious or spiritual matters may rightly call into question the sensible goals of peace and material prosperity. The victory of modern liberalism, the technological progress of modern science, and other developments have, no doubt, resulted in a remarkably stable and tolerant politics. But from Plato's point of view, this victory may have "come at the price of our estrangement from our fundamental concern through loss of self-awareness," an estrangement from "the question in the light of which the world reveals itself as what it is"; for "the most fundamental question" concerns precisely the root of those religious conflicts, the question as to "where the truth of the matter lies" (OPPP 350; ORPT 78; 71 and 76; cf. "the single most important question that we face as human beings" in *SE* 11.14, 156).[10] Now what link is there between Bruell's occasionally polemical interrogation of contemporary orthodoxies, his exposure of persistent elements in our attachments, and the question at the core of these matters? These issues all bear on our self-understanding. "Understanding ourselves requires in the first place that we begin to see the importance to us of judgments of good and bad, right and wrong, judgments which, taken together, amount to an answer to the question of the best way of life. Now judgments of this sort . . . are intended to be judgments of *being*, of what *is*" (ORPT

---

10. Bruell often speaks in the plural of "the fundamental questions confronting human beings everywhere and always," "the fundamental moral-political and religious questions," "our fundamental concerns," and "certain fundamental human longings and demands" (ORPT 66; *AL* 468; DPP 373, 380; QNLS 286; see PR 83-84 for examples of several "fundamental matters"). But he also speaks pointedly in the singular of "the fundamental *issue*," "our most fundamental *concern*," "the fundamental *question*" or "the most fundamental *question*" (SOXS 218, 210; DPP 376, 379; OPPP 350; ORPT 71, 76; my emphasis in each). Contrast "the question which is truly *primary*" with which philosophy "necessarily *begins*" (DPP 368, my emphasis). Note that in the remarks quoted in the body above, OPPP 350 refers to our "fundamental *concern*" and ORPT 71 and 76 to "the most fundamental *question*." This difference may require further exploration.

98; note "in the first place": here we recover the true beginning). Judgments about the best way of life are judgments about what kind of being a human is and what sort of a world humans live in. To state the matter in starker terms than Bruell allows himself in contemporary contexts, the fundamental question concerns "the point of view from which all of life . . . is to be understood"; that is, "in the last resort must our reliance be on the divine or on our own reasoning?" (SOXS 210, taken with 218, citing Strauss, *Natural Right and History*, 74; see also ONRH 279–81, summarizing Strauss; cf. the language of ORPT 77, PR 88) Bruell's effort to lay bare the intentions and assumptions underlying modern developments, aside from achieving an exact historical understanding, offers us an opportunity to rediscover the fundamental character of the question of the truth of any religious creed, and thereby to begin to see what is at stake in the original attempt to philosophize. And his identification of confusions in our opinions about important matters such as "happiness" and "success" shows that our contemporary opinions and concerns coexist with older, weightier opinions and concerns. Occasionally polemical language heightens self-awareness of these unacknowledged attachments. To the extent that traces of the older views become evident to us, precisely in our own views, we see that the questions that occupied the classical philosophers may well have remained our own.[11]

The Stages of Socratic Education

To repeat: Plato shows us no sign that his understanding underwent a "progress" during his composition of the dialogues. He instead shows us a change in Socrates, his turn from the science of nature to his investigation of human things. To undergo this change is to raise for oneself,

---

11. Bruell's own confident articulations of ancient views in contrast to modern ones provides evidence that he too cannot think the break or gulf between ancients and moderns on any of the important matters he explores is complete or unbridgeable. We should be careful, in particular, not to overstate the differences brought about by Biblical religion and the Enlightenment project. At the end of "On Reading Plato Today," Bruell recommends looking, in order to understand the differences between ourselves and "readers of Plato who were raised in earlier times," at a chapter of Churchill's *Marlborough* on societal life in the seventeenth century. Obstacles encountered in life under the "new universalism" emerged more recently than one might have thought (ORPT 77).

as Socrates did, the question of the goodness of the philosophic life. But there is an obstacle here. "The choice to philosophize, to give one's life to philosophizing, is after all a human choice, made for human reasons, on the basis of some human concerns—among which the concern to know is not likely to have played the sole, perhaps not even the leading, part. The thought that philosophy or wisdom or the knowledge of the causes of all things is noble or high or serious may always have had great weight in this choice" (OMPP 192; consider 182 and 191–92 too). Are such thoughts or opinions well-founded? Our motivating assumptions about philosophizing become the object of critical examination only in political philosophy. Bruell is clear in this passage from his interpretation of the *Lovers* that while the silent, older boys undergo a change as they listen to Socrates' examination of two younger boys, their change is only apparently the same as that undergone by Socrates himself in part because of a false impression Socrates gives them (OMPP 191). We wondered about this at the outset, and we now see that even these boys who began with an interest in "astronomy" (i.e., natural science) and are turned to the human things, do not in fact take the same path as Socrates himself (see 7–8 above). Why does Socrates take a different path with his interlocutors and what does he accomplish by turning others toward political philosophy in that way? If political philosophy consists in no small part in examining underlying assumptions about the philosophic life, is it merely preparatory for some fuller sort of philosophic activity? Does the concern to know ultimately take precedence or come to be pursued in an unimpeded way? But what is the content of that life or the goal of the pursuit? Or, if Socrates' post-Delphic activity continues to be, as Xenophon briefly but explicitly indicates, a continuation of his investigation of the beings (*Memorabilia* 4.6.1), what contribution, if any, does his refutative activity make to that study? Following Bruell's lead, let us try to sketch as clearly as we are able the path upon which Socrates puts youths of more ordinary ambition than the boys in the *Lovers* and to identify what is false in the impression that he (also) gives them.

On the Socratic Education 13.12 (179) supplies a frame on which to hang our considerations. The passage occurs in a chapter on Plato's *Meno*, the dialogue whose animating questions include What is virtue? How is virtue acquired? Is virtue One or Many? Is virtue identical to knowledge?—questions of importance to Socrates' second sailing. It would be foolish to attempt an exhaustive interpretation of the passage at the outset (see *SE* vii), but Bruell makes several helpful distinctions here that can serve as starting points. The passage generally takes up the goodness of the good person and its prerequisites. Bruell suggests that one who is to become virtuous may need to possess certain qualities by nature. But if prudence is required as an additional quality, then "the good human beings" are not "good by nature" (because prudence requires for its development experience or teaching or both). Bruell then refers to two senses of "goodness" and says the conclusion drawn above applies to both senses. The first sense is presumably the natural "goodness" which straightforwardly is not good by nature because it requires prudence as an additional component. Goodness in its "secondary, derivative sense," however, requires "a specific 'education' of the original disposition." Since "it is precisely the better natures that give themselves most unreservedly to this education" (see also *SE* 2.10, 14–15), "the natural disposition must in these cases be recovered through an equally specific corruption or 'second' education." The original disposition, Bruell asserts, was lost due to lack of self-consciousness, hence when self-consciousness is attained as a result of the "second" education, that recovery is more than a simple return to the original disposition.[12] Such goodness too, then, is not "by nature." These are difficult remarks, but, for our purposes, we can distinguish four things here. (1) Each of us by nature is born with some set of more or less favorable qualities and an original disposition toward good and bad things. (2) We all receive a first "education," a long "education" that shapes our original disposition in accord with "goodness" as it is understood by the families or political communities or religious orders to which we belong. While this influence was direct in pre-modern times, it is diluted or obscured in our times for reasons we have discussed. (3) The Socratic "second" education is understood, from this point of view, as "corruption" since it involves a critique of the elements of "goodness" that have already taken hold of us. This education, to which the bulk of Plato and an important part of Xenophon's writings are explicitly devoted, itself proceeds in "successive stages of Socratic instruction" (*XHS* 305; also 297). (4) Those who are well-suited to Socratic "corruption" recover in and through it something of their original disposition accompanied now by Socratic self-knowledge. This result, I take Bruell to be suggesting, is

---

12. Bruell's use and non-use of quotation marks in this passage is worth considering: he refers to *the first "education"* and then *the "second" education*, which is *a "corruption."* I surmise Socratic education is in this way suggested to be the one and only worthy of the name.

a necessary if not also sufficient condition of genuine openness to a natural understanding of the world. To avoid a misunderstanding, a remark in "Liberal Education and Education for Citizenship" also tells us that even if liberal education—roughly equivalent to Socratic education in that context—and education for citizenship are distinct, and ought to be kept so, there is an "indissoluble connection" between them (LEEC 57; consider also the last point in ATP 363). That is, self-aware philosophic science requires education for citizenship as a foundation, the experience and "education" of our natural longings, even if Socratic education must appear to be a "corruption" from the citizen's point of view. I suspect that Bruell's conviction that this is so provides one reason for his own extremely careful writing. Now, in what follows, we will try to get clearer about the distinct stages of the "second" education with a view to this broader picture. As we will see, Socrates' attempts to educate others are thwarted above all by certain pre-existing beliefs, chief among which is the belief that one already knows what virtue is. It is very difficult for many of us today not only to see that we do hold such beliefs, but also to pursue the necessary questions that must be raised about them, on account of both our natural longings and the habits of living together developed by our first "education."

The Exhortatory or Protreptic Stage

A cursory reading of Plato or Xenophon reveals a Socrates who is on the hunt for a particular nature or type best suited to join him in his search for wisdom. Socratic education clearly requires unusually demanding intellectual gifts: the ability to learn quickly and remember well, the possession of wide-ranging interests, and especially a desire to know how to rule and make good use of others (Xenophon is explicit about this: *Memorabilia* 4.1.2; consider also Plato *Republic* VI and the general character traits of Alcibiades, Glaucon, and Adeimantus). It requires a certain disposition, certain qualities "of mind and heart" (*SE* 3.1; XEN 317–18, 328–29; also 303–304). These qualities are not always present and need not always coincide. Indeed, in his treatment of the matter, Xenophon goes on to describe three sorts of "worse natures." If we refer to his own standards, we must conclude he never shows us a truly good nature being educated by Socrates. Indeed Euthydemus, Socrates' primary interlocutor in *Memorabilia* IV, quickly proves to belong to the worst class. We are therefore forced to infer and reason through for ourselves what the correct stages of Socratic education are on the basis of incomplete or faulty examples. The situation is fundamentally the same in Plato, though he points to somewhat different defects than Xenophon and shows us several young men who are more promising in different ways.

We can safely say that among the "best natures" are youths motivated by great political ambition. In these cases, Socrates' "first step" is to foster an awareness of one's "concern for justice or for nobility more generally, the concern that burns in the soul of every truly promising youth for whatever, as higher than we are, draws us out of ourselves and, as it appears, disposes us to sacrifice or give of ourselves for its sake" (*SE* 7.1, 75; OPPP 334–35).[13] Ambitious youths possess a noble conviction that one cannot be good unless one is just, for knowledge of justice is "a prerequisite of fundamental importance to political understanding and political action" (XEN 318). Any higher education therefore presupposes the effectiveness of an earlier education that shapes these attachments via habituation to loving obedience in the home or patriotic service to the community or country (e.g., Plato, *Lysis* beg. or *Menexenus* or the conversation with Polemarchus in *Republic* I; LEEC 57–58). Yet the very effectiveness of habituation, the fact that we have not yet adequately reflected on the judgments that have already taken hold of us and implicitly answered for us the question of the right way of life, obstruct any effort to raise that question directly. Socrates therefore works indirectly, leading each promising youth to attend to "the most elementary questions he would have to consider in order to begin to acquire self-knowledge, the foundation and the core of genuine human virtue" (*SE* 3.5, 23; see also 13.5, 168). The better students come to think that nothing is so important as to investigate what justice is, Socrates having revealed to them the "always present, but hitherto unrecognized" need to do so. They conclude that political activity must be postponed until this investigation is completed. The question with which philosophic life begins, then, is not "What is justice?" but "What do I have to do to comply with the demands of justice?"[14] Socratic

---

13. In the immediate context of *SE* 7.1 Bruell refers to a "second step"—investigation as to which are the truly noble pursuits. I believe that this step may be quite far down the line from the first one, and this might be true of similar "programmatic" statements made elsewhere.

14. The importance of this question is not as shallow as my presentation might suggest. At DPP 368, Bruell designates it "the truly primary question" with which philosophy begins. And, in connection with modern doubts about whether we can know what is

exhortations urge ambitious youths to consider whether they know all they need to in this respect, whether that be the mundane details of political administration (Xenophon, *Memorabilia* III.5 and 6) or the grand extent of their own ambition (Plato, beg. of *Alcibiades* 1 and *Lysis*, *Republic* I and II). That good natures are so motivated would alone "have been reason enough for Socratic education to introduce itself to them as education to politics" (XEN 317–18; consider *XHS* 297–98). Contra his denial in Plato's *Apology of Socrates*, Socrates did present himself as a teacher of politics.

Now many of Socrates' politically ambitious interlocutors fall short of recognizing their own attachments to justice. They have doubts about its goodness on account of the harshness or weakness of law, its inability to secure a truly common good, or the apparent prosperity of unjust men, and they are tempted on these or other grounds to conclude justice is merely conventional or unserious (versions of the theme are evident in conversations with Polus, Alcibiades, Hippocrates, and, to a lesser extent, Glaucon). These men may come to be, if they are not already, more attracted to the honor and fame that accompanies rule, or to the private advantages of rule, just or unjust. Via some limited use of protreptic speeches, Socrates calls to the attention of the more ambivalent the importance that they too inevitably place on judgments of good and bad, just and unjust, noble and base. If Alcibiades is any indication, it is very hard for an awareness of that deeper attachment to stick if civic education has, for whatever reason, failed to do its foundational work. By contrast, the better natures are quick and eager to acknowledge their concern for virtuous ends, they pursue virtue with greater determination, and they recognize that obedience even to harsh laws is somehow good for their souls (*SE* 2.10, 13.12; HPP 384).[15] Socrates' exhortations draw

---

just, see DPP 376: What if justice, "so far from being without a hold on our heart, is precisely the form in which our most fundamental concern finds a first, if somewhat enigmatical, expression?"

15. "Somehow"—It would be inappropriate to introduce a full consideration here, but we can make a sketch: burdensome laws shape our appetites; someone without a healthy civic education will likely pursue a thin and inconsistent notion of the human good (e.g., pursuit of random pleasures dignified with the word "freedom"). Because it is true that the laws tend to teach that service to others is identical to one's own good, conventionalists do not have too much trouble finding good grounds to doubt such "goodness" is always good for oneself. But the reach for a good greater than our own also has a natural, erotic root (e.g., OPPP 339: our natural dissatisfaction with the limits to life); conventions direct or channel that longing in various ways, especially

out the belief that justice is good for the soul, and we eventually come to ask the more fundamental question: in what does goodness of soul consist? (*SE* 2.10) Given the oft-unacknowledged attachment to justice or nobility more generally, appealing directly to a concern for our own good or advantage makes for a false start. Socrates instead takes the longer route we have been describing to "the genuine starting point" by opening a gap between authoritative custom, law, or commonly accepted opinions and the good (see *SE* 2.1, and the question whether Socrates' argument deserved to succeed with the noble comrade in *Hipparchus*, *SE* 1). He can do so in part precisely because he bows to authoritative opinion and in bowing calls attention to insufficiently appreciated moral elements of our civic horizon. He presents himself, at least implicitly, as a teacher of the knowledge we require to accomplish what we take to be our noble tasks.

The Refutative or Elenctic Stage

Socrates' protreptic speeches establish the desirability of philosophizing, but that activity is initially understood as a means to an end, namely, to a life governed by attachments that are, at best, accompanied by a self-awareness that is not yet self-knowledge (e.g., the self-awareness of Glaucon and Adeimantus vs. Thrasymachus). The "second step" in the process of turning another toward philosophy in the cases where it is possible to do so, Bruell says, is "to know the identity of the noble pursuits (to which we can dedicate ourselves) or the identity of the noble objects (worthy as such of our devotion)" (*SE* 7.1, 75). The articulation of our noble aims as noble, the deepening of our awareness of our own attachment to them as fulfillments of our greatest good, our awareness of the hopes or expectations characteristic of those attachments—all this must be subjected to examination before our beliefs about noble pursuits can be said to be reasonable or true.

---

via forms of piety. Given the contradictions among the creeds, one could wonder whether eros naturally directs humans toward false beliefs about the whole. But the compulsion to reflect on this, the sting that drives us toward self-knowledge and a true understanding of our good, is much weaker for those in whom an attachment to justice has not taken hold and who have not worked to make such hopes explicit in their way of living. And so long as they remain unarticulated and unexamined, these longings continue to lead an underground life, distorting and ultimately thwarting one's quest for self-knowledge, no matter how seriously undertaken. It is a Socratic theme that "freethinkers" who begin from conventionalism often prove to lack human wisdom.

> [T]he judgments in question come to us and take possession
> of us before we begin to reflect, to reflect adequately, on the
> matters they concern: at this stage, then, however passionately
> we may be attached to them, we do not know those judgments
> to be true. Nor can we simply abandon them at the moment
> we become aware that this is the case, for—apart from the fact
> that we also do not know them to be false—they mean too
> much to us for us to let them go without a struggle. But this
> means that our initial eagerness to learn, though it may put us
> on the path to genuine openness of mind, is not the product
> of such openness nor even truly its companion. Rather, to the
> extent that we become aware that we do not know the truth
> of what we believe regarding fundamental matters, we become
> passionately eager to acquire such knowledge; and, in this spirit,
> we raise the question whether the judgments to which we are
> already attached are true—for example, whether our view of
> justice, of right and wrong, is true. (ORPT 68; see also TVAI
> 94–95, 106; contrast Alcibiades' defect in this regard, *SE* 3.11)

Such judgments are nothing less than judgments about what *is* or being
(ORPT 68; consider also what Bruell says about the "stages" of development
of the city in OPPP 338–40, where the parallel between city and soul is
surely in mind). In most cases, the pursuits or objects in question are, as
we have seen, political ones; but nothing prevents them from including
those connected with astronomy, natural science, or philosophy (see Plato,
Lovers and OMPP 191–92). It seems to me that this second step is a long
one in which the examination of the nobility of political life as the good
life is ultimately replaced by an examination of the philosophic life along
the same lines. Disenchantment with politics, at any rate, often seems to be
accompanied by a transfer of similar hopes or expectations to philosophy
or science. However that may be, the exhortatory stage is followed by a
refutative one which centers on a direct examination of Socratic "What
is . . . ?" questions with a view to producing genuine openness.

In this second stage of Socratic education, Socrates' exhortation
to justice, for example, is "followed by a thoroughgoing critique of [an
interlocutor's] conscious or unconscious conviction that he knows what
justice is" (*XHS* 297). The exhortatory stage may also have led an interlocutor to doubt somewhat that he knows what justice and nobility are, but
only so far as is needed to present philosophy as a means to the (as yet)

unquestioned political ends (e.g., *SE* 3.6, 25, or Polemarchus in *Republic*). In this stage, however, the examination goes much deeper. An inquiry into what justice demands of us is replaced by the question What is justice? Socrates' unyielding pursuit may lead us to wonder whether justice is fundamentally problematic in the sense that the opinions we believe are essential to a definition of justice cannot cohere (e.g., justice cannot be both obedience to the law and giving to each what is fitting or good for each: Plato, *Republic* I generally, Xenophon *Cyropaedia* I.4.16–17). To be at a loss here, to know that one is at a loss here, is to attain for the first time a measure of what Socrates calls his human wisdom. "Not to think one knows what one does not know is to be prepared to that extent to strive for clarity" (SPSK 140; *SE* 13.9, 175). Here the soul turns around. Consequently, "the activity of investigation, which was to be merely preliminary to that of engaging in politics, replaces it instead. What pretended to be an education to politics, a means, becomes the end" (XEN 319).

This stage is the most dangerous for Socrates himself. Socrates' exhortatory speeches appeal to, and even increase, our attachments to pre-philosophic opinions about the good, noble, and just. The politics he seems to be offering to teach, for example, in the *Republic* is radically reformist and it is not until deep into the discussion that Glaucon begins to wonder about the possibility of such reforms. (Polemarchus, to his credit, explicitly raises the question much earlier.) Socrates' initial appeal to a reformist intention by itself runs the risk of a total turn away from even the small good to be done on the political stage. How much worse when Socrates directly examines what justice is and refutes what we think we know about it? How much worse to suspect his ignorance, not yet fully our own, is perhaps incurable? The very attachment he has cultivated will make this a painful experience. The toughness that allows good natures to bear harsh laws may also prepare the toughness that endures hard questions and conclusions. But those who lack such toughness are likely to lash out, and, as Socrates makes clear in his *Apology*, there is no shortage of accusations to level against the philosophers. It is for this reason, as Bruell suggests in connection with his articulation of "the second step," that the *Greater Hippias* "presents an investigation of nobility framed by a consideration of sophistry or a consideration of sophistry whose heart is an investigation of nobility" (*SE* 7.1, 76). Socrates' examinations and refutations of dearly held opinions about virtue look like sophistry to decent people, and to sophists they look like evidence that Socrates' exhortations must be either ironic or hopelessly naive. That, of all people, it is Hippias who comes to blame Socrates for sophistry underlines the point suggested above that all of us share such attachments, consciously or not (see Hippias' remarks about nature and convention in *Protagoras* 337d–e). Socrates' examinations awaken an awareness of the significance of the choice between public and private life, and of the deepest ground of the conflict between the political community and the philosophers (*SE* 8.7–8 and 10.1). The more seriously we take nobility and goodness, the more irritating, infuriating, are Socrates' attempts to show us that we do not know what we think we know (consider also SOXS 209–10).

In one remarkable passage, Bruell refers to the experience of Socratic education as a kind of "purification." At a certain point in book one of the *Republic*, "the focus shifts to a question which is at first hearing almost incomprehensible to someone devoted to justice: the question of whether justice is good or bad." Thrasymachus' outburst, however, helps us become aware that "precisely as lovers of justice, we took for granted all along that it is good." And from this, Bruell offers the following: the *Republic*, as a whole, makes clear that "the love of justice which, among other traits, distinguishes the potential philosopher is in need of undergoing a specific purification which the education conveyed by the *Republic* (if not also that which Socrates outlines within it) is meant to supply" (ORPT 69–70). The result of the *Republic* according to which only the philosopher has a healthy soul and therefore the truest practice of justice supports the suggestion above that in this stage philosophy replaces politics as our end or way of life.

But what exactly is being purified? Even or especially individuals well-disposed to taking up a genuine education are born and bred to certain convictions and a comprehensive outlook more powerful than their attachment to truth. Human beings live in accordance with a set of both natural attachments simply and conventional attachments that have a natural force behind them. On the broadly Socratic view, for example, eros is naturally directed to offspring and to fame, and it is an element of our longing for justice, nobility, happiness, and for the divine care often called upon to support these. Eros, Bruell writes, is "the fundamental longing of our nature prior to its having been educated or purified" (*SE* 4.3; see also PR 89; XEN 329–30; *AAT* 224).[16] I would tentatively suggest that

---

16. As far as I have observed, Bruell speaks elsewhere of such a purification only in an unpublished 1987 conference paper on the *Republic* (REP, third paragraph). Additionally, OPPP 338–40 seem to me to present an exemplary sketch of what purification requires and entails.

"purification" involves the application of the distinction between nature and convention—or, more cautiously, knowledge and opinion—to the objects of our longing, and then the testing of the ends of each in accordance with our expectations of rational coherence. Bruell attends with unusual care to Socrates' profession of ignorance with respect to these matters: "The positive result that it may be possible and even necessary to draw from Socrates' examinations of himself and others . . . would point to or even constitute that knowledge of his . . . while their negative result would uncover and confirm an ignorance of [virtue] which cannot be removed, and thus vindicate the confession of that ignorance that he makes not only on his own behalf but also on that of others" (*SE* 13.6, 170; SPSK 163). It is thus in such purification that we may find the justification of the philosophic life as the end rather than a means. As Bruell suggests, "perhaps the Socratic answer to the question [What is justice?] is available but not openly expressed, and perhaps in that answer, and in the answers to the apparently related questions of self-knowledge and the good, lies a fuller account of the reasons for the superiority—if such it be—of the philosophic life to the political life" (XEN 319). (On this transition from justice to the good, consider also *TP* 27: "More generally, by pointing to our insistence that justice be (a common) good, the Melians point to the fact of the primacy of our concern with the good, a fact which comes to light even and precisely in the midst of any consideration of justice, provided that it goes far enough.") Socrates' refutations or examinations of those who claim to know these matters are, "for their suitable witnesses or subjects, an education toward genuine virtue." Thus it is here that we come at last to the connection between Socrates' moral-political examinations and the question of the goodness of the philosophic life: "if philosophizing is fundamentally inquiry into nature, the examinations or refutations, which were intended to vindicate the possibility of such inquiry over against the most serious challenge to its possibility, serve also to prepare the suitable natures among the youths who are exposed to them to carry it out" (*SE* 14.1, in light of *SE* 10 on *Euthyphro* generally). We come to see that "the civic horizon is constituted by elements which contradict one another" (SOXS 216; LEEC 63) and that the opinions that accompany our natural longings, or the hopes to which they give rise, are less than fully coherent (OPPP 335; consider SPSK 156). A true grasp of the sempiternal, fundamental problems that face us as human beings is finally understood to be the content of human wisdom, perhaps even the core of the knowledge attained by political philosophy. Knowledge of this sort, if it is knowledge, may be accompanied by the persistence of such hopes in some sense, or it may be accompanied by self-knowledge; but it cannot be accompanied by both. Philosophy, as Socrates says on the day of his execution, is the practice of dying and being dead. "To be aware of death is in a sense to die; and, if it should be the case that one sort of awareness of death is a root of the capacity for devotion, another and deeper sort of that awareness would be a necessary product and accompaniment of knowledge of our lack of wisdom" (*SE* 6.4, 72; also 16.1, 212; consider 8.7, 99: Socrates may be "incurable" on the fundamental point). Perhaps such purification is a precondition of theoretical inquiry in part because our natural fear of death is soothed by the pleasure of false beliefs such as are supported by impossible hopes. Someone might wonder, however, whether Socrates has only succeeded in awakening us to longings that cannot be satisfied. (Cf. Plato, *Cleitophon* and *SE* 14.7; Cf. OPPP 336; Socrates' presentation of his daimon surely plays some role here as well.) Socrates, as Plato and Xenophon have portrayed him, leaves us to clarify these things for ourselves.[17] For his part, Bruell indicates more than once that, though clarity does eventually come to sight as pre-eminently good, the philosophic life is nevertheless one accompanied by pleasure mixed with sadness:

> The philosophers, who judge from what they know of themselves and observe of others . . . agree to this extent: the dissatisfaction with the limit that nature sets to our life and therefore

---

17. Granting that Socratic education is a kind of "liberation" from, and break with, conventional opinions about virtue, several questions remain about the character of the philosophic life and the experiences of the philosophic soul. To begin with, while "liberation" emphasizes that from which one breaks, "purification" puts an equal emphasis on the elements of pre-philosophic opinion or experience that are preserved or carried through into the philosophic life. Exactly what elements are these? If there is an Odyssean component of wide-ranging thought, prudential flexibility, attention to one's own good, defensive preservation, and irony with a view to others, is there not also an Achillean generosity or care for others that in important ways remain "one's own," a capacity for frankness backed by confidence in one's strength, a concern for the future good of those like oneself, a vitality in bearing difficult and burdensome things, or the experience of austere pleasures closer to those associated with moral habituation than with amoral hedonism? (One might reconsider 13–14 above and *SE* 8.8 in this light.) To put this differently, even if Polemarchus and Theages both took up the philosophic life, is it perhaps relevant to an understanding of that life that Polemarchus died at the hands of the Thirty Tyrants, while Theages' continued attachment to philosophy was possible in part because he was sickly and unable to pursue the tyranny he desired? (Lysias 12; Plato, *Republic* 496b)

> also with the pursuit merely of the well-being of our mortal
> bodies, the dissatisfaction which the claim made on behalf
> of virtue and the hopes connected with that claim so nobly
> bespeak, is not only apparently inescapable for us, who call
> ourselves human, but also reasonable . . . . The only question
> is whether our situation leaves us any genuine recourse other
> than resignation and the life of serene freedom that such res-
> ignation opens to us. (OPPP 339)[18]

Under philosophic scrutiny, the longing for an unmixed good-in-itself
yields to the recognition that such goods as may be possessed by human
beings are always mixed with evils.

What Is Philosophic Science?

We have come to the place where it is fitting to suggest that the central
theme of Bruell's writings is, in one way or another, the Socratic Turn:
the reasons for Socrates' dissatisfaction with prior natural philosophy, the
character of his own approach (especially his understanding of the "ideas"
or his inquiry into the class character of the beings), the purpose of his
notorious refutative activity, the adequacy of his defense of the philosophic life, the precise character of the philosophic life insofar as it is not
exhausted by that refutative activity. As in the Platonic and Xenophontic
dialogues themselves, Bruell begins by looking at Socrates' philosophic
activity proper in light of immanent political considerations and the cloud
under which Socrates' prosecution, among other older clouds, had left
philosophy. He emphasizes to a much higher degree than other students
of Strauss that it is not possible, in the end, to understand what Socrates
was doing without understanding what his predecessors were trying to
do. (This is true even or especially if one holds that political philosophy
is "the first philosophy," for how else can that conclusion be established?)
Bruell's late works have taken up these themes by focusing on Aristotle's
philosophic science, what it is and on what basis it can be said to rest. His
conclusions are bold. For example, Bruell writes in his most recent paper,
"Theses Bearing on the Understanding of Aristotle's Natural Science," that

---

18. Compare PR 88–89 and HPP 396 on happiness; consider SPSK 140–41, 156,
167–68, 172; *SE* 6.4, 11.12, 16.1; QNLS 285–86; ATP 361.

the theses therein "point to a ground for considering Aristotle's natural science to be the true natural science—not in every respect, of course, but not merely in its general approach, either: rather in his unparalleled grasp of a problem intrinsic to any such science" (TBUA 416; compare similar remarks from Bolotin in the introduction to his translation of *On Soul*, vii).[19] In connection with this claim, Bruell credits Hegel with "in a manner" rediscovering a distinct problem articulated by Aristotle and apparently forgotten until Hegel's time (418). This problem concerns the transparency of the world of our most elementary experience, the given world upon which all reasoning about the world incontrovertibly depends. From this credit to Hegel and Bruell's subsequent criticism of Hegel's approach to that problem, we are tempted to infer that Bruell claims to have seen something in Aristotle that may not have been seen for hundreds if not thousands of years—"no light matter," indeed (416).

In "Aristotle on Theory and Practice," Bruell argues that within the *Nicomachean Ethics* and *Politics* we find alongside an explicit but rather weak case for the superiority of the contemplative or philosophic or theoretical life, a deeper and more compelling implicit case that rests on a dialectical examination of fundamental political opinions. In the unpublished second part of that paper, Bruell takes up the question of the soundness of Aristotle's conception of the theoretical life, "for if theory as he conceived of it should prove to be impossible or fatally flawed, his praise of the life devoted to it will have been bestowed upon a phantom"; this result would then call into question any conclusions we may have drawn based on his critique of the most important alternative (*ATP2* 1). In connection with that implicit case, Bruell tentatively suggests that Aristotle follows Plato in this respect: Aristotle accepted "the view of his teacher as to the necessity of a moral-political preparation for engaging in theory or philosophic science," a version of the "turning around of the whole soul" called for by Socrates in Plato's *Republic* (*ATP2* 3–4; see also TBUA 433).

---

19. I have referred to Aristotle's "philosophic science," as does the subtitle of *Aristotle as Teacher*; but Bruell's most recent paper refers to Aristotle's "natural science." Are these the same or different? I am not yet certain, but my inclination is to say that Aristotle's natural science or physics is a science of bodies that is rooted in his broader philosophic science. Perhaps Aristotle's natural science is what is yielded when the pre-Socratic notion of natural science is modified in accordance with the insights contained in the *Metaphysics*. See *AAT*, 36–39, 121–23, 129–30. Perhaps *AAT* develops the problem of science and the limits of *philosophic* science while TBUA undertakes to introduce Aristotle's *natural* science of *bodies* on that basis.

Yet Aristotle goes much further than Plato in presenting "something of scientific or theoretical activity proper" in a "dazzling array" of theoretical works, albeit ones written in his own reserved or guarded manner. The remainder of the paper gives us some sense of the reserve with which Aristotle presents philosophic science via an examination of his criteria for scientific demonstration in the strict sense. Questions are raised about the indemonstrable principles of demonstration in the *Posterior Analytics*, substance and form in the *Metaphysics*, and the simple but far-reaching first definition of soul found in *On Soul*. Bruell suggests on this basis that beneath his reserve, "Aristotle thinks that there is a *problem* with science or that science, the very possibility of genuine science as he understands it, is problematic"; and in conclusion he ties such philosophic science as Aristotle nevertheless develops to the "new, more rigorous natural science" called for by Socrates in the *Phaedo*, a science which would, "in particular, exercise far more caution than the old one had done in what it accepts as a causal account" (*ATP2* 11, 15). In urging scholars to pursue rigorously Aristotle's defense of science in this regard, Bruell insists we must also emulate Aristotle's "uncompromising strictness as to what must be known or knowable (by a genuine science), together with his unfailing caution as to what we actually do or even can know" (*ATP2* 11). For "it is only on the basis of a grasp of what it means truly to know, that we could even begin properly to assess what our stance toward knowing is" (*AAT* 11; see also 37–38, 44, 57, 85).

Now in Bruell's uncompromising interpretation of Aristotle's *Metaphysics, Aristotle as Teacher*, the central issue proves to be the authentic understanding of the formal cause in its distinctness from the other causes and in relation to ousia (substance; Bruell does not italicize Greek words in *AAT*, and I'll follow him for this frequently used word and its plural, ousiai, only). The *Metaphysics* seeks knowledge of the causes of being, of the beings that are (*ta onta*). Among these beings are the particular things we sensibly perceive and the attributes by which thought identifies and completes those perceptions. What Aristotle calls an ousia is that of which attributes are predicated but which is not itself predicated of anything else. As Aristotle unfolds it, ousia is shown to have two important senses: (1) as each particular thing or "some this" (*tode ti*) or (2) as the essence or the "what it was to be" (*to ti ēn einai*). When we speak of a horse, for example, we may be referring to the particular horse we point to galloping in the field or we may be recognizing the class to which some group of animals belongs by virtue of the shared characteristics we sum up in the definition of the universal, "horse," without which the particular horses are not known as what they are. Which are the authentic ousiai? The particular things (e.g., the living bodies we call horses) or their class character (e.g., the essence or what-it-was-to-be that each possesses and shares with others of its kind)? The bulk of Bruell's argument is an investigation into whether the ousiai in either sense can meet the criteria for science in Aristotle's strict sense. Wisdom seeks, he argues, what is responsible for the beings that are manifest to us, the "things" we encounter in our ordinary experience of the world, the least contestable of which are held by all to be the other natural bodies—animals and plants, inanimate elements like earth, water, fire, and their parts. (Note that to say the manifest beings are the "least contestable" is not to say that each of them or their being is entirely clear to us.) The bodies in this world of our experience manifestly come into being and pass away, as does each of us. Different philosophers sought an account of the unchanging cause or causes of these manifest changes in different ways. Natural philosophy, or physics as it was originally conceived, sought some unchanging element(s) that could account for the coming-into-being, existence, and passing away of the beings we experience (*AAT* 24–26), and in this way the first philosophers tried to find one (or more) necessary and therefore imperishable cause(s). Pythagoreans, for example, were impressed by the enumerability of beings and the necessary relations between numbers. The Platonic doctrine of the Ideas posited universal forms or classes of beings that were said to be somehow beings in their own right. And there is, of course, Aristotle's divine science or theology whose objects are permanent, without motion, and separate or separable (from perceptible being). Divine science seeks the permanent causes of the highest of the manifest beings, some of which are taken to be eternal (123, 129–30), and this is the science that pursues "being as being," what it is and what belongs to it as being, which is universal insofar as it is first (36–37, 121). The conflict between these kinds of science comes down to this: if there are no beings of the sort sought by theology, if there are only the ousiai perceptible to our senses, then physics would be the first science (36–37, *Metaphysics* 1026a27–29).

Bruell draws out Aristotle's deepest criticism of the various schools and the specific confusions at the heart of their accounts while also pressing Aristotle's teachings in accordance with Aristotle's own indications. What are the ousiai or which are the authentic ousiai? What is Aristotle's account of the perceptible beings, mathematical number, matter or forms? And to what extent can we account for their causes in the manner originally sought by the pre-Socratic natural philosophers?

These questions lead to the heart of the work and the most extraordinary difficulties. To get our bearings, we note that Bruell's interpretation begins and ends with reference to a self-conscious awareness of the world of our ordinary experience as something to be both achieved and maintained. In observing the argument of a philosophic work as a whole, he says, we may find that the problems are not alien to us but are rather those "with which our thought, unawares, is already burdened"; in the end, "the land to which such a work can lead us may well be none other than that in which, without truly seeing it, we already dwell" (3; note the generality of this statement, which concludes a short preface that has careful writing as its theme. Consider also *SE* 13.9 on "the problem of definition" in Plato's *Meno*). The arresting, final sentences of *Aristotle as Teacher* hold that the ousiai (in the sense of the things we encounter in our least contestable experience) "are the anchors of that given world which all truly scientific thought must take as its starting point—which, however high or deep it roams, it must never lose sight of and which it must return to in the end" (*AAT*, 268; see also 135–36). Now attaining clarity here requires that we first become perplexed about the matters we have been discussing. Grappling with the perplexities contained in Aristotle's work "is needed not merely for identification of the bonds from which one must free oneself in order to reach a goal already clearly grasped, but also or rather for clarity as to the end or goal itself, what a philosophic science seeks" (*AAT* 38; this remark reminds us again of Bruell's general understanding of the movement of Socratic education: see again 4–5, 12–13, and 23–24 above). Bruell argues that the true task of the *Metaphysics* is to introduce philosophic science by indicating the revisions that philosophy as it was originally conceived (physics), on one hand, and divine science (theology), on the other, "would have to undergo in order to comply with its general requirements" (38). A more thorough review might be able to show that to understand Bruell's account of form as (nothing but) the class character of things—an account that emerges and runs through his writings on Plato and Aristotle almost from the start—is at the same time to come to understand the fatal difficulties of the doctrinal views from which philosophic science is distinguished (difficulties of which Bruell's Plato and Aristotle are fully aware). In the remainder, I limit myself to highlighting some of the crucial remarks from Bruell's writings that help us to understand the character of Aristotle's philosophic science and its necessarily modest aims, beginning with a closer look at what it was the pre-Socratic natural scientists sought and were attempting to do. I hope this may suffice to render plausible the claim that the formal cause rightly understood is the lynchpin of a philosophic science based on Socratic rigor and caution regarding causal knowledge.

Socrates' philosophic predecessors were "conversing about the nature of all things (or beings), investigating the state (or origin) of what the sophists call the 'cosmos' and the particular necessities by which each of the heavenly things (or beings) comes into being" (Bruell's partial translation of *Memorabilia* 1.1.11, XEN2 402; see also XEN 325; *XHS* 298–99; OMPP 181, 191; *SE* 11.8).[20] Science has as its object what cannot be otherwise than it is: what is, and is as it is, by necessity. Science aims to describe and explain the world present to us by identifying the fundamental necessities that limit all possible change. In seeking the elements or principles of all things, the ancient philosophers assumed that these elements or principles always remain the same even as the things or beings manifestly undergo changes in characteristics like size, shape, color, position, etc. The necessities they sought were the causes of this whole, and "they had presumed that they would find them in being or in some beings or in some aspect or relation of beings" (XEN2 403; compare ORPT 70–71). If such causes, as necessities, are incapable of being otherwise and are knowable as the fundamental facts, they cannot simply be mere facts or mere givens: "both their responsibility (for the changing things) and their own unalterability must be intelligible in them" (XEN2 404; on necessity, see also QNLS 291–92 and *AAT* 8). Aristotle, for his part, refers to a "conviction," shared by all the first philosophers, that there must be some fixed and changeless nature—a conviction that "there can be no genesis or destruction of nature as a whole" (*AAT* 12–13). What philosophy or science sought from its inception, then, on the understanding that they were within the grasp of our understanding, are the causes sufficient to account for the beings: for their coming to be, their existence as they are, and their perishing. Plato has Socrates admit to his close companions in his last hours that he too sought these causes (*Phaedo* 96a6–10; cf. the impression he gives of having

---

20. Bruell's repeated reference, in 2000, to "things (or beings)" as alternatives for the object of the inquiry does not occur in a similar passage from the 1987 XEN essay, which refers throughout only to "beings." The distinction between things and beings is retained and explained in 2014's *Aristotle as Teacher*: possessing the principles and causes is not the same as knowing the ousiai as beings that are (*onta*). See 64–66 and 126–28. My own account has not cured the seemingly unavoidable "looseness of speech" with respect to what we call "beings" in these matters.

nothing to do with this in his defense speech, *Apology of Socrates* 19b–d); and when Aristotle claims that all the predecessors held that "being (*tò on*) is just what is perceptible to the senses," he includes himself, as philosopher, among them in this respect (*AAT* 26). Aristotle too insists on strict necessity as the standard of science in the precise sense: "what we know scientifically does not admit of being otherwise"; "what is knowable scientifically exists of necessity"; "the things that exist of necessity in an unqualified sense are all eternal" and "are not subject to generation and do not perish" (*Nicomachean Ethics* 1139b19–24; *AAT* 8, 123; consider also *Metaphysics* 1027a17–21). Can this standard be met? In a rich statement on the task of the *Metaphysics*, Bruell writes that "more adequately stated," the task which Aristotle undertakes is "that of showing what such a science seeks and of uncovering . . . the assumptions on which it actually rests." In the ellipses he asks, "is this the same as vindicating them?" (*AAT* 37–38; see also *ATP2* 5–7 for discussion of Aristotle's criteria for scientific knowledge.)

In the discussion of *Metaphysics* Alpha, as Bruell unfolds Aristotle's criticism of the aims of his philosophic predecessors, he refers more than once to their "audacity." With what right can science assume, as it does, that "being is just what is perceptible to the senses and what the so-called heaven encompasses?" This assumption may well be "audacious in more than one way" (*AAT* 28; cf. 26, 11). Let me dwell at some length on two ways in which the basic assumption of the predecessors is audacious. First, a theological sense: are there not other causes imaginable than those the first philosophers discussed? The *Metaphysics* all but opens with an acknowledgment that philosophy and myth both begin in wonder. Philosophy, if it attains its end and comes to understand of something that it cannot be otherwise, ceases to be perplexed or to wonder (10). But knowledge of the first things is held to be divine or fitting only for the divine, and the poets had made themselves spokesmen for the view that philosophic activity is not pleasing to the divine. The philosophic life is not sanctioned by the divine and in the worst case those who philosophize may be subject to the wrath of the gods. Despite Aristotle's surface dismissal, it is this understanding of the divine that poses the fundamental challenge that the philosophic predecessors had already been seeking to overcome. The predecessors had attempted to discover "not merely the state of the cosmos but 'the necessities' by which each of the heavenly things comes into being or 'the way the god contrives each of the heavenly things' understood as the way he *must* contrive them" (XEN 325, Bruell's emphasis). They "assumed" and "tried also to show" that "divine contrivance has had nothing to do with the coming-into-being of the world or with its actual state," tracing the sources instead to "necessity, in one form or another, if not also to chance" (XEN2 402). If belief in the existence of purposeful gods such as those we find in Hesiod and Homer contradicts the "conviction" or "basic premise" held by the philosophers, which causes are truly primary? The first philosophers had to pursue a knowledge of necessary cause(s) sufficient to rule out belief in divine purposiveness. Now in contrast to these natural philosophers, Bruell underlines Aristotle's indications that philosophic science is concerned merely with "*some* principles and causes" (*AAT* 9, my emphasis). Is this yet another indication of the grave difficulty that faces a philosopher who seeks to meet the challenge posed by the first theologians? Or does Aristotle's philosophic science somehow move beyond "conviction" and successfully supply a foundation in a knowledge of necessary causes that the other natural philosophers could not? This brings us to the second, theoretical sense in which the basic premise is audacious.—An assertion in passing: Bruell identifies this "deeper difficulty" (12; deeper than the immanent theoretical problems?) with greatest visibility and clarity very early in the work. One reasonably expects the subsequent interpretation to address it by finding some fundamental ground in nature, some knowledge of causes in the strict sense, some necessity capable of resolving the issue in favor of philosophy. A reader with some acquaintance with the *Metaphysics* may anticipate that the issue will come to a head precisely in the interpretation of Aristotle's theological teaching in Lambda. Treating the crucial chapters, Bruell indeed provocatively refers to "God" and the Biblical book of *Proverbs*, but many readers are bound to be disappointed by this comparatively brief, perhaps even playful, discussion. (Pages 250–53 must be understood, I think, in light of an admittedly open-ended suggestion at the outset of Kappa that "the case for or against" the "most demanding" sense of philosophic science has been completed by the end of Iota.) Bruell's book may be like Thucydides' *History* or Aristotle's *Politics* in this respect: it appeals to these hopes—and they are hopes of a certain sort (233, 236, 240)—only to subject them to a sober education that sharply observes every obstacle that stands in the way of their fulfillment (cf. LEEC 62). It is in no way clear to this reader that these obstacles are surmountable. On the contrary, the theological problem is, one is tempted to say, necessarily unresolved at the end of the work and no solution to it shall be found in the study of being as being. But knowing why this is and must be the case, from the perspective of the unaided human mind left to its own devices, is crucial not only to a correct understanding of the only defense of the philosophic life available to it, but also to the self-understanding of one who attempts to live it. (Consider the last two paragraphs of the discussion of Lambda, *AAT* 253, also 264.)

As to the theoretical audacity of the basic philosophic contention: Xenophon's brief account of the pre-Socratic philosophers indicates that the necessities sought by them were "the causes responsible for the coming-into-being of things and for their being the way they are"; they presumed they would find these causes "in being or some beings or some aspect or relation of beings." But Socrates judged their efforts in this regard to be a failure and he traced that failure not to a lack of capacity, which could be surpassed by superior genius, but rather "to the impossibility of their goal" (XEN2 403–04). Socrates' contention about natural science in its original form, then, is that it is impossible to find in being(s) or the attributes of being(s) fundamental causes or necessities that are *both* responsible for the changing things of our given experience *and* unalterable themselves. This problem haunts the combatants in the philosophic gigantomachy—the battle between fluxists and monists—and it may very well have been a glimpse of it that gave rise to the two camps in the first place. For if we cannot reconcile motion and rest, it is tempting to assert either that all is motion or that all is rest (consider the discussion of Socrates' predecessors in Plato, *Theaetetus* 177c–183c and *Sophist* 241b–250d). But such assertions are manifestly incapable of explaining the world as we experience it (consider Aristotle, *Generation of Animals* 760b27–33). A glance at Bruell's account of *Metaphysics* Alpha compounds such difficulties. To repeat, we are seeking the first causes or principles of the beings manifest to us, and science has as its object that which cannot be otherwise than as it is (*AAT* 23, 27–28). Aristotle's *Physics* distinguishes four causes—material, motive, formal and final causes—and his review of his predecessors turns in part on how well they saw or distinguished these causes or, glimpsing them, the reasons they refused to admit the distinctions into their accounts. For example, the first philosophers tended to hold that the sole fixed principles are material. They sought to identify the elements that persist through the manifest changes a being undergoes. Now these philosophers had to deny the distinction between material and form so as not to put their fixed principle into motion, as the formal relations between beings in motion are themselves constantly subject to change. But how can the material elements be recognized at all except with reference to their form? The material or matter, taken by itself, is unintelligible. Further, the material cause must be distinct from the motive cause: one might say that the material is in motion or has an internal source of motion, but how is the necessity that draws the movement from what underlies it to be understood? If one cannot explain this necessity then there is, strictly speaking, no natural principle here. And finally, the material cause must be distinguished from the final cause or the causality of the good. How could "fire" or "earth" or any bodily element ever be thought to explain why a being is in a good condition or how it comes to be so? Those who introduce mind as a cause take an important step toward sanity here, but it is of no help to collapse the final cause grasped or chosen by the mind with the motive cause. The movement of a being toward its good condition is knowable as good only by reference to the end it approaches, and this end would therefore have to be regarded as extrinsic—as a distinct cause. (On these problems, which are the tip of the iceberg, see 12–17, 95–96.) To take a second example, opposed to this "atomist" camp are those like the Pythagoreans who came to think that the principles of sciences like mathematics are the principles of all the beings. But in a funhouse mirror image of the problem encountered by the atomists, the Pythagoreans had to collapse their "form-like principles" into material causes to account for the matter the beings manifestly possess. For how could the forms be responsible for the coming-into-being of material things without themselves possessing matter? Or how could even the most general classes be intelligible to us without reference to the material things that bear or exemplify them? In the case of each camp's struggle with and collapse of form and matter, one into the other, a deeper problem comes into view: both camps make a distinction between what is unchanging in the being of their principle(s) and the characteristics subject to change. But, as we just said, to admit this distinction at the level of material principles themselves is to set in motion what was held to be a fixed principle in just the way the atomists had wished to avoid; as for the Pythagorean form-like principles, these too are set in motion to the extent that the forms in matter are subject to changes in the matter. Aristotle calls attention precisely here to the perishability of forms dependent on perishable matter (17–19). To recognize the formal cause is thus to recognize the problem of matter. "The problem of matter, in turn, is at the same time the problem of being, or more precisely, of the transparency or intelligibility of being" (19).[21] Without the formal cause, matter is unintelligible; but to admit the formal cause entails the

---

21. Bruell takes up another problem regarding the "transparency" of the beings at TBUA 424–25.

admission of plurality within being, which runs the risk of "making of it an unintelligible mixture of being and non-being" and thereby failing to attain the fixed and stable knowledge of cause we are seeking (19). This much, then, about the audacity of the philosophic predecessors who, despite some awareness of these problems, nevertheless persisted in their search for the fundamental causes or necessities on the basis of their conviction that being is just what is perceptible to the senses.

Aristotle's account assigns the first full recognition of the formal cause to Plato (and Bruell notices Aristotle is careful in his use and non-use of Plato's name in connection with the doctrine for which his school became famous), so let us take a step back and look at the broadly Socratic account of form that Bruell finds in Plato and Xenophon before returning to Aristotle and assessing whether or how his (or their) view succeeds where the natural philosophers failed. Bruell's work, almost from the beginning, has emphasized a subtle feature of Plato and Xenophon's accounts: Socrates' "activity constituted not simply a break with what the philosophers were doing but also a continuation of it" (XEN2 404; *SE* 11.6–8 generally, especially 143–44, 147; OPPP 349; SOXS 234 on Socrates' turn and 246 on the link between dialectics and *physiologia*). Socrates' philosophic activity is distinguished "by being guided by a greater awareness of its limits." Socrates held that the aspect of nature we have the most access to is "the what" or the perceptible character of each of the beings, rather than their unchanging causes, and the "perceptible character of each being is always the character of a group or class of beings." Socrates associated this knowledge of the beings with "dialectics," and Xenophon draws attention to a twofold sense of this activity: first, conversation, our ability to speak with one another, presupposes some knowledge (or, more cautiously, some awareness) of what each of the beings is; this in turn presupposes a "more elementary form" of separating the beings into classes or kinds. Via dialectics, Socrates thus investigated "each class of beings, in both its similarities with and its differences from the other classes." When Socrates asks, for example, What is just? this question means, "What characteristics or what character is it, that binds together all just things and makes them just, while at the same time distinguishing them not only from the unjust things but also from the pious things, the noble things, and so on?" What character must just things have, must they "necessarily have," if they are to be regarded as just? In seeking to understand all things, the predecessors had sought their causes in terms of necessity, and on Bruell's account, Socrates' investigations too "led toward or to the discovery of necessities." The class character of perceptible being leads toward or to knowledge of an intelligible necessity if only in this respect: the presence of any of these characteristics "entails the presence of certain other characteristics or elements—just as their presence excludes the presence of certain others" (XEN2 404–405; cf. *AAT* 62). We may say that the classes are causes of things to the extent that they set limits to what they may do or suffer while remaining what they are. Socrates' "wisdom" or its "core" is thus a "knowledge of limits, of what is necessary, possible, and impossible" (XEN2 406; strikingly, Bruell says "wisdom," not human wisdom, three times in this context). But the necessities sought by the predecessors were of a "more fundamental kind" (XEN2 405). Can a knowledge of unchanging classes or kinds or "ideas" in this modest sense replace the knowledge of unchanging causes originally sought? Or is this already going too far, since Xenophon's Socrates never speaks of "separately existing 'ideas' "?[22] (XEN 324) The difficulty is that we cannot say that this wisdom is "knowledge of necessity" strictly speaking because "any alleged knowledge of the merely changeable must be as transitory as its object" (XEN2 406; cf. *ATP2* 8). Moreover, the classes share their responsibility, as causes, with something that is other than they are, "something for which they are not responsible and whose existence and nature are guaranteed neither by them nor by anything else we know of" (XEN 324; see also *AAT* 32 and 53). This Socratic understanding of formal causes, expressed in speech as universals, has important consequences for our understanding of science. For "if discovery of the universal, by Plato himself or by Socrates, laid bare the true foundation of science, then it exposed at the same time the fragility of its foundation, since the universals have no existence apart from the particulars" (*AAT* 20; see also 108). The classes, as Socrates authentically understands them, are not beings in their own right, and this means that they are incapable of causally explaining what it is that is responsible for the coming-into-being and passing away of the beings. Aristotle thus agrees with Socrates that the task the natural scientists had set for themselves is impossible (consider *AAT* 59–60; 20,

---

22. As for the more famous Platonic doctrine of the Ideas, see Bruell's reference to "the *so-called* Ideas or Forms (which are *supposed* to supply the Platonic answer to the question of the highest causes)" (OPPP 345 and 349 n. 22, my emphasis). Bruell suggests the version presented by a more youthful Socrates to Parmenides should in fact be understood as a pre-Socratic position, and he understands the intention of that unsatisfactory doctrine to be anti-theological. Consider also *SE* 13.11 on whether even the classes, as such, are fully intelligible to us. The difficult passages in SOXS 220 ff., especially 222–23, on dialectics and order seem relevant here too.

48–49, 172, 175). In exposing how all previous attempts to find such a cause failed, Aristotle makes it possible to see that causal confusion is ineluctable. Indeed, Aristotle is willing to make use of our tendency to conflate ousia in the sense of essence with ousia as a self-subsistent being for his own purposes: to clarify that distinction and what it entails is at the root of the difference, Bruell argues, between Aristotle's theology and his philosophic science (consider 87, 159, 163–64, 231, 237–38).

Socrates is keenly aware that this and other limits on what it is possible for us to know of the beings open the door to claims that divine causes are ultimately responsible for their existence, causes that the natural philosophers had hoped to rule out. This awareness is what turned him toward his "preliminary Socratic investigation" of human things (XEN2 406; *SE* 11.8, 147). What Socrates understood about the formal cause and how the human mind is disposed to be confused or to waver about cause may even have informed the examinations or refutations to which he subjected others, including those who claim to have more than human wisdom regarding virtue and the right way to live. (On confusion and contradiction, see SOXS 225 with 246–47; OPPP 348–49; and *SE* 10.6 with 10.4 end, 1.4, 8.7, 13.7–8, 5.8; note also what Bruell suggests in 10.10, 132 about Socrates' replacement of "a causal statement by one of classification.") To be as clear as possible—if the basic premise of the first philosophers is audacious in more than one way, the broadly Socratic position is that the theoretical audacity is insurmountable. Knowledge of the fundamental causes or necessities such as the first philosophers sought is unavailable to us for reasons intelligible to the unassisted human mind. This result strengthens the challenge posed by claims to more than human knowledge regarding the first causes. And this challenge is met, insofar as it can be met, only by Socrates' dialectical investigation of human things. But exactly how does Socrates' dialectical investigation of human things bear on this theological-political problem? Suggestions—guarded, terse, and tentative—about Socrates' approach to the most fundamental question are laced through Bruell's work, but this question must be left for readers to pursue for themselves. It remains unclear to me, for example, whether Bruell's striking but difficult suggestions about Strauss' view in "Strauss on Xenophon's Socrates" (1984) do not differ in some important ways from claims he makes in his own name in *On the Socratic Education* (1999) and elsewhere (e.g., XEN 326). I will, however, hazard one opinion of my own here that finds some support in Bruell's writings, though it can hardly be the final word: Socratic dialectics is sufficient to recognize whether claims rooted in allegedly divine knowledge are coherent *and* whether such coherence matters to an interlocutor. Because one cannot adequately respond to allegedly superhuman claims merely by demonstrating that alternative explanations are coherent (e.g., to explain an allegedly divine experience as imagined or otherwise unreal, as generated from allegedly more fundamental 'natural' phenomena, etc.), the coherence of the claims themselves must be directly assessed. Socrates' examinations do not and cannot show that Euthyphro (or others like him) has not had the experiences he claims to have had; what they can reveal is that Euthyphro is not a competent teacher of the wisdom he claims to possess on the basis of his alleged experiences. And if Euthyphro cannot coherently convey the opinions he would have someone adopt, then it is not only unreasonable but impossible for anyone to defer to him in that respect. While we may be able to imagine an interlocutor who embraces incoherence as an expected result or sign of divine wisdom, or as a mystery that invites one into a deeper teaching, it is hard to see how an incoherent teaching could, by itself, provide authoritative guidance as to how we should live. Yet Socrates seems to find that men like Euthyphro and even Ion are recalcitrant to abandoning their claims to know what virtue is, and, for this reason, Socrates' dialectical investigations of this kind may be considered a continuation of his philosophic activity proper as well as a defense, however limited, of it.[23]

As some of the citations above already indicate, an awareness of the problems that beset the first philosophers' approach to science informs Aristotle's philosophic science. We have seen that Socrates judged it impossible to find in beings or their attributes fundamental causes or necessities that are both responsible for the changing things of our ordinary experience and unalterable themselves. What basis, then, does Aristotle find for his philosophic science? Is there some other account of being or ousia that discloses necessity in the strictest sense? Bruell's interpretation of book Zeta suggests that the authentic ousiai are just the perceptible things which are agreed to be ousiai (the natural bodies) of which the "what it is" or form is predicated. The claims of both "the shape and the form" and "the what it was to be" to be themselves the first or ultimate substratum are each found wanting. Indeed, because the perceptible ousiai are not and cannot be the same as their what-it-was-to-be, the perceptibles may well remain "the only ousiai, just as they are the only or ultimate substratum" (*AAT*

---

23. One might reconsider 26–29 above from this point of view.

142; see the conclusion drawn on 169). This has consequences for what we can know of the ousiai. For if the particulars are the ousiai, we must acknowledge that each thing would not be an ousia, "and perhaps not even, strictly speaking, a particular, a 'this,' if it were not also delimited or defined by being put into a class" (127–28, 171; 20, 29, 64–66, 99–100). And since each particular thing is recognized only by the attributes it shares with other members of its class, and one or another attribute is only a part of the thing in question, we never truly grasp the whole of the particular thing by or in itself; while there is knowledge of each particular in the class character—the form as a logos of the universal—that knowledge will not and cannot be complete (142, 158 and context). Further, the things that we say are most of all ousiai (human beings, animals, plants, etc.) have matter and thus it is possible for each "not to be, or not to be how it is"; that is, "what are most of all ousiai are perishable" (145; see also 150, 158, 159). But what about the species, which do not come into being or pass away as the perceptibles do? Could perhaps the species exist always? Bruell observes that Aristotle does not insist on this when given the chance. Indeed, it is "the impossibility of insisting upon the imperishability of the species" that is "the authentic source of the problem for science," a problem which "remains unsolved" in Zeta; for the term of validity of a definition depends on the existence of the members of the group to be defined, and we are "necessarily ignorant" of this for the sensible particulars (172–73, 175). Since the class character is dependent on the particulars and has no existence apart from them, the universals are as contingent as the group of things they define (174–75). As this partial look at Bruell's interpretation of Zeta suggests, Aristotle is skeptical that there are any ousiai beyond the perceptible ones.[24] In "his innermost thought, Aristotle may not have been so devout an Aristotelian as some of his followers were and are" (140).

---

24. This is all to say nothing of the impermanence of the human minds that grasp (171) or recognize (172) or hold together the particular things by "the look with which they are regarded" (164). It is also to say nothing of the further difficulty that even if we could insist on eternal species, ousia must be "some this," but a species is always the particulars taken as a class. The attraction of the species as a solution to the problem of science involves the conflation of being as essence with self-subsistent being, a conflation that characterized the doctrine of the Ideas (159–60, 171, 227). Unless, that is, the species is taken to be the particular natural bodies generating and passing away in turn through eternity. But Bruell notices that Aristotle did not assume the eternity of the world was beyond question either (TBUA 418, Thesis 6, and 45–46 below).

Can there be a science of the perceptible, perishable ousiai? Bruell appears to answer this question in the affirmative. The ousiai as we primarily know them are the things or beings as named, each thing known as a member of a class of beings by virtue of the traits that it shares with the others in that class and which distinguish it from other kinds. To name something is to point to "one of those." To make the pre-eminent traits that we perceive explicit is to give the definition of the kind or class. Indeed, each particular is not what it is until it is grasped as a member of the class to which it belongs (*AAT* 167, 171). Now "to have a nature is to be some kind of being, and not another kind" (62). Thus, the nature(s) understood by philosophic science and the necessities implied by the nature(s) are not those responsible for the being or existence of beings but rather "the determinations of being as being, in the sense that they express what it is (for anything) to be or what (its) being a being entails" (62, 102–3). It is in this light, one supposes, that nature as the account of the internal source or cause of motion of a being must also be understood (*Physics* 192b8–23). There is then knowledge of the ousiai—knowledge of them as members of a class and of the necessary relations entailed and excluded by the relations within and between classes. The world we articulate this way, the domain "to which the 'ousiai' belong or which they constitute, is the world as it is given to us in our most elementary and least contestable experience, in the experience that underlies and completes perception"; and "it is perhaps in what is most manifest to us that the necessity sought by science is to be found in its least questionable form" (66 and 245; see 64–66 generally and 70). Bruell suggestively refers in this connection to Aristotle's claim in the *Nicomachean Ethics* that it is from experience that we obtain the indemonstrable principles or starting points of science (see 1142a16–20, *AAT* 66 as well as TBUA 425). It nevertheless remains true that knowledge of a particular ousia or "some this" will never be complete (142, 245); "our awareness of the being or class of beings that we designate by some name—what we 'see' somehow in our encounter with the beings that make up the class—is not exhausted by anything we may be able to say about them" (TBUA 429; see also 430–31). Nor, since the perceptibles are perishable, can we know that the definition we attain will remain valid over time (*AAT* 172–73; see also *ATP2* 5 with n. 6). We cannot know then that the beings we recognize must necessarily exist; yet we do know that they must necessarily possess the characteristics they do in order to be recognized as the beings they are—a contingent, intelligible necessity. Moreover, although we may well come to irresolvable difficulties in our reflection upon the manifest regularity of the world of our experience, we can come to this awareness only on that basis (121, 268). The "genuine solution" to the "problem of the instability of the perceptibles"—the problem of the impermanence we (also) see all around us—to the extent there is one, is that "as limits, the potentialities or possibilities of the perceptibles, which are so long as they are, do not 'flow' as each of them does" (263). "Science is possible then, even if we lack access to beings of the permanence ascribed to the ideas" (264; consider also 83), even if we have now seen that a fixed star and its ancient light can be swallowed up by a black hole.

The thought that the foundation is "merely given, that it lacks itself a knowable foundation, is admittedly difficult from more than one point of view," for reasons I have attempted bring to light (*AAT* 231).[25] Consider again a remark made earlier, quoting now the passage in full:

> Science can content itself with its rather modest causal accounts only so long as it can be confident, and reasonably so, that the causes it can grasp, or the causes to the extent that it can grasp them, cannot be overturned—in such a way as to invalidate its account of them—by the operation of more powerful causes of unknown origin. That is, it can be duly modest or cautious only if it can assume that "being is just what is perceptible to the senses and what the so-called heaven encompasses." And as we have seen, it does make that assumption. But with what right? And if the right or the justification is lacking, if the assumption in question is audacious in more than one way, does not science or philosophy come into a fatal contradiction with itself? (28)

How far does a modest science or knowledge of contingent necessities, one which only partially explains the coming-into-being and passing away of the beings of our given experience, take us in resolving this grave problem? We are constantly tempted, if not compelled, to step beyond this and many other limits Aristotle discerns, to make presumptions about the permanent causes of being or the fundamental necessities to which beings as beings are subject (123, 177; at QNLS 295, note too the distinction between the

---

25. Bruell develops a further account of the difficulty in TBUA 424–26.

"natural beings," which are "manifest," and "nature," which is less than entirely evident). Careful study of the *Metaphysics* (along with *Aristotle as Teacher*) challenges us each step of the way as it relentlessly examines possible foundations for philosophic science. Readers will have to judge for themselves whether Aristotle has ultimately shown that the world manifest to us is, in the end, the only available basis. Despite all the doubts that can be raised about that world, doubts that arise from premises Aristotle did not and in some cases could not share as well as from those premises he does share, Aristotle displays what Bruell is led to call "a manly insistence" on the significance, "in its own way timeless or universal, of what is manifest to us." Aristotle displays an "unwillingness, to begin with, in the face of the thought of an absence of order of perhaps limitless duration, to be so overwhelmed as to refuse to the here and now, to what is around us, to the order in which we live and move, its undeniable evidence" (195; see also 207). It is here too, I think, that the hard moral-political preparation, rooted in civic "education" and purified by Socratic education, makes a fundamental contribution. (Consider the problem intimated on 158–59, the "expectation" referred to on 236, and "confidence" on 240; compare with the "wish" and "concern" on 264 in light of Aristotle's manliness.)

In conclusion, we note a certain pattern in Bruell's work. Whether it is in examining the contemporary obstacles to Socratic education, how Socrates turned himself and others toward a genuine education, or the character of philosophic science, Bruell shows that our thought cannot help but begin in the middle of things. To "begin at the beginning," the true beginning, requires a specific recovery—a recollection, perhaps—of the fundamental questions that are as permanent as the minds that ask them. Bruell admirably, patiently, repeatedly reminds us in his own way that "the problem inherent in the surface of things, and only in the surface of things, is the heart of things."[26]

Acknowledgments

Thank you to Christopher Bruell and the editors for the opportunity to present this essay here. Many friends, old and new, have made it better, especially Paul Diduch. I am grateful as well for the love and patience of my wife, Dana Andreoli.

---

26. Strauss, *Thoughts on Machiavelli*, 13.

Bibliography and Abbreviations

The chapter number for each work included in this volume is noted; abbreviations of works not included are italicized here and in my citations.

AAT   *Aristotle as Teacher: His Introduction to a Philosophic Science*, St. Augustine's Press (2014).

AL   "Ancient Literacy," *The Review of Politics*, Vol. 52, Issue 3, Summer 1990, pp. 466–69.

ATP   *Aristotle on Theory and Practice* (chap. 14).

ATP2   *Aristotle on Theory and Practice Part Two*, presented at the École des Hautes Études en Sciences Sociales in Paris (2006). Unpublished.

CPW   Review of Cropsey, *Plato's World*, *The American Political Science Review*, Vol. 90, No. 3 (September 1996), pp. 623–24.

DPP   *Death in the Perspective of Philosophy* (chap. 15).

FXS   Forward to Leo Strauss, *Xenophon's Socratic Discourse*, and to Leo Strauss, *Xenophon's Socrates*, St. Augustine's Press (2004), pp. ix–xviii and x–xviii.

GPAI   *Gadamer on Plato: The Art of Interpretation*, *The Review of Politics*, Vol. 55, No. 1 (Winter 1993), pp. 167–70.

HPP   *Happiness in the Perspective of Philosophy* (chap. 16).

LEEC   *Liberal Education and Education for Citizenship* (chap. 1).

OMPP   *On the Original Meaning of Political Philosophy: An Interpretation of Plato's Lovers* (chap. 6).

ONRH   *On the Place and Treatment of Classical Political Philosophy in the Plan of* Natural Right and History *as a Whole* (chap. 10).

OPPP   *On Platonic Political Philosophy* (chap. 13).

ORPT   *On Reading Plato Today* (chap. 2).

PR   *Plato and Relativism* (chap. 3).

QNLS   *The Question of Nature and the Thought of Leo Strauss* (chap. 11).

RBG   Review of Goodwin, *Using Political Ideas, Social Science Quarterly*, Vol. 65, No. 3 (September 1984), pp. 914–15.

REP   Untitled and unpublished paper on Plato's *Republic*, presented at the conference Theoretical Perspectives on the Problem of Evil in Twentieth Century Politics, Chicago (1987).

SE   *On the Socratic Education: An Introduction to the Shorter Socratic Dialogues*, Rowman & Littlefield (1999).

SOXS   *Strauss on Xenophon's Socrates* (chap. 7).

SPSK   *Socratic Politics and Self-Knowledge: an Interpretation of Plato's Charmides* (chap. 5).

TBUA   *Theses Bearing on the Understanding of Aristotle's Natural Science* (chap. 18).

TC   "Truth and Consequences," *Boston College Magazine* (Summer 1991), pp. 41–43. Note: the title of this piece was chosen by an editor without Bruell's consent.

TE   "*True Esotericism*" (chap. 9).

TP   *Thucydides and Perikles, The St. John's Review*, Vol. XXXII, No. 3, Summer 1981, pp. 24–29.

TVAI   *Thucydides' View of Athenian Imperialism* (chap. 4).

UAF   *A Return to Classical Political Philosophy and the Understanding of the American Founding* (chap. 8).

XEN   *Xenophon* (chap. 12).

XEN2   *What Xenophon Learned from Socrates About Philosophy and the Philosophic Life* (chap. 17).

XHS   "Xenophon and His Socrates," *Interpretation*, Vol. 16/2, Winter 1988–89, pp. 295–306; republished, in revised form, as the Introduction to *Xenophon, Memorabilia*, translated and annotated by Amy L. Bonnette, Cornell University Press (1994), pp. vii–xxii.

Part I

Introductions

1

Liberal Education and Education for Citizenship

The title of my paper, whether by design or accident, poses a question, a problem: liberal education and education for citizenship—are they the same or not, and if not, what is their relation? Let's call liberal education education simply or strictly speaking, or its highest form, such education as aims at the formation of the best possible human being, or at guiding those capable of it to the discovery of the truth, of those truths most important to human beings as such. What is the relation of education so understood to education for citizenship? The reason why they are not simply the same education is clear. As Aristotle tells us, what a good human being is is the same everywhere, at every time so to speak. This is also what the Bible tells us: "He hath shewed thee, O man, what is good; and what doth the Lord require of thee, but to do justly, and to love mercy, and to walk humbly with thy God?" (Micah 6:8) The admonition of Micah is addressed to man as such; it is intended to have universal validity. But what it means to be a citizen—what rights and duties citizenship entails, what purposes the loyalty of citizens serves—all of this varies from country to country insofar as the forms and purposes of government vary. And therefore, as we also learn from Aristotle, what it means to be a good citizen varies from place to place—so much so,

---

The author dedicated this essay to Allan Bloom, for his unrivaled contributions to higher education in America.

that in some situations, all too familiar in this century, it is impossible to be both a good citizen and a good human being at the same time. In those situations, education for citizenship is deeply at odds with the requirements of education strictly speaking, as is shown most strikingly by the prominence of pseudo-scientific doctrines of various kinds in the education schemes of certain countries. We recognize this state of affairs when we use the term "indoctrination" and distinguish what it designates from true education.

But nothing, that is, no pressing necessity, forces us to dwell on the relation of liberal education to education for citizenship in those extreme cases. We live under a good and decent form of government. What is the relation of liberal education and citizen education in the case where citizenship itself is something decent and admirable? By thus narrowing our question, we free it from most, but not all, of its difficulties. Before taking up thematically some of the positive contributions which, in this case, each sort of education has to offer the other, it might be worthwhile to cast a glance at the difficulty which remains. Its character is indicated by the contrast between two stories in the *Memorabilia* or "Recollections" of Xenophon. These "Recollections" are in fact recollections of Socrates, the citizen-philosopher and educator par excellence, Xenophon's own teacher and friend. I'll tell first the story which involves Socrates and Glaucon, who is familiar to us as Plato's brother and as a leading figure in Plato's *Republic*. When Glaucon was not yet twenty years old, he thought it was time to take the crucial step on the road to fulfilling his ambition to become leader of Athens: namely, to begin to speak out in the Athenian assembly. None of his friends or relatives could stop him from the attempt, which could result in nothing other than his being dragged from the speaker's platform, an object of ridicule. But Socrates brought him to his senses by means of a conversation which went roughly as follows:

> After securing the youth's attention by praising his ambition in extravagant terms, Socrates said, Isn't it clear, Glaucon, that since you wish to be honored, you must benefit the city?
>
> Certainly.
>
> By the gods, don't hold back but tell us where your good work in the city's behalf will begin!
>
> At this, Glaucon was silent. He had, obviously, up to that moment, never given any thought to where he would begin.

Socrates had to help him out: Well, just as in the case of a friend's estate—if you wished to enlarge it you would try to make it richer—so in the case of the city, will you try to make it richer?

Certainly.

Wouldn't it be richer if its revenues were to increase?

Probably.

Tell us then how many sources of revenue the city has now and what they are. Clearly you have looked into this, so that if some of them are not providing what they ought, you can remedy their deficiencies and if more sources are needed you can provide them.

But, by Zeus, these at any rate are things I have not looked into!

Well, if you have neglected these things, tell us at least what the expenditures of the city are: clearly you intend to cut the unnecessary ones.

But, by Zeus, I haven't yet had the leisure to look into those either.

Well, shall we put off making the city richer then? For how can anyone ignorant of its expenditures and revenues supervise these things?

But, Socrates, it is possible to enrich the city at the expense of its enemies [in other words, through war].

Socrates replied that this is indeed possible, providing that the city is *stronger* than its enemies. If it is weaker, on the other hand, it stands to lose rather than gain from war.

Glaucon conceded this.

Tell us first then about the city's power on land and sea and then about the power of its enemies.

But, by Zeus, I wouldn't be able to state it for you just like that, from memory!

Well, if you have it written down, produce it; I would be extremely pleased to hear about this subject.

But, by Zeus, I haven't yet written it down either.

Then war too we will hold off giving our advice about at first. For perhaps, because of the magnitude of these matters, you have not yet examined them at this the outset of your leadership. But surely you have already concerned yourself with the safeguarding of the countryside, and you know which of the guardposts are critical and which not and how many guards are sufficient. And you will advise us to enlarge the critical posts and to cut the superfluous ones.

Glaucon's response appeared to be somewhat rash. Socrates asked him therefore whether his view was based upon an inspection on the spot.

It is an estimate, rather.

Well, here too, shall we give our advice only when we possess knowledge, not merely estimates?

Perhaps that would be better.

When it came to light that Glaucon had not gone to inspect the silver mines, either, an important source of state revenue, Socrates suggested that he might be intending to offer the excuse that the place was said to have an oppressive climate. Regarding the food supply, however—that is, the relation between Athens' annual production and its annual requirements—there could clearly be no excuse for failing to acquire the necessary knowledge.

But Glaucon protested: you are talking of an immense task, Socrates, if it will be necessary to supervise even things like this.

Socrates was now ready to bring the conversation to its conclusion: One can't be a fine manager even of one's own estate unless one both *knows* what it needs—everything that it needs—and takes care to supply all those things; and the city consists of more than ten thousand estates; since it is a difficult thing to supervise all of these at once, why don't you first attempt to enlarge one estate—namely, your uncle's which needs it—and if you can do *this, then* try to supervise more? If you can't benefit one, how would you be able to benefit many?

But I *would* benefit my uncle's estate, if he would listen to me.

So, you are unable to persuade your uncle, but you think you will be able to make all the Athenians, your uncle included, listen to you? Watch out, Glaucon, lest desirous as you are of fame, you meet with the opposite. Haven't you observed how dangerous it is for one who lacks knowledge

> to speak or act? . . . If you wish to be famous and admired
> in the city, try to acquire knowledge regarding those things
> you wish to do. (III, 6)

Thus Socrates reminded Glaucon of the range and magnitude of the responsibilities of a public leader and led him to see what sort of knowledge is needed to carry out those responsibilities in a competent manner. In doing this, Socrates fulfilled his own responsibilities as a citizen and a friend—though it is perhaps also fair to note that he did not offer to supply Glaucon with the necessary knowledge; it is even possible that he did not possess it in every case.

The other story concerns a conversation of a quite different tenor. It too involved a youth "not yet twenty" years old, one named Alcibiades. The conversation took place, at Alcibiades' initiative, with his guardian, who happened to be the renowned Pericles, the great leader of the Athenian democracy, then at the peak of his fame and power. It thus did not directly involve Socrates, but Xenophon includes it in his "Recollections" because, at the time it took place, Alcibiades was still a close companion of Socrates; in fact, the conversation revolved around the sort of questions Socrates himself was always asking. In other words, the Socratic influence—in however distorted a form—is unmistakably present in it.

> Tell me, Pericles, would you be able to teach me what law is?
> By all means.
> By the gods, teach it then. For when I hear people being praised as law-abiding men, I think that anyone ignorant of what law is wouldn't deserve this praise.
> In wanting to know what law is, Alcibiades, you don't desire anything difficult: whatever the assembled multitude approves [remember here that Pericles is the leader of a democracy] and puts in writing—declaring what must and must not be done—all these are laws.
> Does the multitude believe that the good things or the bad must be done?
> The good by Zeus, boy, and the bad must not be done.
> And if it is not the multitude but, for example, where the government is oligarchic the assembled few put in writing what is to be done—what are these things?

To which Pericles replied: All that the dominant part of the city, upon deliberation, puts in writing regarding what must be done, all that is called law.

Even if it is a tyrant who is dominant in the city and who puts in writing for the citizens what must be done—are these things law?

Even what a ruling tyrant puts in writing, even those things are called law.

To which Alcibiades responded: But force and lawlessness—what are they, Pericles? Aren't they found whenever the stronger compels the weaker—not persuading him but through use of force—to do whatever the stronger decides?

That's my opinion at least, Pericles said.

Then, whatever a tyrant compels the citizens to do, not persuading them, and puts in writing—is this lawlessness [rather than law]?

In my opinion it is, Pericles replied, for I retract my former answer to the extent that it held that what a tyrant puts in writing, without using persuasion, is law.

And what the few put in writing, not persuading the many but exercising dominion over them—shall we or shall we not say that these things are force [rather than law]?

In my opinion, Pericles said, everything that one compels another to do without persuading him, whether he puts it in writing or not, is force rather than law.

Then whatever the whole multitude puts in writing, not persuading the rich but exercising dominion over them—would these things be force rather than law?

At this point, Pericles ceased to answer Alcibiades but said to him instead: You know, Alcibiades, we too, at your age, were very sharp in discussions of this sort; we practised them and played the sophist as you appear to me to practise them.

To which Alcibiades replied: O that I had known you when you were at your sharpest, Pericles. (I 2.40–46)

Now, to bring our two stories together: nothing further, at least nothing bad, was heard of Glaucon. Socrates had apparently restored him permanently to the path of responsibility and good citizenship. But Alcibiades—an equally close, in fact a closer companion of Socrates than Glaucon was—became the most notorious traitor of his age, doing irreparable harm to Athens in the process; even prior to his treasonous activity, he was conspicuous for the lawlessness of his private behavior. Now it would be foolish and unfair to blame Socrates for all of this; but it is, also, difficult to be certain that his undoubted influence on Alcibiades was entirely harmless. I draw the following simple, but perhaps far-reaching, conclusion from the stories: while liberal education has an important contribution to make to education for decent citizenship, and while, as we will see, the converse is also true, liberal education should not be thought to be identical with education for citizenship even in the best case of citizenship in a decent community. Even here, at a certain point the paths of the two sorts of education diverge, for the one culminates in the raising of questions which, for the most part, it is not necessary to raise for the purposes served by the other. It would probably be a disservice to both sorts of education to fail to respect their distinctness, just as it would be to fail to recognize their indissoluble connection.

Let's turn then to that connection—more precisely to some aspects of the contribution which liberal education can make to education for citizenship in our country, taking liberal education now to mean the education which is or ought to be available in our colleges and universities. The citizens who can be expected to come in contact with this education will be especially leaders or rather potential leaders of their communities. What attributes would qualify them to exercise such leadership? Turning to Aristotle's *Politics* (V 9) for an answer, we find that he mentions these: friendship toward the established form of government; capacity for the great tasks of office; and virtue, including the sort of justice upheld by that particular form of government. That liberal education as we are familiar with it has some contribution to make to the development of such qualities is clear, I think; that there are certain limits to its contribution is perhaps also clear. For example, the role of church and family and of education at the primary and secondary levels in the development of moral virtue and of loyalty toward American democracy is clearer than the role of liberal education here, and almost surely more important. No amount of so-called higher education is likely to be able to make up for what is lacking at earlier stages; rather the usefulness of the higher education may well presuppose the effectiveness of what has come before. To mention just one point, there is an emotional bond to our country and what it stands for that must, in most cases at least, precede and accompany further education in its political principles if that education is to have its greatest impact. With regard to capacity for great tasks, to take another example, liberal education can point out, as Socrates did to Glaucon, the various sorts of knowledge necessary for the accomplishment of those tasks; given the current constitution of our universities, it can even supply much or all of that knowledge; but it is more difficult to say how, and even whether, it can contribute to the development of prudence—the judgment which enables one to *use properly* the otherwise merely technical knowledge. The difficulty here is due partly to the fact, which Aristotle points out, that the development of prudence presupposes the presence of moral virtue—to take just a small but not insignificant example, the courage to look harsh facts in the face without blinking or turning aside. We could make liberal education our sole reliance for the development of prudence, then, only if we could make it our sole reliance for the development of moral virtue. Here again its utility depends to some extent on what has gone before, as well as on the presence of a suitable nature.

Nevertheless, the utility of liberal education—both in the development of prudence in those who have the capacity for it and in the development of an educated devotion to American democracy—is far from negligible. To turn first to prudence or judgment, this cannot be *taught*, strictly speaking, not only for the reason already given but also because it does not consist solely in having, and holding on to, the right opinions. There are no infallible rules that can simply be memorized or mastered and then applied—rules, for example, that would let us determine when it is or is not proper to take an action involving risk to life. Nor are there rules to guide the gathering and absorption of the myriad bits and pieces of information necessary to informed decisions—still less rules to insure the correct assessment of the information available so as to yield accurate estimates of an opposing leader's character, for example, or his influence. But liberal education can help by fostering the habits of observation and reflection which are integral elements of prudence or judgment. The unsurpassable model in this regard is Thucydides' history of the twenty-seven-year war between Athens and Sparta, a work which is designed to make of its reader almost a participant in the great political events narrated in it. As a quasi-participant, the reader is all but compelled to make judgments and decisions as the actual participants did: Should the Athenians make an alliance with the Corcyraeans as the speech of the latter in the Athenian assembly urges; or should they refrain from doing so as the answering speech of the Corinthians insists? What information is relevant to the decision, and what is available; what considerations of right or interest should guide it? Thucydides confronts his readers with such questions in scores of concrete situations, giving them as much but generally no more information than the actual participants possessed at the time the choices had to be made, the actions taken or abstained from. And he rarely obtrudes his own judgment to relieve the reader from the task of thinking for himself and thus developing the habits of observation and reflection referred to. But the education which Thucydides' history and similar works provide in this way may make a still more significant contribution to the development of prudence. If prudence does not consist solely in the possession of the right opinions, it can be impeded by false opinions which pose obstacles to its development even where the other requisites are present and which thus distort the capacity for judgment of good and bad men alike. To clarify this notion of *obstacles* to prudence, it will help to give a few concrete examples. The first is from Thucydides—a passage toward the end of his account of the Sicilian expedition, the unsuccessful Athenian attempt to conquer Sicily and thus begin to expand their empire to dimensions later achieved by Rome. With their cause in Sicily clearly lost, the Athenian generals made a much-delayed decision to withdraw their army and navy from the island and thus prevent defeat in Sicily from becoming defeat in the larger war with Sparta: for it was difficult to see how Athens could hold out in that war if she should be deprived of the forces then in Sicily, the cream of her military strength on both land and sea. The generals' decision came at the last possible moment for the Athenians to get away; the enemy forces on the spot were gaining strength daily and were eager to inflict a crushing defeat on the Athenian force before it could escape. When preparations for the departure were complete, and the Athenians were on the point of leaving, there was an eclipse of the moon. (Thucydides remarks that the moon was full; he seems to have made a point of noting when such things occur.) At this Nicias, the general with the greatest authority, declared that he would not even consider departing before waiting "thrice nine" days, as the diviners were advising (and the bulk of the soldiers—but not the other generals—were urging). Thucydides is sufficiently moved by this decision, which sealed the Athenians' fate, to permit himself a rare comment: "Nicias was somewhat too inclined toward divination and such things." A more recent example comes from Churchill's reflection (in *The Gathering Storm*) on what might have led the responsible ministers to the grave error of judgment constituted by the Munich agreement with Hitler. As Churchill emphasizes in the narrative leading up to the reflection, Chamberlain did not believe that the peace purchased at such a price would last even three months:

> It may be well here to set down some principles of morals and action which may be a guide in the future. No case of this kind can be judged apart from its circumstances. The facts may be unknown at the time, and estimates of them must be largely guesswork, coloured by the general feelings and aims of whoever is trying to pronounce. Those who are prone by temperament and character to seek sharp and clearcut solutions of difficult and obscure problems, who are ready to fight whenever some challenge comes from a foreign Power, have not always been right. On the other hand, those whose inclination is to bow their heads, to seek patiently and faithfully for peaceful compromise, are not always wrong. On the contrary, in the majority of instances they may be right, not only morally but from a practical standpoint. How many wars have been averted by patience and persisting good will! Religion and virtue alike lend their sanctions to meekness and humility, not only between men but between nations. How many wars have been precipitated by firebrands! How many misunderstandings which led to wars could have been removed by temporizing! How often have countries fought cruel wars and then after a few years of peace found themselves not only friends but allies!
>
> The Sermon on the Mount is the last word in Christian ethics. Everyone respects the quakers. Still, it is not on these terms that Ministers assume their responsibilities of guiding states. Their duty is first so to deal with other nations as to avoid strife and war and to eschew aggression in all its forms, whether for nationalistic or ideological objects. But the safety of the State, the lives and freedom of their own fellow countrymen, to whom they owe their position, make it right and imperative in the last resort, or when a final and definite conviction has been reached, that the use of force should not be excluded. If the circumstances are such as to warrant it, force may be used. And if this be so, it should be used under the conditions which are most favourable. There is no merit in

putting off a war for a year if, when it comes, it is a far worse war or one much harder to win. These are the tormenting dilemmas upon which mankind has throughout its history been so frequently impaled. Final judgment upon them can only be recorded by history in relation to the facts of the case as known to the parties at the time, and also as subsequently proved. (Churchill, *The Gathering Storm.* Boston: Houghton Mifflin, 1948, pp. 285–286)

The choice of these two examples may have left a misleading impression. It goes without saying that neither the sole nor, in our time at least, the gravest obstacles to prudence have their source in an insufficiently educated piety. That source is much more likely to be the one indicated in the final example, taken from some reminiscences of Trotsky regarding Lenin (*On Lenin: Notes Towards a Biography*). The remarks in question concern some theses written by Lenin in January of 1918, where he seems to regard the success of socialism in Russia as requiring only a few months. Trotsky wonders whether Lenin could have meant seriously these and other similar, apparently unrealistic statements: "*He believed in what he was saying.* [This is emphasized in Trotsky's text.] And so the fantastic date for socialism—six months hence—testified also to the same Leninist spirit which showed itself in his realistic approach to every immediate task. The deep and unyielding conviction that there were tremendous possibilities of human development for which one could, one should pay the price of suffering and sacrifice, was always the hall-mark of Leninism." It would be difficult to put the matter in a nutshell better than Trotsky does—one might only wish to add that the sacrifices Lenin referred to were, of course, to be made by others.

If certain false opinions, for example the opinion that there are possibilities of future human development so tremendous as to justify the inflicting of unspeakable suffering on the present generation in order to bring them about—if false opinions of this sort are obstacles to the development of a humane and truly prudent judgment, then liberal education can make a contribution to the development of such prudence by combating them, by showing us how the world is, the world God gave us and must expect us to act in, by calling our attention to the permanent features of the world we know. This is what Thucydides does. He is sometimes compared in this respect to Machiavelli, who regarded his superiority to ancient political philosophy as consisting in his greater realism.

But Thucydides shows us the way the world is not, as Machiavelli does, to shock and ultimately overcome our attachment to justice but rather to educate and refine it. To this end, his severe but beautiful prose first calls forth that attachment and nourishes it: he continually invites us to judge the participants in the history and their actions, both nations and individuals, in moral terms. But he insists in return that we familiarize ourselves with all of the relevant features of the situation in which the actions we judge must be taken, all of the features which moral judgment must take into account if it is to be truly moral. To recall an example mentioned earlier, would the Athenians be in violation, as the Corinthians claim, of an already existing treaty if they make an alliance with the Corcyraeans? And if this is the case, are the defense requirements imposed by an impending and all but unavoidable war sufficient to excuse such a breach of their word? Or, to take another example, is a small nation to be condemned for taking Athens' side in her wars of expansion and thus helping to enslave her neighbors? What were the concrete choices available to that nation at the time? Does a truly moral course of action require that one possess the strength to be independent? What, in turn, are the foundations of such strength? Properly used, Thucydides' work provides an education in the unchangeable necessities that limit all possibilities of human development but also, for that very reason, provide the arena within which truly moral action and judgment is possible and needed. And the works of Aristotle, among others, do the same. When we turn for example from the end of his *Ethics* to its sequel the *Politics*, we are likely to do so with the expectation and hope that we are about to learn how to increase vastly the amount of virtue in the world through the use of appropriate legislation. Read from this perspective, the *Politics* comes to sight as the gentle but thorough and relentless account of the difficulties preventing the fulfillment of that expectation; it is the required political education of the moral man. It is intended, like Thucydides' book, to foster a manly acceptance of what cannot be changed, while at the same time—and only in this way—encouraging the calm but determined effort to do that which can be done.

To turn just briefly now to the place of liberal education in the development of an educated devotion to American democracy, I think it is clear that at each stage of learning, the pre-existing bond of attachment to country must be deepened by the learning appropriate to that stage. At the college level, this would include the assiduous study of the fundamental documents of American democracy as well as the writings of those who have reflected most adequately on our politics and way of life. The Declaration of Independence, the Constitution, the Federalist papers, and writings of Washington, Jefferson, Lincoln and de Tocqueville would be included on any such list. This study would be significantly assisted by attention to some of the great philosophic teachers of modern republicanism, Locke and Montesquieu especially. One additional point needs to be mentioned. In the same chapter of the *Politics* in which he puts "friendship toward the established form of government" first among the attributes desirable in a leader, Aristotle also says that education in the spirit of the regime is the greatest of the means of preserving a particular regime (or form of government). Then, however, he adds remarks to the effect that the intention of such education should be to foster a moderate or sober, rather than an extreme attachment to the spirit or principles of the government. The reason, which he develops at length elsewhere in the *Politics*, is that the principles of any actual government can never be free from flaws. The unbending application and extension of them, while gratifying to extreme partisans, is likely to undermine, in the long run, the very survival of that form of government by making the government worse. An educated attachment to American democracy must include, then, awareness of its blemishes and flaws—not those which are held to consist in the insufficiently rigorous application of its principles; rather it is the principles themselves which have to be looked at in this light. And for this purpose, the use of the writings of the non-democratic thinkers (I don't say anti-democratic, but non-democratic) of our past, of the philosophic tradition, is probably indispensable.

In conclusion, I want to mention just one contribution which the concern with education for citizenship can make to liberal education—but an essential contribution, at least in my view. When we turn to the generally old and difficult books which must constitute the core of a true liberal education, we are confronted too often with the situation that guides to help us uncover their riches are lacking. For whatever reasons—some are not too hard to seek: it is much easier to specify the training of a competent physicist than that of a competent interpreter of Shakespeare—this is often our situation. And that means that we have no other guidance than what is supplied by our own seriousness. That is, it must be the seriousness of our purpose in seeking out these books which grants us some access to their contents. And it is difficult to think of a more serious purpose than the desire to develop in oneself or another the capacity for a high sort of citizenship. It is when we turn to the old books with our political and moral concerns foremost in mind—to learn more about justice and war, about the strengths and weaknesses of various forms of government, about the temptations and dangers of tyranny—it is when we do this that these texts cease to speak to us in an alien, if charming, idiom and begin to speak instead in plain terms of matters which touch our lives and concern our role as citizens and our place in the world.

2

On Reading Plato Today

My theme is "On Reading Plato Today" and, in particular, the obstacles or difficulties one is likely to encounter in reading Plato today. In what context, in the light of what concerns, does this topic present itself as worthy of consideration?

It is clear to just about everyone that we are living in extraordinary times. The confrontation—not to say undeclared war—which divided the modern world for forty-five years has been settled by the all-but-complete surrender of one of the two opposing sides, a surrender not less but rather more remarkable for being offered not to the armies but to the ideas and principles of its opponent. On the winning side, newspapers and television news programs, reflecting the desire to celebrate such a victory, were filled with accounts of the events associated with the demise of the longtime foe. At the same time, though this was and is less often noted, the status accorded by the victorious side itself to its triumphant principles has never been less clear. In this country, for example, a recent nominee to the Supreme Court felt obliged in his confirmation hearings to depreciate the significance of his adherence to natural law or natural right—to the notion that there are principles of justice whose validity is independent of human fiat or choice—and to speak instead of his "values," of his personal commitments and merely subjective judgments. And partly for this reason—because the status of the Western principles has become unclear in the West itself—many individuals in Western countries are more than ever at a loss not only as to the direction their lives should take but even as to where to look for guidance in answering that question. This situation, in turn, in which many individuals in the West find themselves, may help to account for a development that is, in its way, as surprising and, perhaps, hardly less significant than those already mentioned. In small but growing numbers people are again, today, taking Plato seriously—that is, reading him not merely "for pleasure" or to trace the antecedents of contemporary ideas or for any other light or frivolous reason, but in order to gain from him guidance about how best to lead their lives. To me, this seems a salutary development—in the first place, for our liberal democracy for, although Plato was not a liberal nor even a democrat, he was a friend to decent government based on the rule of law, and he made a powerful case on its behalf. And, in the second place, it seems to me even more salutary for the individuals concerned. It makes sense then to encourage them and, so far as we can, to assist their efforts. But those efforts can be assisted, assisted effectively, only to the extent that we appreciate the obstacles which lie in the way of their reaching their goal. The most important obstacles, which stem from the intrinsic difficulty of the problems treated by Plato, would have been encountered by readers of any period, including Plato's own; and we can assume that he has supplied in the dialogues themselves the most suitable assistance for overcoming them. But there may be other obstacles which arise from subsequent developments that have affected the upbringing which readers of later ages bring with them to the text. It is possible that some of these developments were not foreseen by Plato. This possibility need not cast doubt on the permanent validity of the guidance supplied by the dialogues: the questions addressed by Plato may remain the fundamental questions confronting human beings everywhere and always. But developments not foreseen by him may have affected our awareness of the fundamental questions and hence our capacity to recognize and to comprehend his treatment of them. And, if this is the case, we might have to supplement our reading of the dialogues by reflection on special features of our own situation, if we wish to understand him.

Plato's dialogues are intended, with a singleness of purpose rarely if ever matched by the works of any other philosopher, to attract young readers to philosophy and to lead them toward it. By philosophy, Plato appears to have meant a certain way of life—namely, the *best* way—and a certain understanding of the world, insofar as it is capable of being understood—namely, the *correct* understanding. Today, most of those who have anything to say about these matters deny that there is one best way of life, best for human beings as such; and their denial is welcomed by many others as contributing to tolerance. But this has not succeeded entirely in preventing readers of Plato from falling under his spell; some, those I mentioned earlier, are still or again enchanted by him and tempted by the vision of philosophy and the philosophic life which he holds out to them. Turning to the dialogues with eager anticipation and passionate desire to learn, such readers are deterred neither by the denial of all objective truth regarding the most important matters nor by the prospect of the social good which is, according to many, dependent on the universal acceptance of that denial. Nor should they be deterred. For, as for tolerance, it is reasonable to doubt that genuine tolerance requires the denial of all objective truth or is even compatible with that denial. Moreover, those who, in the name of tolerance, condemn the search for the way of life best for human beings as such are presumably convinced that it is best for human beings as such to be tolerant: they surely urge others to be tolerant and condemn those who fall short of what they themselves take tolerance to be. They thus give unwitting testimony to the inescapability of judgments of good and bad, right and wrong; they have succeeded in freeing themselves, not from such judgments, but only from the inquiry and reflection on which any reasonable judgment is based. They might make the objection, at this point, that this is precisely what they deny: the very possibility of reasonable judgment; all judgment, whether we like it or not, rests finally on "values" or personal commitment. The search for a rational answer to the question of the best way of life ought therefore to be given up as futile even if it cannot be persuasively or even consistently condemned as harmful or wrong. But now we are entitled to insist in turn that *that* assertion, at least, be defended with adequate reasons—the assertion that no rational or objectively true answer can be given to the question of the best way of life. Or what else could oblige us to accept that assertion as true and act in accord with this acceptance? Nor can we regard as adequate, reasons whose adequacy we have not seen *for ourselves*. And we are unlikely to be in a position to determine for ourselves whether a given question is susceptible of receiving a rational or objectively true answer, unless we ourselves have had some experience in thinking about that question, unless, that is, we have made the attempt to find its true answer. So far then from affording sufficient cause to give up the search for a rational answer to the question of the best way of life, the contemporary denial of the possibility of such an answer supplies to serious readers of Plato today—even or precisely if they are troubled by that denial—a reason for sticking to their guns, for acting as their inclination to think that they can learn from him something of fundamental importance bids them to act, for studying the dialogues with mind and heart open and eager to learn.

Indeed, the reflection just summarized may serve to indicate more clearly not only why these readers, or anyone else with a modicum of self-understanding, must be eager to take a step like this one but also what such eagerness means. Understanding ourselves requires in the first place that we begin to see the importance to us of judgments of good and bad, right and wrong, judgments which, taken together, amount to an answer to the question of the best way of life. Now judgments of this sort, as we can also see—so long as we do not seek to hide this from ourselves by cowardly recourse to the language of value and commitment—are intended to be judgments of *being*, of what *is*. But the judgments in question come to us and take possession of us before we begin to reflect, to reflect adequately, on the matters they concern: at this stage, then, however passionately we may be attached to them, we do not know those judgments to be true. Nor can we simply abandon them at the moment we become aware that this is the case, for—apart from the fact that we also do not know them to be false—they mean too much to us for us to let them go without a struggle. But this means that our initial eagerness to learn, though it may put us on the path to genuine openness of mind, is not the product of such openness nor even truly its companion. Rather, to the extent that we become aware that we do not know the truth of what we believe regarding fundamental matters, we become passionately eager to acquire such knowledge; and, in this spirit, we raise the question whether the judgments to which we are already attached are true—for example, whether our view of justice, of right and wrong, is true. It is impossible however to pursue that question very far without raising the more comprehensive one, "What is justice?" Now, the question "What is justice?" is nowhere raised with greater seriousness than in the Platonic dialogues; nor is its treatment anywhere given a more central place. So much attention, in fact, does Plato's Socrates give to this question that the philosophic life represented by him first comes to sight for many readers as devoted above all to discovering the truth about justice and as consisting in large part in the pursuit of that truth.

Such readers are more than likely to focus their attention, first and foremost, on the *Republic*. The *Republic* is the most famous of the works of Plato devoted to the theme of justice; indeed, it is the most famous book, simply, devoted to that theme, at least if we disregard for the moment the Bible. The discussion of justice begins in the *Republic* when Socrates raises the question whether what a certain elderly man takes justice to consist in—as can be inferred from the account the man gives of his actions—is *truly* justice. The consideration of what justice is continues with the old man's son, Polemarchus, after he himself has departed. When Socrates and Polemarchus reach an impasse in their investigation, the way is opened for the entry into the conversation of Thrasymachus, a teacher of rhetoric who has his own views as to what justice is. Then, at a certain point in the conversation with Thrasymachus, the focus shifts to a question which is at first hearing almost incomprehensible to someone devoted to justice: the question of whether justice is good or bad. For what can this mean? Can justice be bad? Can it be judged in terms of, and thus subordinated to, any standard other than itself? At any rate, it would apparently not even occur to a lover of justice to raise this question, as can be seen from the case of so impressive a man as Polemarchus. (He is the only interlocutor of Socrates in the *Republic* who is said later on to have turned to philosophy.) Thrasymachus, on the other hand, who forces Socrates to take up the consideration of it, gives little evidence of being a lover of justice. Still, as things stand, we owe him some gratitude. For his action enables us or helps us to become aware of the fact that, precisely as lovers of justice, we took for granted all along that it is good. (A rereading of the conversations with Polemarchus and his father, among other things, would confirm this.) Moreover, it would be difficult, not to say impossible, to overestimate the importance of this fact for the development of the argument of the *Republic* as a whole, and therewith for its treatment of justice. It is this that authorizes or enables Socrates to elaborate the essential features of a good political community without reference to justice, without taking his bearings by it—so that, when it comes time to consider where justice is to be found in that community, Socrates and his interlocutors are at first unable to discover it and succeed in doing so only with some difficulty. It is this fact, again, which enables Socrates to complete his first sketch of an education for the highest class in the city without settling the question of how, or even whether, education to justice is to form a part of it. The ambiguity may be thought to remain even in the still higher version presented later in the work, where the education outlined by Socrates, an education meant to prepare the ascent to knowledge of the idea of the good, is more obviously an education to philosophy than it is to justice. This is not to deny that only those who possess a certain nature are to be given this education and that among the required natural characteristics is love of justice and kinship to it (or a just character). But, as the *Republic* as a whole makes clear, the love of justice which, among other traits, distinguishes the potential philosopher is in need of undergoing a specific purification which the education conveyed by the *Republic* (if not also that which Socrates outlines within it) is meant to supply. Nor are we able to deny the conclusion which follows from the definition of justice that is offered by Socrates in the course of the work. According to that definition, an individual is just when each part of his or her soul does (and does well) only its own work. Now, this is something which can occur when each part of the soul is healthy or in the proper shape. Thus it follows that only the philosopher can be completely just, for only in the philosopher is the highest part of the soul, the rational part, in the proper shape. Philosophy, then, and only philosophy, is the truest practice of justice and this, by itself, would appear to constitute it the best way of life.

The conclusion that philosophy is the truest practice of justice will be especially attractive to many readers for its apparent similarity to an opinion with which they began their serious study of the *Republic*, the opinion that philosophy consists largely in the pursuit of the truth about justice. But, apart from other questions that might be raised about that conclusion, there is the question suggested by this very comparison: what does philosophy, as it is now understood, as itself the truest practice of justice, consist in? For our new understanding of philosophy implies that we know now what justice is. Has the task of philosophy, and hence its activity, come to an end with this discovery? Or has our very success, with the help of the *Republic*, in answering the question of what justice is—however that success may ultimately have to be understood—brought to light the insufficiency of limiting philosophy to little more than the pursuit of that question? What, then, does philosophy or philosophizing consist in beyond the pursuit of the truth about justice?

Unless and until we can give a satisfactory answer to this new question, we must regard as merely provisional anything we may think we have learned from the *Republic* about the necessity and desirability of the philosophic life.

At first glance, the task of answering it would not appear to be a particularly difficult one. We have already spoken of Plato's view of philosophy as not only a certain way of life but also a certain understanding of the world. And the *Republic* confirms that what philosophy seeks to understand, over and above justice, is the *world*, the world as a *whole*, the *natural* whole within which human life and its strivings for justice take place. The philosopher seeks to discover the permanent and intelligible causes of all things, together with the natural articulation of those causes or their intrinsic relation to one another, causes which Plato calls the "ideas." But the very mention of the term "ideas" suggests at once the presence at least of a complication in this picture, if not a difficulty. Is not the "theory of ideas" a doctrine whose inadequacy has been shown long ago? And, more generally, has not philosophy as such, at least in all of its premodern manifestations, been able to provide only a very defective understanding of the world, of the natural whole, an understanding far inferior to that provided by modern natural science? Has not philosophy, insofar as it consists in the attempt to understand the world, been definitively replaced or superseded by modern science? If so, the most that the *Republic* can have shown, in demonstrating the necessity and desirability of the philosophic life, is the necessity and desirability of turning, at a certain point, to modern natural science.

And yet, while unable and unwilling simply to deny this, we may sense, however dimly, that what modern science is able to tell us about the world is not identical with what philosophy, especially in its premodern forms, originally sought to understand about it; we may suspect further that the entire stance of philosophy toward the world it wishes to understand is affected by the fact that the question which it addresses initially is different from the question or questions asked by modern natural science; and for these reasons, we may resist, perhaps unjustifiably, the simple replacement of the philosophic attempt to understand the world by the modern scientific attempt. To see whether what we dimly sense to be the case is truly the case, we would (among other things) have to see how the problem of understanding the world appeared to premodern philosophy, of which, at least for present purposes, Platonic philosophy can be taken as the preeminent example. Now the question which Plato initially addresses emerged directly from nonphilosophic or prephilosophic life as Plato and his contemporaries experienced it. That is, Platonic philosophy initially sought to address a question which arose in ordinary life and which was recognized as the most fundamental question by ordinary life itself. One might suppose therefore that we could recover that question—in the sense of making it our own—simply by consulting ordinary or nonphilosophic life as *we* know it. But this would suffice only if ordinary life as we know it today had not been transformed by post-Platonic developments which have tended to make us oblivious of the fundamental character of the question we seek to recover and even of its very existence as a question.

The contemporary effects of these developments, which is all we are concerned with here, may perhaps be brought to light by an examination of the controversy that claims the most attention today in American colleges and universities, while having at the same time important implications for the country at large: the controversy between those who would put much greater stress on "cultural diversity" in college and school curricula and those who resist these changes. The controversy has an intellectual or philosophical aspect—insofar as it raises such questions as those of the relativity of truth or the allegedly cultural basis of all thought—and it also has a political aspect. That is, those who urge the adoption of curricula of "cultural diversity" generally anticipate that significant political benefits will result from the changes they wish to promote, while those in opposition anticipate political harm from these same changes. It is more helpful, for our purposes, to approach the matter from its political side.

Let me start with the camp of the resisters, the conservative camp. On closer inspection, these conservatives often turn out to be none other than old liberals, the remaining adherents of the liberalism in which my generation, among many others in this country, was raised. That liberalism, effective not only in the schooling we received but also, in many cases, in the precepts we imbibed at home, stressed what we all had in common as human beings and what united us as Americans: black and white, Christian and Jew, native-born and immigrant. It sought to unite the diverse groups to be found in our country by means of their common recognition of a principle it believed all could accept: that what really matters about someone is not origin or group identity but one's own individual worth—one's character, ability, purpose in life. Those on the other side of the diversity controversy tend to be more doubtful than the liberals that what I have very loosely called "group identity" falls outside of what matters most about a human being. For this reason, among others, they regard it as the task of education at every level to make the young more aware than they have hitherto been of the differences among them, of what distinguishes them from one another. At the same time, they agree with liberalism on the goal of a society in which members of different groups, as well as the diverse groups themselves, coexist in mutual respect and harmony. They must therefore regard the self-assertion on the part of these groups which they seek to encourage as compatible with such harmony. Where liberalism feared and fears the consequence of almost any group self-assertion, the newer movement is able to contemplate much more of it in the confidence that it will not bring the groups so disposed to blows. What is the source of that confidence? It is impossible to answer this question without taking into account a little-noted agreement of the two opposed camps which betrays itself most fully just here where they seem most at odds.

The old liberalism was and is, by intention, cosmopolitan or universalistic. We see this, for example, in its view that our common humanity is more important than anything which could or does divide us, more important, in particular, than the differing stands we might take on any question about which we might disagree. A Christian or a Jew or a member of any other such group is, in its eyes, best seen as "Nothing But a Man"—to borrow a film title of the early 1960s which, in so referring to the black hero of the film, gave expression to this older outlook. The newer movement, as we have seen, tends to regard this view and the "humanity" it promotes as shallow. And yet, despite its best or worst intentions, it reveals itself as an heir of the liberal universalism it would like to discard. This becomes apparent the minute one considers its very concern for the self-assertion of groups as such: this is not a concern of any of the particular groups themselves, each of which, precisely as self-assertive, is preoccupied with the promotion of its own "agenda"; rather it presupposes a universalistic perspective. Such a perspective is apparent also in the emphasis the movement places on the harmony and mutual respect of the groups: harmony and mutual respect are, from the particularistic perspective of any one group, merely tactical or at best secondary goals. But it is above all the movement's confidence that the self-assertion of groups is not incompatible with their harmony and mutual respect that reveals its universalistic perspective. For that confidence, as much at odds as it is with liberalism's fears, shows the newer movement to be in conscious or unconscious agreement with liberalism that no difference which might divide us—and, in particular, no differing stands we might take on questions about which we disagree—can ever be so important as to *deserve* to call into question the goal we are all taken to share of living in peace and harmony together. In fact, the agreement is more likely to be unconscious than conscious; for it is more precisely the newer movement's lack of awareness of its own distance from a genuinely particularistic or group perspective—its ignorance, that is, of what such a perspective truly entails—that enables it to be so sanguine with regard to the consequences of the fostering of particularity. Liberalism, by contrast, being more consciously universalistic, is also more aware of the alternative to universalism; as a result, its political instinct is far sounder than that of the movement which would replace it. However that may be, for our purposes, the chief point brought to light thus far by our examination of the struggle of the two opponents is that the triumph of the diversity movement would not mean the immediate end of the influence of liberal universalism. On the contrary, insofar as it supplies the (unacknowledged) basis of the thought of the promoters of "diversity," this universalism would survive, at least for a time. And this, in turn, is no small indication of its power today more generally. For what is true even of opponents of liberalism is likely to be still more true of others, including perhaps most of those who do not belong to the diversity camp. Liberalism, in the form of what I have called "liberal universalism," is likely to supply the basis of *our* thought—and therewith of the way in which we approach Plato—a basis that we are aware of to varying degrees.

This conclusion may seem trivial (if not also obvious): what we wish to understand is not merely the fact but also the character of the influence of liberal universalism on our thought. But here, too, we may get some assistance from an examination of the relation of the diversity movement to the position it seeks to replace.

I must note first that, in all such controversies, there are the ranks in which the battles are fought, the arguments made and responded to, and, on the other hand, the ranks of the perpetual followers. The latter, ever prepared to take their orders from the victorious side, whichever it may happen to be, to conform in thought as well as deed to the new outlook, are anxious only that they not be behind-times in demonstrating their allegiance. This anxiety of theirs sharpens their senses for the detection of any shift in the prevailing winds; and, as a result, they are not unlikely to signal the eventual outcome of a struggle, and to expose to view its consequences, by a premature act of deference. Hence the significance of a brief biographical sketch included in an article in the August 1991 issue of the *National Geographic* magazine. The subject of the sketch, a National Park Service employee, was a Navajo woman who, after a childhood spent with Barbie dolls and Girl Scouts, had, in the spirit of the dawning age, later come "to understand her identity as a Navajo," as the article tells us. It continues as follows: "Fourteen years ago she suffered an automobile accident and the loss of a job and boyfriend in one week. A relative suggested she see a medicine man. He *discovered* a curse had been placed on her; through ceremony it was *broken*."[1] I have emphasized the words "discovered" and

---

1. Paul C. Pritchard, "The Best Idea America Ever Had," *National Geographic* 180.2 (1991): 51.

"broken": they are not placed in quotation marks in the *Geographic* report but presented rather as part of the facts of the case. Has the *National Geographic*, which is published by a Society whose motto declares its purpose to be "the increase and diffusion of geographic knowledge," come to believe in the efficacy of curses along with the power of medicine men and their ceremonials to break them? Or, as is more likely, does the question of the truth of such claims not even arise for it? The stance of the *Geographic* may be brought into even sharper focus by comparison with an apparently similar treatment of a locally well-known happening which V. S. Naipaul tells of having come across in the sole daily newspaper of the Ivory Coast:

> Seventeen kilometers out of Abidjan in a village on the great auto-route to Yamoussoukro, there was a school-teacher's house which from time to time blazed with mysterious fires. A reader had written to the paper that weekend with the suggestion that there was probably some escape of natural gas in the neighborhood. But this letter, headed "A Scientific Solution," was placed at the bottom of the right-hand page [of the two-page treatment]. The main story, the *reportage*, was that the mystery of the fires at Kilometre 17 had been solved.
>
> It had been solved by a preacher of the Celestial Christian sect. Even before they had been called in on the case—and while the teacher was spending a fortune on fetish makers and Muslim magicians—the Celestial Christians had "discovered" through some divine communication that the Evil Spirit was at the bottom of the business. . . .[2]

This "discovery" then enabled the Celestial Christians to solve the problem in a manner which Naipaul, following his source, details as well. Unlike the *Geographic* and, presumably, unlike the African daily as well, Naipaul puts the term "discovered" in quotation marks. The presumed failure of the newspaper to do this can safely be traced to its editors' belief in the genuineness, the truth, of the discovery in question. As a result, they are aware that acceptance of such truths entails doubt of the validity of a "scientific solution." The contrast between these editors—with their awakeness to this issue, their grasp of its significance—and their American counterparts could hardly be greater.

---

2. V. S. Naipaul, "The Crocodiles of Yamoussoukro," *Finding the Center: Two Narratives* (New York: Vintage Books, 1986), 87–88.

Now, in the stance of the American magazine, we detected both a sign of the coming victory of the diversity movement and an indication of the consequences of that victory or of the character of the new outlook. But, as we have also seen, the new outlook owes much to its older rival. If that should prove to be the case here, too, with regard to the matters our two stories are concerned with—that is, if liberal universalism is at work here, too, if only to the extent of preparing the ground for the newer attitude toward these matters—then our stories will have pointed to something else as well. They will have provided an indication of the character of the influence which liberal universalism exercises also on those who are not partisans of the new order of things.

We begin by noting what the Naipaul story, with its reference to the rivalry among religious sects, might help to remind us of: the diversity whose effects liberalism most feared and most wished to control was not racial or ethnic but rather religious diversity, a diversity whose root is differences of belief as to the answer to the most fundamental question, disagreement as to where the truth of the matter lies. And the liberal approach to that diversity, which prevailed especially in this country, involved, among other steps, its proponents' insisting—that is, saying if not necessarily believing—that differences on this matter are unimportant in themselves. Hence Jefferson's comments on the religious diversity to be found in the two states of early post-Revolutionary America which had dispensed with an established church: "Religion is well-supported; of various kinds, indeed, but all good enough; all sufficient to preserve peace and order. . . ."[3] The chief thing, in other words—the only consideration to be brought to bear in judging a religion—is its contribution to the preservation of peace and order. And, as Jefferson had also said, "it does me no injury for my neighbor to say there are twenty gods, or no God. It neither picks my pocket nor breaks my leg."[4] We might note in passing that, in thus preparing the ground for the still more radical indifference to truth evinced by the diversity movement, political liberalism marched in step with a natural science which, to judge at any rate from the account of it given by Einstein and Infeld, fails to address the fundamental question:

---

3. Thomas Jefferson, "Notes on Virginia," *The Life and Selected Writings of Thomas Jefferson*, eds. Adrienne Koch and William Peden (New York: The Modern Library, 1944), 276.

4. Jefferson, 275.

> Physical concepts are free creations of the human mind, and are not, however it may seem, uniquely determined by the external world.
>
> Science is not and will never be a closed book. Every important advance brings new questions. Every development reveals, in the long run, new and deeper difficulties.
>
> Without the belief that it is possible to grasp the reality with our theoretical constructions, without the belief in the inner harmony of our world, there could be no science.[5]

For it appears from these remarks that modern natural science has no means of its own for confirming the belief referred to, although it depends on the belief; or, in other words, that it rests on the assumption of a particular answer to a question it does not address. To return to Jefferson, one can have every respect for the political instinct which is part of what lies behind his remarks; one can regard as correct its assessment of the dangers posed by any religious rivalry whose intensity has not been dampened by the application of the liberal message. But what becomes of us as individuals when we allow ourselves to be guided by that message as to the fundamental point (as many are bound to do when remarks such as Jefferson's articulate the "nomos" or unwritten law that broadly determines the public understanding of the matter)? What becomes of our awareness of the importance of the question which is truly most important, an awareness which is a necessary condition of our making the effort to find the true answer to it? And what becomes of the disputes which the effort to find the truth is bound to spark and which are so fruitful, in return, for testing and modifying opinions we have received as well as those we have begun to arrive at on our own? Among Jefferson's comments on the experience of the nonestablishment states, we find also this remark: "They have made the happy discovery, that the way to silence religious disputes, is to take no notice of them."[6]

It is, as we have seen, a mark of the liberal universalism we have been considering that it is able to disregard not only race and national origin

---

5. Albert Einstein and Leopold Infeld, *The Evolution of Physics* (New York: Simon and Schuster, 1966), 31, 292, 296.

6. Jefferson, 277.

but also "creed"—especially, religious creed—in judging of the worth of someone. In this respect it recalls an older universalism which held that the truth is in principle accessible to people everywhere and always and that the rare combination of natural qualities which is required for a successful search for the truth is as likely to be found among the barbarians as it is in Athens. That universalism, too, disregarded creed in judging, for example, of a young person's worth; but it did so only because it was interested solely in whether the youth possessed a good nature, by which it meant a nature that would enable its possessors to raise and pursue the question whether the creeds they had been raised in were true. The good natures who in fact undertook this search were bound to adopt, in due course, the universalism by which they themselves had been judged. But such searchers are at any time a tiny proportion, at most, of the body politic.[7] The universalism they represented and kept alive was therefore perpetually adrift in a sea of "particularism" of a virulence undreamed of by our contemporary promoters of particularity. Liberalism, by transforming the character of universalism, purchased a broader influence for it, but only at the price of obscuring the access of many individuals to the question in the light of which the world reveals itself as what it is. It is for this reason that we who are the offspring of the new universalism must make the special effort, whose beginnings I have tried to sketch, to uncover the differences between our situation and that of readers of Plato who were raised in earlier times. We can derive invaluable assistance in that effort from the writers who have given us thoughtful descriptions of those times. The most accessible and at the same time profound such description that I know of is to be found in the second chapter of the first volume of Churchill's *Marlborough*.

---

7. Compare Walker Percy, *The Moviegoer* (New York: Avon Books, 1982), 18.

3

Plato and Relativism

I.

My talk is intended to provide an introduction of sorts to the reading of
Plato. And, as this implies, I regard the reading of Plato as a good thing.
But I will begin by speaking of an objection that one might make to Plato.
And this manner of proceeding requires some explanation. The objection
that I have in mind is, as I suspect, widely felt today, though less widely
acknowledged. And if this suspicion is correct, many readers of Plato
will be approaching him today with a "mental reservation" of which they
are not fully aware. Now, the difficulty with entertaining a reservation or
objection of which we have not made ourselves fully aware is that we
have no opportunity of testing it to determine its validity; moreover, the
inevitable result of this failure to test is exposure to a number of dangers.
Since an unacknowledged objection is one which we merely feel (having
failed either to confirm or to dispose of it by testing), we are likely, even
or precisely if it is a valid one, to waste our time on an author who is
unworthy of our attention; while, if the objection is invalid, since we still
feel it we may pay insufficient attention to an author who demands and
deserves our utmost seriousness, or—what is still worse—we may seek

___

This is a slightly revised version of a talk written for young students and given at
Middlebury College on October 1, 2001. Its inclusion here enables me to acknowledge the help that I received, both as a young and not-so-young student, from the
instruction of Ralph Lerner, whose writings were the first to show me how I might
learn from Maimonides.

to get rid of that in him which causes our vague uneasiness by means of a "sympathetic" interpretation which assimilates his thought to our own just where he is right and we are wrong. It is with an eye to these dangers, then, that I will begin my talk with an attempt to bring to light the objection to Plato that I seem to discern and make the best case against him that I can, on its behalf.

The very title, "Plato and Relativism," is meant to suggest the possibility of a problem with Plato. Relativism is a constituent element of our world: we are all somewhat familiar with it, however uncertain we may be as to what precisely it is or whether it is a good thing or a bad one. Plato's writings, on the other hand, are old, possibly out of date. Could this possible obsolescence of theirs not have something to do with relativism, perhaps with a failure on Plato's part to consider it? As a matter of fact, he did consider it: in a dialogue called *Theaetetus*. We must take a brief look at that dialogue, therefore, if we are to bring to light the objection to Plato to which the title, "Plato and Relativism," is already meant to point.

The *Theaetetus* is concerned with the question, "What is knowledge?" In the course of its consideration of this question, it takes up a saying of a famous Greek sophist (or teacher) by the name of Protagoras. (Protagoras is not a character in the *Theaetetus*—he was already dead when the conversation it reports is supposed to have taken place—but he is a character in another Platonic dialogue, the one named, after him, *Protagoras*.) According to the saying of Protagoras with which the *Theaetetus* is concerned, "Man is the measure." And that saying is taken there to mean that, for each of us, the world is such as it appears to us to be or as each of us takes it to be. If, then, the world or the beings that constitute it appear differently to different individuals (indeed even to the same individual at different times), as might seem to be the case, Protagoras' saying—according to which what *appears* to each of us, *is* for each of us—amounts to the thesis that each of us has his or her own private truth or that being and truth are *relative* to each of us. And from this we can perhaps understand why the *Theaetetus*, Plato's dialogue on knowledge or science, undertakes first to explicate Protagoras' saying and then to subject it to a long and searching scrutiny: only if the thesis to which that saying can be taken to give expression is in some sense wrong, can there be any such thing as science or knowledge at all.

The objection that can reasonably, or at least plausibly, be made to Plato cannot, then, be that he failed to consider the question of the truth or falsity of the relativist thesis or that he did not take the question of its truth or falsity seriously. As we are now in a better position to appreciate, it concerns rather the reason that he did take that question seriously. For Plato assumed that knowledge is a good, indeed a necessary thing: something which, if we are to live well, we cannot do without. And this is an assumption that we today *can* no longer make and *do* no longer make—not to say that we have rejected it entirely. But if this is the case and if to make an assumption that need not be made, to take for granted what can be questioned, is an intellectual flaw, we would seem to have uncovered a respect in which Plato must be judged wanting. And not just Plato, together with his spokesman Socrates—the opponents of the latter, the foils with whom Plato confronts Socrates in his dialogues, even the very radical Protagoras, will all be found to have made the very same assumption. Here I appeal to your own experience in reading Plato: do not Thrasymachus, for example, in the *Republic* and Callicles in the *Gorgias* assume, along with Socrates, that knowledge is necessary to us if we are to live well, however much they may differ with him as to the content of that knowledge or as to what the truth that we need to know consists in? And this tacit agreement with Socrates of even his most determined and articulate opponents would seem to confirm that the intellectual atmosphere in which Plato lived and thought and which he has so unforgettably recreated for us in his dialogues—an atmosphere that appears to have allowed the agreement in question to go unchallenged—was more narrow or shallow than the one in which we live and breathe. How, then, can Plato, for all of his undoubted merits, be of any serious use to us?

But isn't it absurd to say that we are any less convinced than Plato was that knowledge is necessary to us, if we are to live well? And is not the assumption that it is necessary—so far from being a questionable one—evidently sound? Does not the whole modern experience of scientific and technological progress bear, day by day, ever more impressive witness to its soundness?—Leaving aside the question whether the whole modern experience of scientific and technological progress bears adequate witness to our need for knowledge, let me hasten to explain that it was not primarily this sort of knowledge that I had in mind in suggesting that Plato and Socrates, together with those who converse with Socrates in the Platonic dialogues, assume that knowledge is necessary to us—and that we do *not* assume this. Here again I appeal to your own experience in reading the dialogues: what is the question that Socrates is always raising in them and always seeking to answer by way of learning something (about justice, for example), that is, by way of knowledge? Is it not the question of how he should live his life? And this means that the knowledge which he primarily seeks is not that of the means to some pre-determined goal (whether it be wealth or health or pleasure or fame or political power) but that of the goal itself, of what it should be, of the end or ends of all our striving. It is *this* knowledge, I meant to suggest, whose necessity Plato and all of his characters take for granted—whether, like Socrates himself, apparently, and some few others, they regard it as still to be sought or, like the majority of those he converses with, as already possessed. It is knowledge of the best or right or correct way of life, understood as the best way of life for man as man.

Still, what does it mean to say that we are no longer convinced of the need for this knowledge?—First, if not we ourselves, many of our contemporaries have doubts whether there *is* a life, *one* way of life, best for man as man; and, even if we are not inclined to share these doubts, we are bound to take account of them and to consider their ground or grounds—and to hold it against any thinker who should fail to do so. And second, for the determination of which life is best for each of the infinitely many individuals, with their infinitely various abilities and inclinations, we are less likely to look in each case to knowledge, even to knowledge of the particular abilities and inclinations of the individual in question, than to something else. Let me sketch for you here, in its broad outlines, a version of a view with which you are surely already familiar, since it is not among the least loudly proclaimed of the views of our day.

II.

According to the view in question, which has some affinities with the Protagorean view but owes its present form to more recent influences, nothing is right or wrong, good or bad, in itself. What comes to be right and good for each of us is only what we have *chosen* to regard as such. What is right and good for each of us owes its rightness and goodness to that choice of ours and to nothing else. In particular, our choice need not be and cannot be guided, in any fundamental sense, by knowledge or reason. If it were susceptible of guidance by knowledge or reason, it would be by that very fact *subject* to reason, at least to the extent that it would be subject to the judgment of reason, to reasonable praise or blame. Choice itself would not be sovereign. Our freedom would be limited. But freedom, according to the view I am sketching, or the sovereignty of choice is the fundamental fact, beyond or behind which we cannot go and have no need to go. Or, to spell out this last point, in particular: our natural concern to do the right thing or to pursue a good course of action is fully satisfied by the consciousness that we have *chosen* to regard an action that we take as good or right. And, if this is truly the case, *knowledge* of what is right or good, the kind of knowledge that Socrates was apparently always seeking, is so far from being necessary to us that it is not even desirable. Such knowledge is not merely unobtainable, as the older relativism would seem to have contended: it is not even to be missed.

A complication, perhaps calling for the exercise of reason, might seem to arise in connection with the diversity of choices made—or to be made in some freer society of the future—by the infinitely many and infinitely diverse individuals. What if my "right"—what I choose to call right—turns out to be your "wrong"? How will we be able to live together harmoniously or even peaceably in the same society? We may take the dispute over abortion as an example. An action which one party to the dispute holds to be the exercise of a right is held by another to be an act of murder against a defenseless child, that is, an action which could not be more wrong.—An intransigent adherent of the view I am sketching might respond, however, as follows. "The example that you have selected, the abortion controversy, is most apt for elucidating the true nature and extent of the difficulty that you raise. For what is it here that gives rise to controversy? It is not the exercise of an unfettered, that is, a genuine value choice on the part of all of the parties to the dispute. For what can only loosely be called the 'choice' of one of those parties is distorted by prejudice, tainted by the influence of unevident belief (as to when human life begins, as to the allegedly divine origin of such life). And there is no reason to think that, in the absence of such prejudices or once the influence of such beliefs has been weakened or destroyed by a true education, the disputes that will then remain cannot be disposed of by compromises acceptable to all sides or by majority decisions that all sides are content to abide by. There is no reason, in other words, or at least none that is brought to light by your example, why we cannot look forward to a time when each human being, through the unfettered exercise of his or her choice as to what to regard as right and wrong, good and bad, will be a genuine individual and all individuals will be able to live together harmoniously through the respect that they all have for that in others which they recognize as highest in themselves: choice itself."

So, at any rate, might an adherent of the view that I have been sketching claim. But if a claim like this can plausibly be made—and if, as was suggested a moment ago, our deepest concern as individuals can be satisfied by the consciousness that our stance on fundamental matters is due to (nothing but) our own choice—the self-evidence, at least, of any necessity for the knowledge sought by Socrates vanishes. Or, to conclude for the time being the case that I have been trying to make against Plato, even if the need for this knowledge was once so evident as Plato thought it to be, even if there once was such a need whose evidence was generally felt and acknowledged, we of the present generation would seem to have outgrown it.

III.

But, to begin to look now at the other side of the question, *can* such a claim be plausibly made? Disagreements of a fundamental sort can be settled in only two ways: either by reason (that is, by knowledge) or by force—for persuasion, if it is not reasonable persuasion, amounts to force by another name. The proponents of the view we are considering must therefore rest their hope for a harmonious, or at any rate peaceable, society (whose basis is not laid in knowledge of fundamental matters) on the alleged possibility of the disappearance of all disagreements as to fundamentals. And this possibility has been said to rest, in turn, on an education that will free us or our fellow citizens of their "prejudices." But do we *know* that the "prejudices" in question are mere prejudices—that is, opinions for which there is no sufficient ground? Who would dare to claim that modern natural science, in particular, which apparently remains perplexed about so fundamental a matter as the origin of the universe, has progressed far enough to have proved beyond a reasonable doubt the groundlessness or falsity of our or our neighbors' "prejudices"? And, in the absence of such proof, can we expect, or even reasonably demand that the alleged prejudices be given up? Furthermore, even if all such opinions as might be considered prejudices were to be given up, is it certain that disagreements as to fundamentals would cease? According to a suggestion of Socrates (*Euthyphro* 7c10–d5), disagreements over justice and injustice, nobility and baseness, good and evil (or bad), bring us and all human beings to anger and enmity with one another—when we are unable adequately to resolve them—and will continue to do so. Or, to return for a moment to the abortion example, is it not thinkable at least that, even in the absence of the particular beliefs referred to, a disagreement worthy of being called fundamental would remain, perhaps regarding the "right" to destroy a fetus that, given the state of modern medicine, would otherwise have been viable outside of the womb? And if there is even one disagreement of a fundamental sort remaining after the hoped-for disappearance of "prejudices," is it clear that such peace as might be obtainable by compromise in its regard, or acceptance of a majority decision, *should* be preferred or *would* be preferred to making a principled stand? A consideration of what is required for societal peace alone, then, mere peaceableness, is able to uncover sufficient ground for Socrates' suggestion that there can be no cessation of evils for "the cities," nor for the human race generally, until philosophers become kings or kings (rulers) philosophize: that is, until knowledge rules our common life (*Republic* 473c10–d6). Or what one can call the social or political component of the necessity for knowledge remains as evident today, for us, as it was to Plato, however much and for whatever reason or reasons we may wish to deny or ignore its evidence.

But there was also an individual component to that necessity, as Plato saw it, a need of each of us for knowledge, if we are to live our lives well as the individuals that we (also) are. Perhaps it is here, then, that the radical change which is alleged to have taken place has taken place, so that the need apparently so evident to Plato and his contemporaries is no longer felt. To see whether this is truly the case, however, we must consider not simply "value" choices in general—and, therefore, as pertaining to matters many of which have very little bearing on our lives, little connection with what touches our hearts and souls. We must pay particular attention to those choices that affect us every day and determine our life's course. We might take as an example our response to the question whether we should make "success" or the so-called "bottom line" our single or highest goal and regard as good whatever contributes to it, as bad whatever detracts from it or distracts us from it. There is certainly considerable pressure on us in this direction, stemming not only from society at large (whose influence in this respect has been strengthened to no small degree by the victory of the West in the Cold War and the manner in which that victory is often understood), but sometimes even from our nearest and dearest. And yet many of you surely feel that this is pressure to be resisted, that, however desirable "success" may be, there are some things which must not be done to attain it. You refrain, therefore, from doing those things, even at some cost to yourselves; you willingly, if necessary, fall behind others who do not place upon themselves the same sort of restrictions. This is your *choice*—what is right for you—and that other choice, of those who place no restrictions of their ambition, is right for them and must be respected as such. Or so it is claimed. But does anyone, on questions that really matter, see it this way in fact? (There is a character in Dostoyevsky's *Possessed* who claims to believe that everything is good; someone therefore mentions to him an atrocious crime that might be committed against a small girl who happened to be in the room and asks whether that, too, is good; whereupon the first man—his name is Kirilov—replies that when everyone knows that everything is good such crimes will not be committed! [Part Two, I 5].) And don't we, to come back to the question before us, truly believe that the choice of the unscrupulous does *not* suffice to make their unscrupulous actions good or right, even for them? But this would imply that we believe also that our own restraint is right *for us* not merely because we have chosen it but because, in choosing it, we have chosen what is right *in itself*.

But is it sufficient merely to believe this? What we believe to be right in itself, and therefore right also for us, the others (the unscrupulous) clearly regard as bad for us—though good for them, since it makes us their dupes. In this way or to this extent they contest the correctness of our belief, while for us very much, not to say everything, lies on its being correct. We can't help then being passionately concerned with its correctness, concerned that what we believe to be true, be true in fact and *known* by us to be true in fact. But to know this, we must convert belief into knowledge. And that, in turn, we cannot do without subjecting our belief, the one on which our choice is based, to the most rigorous scrutiny. We must follow the example of Socrates, after all. The insistence that choice is sufficient to make something right—that is, the concealment, even from oneself, of the belief that underlies one's choice—serves only to blind one to the necessity of this conversion and thus to delay one's attempting it, in some cases indefinitely. At this point, however, we are forced to confront directly a difficulty that we have touched on up till now only obliquely. Is the knowledge that Socrates sought and that we, too, would be seeking in any such attempt obtainable? Is it not doubts on this score—doubts passed down to us from whatever source—that induce us to hesitate even to attempt the necessary conversion of belief into knowledge and that make us, in the same degree, anxious to conceal from ourselves its necessity? Is this not the deepest reason for the inclination to insist that choice alone suffices to make something right? "For you, yourself," as someone might now object to me, "have contended throughout your talk merely that Plato was correct in thinking that knowledge is evidently necessary to us, if we are to live well. You have said nothing at all as to whether the knowledge that we may need is obtainable. And what can be the result of making us more aware than we were of a need for something that, in the nature of things, we cannot obtain—what other result can this have than to plunge us into despair?"

In response, I would say that despair is premature, and not only because there is always the possibility that someone (someone of the present generation) may well discover what no one has yet discovered, but above all because we are in no position to rule out that genuine knowledge of good and evil is already available to us in one or another of the teachings that have come down to us in our tradition. By way of conclusion, then, I will give a brief outline of these teachings, so as to place Plato's among them.

IV.

The oldest or most venerable sources of the knowledge—at any rate, of the truth—that we need present themselves to us in the Bible. "He hath shewed thee, O man, what *is* good; and what does the LORD require of thee, but to do justly, and to love mercy, and to walk humbly with thy God?" (Micah 6:8). "Thomas saith unto him, Lord, . . . how can we know the way? Jesus saith unto him, I am the way, the truth, and the life: no man commeth unto the Father but by me" (St. John 14:5–6). As these verses imply—the one from the prophet Micah, the other from the gospel of St. John—the Bible in each of its Testaments raises a call which is addressed to man as man, which is intended to have universal validity, which makes demands binding on all of us (whether we choose to acknowledge them or not). Now this call, universally binding as it may be, comes to us through particular men and women, who address us on the basis of something which they have experienced, have seen or heard or felt. And therefore the question might reasonably be put to the Bible, or its spokesmen, whether the truth proclaimed by it as valid for man as man is *accessible* to man as man, that is, to reasoning based on our common experience, or by way of knowledge. To this question, our authority gives a rather complex answer. To begin with, we or our first ancestors were forbidden to eat of the fruit of the tree of the knowledge of good and evil; initially, it seems, an unquestioning faith or reliance was to be our guide. As Paul says of Abraham, he "believed God, and it was counted unto him for righteousness" (Romans 4:3). But our first parents *did* eat of the fruit of that tree; and thus this same Abraham was able to dispute with God as to the rightness of the destruction of Sodom (Genesis 2:9 and 17, 3:1ff., 18:17ff.). Moreover, the laws whose revelation is the high point or purpose of the Old Testament are said by Moses to be our "wisdom and . . . understanding in the sight of the nations, which shall hear all these statues, and say, Surely this great nation is a wise and understanding people" (Deuteronomy 4:6). And if "the nations" (which have, as such, not been the beneficiaries of a special revelation) are able to appreciate the wisdom underlying the Jewish laws, or their truth, that truth must be accessible also to man as man, to merely human wisdom.

But whatever may be the final word of the Bible as to the sufficiency of our merely human understanding for the recognition or discovery of the truth we need, a number of human beings in another part of the ancient world, anticipating perhaps a permission that may or may not have been granted or (as is more likely) caring little for any such permission, had the audacity to begin to seek that truth on their own. They relied in their search on the common experience of human beings, or on reasoning that begins from what all human beings can see and feel. And this compels me to another digression, which will, however, be the last. For someone, as we have to some extent already seen, might object today that, in the decisive respect, we have no common "human" experience: that the term denotes a fiction, "the thing that is not," since what we most deeply feel or long for, each of us, is something which belongs to each of us alone, something neither shared nor shareable. And, if this is the case, we are so far from being able to appeal in our reasoning to a common experience of any significance or depth that, in the most fundamental respect, we are not able even to understand one another. (Cf. *Gorgias* 481c5–d1.) By way of a brief response, let me grant, therefore, that there is a great, not to say infinite, variety in what we seem most to want or to long for. But must it not be granted also, on the other side, that what we want or long for is, in the case of each of us, not perfectly clear? That is to say, we may well know, each of us, to a certain extent what our highest goals are—to be President, a famous writer or inventor, or whatever—and these, our readily identifiable goals, vary greatly. But, in each case, is it not also true that what we most deeply long for is not simply the realization of the goal that we have put before ourselves, but also something else that we hope to attain by reaching that primary goal, something (as this implies) even more fundamental, even dearer to our hearts, yet resisting precise articulation, though we sometimes call it "happiness"? And isn't it possible, therefore, that this further goal (which each of us "divines" without being able, absent great effort at least, to identify it [cf. *Republic* 505d11–e4]), is the same for all of us? But, in that case, what is perhaps our deepest experience would—insofar as it consists to begin with in our *longing* for this truly highest goal, in what Plato calls "eros"—indeed be a common one. And the attempt to acquire knowledge of the best way of life, or of what is truly good and bad for us, by reasoning that begins from common human experience, would not be absurd.

To return, then, to my sketch of that attempt, an attempt which is the original meaning of what we still call philosophy, those who had the boldness to take it up divided almost at once into two camps. And, in closing my talk with a description of this fundamental division or controversy within philosophy, which retained its vitality for as long as philosophy itself was more that just a name, my intention is not to shock anyone but simply to place matters in the clearest light that I can.

The first of these camps—first at least in time, if not also essentially—consisted of those who regarded justice as a mere burden which we, or some of us, impose upon ourselves or others in order to secure social peace. Our true good, on the other hand, (happiness, so far as it is attainable) consists not in compliance with the rules of justice—which is at best a necessary evil—but in the maximum enjoyment of the natural or true pleasures. Indeed, insofar as justice claims to be good (in a higher sense essential to our happiness—as a component of it, so to speak), it is nothing but a (socially useful) fiction, which it is wise to pay lip service to but not always wise to comply with. Disraeli, in his novel *Coningsby*, describes a crude version of this outlook, as it came to be shared by certain European aristocrats, in the following terms: such people believed "that the exoteric public were on many subjects the victims of very vulgar prejudices which these enlightened personages wished neither to disturb nor to adopt."[1] The outlook in question has more than a little in common with the view in fact adopted by those we considered earlier, who place no restrictions on their own pursuit of "success." Its philosophical exponents differ, however, from the "success" people both in their greater consistency and self-awareness and in their utter freedom from crudity. Their most famous representative was Epicurus, who sanctioned the pursuit only of

---

1. Benjamin Disraeli, Earl of Beaconsfield, *Coningsby* (London: J. M. Dent & Sons Ltd., 1959), 242.

the natural or true or pure pleasures. Still, one must admit that even or precisely in its philosophic version, this position differs from the Biblical one not only regarding the ultimate source of the truth we need but also as to the content of that truth. One of the Jewish sages enjoins us therefore, to "know how to answer an Epicuros."[2] And, in a commentary on that sage, we find the remark that this statement of his "is the source of the permission which we have taken to study philosophy, so that we may know how to refute the philosophers in their own words . . . ."[3] That is, Jewish tradition authorizes the study of philosophy to this extent: to the extent that it is necessary to effectively combat the teaching of one of the two great philosophic camps. And it does so reasonably. For, whether that commentator was aware of it or not, the task of "answering an Epicuros" had already been taken up by the other of those camps, that of our great teachers of natural right, the thinkers who undertook through the years to refute the "fool" that, in Hobbes' unforgettable formulation, "hath said in his heart, there is no such thing as justice; and sometimes also with his tongue."[4] Now, as I think most observers would concede, not only the first but the greatest of these natural right teachers, these philosophic defenders of justice, was Plato. And, as Plato himself insists, to be a philosophic defender of justice is not merely to *praise* justice (as one might do in a commemorative day speech) but to show what it is and that it is good: to provide genuine *knowledge* of justice. The record of Plato's attempt to do this has been left to us in the *Republic* and other dialogues. And the whole burden of my talk has been to suggest that the effort to which those dialogues bear witness is no less necessary for us to make than it was for him, that the difficulties which they show him to have grappled with are not only Plato's difficulties, but our own.

---

2. Judah Goldin, Editor and Translator, *The Living Talmud: The Wisdom of the Fathers* (New York: The New American Library of World Literature, Inc., 1959), 113.

3. *The Living Talmud*, 114.

4. Thomas Hobbes, *Leviathan* (Oxford: Basil Blackwell, 1960), 94.

Part II

Beginnings

4

Thucydides' View of Athenian Imperialism

Our topic appears for more than one reason to be an historical or merely historical one, for it concerns the thought of a man of the past who was himself an historian, i.e., who was concerned above all with what belongs to the past. The appearance is deceptive at least to this extent: Thucydides is not properly classified as an historian. He never calls himself an historian, and he claims that the war which he "put together in writing" is of such a size and character that it is able to reveal to him and to those for whom he writes the comprehensive and therewith eternal truth of human or political life. His study of Athenian imperialism as a cause or ingredient of that war serves his great task and to that extent its seriousness. But this means that precisely if our study is to be historical it must not be merely historical. We must try, to begin with, to understand Thucydides as he understood himself; we must take seriously his claim, however extravagant it may appear; we must be open to the possibility that he is correct. We are not averse to such a possibility, despite the austerity or sternness of his work; for that austerity is suffused with gentleness, his exactingness with humanity, and we sense in and through his work the presence of a nobility which is lasting because it is undeceived (cf. Book III, Chapter 83).[1]

This perhaps would be sufficient introduction to our study if the problem of our openness to or ability to learn from Thucydides were

---

I am indebted in many points, both general and particular, to the discussion of Thucydides in Leo Strauss, *The City and Man* (Chicago: Rand McNally, 1964).

1. These references, which will hereafter be indicated by number alone, are standard for any Greek edition of Thucydides and are referred to in most translations.

solved by our willingness to consider the possibility that he is correct. But, as it is, that willingness itself, insofar as it implies that we are somehow competent to judge of his correctness, is not free from problems. An essential part of such competence would be freedom of mind or openness to the truth. Now, Thucydides does not seem to assume that his readers approach him with this openness, although he clearly writes for those who are capable of it (I, 22). The problem is not merely the unwillingness of the many to toil at the search for truth (I, 20), but rather something which affects even the well-disposed few. For all of us, he seems to feel, are born and bred to certain convictions and to a certain comprehensive outlook which shape our understanding of the great matters that he deals with and which perhaps reflect the truth but remain nevertheless at a certain remove from it. Those convictions, further, answer to concerns more powerful than our concern for truth; our attachment to them defies attempts, by dedication to the truth, to loosen its bonds. The concerns in question, together with the views which answer to them, would block completely our access to the truth they conceal if there were not a link between them and the concern for truth, or a path from the ones to the other, as well as a path between the primary or naïve views and the adequate view which Thucydides intends to teach. But this means that his teaching must begin with powerful opinion as opposed to truth and must appeal in the first place to concerns other than the concern for truth. The openness to truth is not a precondition of study so much as it may be the outcome and reward of a certain kind of study.

As more than one commentator has observed,[2] Thucydides makes of his reader a witness to the deeds and speeches he puts down: so penetrating is his narration that the men and nations of which he writes come to life before us; we hear their speeches and see their deeds. And since the matters with which they are concerned—war and peace, justice and injustice, freedom and empire—retain their place in the economy of human life, we not only hear and see but we are also moved. We are moved by, we respond to his narration in accordance with our fundamental view of these matters, however vague or undefined that view may be. In being moved, we are taking a stand that reflects that view; we cannot read Thucydides

---

2. Cf. the introductions to the Penguin (Thucydides: *History of the Peloponnesian War*, translated with an introduction by Rex Warner [Baltimore: Penguin Books], p. 5) and Loeb (*Thucydides*, translated by Charles Foster Smith [London: William Heinemann Ltd., 1919], p. xvii) translations.

without taking a stand and to that extent articulating our fundamental position. It is by the sympathetic fostering of the articulation of our position, it seems, that Thucydides begins to lead us to the considerations in the light of which it can be corrected or abandoned.

Part One

We are confronted then almost at the outset of the tale by the fact of Athenian imperialism. Not long after the Persian war there arose in the Greek alliance which had repulsed the barbarian a division followed before long by intermittent warfare between those who were attached to the Athenians and those who remained under Spartan leadership (I, 18). In time, the Athenians took over the ships of most of the cities allied with them and imposed tribute on them all. As a result, their military establishment at the start of the Peloponnesian war was greater than that of the united alliance at its height (I, 19). We can say then that Athenian imperialism is a condition of the greatness of the war and therewith of its particularly revealing character (I, 1; cf. I, 15). We remain perhaps truer to the proper perspective if we limit ourselves at this point to the assertion brought forward by the Corinthians and the Spartans, and indeed by Thucydides himself (I, 23 and 88), that the imperial greatness of Athens brings on the war.

The two incidents which constituted the proximate provocations to war and furnished the immediate grounds of quarrel had given confirmation to her enemies of the character and scope of the Athenian threat. First, the Athenians accepted a defensive alliance with Corcyra, perhaps the second naval power in Greece (I, 33), which was bound to bring them into conflict with a leading city of the Peloponnese, Corinth. They did so partly because they thought that war with the Peloponnesians was coming in any case, and they wished to wear out the Corcyraeans and Corinthians in mutual combat. At the same time, they were impressed by the location of the island with regard to Italy and Sicily (I, 44). It is not said whether this fact impressed them from an offensive or defensive point of view, but just as subsequent events may be sufficient to settle this question for us, we may expect that the aggressive Athenian policy of the previous fifty years was sufficient to suggest an answer at the time to the anxious minds of the non-Athenian Greeks. At any rate, this alliance led to a clash between Athens and Corinth. After this, anticipating a Corinthian move to detach from them their ally, Potidaea, which was linked by ancestral ties to Corinth, the Athenians demanded of the Potidaeans that they take down their walls, hand over hostages, and expel, to admit no further, their Corinthian magistrates (I, 56). The Potidaeans then revolted from Athens with Corinthian encouragement and help, and in attempting to put down the revolt, Athens again clashed with Corinth.

The sequel to these events was a conference of the Spartan allies in which the question of war with Athens was mooted. It is not surprising that it was Corinth which took the lead in summoning this conference and in urging the injustice of Athenian policy and the necessity of war; but she was supported by other cities, each with its own charge to lay against the Athenians. After these cities had had their say, the Corinthians advanced to conclude the arguments. They directed the greater part of their complaints against Spartan inaction, for the case against the Athenians appeared to be clear enough: the injustice they are committing against Greece is manifest—some are already enslaved by them, others are being plotted against, and they are making great preparations for war (I, 68; cf. 103, 105–106, 119). But the Corinthians also painted a memorable picture of the Athenians as people who would never have peace themselves or permit it to others (I, 70). The response of the Spartans was to vote that the treaty between Athens and Sparta had been broken and that injustice was being done by the Athenians (I, 87; cf. 79).

There are many reasons to sympathize with democratic Athens in the war to which this vote led, and therefore many temptations to make light of the arguments brought against her. We cannot tell at this stage whether even Thucydides does not share that sympathy. But he lets us hear the Corinthian condemnation of Athens before a single Athenian has spoken, and he takes the trouble to tell us that Greek opinion at the outset of the war was heavily on the side of the Spartans, who were promising to liberate Greece (II, 8; cf. I, 124). The anti-Athenian view seems to be primary for Thucydides; we can perhaps best understand the truth which underlies it if we turn to the Athenians' own accounts of their imperial policy.

At the time of the conference of the Spartan allies, a delegation of Athenians happened to be in Sparta on other business. On their own initiative, they came forward and were allowed by the Spartans to speak. They declined to answer the charges brought against Athens by the various cities (I, 73), but their words amount at least to a statement of the Athe-nian view of Athenian imperialism. They can say that the allies themselves asked them to assume the leadership after the Spartans withdrew. But they must then explain the transformation of the voluntarily offered hegemony into an empire over unwilling subjects. They say therefore that they were compelled to bring their rule into this form, above all by fear, then by honor as well, later by profit as well (i.e., by desire for honor and desire for profit). Subsequently, they seem to take the necessary further step of extending this "compulsion" to the original act of accepting the leadership: in accepting (and not abandoning) the empire, they were overcome by the greatest things, honor, fear and profit; nor were they the first to do such a thing, but it is forever laid down that the weaker is kept down by the stronger (I, 75, 76). The Athenians would thus appear to fulfill, by the offer of an inadmissible defense, their promise not to defend themselves: for what under certain circumstances might be allowed to fear, could not without the gravest consequences be granted to the desire for honor and profit. Other of their arguments tend to confirm this impression. It may be true that the Spartans, if they had remained in the leadership, would have found themselves under a like compulsion or necessity to become "painful" to the allies and to rule forcefully (I. 76); but does not this "if" strike directly at the Athenian case for "compulsion" to rule? We may grant that it is now hazardous for the Athenians to do the right by letting their subjects go (I, 75 at the end); but if it is former wrongs which produce the hazard, is their failure to face it to be excused? And with regard to their arguments as to their worthiness to rule and their acting with measure or with greater justice, given their power, than they have to (I, 76), might one not reply that moderation in crime is no great claim to merit among the noncriminal? It was perhaps with such considerations in mind that a Spartan leader said of the Athenian speech that it nowhere contained, despite its length, a denial that the Athenians were committing injustice against the Spartan allies and the Peloponnese (I, 86 at the beginning).

During the war itself, the thought underlying Athenian policy was restated by the Athenian ambassadors at Melos in the course of the negotiation which preceded the Athenian invasion of that island. Their situation (i.e., the weakness of the Melians) allowed the Athenians to speak with even greater frankness than their countrymen had employed on the earlier occasion at Sparta. Accordingly, whereas the earlier speakers had declined to reply to the accusations brought against Athens on the ground that the Spartan assembly did not constitute a court of law (I, 73), the ambassadors at Melos decline to justify the empire or their aggression against Melos in the expectation that the parties to the discussion belong to those who know "that just things in human reckoning are determined of the basis of equal power to compel [literally: 'necessity'] while the superior do what they can and the weak yield" (V, 89). And in the course of a contemptuous dismissal of the Melians' hopeful trust in the favor of the gods—"because, free from sin, we stand against the unjust" (V, 104)—the Athenians go perhaps even further:

> As for good will on the part of the divine, we do not think that we will fall short either; for we don't claim as our right or do anything outside of what humans hold with regard to the divine or wish with regard to themselves; for as we believe on the basis of opinion with regard to the divine and on the clear basis of unremitting natural necessity with regard to humanity, where one gets the upper hand, he rules. And neither laying down the law, nor being the first to use it as laid down, but taking it as it is and will be forever when we have left it behind, we use it, knowing that you and others, if you became as powerful as we are, would do [the] same (V, 105).

On the other side, we are able to find that on a subsequent and less favorable occasion an Athenian by the name of Euphemus (otherwise unknown)[3] puts the case for the empire in more moderate terms. Above all, he ascribes its acquisition to fear alone (i.e., he excludes desire for honor and profit), for, as he explains, all are permitted to provide for their own safety without incurring envy (VI, 83; cf. 87 and 82). But in determining the weight to be given this un-Athenian instance of moderation (cf. Euphemus' own reference to the difficulty of "moderating" the Athenians, VI, 87), one must not overlook the context. The Athenians are in Sicily near the start of their disastrous attempt to enslave that island; they have already encountered some difficulties (e.g., VI, 71, 74–75); they are seeking to renew an alliance with a people who are among their intended victims. The situation seems to call for euphemism if not for a spokesman called Euphemus.

To all this we might add that even Pericles, who can with some justification be regarded as the most moderate of the great Athenian leaders—consider his advice on the war (I, 144 and II, 65) as well as

---

3. Arnold Wycombe Gomme. *A Historical Commentary on Thucydides* (Oxford: Clarendon Press, 1945) on III, 41.

Thucydides' eulogy more generally (II, 65)—tells the Athenians not long after the outbreak of the war that they hold their empire, by this time, "as a tyranny, which it is *deemed* wrong to take, but is dangerous to let go" (II, 63; my emphasis). And he advises them to put up with the hatred in the present which is the lot of all who think fit to rule others, not merely on account of the dangers of letting go but also in light of the advantages which do and may in the future accrue to them from empire, and perhaps above all for the sake of the ever-remembered renown which it brings (II, 64 and 62).

We should also take note of the account of the establishment of empire which Thucydides gives in his own name in the form of a digression from his narrative (I, 97) after his account of the conference at Sparta. He confirms the Athenian claim that it was the allies who first asked them to assume the leadership of the alliance (I, 95, 96, 97). And he adds that the pretext for the Athenian transformation of alliance to empire was provided by revolts on the part of allies who did not wish to fulfill their obligations—strictly enforced by the Athenians—under the league. He explains that the suppression of these revolts was made possible, or at least easy, by the shirking of these same allies from the military exercise and exertions that would have prepared them to defend themselves (I, 99). But he also makes clear that the Athenian response to these coincident provocations and opportunities was the enslavement of the allied cities contrary to "that which had been established" (I, 98). (According to the *scholium* cited by Gomme, *ad. loc.*, this means "contrary to the lawful and proper." Other commentators mentioned by Gomme understand it to mean "contrary to the covenant of the league.") More generally, his account here of Athens in the fifty year period between the wars (Persian and Peloponnesian) is one of almost constant motion, as the Athenians, now in one place, now in another, against allies and nonallies, Greeks and foreigners, sometimes called in by others, sometimes, apparently, uncalled (e.g., I, 112), seek to extend their power and dominion. Nor did a corresponding Spartan activity in those years make less impressive, while it required, the Athenian policy. Thucydides closes this summary as follows: "[In these years] the Athenians established their empire on a firmer footing and themselves advanced greatly in power. But the Spartans, while they perceived this, did not prevent it, unless to a small extent. They kept quiet for most of the time, being even before this not quick to go to war, unless they were forced, and also prevented to some extent by domestic wars. . . ." Only when the power of the Athenians was clearly exalted and they were already laying hands on the Spartan alliance, did it seem to the Spartans that it was time, if they could, to bring them down (I, 118).

Part Two

The policy of the Athenians is not only imperialistic, it is admittedly so; their imperialism not only lacks for the most part legitimate pretext, but such pretext is rarely claimed. And if their frankness does not increase their guilt, it at least makes it plainer for all to see. This is the substance of what one may call the Spartan case with regard to the war, but could it not be Thucydides' view as well? If one accepts it one is able to discern a striking and oft-noted unity and indeed beauty in the movement of the work as a whole. For Pericles' funeral speech with its boundless praise of Athens and Athenian greatness, where Pericles does not hesitate to speak, not to say boast, of the eternal monuments of bad and good everywhere left by the Athenians (II, 41), is followed by the plague, by which Athens is brought so low. The Melian dialogue, in which the Athenian ambassadors put forward the claims of empire with the insolence already noted, is followed by the Sicilian expedition in which Athenian imperialism is seen finally to have overreached itself. And the work as a whole is the story of the setting of that Athenian greatness which, at the work's outset, rode so high. But this understanding of the book would call for satisfaction that punishment was indeed meted out where due, whereas the passion with which we are likely for the first time to put it down is rather sadness or melancholy. The reason is not so much that Thucydides does not permit us to see the final defeat of Athens, that the work closes shortly after the Athenians have managed to repair somewhat their political and military affairs, for his account of the terrible sufferings of the Athenians in Sicily would amply or more than amply fill that lack. It is rather that this great instance of the apparent victory of right does not succeed in diverting our attention from the many instances in which it does not appear victorious. The Sicilian narration itself is interrupted by an account of the almost senseless slaughter of the inhabitants of all ages of Mycalessus at the hands of Thracian mercenaries being sent home from Athens (VII, 29); and this may recall to mind the atrocities of the Spartan Alcidas, who slaughtered his prisoners, friend and foe alike (III, 32). We are not likely to have forgotten the Melians, who, however right their cause, were slaughtered by the Athenians, or the Plataeans, who suffered a similar fate at the hands of the Spartans (III, 68), or the willingness of the Spartans to abandon, as the price of peace, cities promised protection by their agent Brasidas (compare V, 18 with the account of Brasidas in Thrace), or the Corcyraean civil war, in which, under the color of party strife, men were killed for private hatreds or because they were owed money by their murderers (III, 81). The party strife itself, passing these bounds, became so savage that father killed son and men were murdered next to the very temples from which they had been dragged; this savagery in turn was surpassed—both in other respects and in the singularity of the revenges exacted—by that of the civil wars which, following this one, moved so to speak the whole of Greece at this time; revenge became more important than not suffering oneself; it was not limited by the just or the good of the city, but only by the pleasure of the avenging parties, each side having made the common things it professed to serve its prize; in the course of events, the citizens in the middle were destroyed by both sides, the clever by those of the meanest capacities, so that the latter, for the most part, were the ones who survived (III, 81–83). Such is the context in which one must understand the comment of Thucydides on the execution of Nicias: of the Greeks of that time, he least of all, in view of his attention to conventional virtue, deserved such a fate (VII, 86). It would appear to be rather the weakness than the strength of right that is Thucydides' theme, the consistent defeat or going down of right or at least the righteous before force, compulsion, necessity. That defeat is not in his view particular to the time of the Peloponnesian war but, as his "archeology" (account of olden times) and also his account of the settlement of Sicily—marked as it is by repeated invasions which drive whole peoples from their homes—indicate, it is true of all times. We must try to indicate somewhat more fully its character or what underlies it. In speaking of the effects of the plague, Thucydides says that, pressed by the greatness of the evil, people abandoned the laments for the dead, the respect due to temples, and the laws regarding burial (II, 51–52). Earlier he had spoken of an extraordinary necessity which forced the Athenians to transgress an oracle and occupy an accursed ground (II, 17). The Athenians, accused by the Thebans of treating sacred ground as profane, allege the necessity that forced them to it (IV, 98). The war which convulsed the Greek cities in both civil and foreign strife proved to be a violent teacher which assimilated the tempers of most men to their harsh circumstances (III, 82). Behind the defeat of the righteous by necessity or force, we discern the defeat of the righteousness of the previously just by a necessity or force whose character however has not yet been sufficiently brought out. In the course of the aforementioned civil wars there occurred such harsh things as "have been and will be always, so long as there is the same nature of human beings" (III, 82). In the course of the Athenian plague, the increase in general lawlessness as men turned openly to the pursuit of pleasure was caused precisely by the release of men from the constraints of fear of gods and law of men (II, 53). Neither release need always await a plague: the latter, for example, could be accomplished by great strength. But what of the Spartans, who, powerful as they were, were not emphatically imperialistic? Toward the end of his work, Thucydides tells us that next to the Spartans, the Chians were the most moderate in prosperity, i.e., refrained most from the use of the power they possessed (VIII, 24). A little later he tells us that next to the Spartans the Chians possessed the most slaves (VIII, 40). The moderation of the Spartans with regard to empire, which had seemed to refute the contentions of the Athenians who spoke at Sparta, is due to nothing so much as their possessing many slaves, whom they must remain home to watch. On the other hand, the resort to justice on the part of the Melians, the most conspicuous spokesmen for justice in Thucydides, is explained by the fact that they have no other resort, and Thucydides as a rule entrusts the arguments which resort to justice either to the weak or to the insincere (for example, Cleon).

But if Thucydides is willing to grant this much to the argument of the Athenians at Sparta, he is far from condoning the mood of triumph which characterizes its Athenian utterance: if right does indeed bow in this way before necessity, no profit which one might derive from this fact would compensate for the ultimate loss. Thucydides begins the first speech in his book with the word "Right" and the second with the word "Necessary." Is not the tragedy to which that juxtaposition appears to point *the* theme of the work, a theme developed in the somber tones appropriate to it? Thucydides would appear to have replaced the Socratic question, What is justice, by the spectacle of the worldly weakness of the justice which we all know, perhaps foreshadowing in this respect Machiavelli, for whom the weakness of right rather than its character is the theme. But Thucydides has not abandoned the sense of what is lost.

Part Three

The conclusion reached is exposed at least to this difficulty: one cannot continue to call unjust that which is done by a universal necessity; it belongs to the notion of right that the actions it requires be possible. This seems to be the meaning of the correction made by the Athenians at Melos on the argument of their predecessors at Sparta. For they either deny that such as action as theirs is unjust, or they dare to suggest that it is just by an eternal law that is both human and divine.[4] It appears that we have not yet properly understood the thought contained in the juxtaposition of the terms right and necessity, for we failed to understand that precisely if that juxtaposition has the meaning previously suggested, the question of the character of right, the question what is right, is necessarily raised by it.

We must then examine more closely than we have as yet done the alleged necessity for the powerful to do wrong. Surely the fact, that those who are able to do wrong do not refrain from doing wrong, does not establish the necessity for them to do wrong. The manner in which the extent and character of such necessity can be established is indicated in the Melian dialogue. The Athenians had forbidden the Melians to speak of justice. They are to confine themselves to what is possible in view of what each side truly intends to do (V, 89). The Melians respond, forced, as they assert, to abandon considerations of justice for those of advantage, that they regard it as useful to the Athenians that the Athenians not destroy the common good, which holds that for him in danger whatever is plausible is just, and which allows him to derive benefit from persuading some one by arguments that fall short of precision: will not the Athenians one day be in more need of this common good than any one, destined, as they are, to be by their punishment an example to others (V, 90)? The Melians thus, contrary to their assertion, introduce the consideration of justice, for do we not mean by justice the common good? They also indicate the limits to their ability to demonstrate that it is to the Athenians' advantage to let them off. And indeed the Athenians, by arguments which there is no need to detail here, have no difficulty in showing them that it is not. But then there is no common good with regard to the Athenians and Melians; the Athenian invasion is dictated by a sound calculation of Athenian interest. Such interest, or the good, is a kind of necessity—it can be overridden, one can make mistakes, but not without its exacting the consequences of them. Nor, as the dialogue also indicates, are there any irremovable barriers standing between the good and our necessary desire to have it or directing our desire for the good away from its object. These then are

---

4. The Athenians at Sparta perhaps themselves move in the indicated direction in I, 76: . . . *aei kathestōtos ton hessō hupo tou dunatōterou kateirgesthai* . . . Cf. the discussion of their speech in Part One above.

the ineradicable roots of the "necessity" for those who can to do wrong, although for the reason indicated above, as well as because the Athenians and others cannot be accused of destroying what (in such cases as this at least) does not exist, we no longer speak of the necessity to do wrong.[5]

Because the Melian dialogue is followed eventually by the slaughter of the Melians, one might conclude that there is no more important task than the encouragement of the all too rare "mistakes" referred to or the creation or strengthening of the indicated barriers. But that conclusion would not be entirely correct, and not only because the slaughter is not required by the dialogue. The Athenian thesis is indeed compatible with, and to some extent conducive to, a remarkable gentleness. It goes without saying that it does not excuse the senseless butchery engaged in by Alcidas or the Thracian mercenaries (see Part Two above). But further, it is the Athenians who, whether or not their being more enlightened in this respect than others (e.g., the Spartans) is a spur to their imperialism, are also in their dealings with foreigners more gentle than, in particular, the Spartans. The quality in question and its cause appear most clearly in the thought and speech together with the deed of the singular Thucydidean character, Diodotus. Like his countryman Euphemus, Diodotus is unknown outside the pages of Thucydides;[6] his name means "Gift of Zeus"; and indeed he appears once to play his amazing part and then is gone. His speech abounds in subtlety and we are tempted to say of him—borrowing to some extent from what Nietzsche says of Machiavelli (*Beyond Good and Evil* #28)—that he derives a certain joy from the contrast between the quickness and lightness of his utterance and the gravity of his thought. For what other speaker in Thucydides, in a private capacity and to fellow countrymen, states so fully what we have called the Athenian thesis, making clear its applicability to individuals as well as cities; and what other speaker alerts his audience in advance

---

5. Given my argument—see the preface—for the necessity of a naïve—as opposed, for example, to a scholarly—starting point in the study of Thucydides, it may perhaps be helpful to point out that the differences between my conclusions and those of Jacqueline de Romilly in *Thucydide et l'impérialisme athénien* (Paris: Budé, 1951, 2nd ed.) on the meaning of the opposition of right and force or compulsion—cf., for example, with Part Three above, de Romilly pp. 256–59, esp. 257, as well as 280–82 and 243–44—are not unrelated to the greater seriousness with which I take, and argue that Thucydides takes, the issue of justice, the issue of the justice of Athenian imperialism, in the first place (cf. de Romilly, pp. 89–91).

6. A. W. Gomme, on III. 41.

to his intention to deceive them? We should resist the temptation to say that because of the seriousness of the occasion on which he speaks. The Athenians are debating for the second time the Mytilenian question, having decided the day before to punish the Mytilenians for their revolt by killing the men and enslaving the women and children. Diodotus supports the repeal of that decree, not, as he insists, on the ground of justice, but on that of "good counsel," of what is best for Athens (III, 44). His speech opens with a consideration of the complicated relation between the private good of the speakers who advise the Athenian assembly and that of the city advised: i.e., it opens with a reference to the problematical commonness of the common good of the city (III, 42–43). Its heart is an attack on the death penalty in general on the ground that it is in the nature of all, both privately and publicly, to err (or make mistakes) and that there is no law which can keep them from this (III, 45). It is perhaps true that Diodotus does not go so far as to draw the conclusion ascribed by us to the Athenians at Melos, but this is only because the circumstances prohibit the utterance of that conclusion, not because it does not belong to his thought. The Athenians—i.e., the Athenian *demos*, which did not necessarily share nor always permit itself to be guided by the enlightenment of some of its leaders—had passed their terrible decree against the Mytilenians under the influence of anger; they were indignant that the Mytilenians, who had not been treated badly by them, had nevertheless revolted. Their anger had been fired by two speeches of Cleon ("also in other respects the most violent of the citizens and by a large margin at that time the most trusted by the demos" [III, 36]). Cleon had spoken repeatedly of the "injustice" committed by the Mytilenians and had praised the anger which seeks swift revenge (III, 38 and 37–40 generally). Diodotus could not persuade the Athenians to repeal their decree and thus save the Mytilenians, if he did not first free them to some extent from their anger. He tries to do this by encouraging them to think rather of their interest than of the "wrong" which they suffered; the necessary compulsion of interest or advantage is to retrieve its place from the compulsion of anger and revenge, the compulsion which had rendered the Corcyraean civil war so terrible (Part Two above). Diodotus is able to free the Athenians somewhat from their anger because, in the first place, he never shared it; he does not share it because he does not blame the Mytilenians. Anger is the companion of lack of education and a narrow mind (or of folly) (III, 42). The thought of Diodotus leaves as little room for anger and indignation as that of Socrates.

Part Four

Diodotus' action is a typical Athenian action, or an action belonging to Athens at her best, such as we would expect also of Demosthenes and perhaps even of Themistocles. There is a definite hierarchy of men in Thucydides, and the placing of Diodotus among its heroes suggests, as it appears, nothing so much as the unity of enlightenment and gentleness. At the same time, the fact that he shares that eminence with Themistocles, the founder of the Athenian empire, and above all with Alcibiades, and the fact that the thought of Diodotus would not lead necessarily to the abandonment of empire, indicate the limits to that unity. It remains true, however that may be, that the thought ascribed to Diodotus is inseparable from a certain kind of right.

Alcibiades, more than anyone else in Thucydides, represents another side to Athenian greatness, the boundless striving for preeminence and immortal glory, a striving characteristic perhaps of Thucydides himself. It is fitting, then, that he should be the one to point to a connection between this striving, indifferent as it is to anything but its object, and the kind of right of which Diodotus has given evidence. Alcibiades maintains, as he had good reason to discover, that men are envious by nature, with the result that the eminent, while they live, cause pain especially to their like but also to others (VI, 16). Does not this pain obstruct our view of the excellent and therefore of human excellence itself? If this is so, then for this reason if not also others, only one who has striven successfully to be best would be able to assess every human type at its worth; and this clear-sighted giving to every man his due—compatible as it is with the aims of practice and essential to that of theory—would be that genuine right of the stronger which is necessary to the lion himself, Thucydides.[7]

---

7. An ancient commentator reports the saying of "some" who were surprised that the sober Thucydides went into such detail to explain a curse: "Here the lion laughed." (See the *scholia* collected by C. Hude, at about I, 126.)

5

Socratic Politics and Self-Knowledge

An Interpretation of Plato's *Charmides*

In Plato's *Charmides*, Socrates has a discussion about moderation with two cousins, Charmides and Critias. The conversation shakes the conviction of Charmides, a youth of great beauty and of promise, that he possesses that virtue and persuades him that he must seek it from Socrates, who claims to have learned an incantation or song capable of producing it in one who listens. The end of the dialogue will be the beginning of Charmides' association with Socrates for that purpose. Some thirty years later, Charmides joined his elder kinsman Critias in an oligarchic regime whose rule over Athens was such that in a short time, according to a letter ascribed to Plato, it made the discredited democracy look golden.[1]

The *Charmides* thus takes its place beside the *Alcibiades I*, where Socrates has a conversation with the young Alcibiades, then at the eve of his entrance into politics, which convinces Alcibiades that he must begin at once to be concerned with justice. The end of the dialogue will be the beginning of his association with Socrates for that purpose. Yet Alcibiades' later career (during which he played a major part on three different sides in the Peloponnesian war, Athenian, Spartan, Persian), while conspicuous in other respects, does not seem to have been remarkable for its attention

---

The text of the *Charmides* used is Burnet's OCT, except where differences from Burnet's readings are noted.

1. *Seventh Letter* 324 d7–8. (Unless otherwise noted, works cited are by Plato.)

to justice. By presenting what appear to be Socratic exhortations to concern for justice and moderation in such settings, Plato invites our wonder about the efficacy of such Socratic exhortations; in this and other ways, he leads us to wonder about their true character and purpose.

I. The Context in Which and the Manner in Which Socrates Turned His Attention to Charmides

The dialogue is narrated by Socrates to a companion whom he does not address by name. Socrates begins by saying that they (i.e., Socrates and other Athenian soldiers) had come the preceding evening from the army in Potidaea. Since he had been away for some time, he (Socrates) went gladly to his accustomed haunts. (Socrates, who makes no mention of home, was perhaps not yet married.)[2] In particular, he went to the palaestra (wrestling school) of Taureas, which is opposite the Queen's temple, and found among the many there a few he did not know, but most were known to him. When they saw him enter unexpectedly, they at once greeted him from wherever they were; but Chairephon, inclined as he was even to madness, jumped up from their midst and ran toward Socrates, and taking him by the hand said: "Socrates, how were you saved from the battle?" Before recounting his reply to Chairephon, Socrates pauses to explain to the companion that there had been a battle at Potidaea shortly before they had left there, of which those in the palaestra had recently learned. Socrates does not assume that the companion has any knowledge of or interest in that battle, just as he does not seem to assume that he is familiar with the palaestra in question or with such a conspicuous Athenian as Critias (153c7). The companion, who is a stranger to these things although he knows of Socrates' companion Chairephon, is perhaps a foreigner led to Athens by his interest in the way of philosophizing practised by Socrates. Socrates repays his interest by narrating to him his encounter with Charmides and Critias. Is that encounter especially revealing with respect to the companion's interest? That this is so is suggested also by the presence of Chairephon. Chairephon reminds us of the Delphic story of the *Apology of Socrates* (20c4 ff.). According to that story, the oracle's response to a question about Socrates, directed to it by Chairephon, was responsible for the change in Socrates' activity which distinguished him

---

2. Cf. however Xenophon, *Symposium* 9.7 with 2.10.

so markedly not only from his fellow citizens but also from other theoretical men. (When Socrates had this meeting with Charmides, though not necessarily when he told the story to the companion, he was quite young, perhaps thirty-eight, almost as young as he was at the time of the *Alcibiades I*: the *Alcibiades I* takes place before, perhaps shortly before, the battle of Potidaea[3] and the action of the *Charmides* takes place just after that battle. Whereas Socrates was all but unknown to Alcibiades when he first addressed him, he already had a reputation among the boys at the time of his meeting with Charmides.[4])

The companion, if he has indeed travelled to Athens to see Socrates, differs to that extent from him; for Socrates appears never to have left home except to perform his citizen's duty as a soldier. Perhaps Socrates had more need than other theoretical men to be a citizen.[5] Socrates implicitly distinguishes himself in turn from the "mad" Chairephon. Madness is an opposite to moderation (see, e.g., *Protagoras* 323b4–5). Chairephon's madness seems to have been shown by his excessive joy at the survival of Socrates, rather than by his unrestrained display of that joy before others who may have suffered or fear to have suffered a recent loss (153b9–c1). It does not, at any rate, consist in an indifference to the city, for Chairephon, who was later to provide Socrates with a link to the Athenian demos[6] and who here brings Socrates to sit down beside the future oligarch Critias, was more political than Socrates. (Consider also Chairephon's connection with Gorgias,[7] and note here that Socrates appears to share the nameless companion's indifference to the details of the battle rather than Chairephon's interest in them.)

After politely fulfilling the curiosity of Chairephon and the rest of the circle around Critias regarding the battle, Socrates in turn asked about things in Athens: about philosophy—how things were now—and about the young—whether any of them were outstanding in wisdom or beauty or both. Critias, looking toward the door, where he saw some youths (who were reviling each other) entering, with another crowd behind them, said: "About the beautiful, Socrates, I think you will know directly; for those

---

3. *Symposium* 219e5–6.

4. *Alcibiades I* 104c7–d5; cf. *Charmides* 156a5–8.

5. *Crito* 52e3–53a4; *Meno* 79e7–80b7.

6. *Apology of Socrates* 20e8–21a2.

7. *Gorgias* 447b2–3 and c9.

now coming in are the forerunners and lovers of the one thought to be most beautiful at present, and he himself appears to me to be already near to entering." Critias' partial answer to Socrates' question brought it about that a youth rather than philosophy, and the youth's beauty, rather than any wisdom he might possess, commanded the immediate attention of those present. We do not know whether this accorded with the order of Socrates' concerns. His concern with beautiful youths—about which he was here and elsewhere so open[8]—gave, so far as ordinary Athenians (and perhaps others) were concerned, an only slightly objectionable color to his pursuit of youths; its display may therefore belong, together with his soldiering, to his deference to the city. But this is not to say that he was insensitive to beauty, or that there was no intrinsic connection between that sensitivity and his philosophy.

Soon after, the youth in question, Critias' young cousin and ward Charmides, entered. Now Socrates is no judge of beauty, as he explains here to the companion, for just about all those of age appear beautiful to him; therefore, although Charmides appeared to him then of wondrous height and beauty, Socrates emphasizes the reaction of the others. All the others seemed to Socrates to be in love with Charmides, so affected and disturbed were they when he entered. The reaction of those to whom Socrates belonged, the men, was less to be wondered at; but Socrates applied his mind also to the boys: not one of them, not even the smallest, looked elsewhere, but everyone gazed at Charmides as if he were a statue. Only Socrates, it appears, looked elsewhere. He was forced, one can say, by his undiscriminating sensitivity to beauty, to look away from the beautiful Charmides in order to gauge or confirm that beauty, or his impression of it, by observing the reaction of others; he had to turn from the beautiful to the human response to the beautiful. But from what source did he derive the strength to do this?

Chairephon asked Socrates whether Charmides was fair of face. " 'Supernaturally so,' I said. 'If he would be willing to strip,' he said, 'he will seem to you to be faceless, so all-beautiful is he in form.' The others too joined in these assertions of Chairephon." If Charmides would strip, the beauty of his form would prevent one from observing his beautiful face: it is impossible apparently to behold the two beauties together. His

---

8. *Charmides* 153d4–5, 154b8–c2, 155c5–e3; *Protagoras* 309a1–b7; *Lysis* 204b1–c2, 204e1–205a2; *Erastai* 132a1–3, 133a1–6; Xenophon, *Symposium* 8.2. Cf. *Protagoras* 309b7–d2; Xenophon, *Memorabilia* IV 1.1–2.

stripping would not diminish or lessen his beauty, but it would in a sense make it less his by concealing the characteristic features of his face. As it is, as Charmides comes into view, his form is concealed by his clothes, by the artifice or convention of clothes.

Socrates proved to be interested in seeing Charmides' soul rather than, or before, his form. Responding to Chairephon's and the others' assertions of Charmides' beauty, Socrates said: "Herakles, the man, as you speak of him, would be irresistible [not to be fought against]," if only he happens in addition to be of a good nature in his soul. (Did Socrates wish to fight with Charmides?) Passing by Critias' assertion that Charmides was noble and good in his soul too, Socrates suggested that they strip Charmides' soul and contemplate it before the form: "for surely, at the age he has reached, he will already be willing to have a conversation [*dialegesthai*]." The means of stripping was apparently to be a conversation. Critias, after his fashion, said that Charmides would be willing to converse. Would he be willing if he knew the purpose of the conversation? (Cf. 158c–159b.)

Socrates implied that Charmides' soul too was concealed, so that its nature would not be visible without a stripping. Since it is not immediately clear what Socrates meant by "a good nature in his soul," we are forced to look for clarification of this point to the sequel, where Socrates reveals his understanding by deed, by his examination of Charmides. From a very simple reading of that examination it might appear that Socrates wished to find out whether Charmides possessed by nature the virtue of moderation (cf. especially 158b2–4 with 154e1). On a closer look, we might find more plausible the suggestion that Socrates wished to find out whether Charmides was able to resist claiming or believing that he possessed that virtue.[9] (If Charmides had by nature a good soul in either of these senses, we are tempted to say, he would have been as impossible to fight against as that son of Zeus, Herakles.) The analogy of soul stripping with body stripping is then not quite apt. Socrates seems to seek to discover whether Charmides' soul believes that it is good (cf. 160e9): soul stripping might uncover a further layer of clothes. But this

---

9. Since moderation will be spoken of in the *Charmides* as both beautiful (simply beautiful, most beautiful of all) and good (simply good) and since it will be said to lead to happiness, we feel justified in calling it a virtue. But it is not so called anywhere in the dialogue. Indeed, the term virtue (*arēte*) occurs only at 158a1, in a reporting of praises composed by poets. Perhaps Plato wished to anticipate, by this act of moderation, the conclusion which the dialogue would reach.

is not to say that these too might not be stripped. Indeed, it might be impossible to see their importance before they were.

Socrates then asked Critias to call Charmides to him. Although it was not clear from anything Critias had said that Critias had an objection to Socrates conversing with Charmides, Socrates pointed out to him that, even if Charmides were younger, such a conversation would not be shameful in the presence of Critias, his guardian and cousin. Critias then sent his slave to fetch Charmides, with the message that Critias wished to introduce him to a medical man for his sickness. Then Critias explained to Socrates that Charmides had been suffering from headache, and he suggested that Socrates pretend to know a drug for the head. Since Critias had said earlier that Charmides would be most willing to converse, it is not clear why he thought the pretense was necessary. Perhaps he thought that Socrates would not want to reveal to Charmides the purpose for which he wished to converse with him; but perhaps he wished to put an obstacle in the way of the accomplishment of that purpose. Whatever his reasons, Critias, who was later to become his city's ruler, forced Socrates to pretend to a capacity to heal which Socrates did not possess. There may be some correspondence between this occurrence, which the next section elaborates, and what occurs at the very end of the dialogue.

II. What Socrates Suffered from Charmides
and Learned from a Thracian

When Charmides came, he produced much laughter. For the earnestness or seriousness with which each of those in Socrates' group pushed his neighbor, so as to make room for Charmides to sit by him, forced from their places those sitting at the ends (cf. 154a1–2 *loidoroumenous*). There was something comic to that seriousness about the beautiful.

Charmides sat down between Socrates and Critias. At this point, Socrates lost his former boldness that he would be able to converse with Charmides with ease, and, as he says to the companion, he was at a loss. Socrates' discomfiture was increased by the gaze Charmides turned upon him when Critias presented him as the one who knew the drug, while the crowd pressed around them; it was completed when, as he says to the companion, he saw inadvertently what was within Charmides' cloak, became "inflamed," was no longer in himself, and held that Kydias—who in counseling another in verse had compared a beautiful boy to a lion who makes his meal of the approaching fawn—was wisest in erotic matters: Socrates seemed to himself to have been caught by such a beast. On other (later) occasions, Socrates claimed for himself an expertise in erotic matters.[10] Here he was led by an apparently overwhelming erotic passion to acknowledge a poet's superior wisdom in these matters. (There had been an earlier intimation that whereas Critias and Charmides fancied themselves to combine philosophy and poetry, Socrates' own philosophy was unpoetic, which is not to say that his presentation of that philosophy to the companion is unpoetic.[11] Coincidentally with his succumbing to the attractions of Charmides, Socrates became aware, or more aware, of his audience.) Nevertheless, when Charmides asked if Socrates knew the drug for the head, Socrates managed, with some difficulty, to answer that he did. Socrates resisted that passion. The key to the success of his resistance appears to be his reflection that Kydias was wisest, i.e., that he himself was defective in wisdom. By coming to that conviction (*enomisa* 155d4) at the height of his passion's intensity, he must have become aware that the passion was not simply overwhelming: it was accompanied by his concern for his wisdom. Socrates was not simply outside of himself; he also thought, he was aware of himself—of how he stood in relation to Kydias with respect to wisdom; that thought was part of the experience, so to speak. And his awareness of all this, together with his concern for his wisdom, gave him some power to resist what had been an irresistible passion because that passion had seemed to point so simply and unambiguously to all that was longed for.

Charmides asked what the drug was. Socrates replied that it was some leaf, but there was a song applying to the drug in such a way that if one sang it at the same time that one used it (the leaf or drug), the drug would make one entirely healthy, but there was no benefit from the leaf without the song. (It was not said whether there was a benefit from the song without the leaf.) Charmides was prepared to write down the song at the dictation of the one who told him of it.[12] But Socrates asked, "If you

---

10. *Theages* 128b2–6; *Symposium* 177d7–8; *Phaedrus* 257a7–8. (Two of these dialogues happen to mention Charmides: *Theages* 128d ff.; *Symposium* 222b1–4.) Cf. *Lysis* 204b8–c2, 205a1–2 and 210e1–5.

11. *Charmides* 154e8–155a3; cf. *Timaeus* 20d7–21d3.

12. If Socrates' purpose was to get Charmides to listen to the "song," it appears at this point that the Thracian story he is about to tell is superfluous. But perhaps the song required a truly willing listener, one, that is, who knew what he was being subjected to.

persuade me or even if you don't?" (Cf. 176e5–7.) Charmides said with a laugh, "If I persuade you, Socrates." It thus came to light that Charmides knew Socrates' name: there was no little talk of him among the youths and Charmides remembered Socrates as a companion of Critias, when he himself was a boy. Socrates was not disconcerted by the revelation that Charmides all along had seen through the disguise which Critias had forced upon him. At any rate, he did not take the opportunity to begin so to speak the conversation anew. He said rather that he would now be more frank with Charmides as to the character of the song, for he had just been at a loss as to how to show him its power. (He admits that there are circumstances in which he is not entirely frank or outspoken; he admits that the present situation is still not altogether free from such circumstances.) Did the explanation of the song require that Socrates reveal to some extent what or who he was?

The explanation proved to entail a comparison of Greek and Thracian medicine. Socrates characterized Greek medicine by describing to Charmides a familiar case. (Since it is not yet identified as Greek, one should perhaps speak here of medicine simply.) If one goes to the good medical men, suffering in one's eyes, they say that they are unable to cure the eyes alone, but that it would be necessary to minister to the head at the same time, and, again, that it is extremely foolish to think that one can minister to the head by itself to the neglect of the whole body. For this reason, prescribing regimens for all of the body, they undertake to minister to and heal the part with the whole. At this point, Socrates asked for Charmides' assent both to the accuracy of his characterization of the medical men's words and to the words themselves and the reasoning; to both Charmides' assent was emphatic. And Socrates, hearing his praise, took heart again and little by little his boldness came back, and he came to life again, as he says to the companion.

Socrates began the continuation of his explanation by asserting that the case of the song (of which he had already said that it could not make healthy the head alone) was similar to that of the medical procedure he had described. That assertion was insufficient because the procedure in question belonged, as it now appeared, to Greek medicine, while the song, which Socrates had learned from a Thracian medical man, belonged to Thracian medicine. Thracian medicine was distinguished in the first place by its alleged attempt to produce immortality. It understood itself to have been handed down from Zalmoxis, a god who is also a king. The Thracian told Socrates, as Socrates now tells his companion that he told Charmides, that

Zalmoxis said that, just as one must not undertake to cure the eyes without the head, or the head without the body, so also not the body without the soul; this was the cause, as Zalmoxis or the Thracian himself went on, of the failure of the Greek medical men in the case of many diseases—the ignorance of the whole to which care must be applied and whose fine state is a condition of the good state of the part.[13] For, he said, all the bad and the good things for the body and all of the human being start from the soul and flow from there to the body. One must then minister to the soul first and above all if the things of the head and of the rest of the body are to be in a fine state. The soul is ministered to, the Thracian continued, by certain songs, and these songs are the speeches which are noble (or beautiful); from such speeches moderation is generated in the souls, the immanence and presence of which makes it easy to provide health to the head and the rest of the body.

"Thracian" medicine then is distinguished from Greek by its attempt to immortalize and by its assertion of the power of the soul over the body. (The self-limitation of the Greek medical men to the body was perhaps connected with their self-limitation regarding immortality.) There is no evil for the body which does not originate in the soul; the soul can be imbued with moderation by the noble speeches; and, when this has been done, the health of the body is easily provided. What we call moral education is the key to health, if not also to immortality. If we were not held back by our ignorance as to what moderation is, we would be tempted to say that Socrates' Thracian teacher was not conspicuous for possessing it. It is perhaps true, on the other hand, that he did not claim to possess moderation; but he claimed to be able to bring it into one's soul, and who, if he possessed such ability, would fail to use it on himself?

After teaching Socrates the drug and the songs, the Thracian bid him not to be persuaded by anyone to minister to that person's head, who had not first provided his soul for Socrates to minister to with the song, "for now this is the mistake regarding human beings, that some undertake to be doctors [medical men] of each separately, moderation and health." Did the Thracian thus inadvertently advise Socrates not to be a doctor (medical man) of moderation without also professing to be one of "health"? Socrates swore an oath to the Thracian and, as he also

____

13. Zalmoxis, or the Thracian medical man, appears to regard the body as a part of the soul. See T. M. Robinson, *Plato's Psychology* (Toronto: University of Toronto Press, 1970), pp. 5–7.

told Charmides, it was necessary for him to obey. So if Charmides, in accordance with the stranger's injunctions, wanted to provide his soul first to be sung to with the Thracian's songs, Socrates would apply the drug to his head; if not, they would not know what to do for (or with) Charmides. Socrates thus offered to minister to more than Charmides' bodily health, while, on the other hand, he treated Charmides as if Charmides was in need of moderation, or at least as if there was reason to think that he was. Moreover, according to the presentation that he gives, Socrates was forced to proceed in this way by his adherence to Thracian medicine, or by his piety, or both: he did not make such a grave charge, even if only by implication, on his own authority. (Cf. *Apology of Socrates* 29d2–30a5.)

On the basis of the assumptions underlying Thracian medicine, one is forced to hold that whoever suffers from a bodily ill is or has been defective in his soul in such a way as to need moderation. (It is possible that he has acquired moderation but has not yet been cured in his body: as the leaf indicates, moderation is only the necessary condition of health.) We may therefore call such a person, if he has not yet acquired moderation, immoderate. This seems to leave open however the possibility that there is an original good state of the soul whose goodness, while securing the health of the body, consists in something other than the possession of moderation (in innocence, for example): moderation would then become necessary to those who have left this state, for the reason that it itself is not recoverable. Whether or not, in the Thracian view, there is such a state and, if so, whether the soul in that state is better or worse off than the moderate soul, the Thracian seems not to have told Socrates, just as he seems not to have taught him what moderation is. (Socrates, despite his possession of the Thracian songs, claims at various times in the dialogue still to be in the dark in that respect.) Perhaps the Thracian thought that it would be difficult to account, consistently with his principles, for the passage from such a state to the defective one. However that may be, since every human being suffers at one time or another from a bodily ill (if only that of aging), everyone comes to be in the need of moderation; moderation is inculcated by songs or speeches: no one is born with a soul sufficient by nature with a view to moderation[14] or another kind of

---

14. Socrates seems to leave open such a possibility at 158b2–3 (note however *pros*). But at 158d8, he proposes to examine with Charmides whether Charmides has acquired (*kektēsai*), and thus possesses, moderation, while at 158c1 he wonders whether Charmides is still (*eti*) in need in this respect.

goodness, for even granting the existence of such goodness we are forced to say that it does not last.

There is a certain correspondence between the two ways in which the Thracian view permits us to understand the good or noble state of the soul and the two interpretations of Socrates' phrase "a good nature in his soul" that were suggested above (p. 111). There it appeared more plausible that Charmides' nature might abstain from claiming or thinking to possess the virtue of moderation than that he possessed such a virtue by nature. If we incorporate the suggestion of the present passage, we are forced to expect that neither Charmides nor anyone else will prove to have a good nature in either of those senses. On the other hand, even by virtue of that very suggestion, this passage holds out the prospect that we may become moderate—whether in the Thracian sense and manner or in some other.

III. The Examination of Charmides

Socrates' Thracian story, culminating as it did in his offer to apply to Charmides the songs which induce moderation, must have put Charmides on the spot. For that offer carried with it, as we have seen, the suggestion that Charmides was not moderate, a suggestion which would appear to be confirmed if he should accept the offer. Charmides might have replied however that the offer was one which no one could refuse, since it is sensible even for a moderate man to neglect no opportunity to make sure of or strengthen his moderation. He was prevented from making such a reply in the first place by Critias, who saw the implication of Socrates' offer and answered for or in the place of Charmides: the headache would be a fine piece of luck, he said, if the youth will be forced, on account of his head, to become better also in his understanding or mind. (Critias differed from Socrates' Thracian in speaking of the understanding rather than the soul as what was to be imbued with moderation. Perhaps he drew an inference from the suggestion that moderation can be imbued by listening to speeches, without paying sufficient attention to the fact that the Thracian calls those speeches "songs.") But Charmides is already reputed to be far the most moderate of his contemporaries and is in all other respects, so far as his age permits, inferior to no one. Hence, Critias implied, the song is unnecessary. Critias appealed to Charmides' reputation to prevent an action on Charmides' part which, he may have feared, would damage that reputation and therewith his own; but can he be sure that Charmides is sufficiently moderate and that he, Critias, is not standing in the way of his becoming so? But one can also say that Critias had in mind not Socrates' offer regarding moderation, but his intention regarding stripping; and it is perhaps not immediately clear how such a stripping will contribute to Charmides' becoming moderate. Or, perhaps, Critias wished merely to prevent any conversation between Socrates and Charmides which might endanger his own influence over the youth.

Socrates responded, to Charmides, that it was right that he stand out from the others in such respects, for his ancestry would make this the likely or expected thing. And he then spoke of the two "houses" from which Charmides descended. One could perhaps have taken his words to suggest how unlikely it was that a youth with so much to puff him up (not to mention Critias as a guardian) should be moderate in any sense. Socrates surely left it open whether the expected had in fact occurred: "if also with regard to moderation and the other things, in accordance with [Critias'] account, you have been sufficiently endowed by nature, blessedly happy did your mother bear you, dear Charmides." Nature, not ancestry, is decisive with regard to moderation; and moderation in turn appears necessary to happiness. Socrates had departed from his Thracian teacher by his mention of nature and—in letter though perhaps not in spirit—by speaking of happiness. (Does health in the Thracian sense [156d6] take the place of happiness?) He thus underscored the importance of moderation—but also brought into some question his ability to induce it, in all cases, by speeches or songs—before offering Charmides a choice and thus posing his question anew, this time more directly. If Charmides was already sufficiently moderate, as Critias said, he would have no need of the songs of Zalmoxis or of those of Abaris the Hyperborian, but it would be time to give him the drug for the head; if on the other hand, he thought he was (or seemed to be) still in need of these, one must sing to him first. "Tell me then yourself whether you agree with [Critias] and claim to partake sufficiently of moderation already, or to be in need." It is not clear that Socrates was not in violation of the letter of his oath to the Thracian in giving Charmides this choice; but his adherence to the Thracian spirit is indicated by his reference to the Hyperborians, a people of the far north who might perhaps be called the Thracians' Thracians.

Socrates' question again, and more obviously, put Charmides on the spot. He replied, with a blush, that "It would not be easy in the present circumstances either to agree to it or to deny it: for if I deny being moderate, it is both odd to say such things against oneself, and, at the same time, I will show up both Critias as a liar [or mistaken] and many others, by whom I am reputed to be moderate, by his account; if again I claim [to be moderate] and praise myself, perhaps it will appear offensive." On these grounds Charmides refused to answer: I do not know how I should answer you. He did not answer above all because each of the two answers he considered was in some way offensive: it would be offensive to call Critias and "many" others liars, and it would be offensive for Charmides to reveal that he held a high opinion of himself. Moreover, to deny being moderate would be odd.[15] Charmides was prevented by what we can call "good manners" from accepting Socrates' offer or explicitly declining it: he declined it in fact. (Socrates characterizes this response to the companion as not ignoble or low born.) It was not a question either of shame at revealing a defect (cf. 164d1; 169c7–d1) or on the other hand of a high opinion of himself which Charmides blushed to acknowledge even to himself and which Socrates' question had threatened to make public.

This account of his action—the one which Charmides wished Socrates to form—was belied in the first place by his blush, of which Socrates says to the companion that it made Charmides still more beautiful, for his sense of shame was becoming to his age. His revealing blush, rather than his concealing, well-mannered words, enhanced Charmides' beauty, as is emphasized by the formulation in the text: "first he became more beautiful . . . then he answered . . ." In the second place, Charmides' words were perhaps not so concealing as he may have hoped or supposed. For if he had believed to need Socrates' assistance, would he not have sought a way to accept it without offense to others or embarrassment to himself? But perhaps no way occurred to him.

Socrates' response to Charmides' objection must have been reassuring. What Charmides had said appeared to him fair or plausible. Socrates therefore suggested that they examine in common whether or not Charmides possessed what Socrates inquired about, so that Charmides would not be forced to say what he did not wish, and Socrates would not turn to the medical art without an examination (of Charmides). "If then it is welcome to you, I am willing to examine with you; if not, to let it go." Charmides apparently would never be required to reveal his belief as to whether he possessed moderation: they would examine only the fact of

---

15. Cf. *Protagoras* 323a7–c2.

possession or non-possession. His emphatic assent to Socrates' offer per-haps reflected his relief at this, together with his interest in the question. He went so far as to say that for his part, Socrates was free to examine in the manner that he thought best. Charmides did not fear the result of that examination.

Socrates' suggestion as to procedure was based on the following considerations: if moderation is present to Charmides, he will clearly be able to form some opinion about it; for being in him, if it is in him, it will necessarily furnish some perception from which there would be some opinion about it as to what and what sort of thing moderation is; more-over, since Charmides knows how to speak Greek, he would be able to say what it is that appears to him. Charmides responded to these premises of Socrates' proposal in a way that passed for assent. Whatever might be behind his hesitation, it does appear that they deserve some further scrutiny. For even if we grant that moderation, if it is in one, will furnish some perception about which an opinion may be formed, is it necessary that the opinion will assign to the cause of that perception the name "moderation"? On the other hand, does not "speaking Greek"—and therefore, what one has heard—have more to do with one's opinion about moderation than Socrates' formulation allows? By not permitting such questions to arise, Socrates brought it about that Charmides accepted the proposition that an experience, so to speak, of moderation will always make itself known as (or believed to be) such; while he left it in the dark whether there is any other source of opinions—not excluding correct opinions—about moderation. But this very "success" called into question the validity of the procedure for discovering whether or not Charmides is moderate which is about to be proposed. Socrates' action would be unintelligible then if that procedure did not have other objectives than the one stated.

Having more or less secured Charmides' assent to his premises, Socrates proceeded at once to ask him—"so that we may guess whether it is in you or not"—to say what moderation was according to his opinion. Now one who, having accepted the Socratic premises, ventures to give an answer to a question so phrased all but admits that he believes he is mod-erate: he states what, in himself, he believes to be moderation. (Moreover, if his answer or answers should be shown to be incorrect—or if he should be unable to answer at all—he would be led by those same premises to doubt that he is moderate.) But this is just what Charmides did. At first he held back and was not very willing to answer; then however he did so. Socrates does not tell the companion what further inducements, if any, were necessary to produce this step; he concentrates his attention on the step itself. Socrates had led Charmides, after all, to reveal his belief that he possessed moderation. Did he not intend this all along? For whatever reasons, he was more interested here in discovering (and subsequently shaking) Charmides' opinion about himself with regard to moderation than in answering the question whether Charmides was moderate or not, to say nothing of any other question (see pp. 124–25 below). But one may object that this presupposes that Charmides was aware of some of the implications of Socrates' procedure, while being unaware of the difficulties. We must see whether the doubts which this objection may justify are cleared up in the sequel.

Charmides' answer was to the effect that moderation seemed to him to be doing everything in an orderly and quiet manner, both walking in the roads and conversing and all the rest; that some sort of quietness was what Socrates asked for. Socrates said: "Do you speak well? They say at least, Charmides, that the quiet are moderate: let's see if they have a point." He implied that the answer reflected what Charmides heard rather than what he felt. Had Charmides really looked into himself? It corresponded however at least to Charmides' behavior hitherto, especially if we include under "doing quietly" refraining from asserting oneself. Socrates had raised the question whether Charmides "spoke well" or correctly. It thus came to light that they were now to examine the correctness of Charmides' definition. From what source did Socrates expect to derive the standard to make that determination? (Cf. p. 174f. below.)

The examination began with Socrates asking whether moderation belonged to the beautiful (or noble) things. Charmides said, very much so. Socrates then enumerated activities in which, as he easily got Charmides to agree, slowness was less beautiful than swiftness, if it was not also ugly or base (159d2). (It will be seen that he ignored Charmides' reference to orderliness and understood quietness in a particular way.)[16] Socrates failed to mention activities—e.g., dancing—where a certain kind of slowness may be beautiful.[17] He did not raise the question whether some quietness or

---

16. Cf. 160c7 where "orderly" (*kosmios*) makes an enigmatic reappearance.

17. Cf. 159d2; *ta de* [*bradea*] *mogis te kai hēsuchē ta tou aischrou.* The word excluded by Burnet following Heindorf shows the problem: slowness without difficulty may not be ugly. Cf. *Statesman* 307a1–b3. The kinship of the *Statesman* passage to that in the *Charmides* is noted by J. N. Findlay, *Plato The Written and Unwritten Doctrines* (New York: Humanities Press, 1974), p. 279.

slowness might not be a presupposition of the swiftness he praised—e.g., sleep for a runner. He thus exalted the swift and sharp, the intense, the easy above the quiet, slow and difficult, in reaching the conclusion that "moderation would not be some quietness, nor would the moderate life be quiet." (Cf. *Apology of Socrates* 37e3–38a8.)

Socrates' list of activities consisted of two parts of eight items each. Although it did not include walking or conversing (cf. 159b4 and 160c6), it made some claims to comprehensiveness (159c13, d4, 160b3–4): the first part (in which he included reading, writing, and cithera playing, perhaps because he started with Charmides' school activities) consisted, according to the impression given by Socrates' summary, of bodily activities, the second of activities of the soul. Socrates spoke as if all human activities are activities either of the body alone or of the soul alone. Moreover, the activities ascribed to the soul are all, as we would say, activities of the "mind": there is no reference to desire, hope, fear, etc., or even to perception (cf. 167e–168a). Can a better case be made for a kind of quietness if one considers our composite nature? After his summary of the first part, Socrates said, "then with respect to the body not quietness but swiftness would be more moderate . . . . " After his second summary, which referred to both the soul and the body, he said, "Then moderation would not be some quietness . . . ," adding the qualification, "from this argument." His conclusion was based on the consideration that the slow activities in life are either nowhere or in few places more beautiful than the swift and strong; but even if no fewer of the slow (activities) than of the intense and swift were more beautiful, not even thus would acting quietly be moderation any more than acting intensely and swiftly. Socrates, following Charmides (159b3–4), required that the moderate way of acting be beautiful, even preeminently beautiful, everywhere or always.[18]

Charmides said that Socrates seemed to him to have spoken correctly. Socrates thereupon urged him to apply his mind again to a greater extent and to look away from everything else into himself; to turn over in his mind what sort of thing moderation makes him to be, and what sort of thing it is that it should work that effect; to reckon up all these things and then to say well and courageously what it appears to him to be. After a manly or courageous examination with regard to himself, as Socrates

---

18. Not only must moderation, wherever it is, be beautiful or more beautiful, but they refuse to limit it to certain actions—to say, for example, that to do certain things slowly is moderation. Cf. Findlay, p. 92.

explains to the companion, Charmides said that moderation seemed to him to produce shame and make the human being such as to feel shame and that it seemed to be what reverence or awe or shame (*aidōs*) is. Socrates did not say of this answer that it is what people say. He wished to consider it on the basis of Charmides' agreement that moderation is (always) good, as in the case of Charmides' first answer he had proceeded on the basis of Charmides' agreement that moderation is (always) beautiful or noble. But this time he did not ask for that agreement directly: he acted as if the goodness of moderation, as distinct from its nobility or beauty, were in need of proof; yet that goodness is implied somehow in its nobility. For the "proof" was as follows. Socrates asked whether Charmides had not just agreed that moderation was noble (beautiful). Very much so, he said. From this it seemed to follow that moderate men were good men and that moderation itself was not only noble but also good. The proximate ground of the goodness of moderation would appear to be its responsibility for the goodness of moderate men. (Can this be the ground also of the goodness of the good men, that they make men good?) For some reason or other, this ground was stated initially as a necessary condition of (any) goodness, and then treated as a sufficient condition of the goodness of moderation. Socrates asked, "Would that be good then which did not make men good?"; and on the basis of Charmides' strong denial, he asserted the goodness of moderation. Having established, after this fashion, that moderation is good, Socrates employed the authority of Homer to show that reverence or awe or shame is not always good; it is not good for a needy man. (Socrates was perhaps somewhat more gentle or cautious here than he had been with "quietness.") It followed that moderation would not be reverence or awe or shame. Socrates, together with Charmides, insisted that moderation be simply, always, good. (The needy man referred to by Homer or by the Homeric speaker was Odysseus disguised as a beggar. Odysseus, to whom Socrates occasionally likened himself[19] had disguised his true need by taking upon himself the appearance of a false one. See p. 110 above.)

Charmides readily agreed to the correctness of what had been said and now proposed on his own initiative a new definition for Socrates to examine. "For I just remembered, what I have already heard someone saying, that moderation was doing one's own things; examine this then, whether the speaker seems to you to speak correctly." "Wretch," Socrates

---

19. See, e.g., the entrance into the house of Kallias in the *Protagoras*, esp. 315b9 and c8.

says that he said, "you have heard this from Critias or some other one of the wise." (Cf. 174b11 where Socrates addresses Critias, immediately after Critias has spoken of a science of the good and the bad, as "wretch." If Charmides had heard this definition from Critias, had not Critias in turn heard it, as he had doubtless heard of a science of the good and the bad, from Socrates? Is one a wretch for repeating what seems to be a Socratic teaching?) Critias denied that Charmides had heard it from him. Charmides then asked Socrates what difference it made whom he had heard it from. None, Socrates said, for what is to be examined is not who said it but whether it is true or not. Charmides, the truster in Homer (161a2–5), said, "Now you speak correctly." Socrates, who responded with a "by Zeus," is a better guide to the scope or bearing, and therewith the difficulty of application, of Charmides' principle. Socrates went on to say that he would be amazed if they were to discover even the meaning of this definition, for it had the look of a riddle.

It is clear by now that the situation has changed in a number of respects. When Charmides, referring to the definition he had just proposed and for which he had denied responsibility, asked Socrates to examine whether the speaker seemed to him to speak correctly, he clearly did not mean by that speaker himself. He had perhaps become so concerned to find an answer to the question what is moderation that he had forgotten the purpose which his attempting to answer that question from his own experience had been said to serve. But it is at least equally likely that he had already formed the wish or purpose to escape Socrates' examination by provoking Critias (cf. 162c). Did he now regard Socrates' procedure as faulty? He raised no question about it. Had that procedure and the failure of his first two answers led him to the conclusion that he was not moderate? The definition he has just proposed would not tend to support this conjecture, since he appears not to regard himself as a busybody (161d11–e2). Perhaps then he wished either to avoid facing that question or, at least, to have it resolved in a less public manner. For to continue the discussion in the way he now proposed was to divorce it from the Socratic procedure for discovering whether or not he possessed moderation and to that extent to leave that question behind.

Socrates nevertheless accepted Charmides' proposal and not long thereafter (162d) his replacement as an interlocutor by Critias. Whatever Charmides' motivation or intention, and whatever Socrates' own preference or intention, it would have been difficult for Socrates, especially after the way in which he had introduced the theme of moderation (see especially 158b4), to avoid taking the lead in a discussion that professed to aim above all at answering the question what is moderation, that professed to subordinate all other considerations to that end. It may also have been difficult for him to avoid allowing Charmides a way out or Critias the chance to speak he all but demanded (162c–d). These considerations lead us to wonder whether Socrates had finished with Charmides or learned from him as yet all that he wanted to learn, or whether he was not forced in this way to turn aside from his examination before completing it. But this is not to say that Socrates, given his Odyssean versatility, might not find a way to complete the examination despite the turn the conversation has now taken, might not indeed make that very turn serve his purpose.

However that may be, coincident with the apparent change in purpose of the conversation or in what appears to be at stake, there is a change in Socrates' treatment of the definition proposed. Whereas he had been content to "refute" and apparently cast aside the two earlier definitions, he indicates that the one they are now about to consider is to be approached as a riddle. This appears to mean that their failure to find for it a reasonable or acceptable meaning will not necessarily be taken to bear on its ultimate validity. It might even be that such an answer as is given in the dialogue to the question, what is moderation, can be understood as a modification or development of the answer now given. (This would not necessarily imply a modification of the intention of the one responsible for the definition, for what he had in mind was not clearly but only enigmatically indicated by what he said [161d1–2].) For we do not mean to say that the dialogue is not concerned to consider and even answer the question, what is moderation.

Doing one's own things is the famous formula of justice in the *Republic* (e.g., 433a1–b4). It is understood there in the first place to mean that each man will perform the task of one art; in doing so he will of course serve those who have need of the product or service of his art, just as they will serve him with their arts; indeed as an artisan or knower, as one who is concerned wholly with his "own" art, he is perfectly indifferent to the distinction between "mine" and "thine," and this has much to do with his justice. The formula, so understood, was the basis on which Socrates, Glaucon, and Adeimantus built their city (433a1–6). Here, on the contrary, Socrates understands the formula to require that one write or read,[20] for example, only one's own name or at the most the names of one's friends, and not those of one's enemies; and that an artisan work only for himself—e.g., make only his own cloak, if he is a weaver, or his own shoes, if a shoemaker. (One is tempted to say that whereas in the *Republic*, Socrates looks at the formula from the point of view of justice, here he looks at it from the point of view of moderation.)[21] But to write or read the names of others, at least in school, does not make one a busybody or immoderate.[22] And, although a moderately managed city would be well managed, a city which was managed according to the law bidding each to make or do things only for himself would not be well managed. Since the failure to do only one's own things in this sense does not lead to immoderation for the individual, while the doing by each only of his own things in this sense does lead to immoderation for the city, doing one's own things in this way and with regard to the sort of activities referred to is not moderation. The exchange between Socrates and Charmides which we thus summarize introduced moderation as belonging to cities (or at least to their management) as well as to individuals into the dialogue. The understanding of moderation (or of the formula) proposed is called into question more with regard to its political consequences than with regard to its consequences for the individual. Sound or moderate politics, more obviously and to a greater extent than a sound or moderate life, require an interdependence or cooperation which Socrates took the literal meaning of doing one's own things to oppose; yet this was accepted, by Charmides at least, as ground for rejecting that meaning as a definition of moderation.[23]

---

20. 161d3–e5; cf. 159c3–6 ff. Socrates began here, as he had in the examination of Charmides' first answer, with examples from school; in the examination of Charmides' central answer, Socrates had relied on Homer. In questioning the first and third answers, Socrates could appeal to some extent to Charmides' experience. But Charmides had not yet come upon a situation where he could understand *aidōs* to be not good—or, if he had, Socrates did not now wish to call it to his attention. (One might find, however, that the general criticism of *aidōs* prepared such a step).

21. Cf. *Erastai* 138a9–b5; *Protagoras* 323b2–7.

22. At this point, Socrates does not challenge the identification of moderation and minding one's own business, or at least of immoderation and the opposite of minding one's own business, but questions a certain understanding of the latter.

23. Note, however, the lack of conviction in his answer (*ou phainetai*). 162a9; cf. 162a3 and 6.

When the result we have described had been reached and agreed to, Socrates repeated his assertion that the one who said that doing one's own things is moderation was riddling, for he would not have been so naïve—or did you hear this from some fool, Charmides? Charmides strongly denied this; the one who said it seemed very much to be wise. Then, according to Socrates, he must have thrown out the formula as a riddle, something difficult to understand. (It was of some importance after all to know the source of the definition: it is worth pondering the enigmatic sayings of the wise.) Perhaps, Charmides said. Socrates then asked Charmides whether he was able to say what doing one's own things means. "For my part, by Zeus, I don't know," Charmides said, "but perhaps nothing hinders that not even the one who said it knows what he had in mind." And here, Charmides, who not long ago (in refusing to answer Socrates' question about his moderation) had professed consideration for Critias, laughed gently[24] and looked in Critias' direction. He was becoming liberated from his respect for Critias, if not also from the constraints of his good manners.

For it had almost surely been Critias—as Socrates says to the companion in the course of a rather lengthy explanation of the dramatic situation, as we can call it—from whom Charmides had heard that answer about moderation. Wanting Critias rather than himself to give the defense of the answer, Charmides gently provoked him (not, as it appears, without Socrates' help). And Critias, whose anxious striving and yearning for honor before Charmides and the others had long been clear, who had barely held himself in before, was now no longer able to restrain himself. When Charmides concluded, he did not bear it but seemed to Socrates to be angry with Charmides as a poet is angry with an actor who has badly played the poet's lines. Looking at him, Critias said: "So, Charmides, do you think, if you do not know what he who said that moderation is doing one's own things had in mind, he doesn't know either?" It was now Socrates who came to Charmides' defense and answered in his place (cf. 157c7 ff.). He excused Charmides before Critias for his ignorance: it is not surprising given his age. (Who had put that ignorance to the test in the first place?) It is on the other hand perhaps to be expected that Critias know, given both his age and his

---

24. Charmides' previous laughter too (156a4) had been occasioned by what looked like a sort of pretentiousness or boasting: Socrates' professed reluctance to dictate the song unless Charmides persuaded him.

care or practice. If Critias therefore agreed that moderation was what Charmides had asserted it to be and took in inheritance the argument, Socrates would be more pleased to examine with Critias whether what was said is true or not. "But I certainly agree and accept it," Critias said. Socrates, with his highly selective statement as to Critias' qualifications, permits us to wonder whether it is Critias' competence which is responsible for the pleasure of conversing with him.

Before undertaking to examine the definition with Critias, Socrates asked him to accept responsibility for it. (See also 163e6–7.) But Socrates had not spoken of or indicated a desire to examine or strip Critias; for all we know, he had done so on some former occasion. It is therefore unimportant that we do not know whether Critias' inheritance of the argument implies that he has taken over the procedural agreements made by Charmides; that we do not know whether Critias' believing to know what moderation is, implies that he believed to possess it. Surely it is never said that Critias' answers are to be based on his experience of moderation. On the other hand, he cannot believe to possess moderation without believing to know what it is, for how otherwise would he know he possessed it? What Socrates claimed to want of Critias was to examine with him the truth or untruth of what had been said about moderation; or, as Charmides had demanded earlier (161c3–7) and as Socrates seems to indicate somewhat later (166d8–e2), the discussion is to be concerned not with "personalities" but with the argument. But will this be possible when Critias is the interlocutor? While the entrance of Critias thus appears to complete the shift in the purpose of the discussion—from examination of Charmides to attempt to answer the question, what is moderation—noted above, it in fact tends to confirm our impression, also noted above, that the character and extent of that shift are not unambiguous. For to the uncertainty as to the intention of Socrates, as he guides the inquiry into moderation, we must now add the uncertainty as to the effect on it which Critias' character, the nature of his abilities, and his experience will have. It becomes still less possible then to assume that the inquiry about to commence, or continue, will be a simply "philosophic" one in our sense, either in its manner or its purpose. In evaluating the suggestions that it may make regarding the truth about moderation, together with those which have already been made, we can never forget the action or drama of the dialogue, Socrates' deed as it is thus presented to us. (According to the views which have already been rejected, either simply or as stated, moderation is not: quietness; reverence or awe or shame; doing one's own things. This does not in itself mean that moderation is the opposite of these things.)

IV. Moderation and Self-Knowledge

A. Introduction of the Theme "Self-knowledge"

We have been led to suggest that Socrates' approach to Critias and his examination of Critias' definition of moderation will be determined by Socrates' present intention or aim as that is affected by Critias' character, abilities and experience. The usefulness of that suggestion is however somewhat limited: we cannot at this point be certain of Socrates' aim, and we are not sufficiently familiar with Critias. We have no other recourse than to try to remedy these deficiencies by following the twists and turns of the argument itself.

After Critias affirmed his agreement that moderation is doing one's own things and took over the defense of that definition from Charmides, Socrates began by raising with him the same difficulty that he had raised with Charmides, the difficulty which comes to light particularly in the case of the arts. But whereas with Charmides, Socrates had been most careful to secure his agreement that the artisan in question was "doing something" (161d3, e4, e8), Socrates now asked Critias whether the craftsmen all "make something" (162e9).[25] This proved to give Critias an opening. For after he had agreed that the craftsmen make something and also that they make not only their own things but also those of others, he was asked by Socrates whether, in "making" not only their own things, they are moderate. He replied, "What prevents it?" When Socrates objected that this was for the one who defined moderation as "doing" one's own things to assert that nothing prevented those who "do" the things of others from being moderate, Critias suggested that he had not agreed that those who "do" the things of others are moderate if he agreed that those who "make" the things of others are. When Socrates asked him whether he did not call the same thing "making" and "doing," Critias responded at some length. He certainly did not, he said, make that identification, nor that of "working" and "making." For he had learned from Hesiod that no work

---

25. The words are respectively *prattein* and *poiein*. The shift executed by Socrates is facilitated by the fact that *poiein* may also mean "doing."

is a disgrace.[26] Critias took this to mean that the obviously disgraceful activities—e.g., shoemaking, selling salt fish, prostitution—were not held by Hesiod to be "works" nor being engaged in them "doing" or "working." Hesiod held, as Critias thought, "making" to be different from "doing" and "working"; and what was made to be sometimes a disgrace—whenever it did not come into being with what was beautiful; but a work was never disgraceful. For what was beautifully and beneficially made he called "works," and those sorts of makings he called "workings" and "doings."

If the bearing of Critias' argument to this point is to support or elaborate (with the help of Hesiod's name) his position that craftsmen are not prevented from being moderate by making the things of others, since that "making" is not "doing," his argument would seem to leave open the question whether these craftsmen are not immoderate because they fail to do their own things. If, on the other hand, he means to say that in making the things of others, some craftsmen, those whose making is beautiful (or productive of beauty) and beneficial, may be engaged in working or doing, he would still have the problem that they would be doing the things of others. He therefore went on to say in conclusion that one must say that such things alone—i.e., the things beautifully and beneficially made—are one's own, but all the harmful things are others', so that one must believe Hesiod and any other sensible man to call the one who does his own things moderate.

In this way Critias established that the craftsmen, in making the things of others, may be moderate: they are moderate if their "making," being beautiful (or productive of beauty) and beneficial, is actually a "doing" and if the "things of others," being beautifully and beneficially made, are in fact their own; or, they are moderate if their making of the things of others is in fact a doing of their own things. One could perhaps have objected that Critias thereby withdrew the assertion that had created the problem; but Socrates did not raise that difficulty. He said that he had grasped Critias' point just about at the start of his speech—that Critias would call one's own, and the things of oneself, "good" and the making of the good things "doing." (Socrates had then grasped at least the point he puts first before Critias had stated it. Moreover, he restates that point: he implies that Critias' real intention or wish is to call his own things good rather than the good things his own.) One can hear ten thousand such distinctions from Prodicus. Socrates granted to Critias to dispose

---

26. Cf. Xenophon, *Memorabilia* I 2.56–57.

of the "names" as he wished; he should only make clear to what he applied the name he said.[27] Socrates therefore asked Critias to make his definition again from the beginning with greater clarity. "The doing or making or however you wish to name it, of the good things, is this what you say moderation to be?" (Socrates did not take up Critias' reference to the beautiful or noble; and he spoke here of the good rather than the beneficial—but cf. 164b1, 7, 9, 11, c1, 5.) Socrates thus disdained to be concerned with subtleties regarding "names"; he aimed only at the clarity of the argument. But perhaps he had reason to be satisfied with the turn the discussion had taken, a turn which had been made possible by his "mistake" regarding "making" and "doing."

Critias accepted Socrates' revision or restatement of his definition of moderation. Socrates then asked, "The one who does the bad things is then not moderate, but the one who does the good things?" Critias said, "And you, best of men, don't hold that opinion?" Socrates said, "Let it go: for we are not yet examining my opinion but what you now say." Socrates refused to state his opinion. Why had Critias presumed to know it? It seems more likely that he was drawing upon recollections of the time he had spent together with Socrates (156a8) than that he believed himself to be stating a truth so obvious that Socrates could not fail to give it his assent. This remark of Critias gives some confirmation then to the inference we were tempted to draw from the fact that, after giving Critias an opening, Socrates had guessed almost at the outset of Critias' speech the use that Critias was going to make of it: had not Socrates given Critias that opening with a view to getting him to assert that craftsmen may be moderate and above all to replace, in his definition of moderation, "doing one's own things" with "doing the good things," or to understand one's own as good? This is not to assert that the new or revised definition, any more than the old one, represents Socrates' views, or that Critias knew those views—only that Socrates and Critias were on familiar ground and that Socrates chose to exploit that fact in order to move the conversation, for some reason, in this direction.

Critias now restated more completely his revised definition. He made it somewhat clearer than had Socrates' last statement that one must not only do good but also refrain from doing bad things to be moderate. He did not specify in any way which are the good things whose performance is moderation; nor, if all good things are included, did he indicate how

---

27. The license Socrates grants has an obvious limit: it comes to a halt before the name "moderation." Cf. 165e2, 175b4.

the good things are to be distinguished from the bad (unless one is to take as sufficient indication his earlier exclusion of making shoes, selling salt fish, and prostitution).

Having brought the conversation to this point, Socrates said that nothing perhaps prevented Critias from speaking the truth; but he wondered about one point: whether Critias thought the moderate human beings do not know that they are moderate. (As T. G. Tuckey points out, this reminds us of the procedural agreements wrung from Charmides earlier.[28] But Socrates makes no effort now to revive those agreements or to explain his question on those grounds.) Critias did not think this. Socrates then showed that this admission was incompatible with Critias' revised definition: there is no necessity that those who do the good things and not the bad are aware of their doing so. More precisely, the admission proved to be incompatible with an assertion that an artisan is moderate by virtue of the practice of his art. For while one might say that the doers of good things are moderate only insofar as they know the goodness of what they do, an uncertainty about the goodness of what he does belongs to the artisan as such. He cannot know, without divination, whether his work will have a successful outcome;[29] he does not know as artisan the goodness of the end his art serves (e.g., it is not by his science that a medical man knows the goodness of health); and he does not know by his art the circumstances in which its practice is beneficial. Socrates' refutation of Critias here was made possible then by his leading Critias, who had not asserted that artisans as such are moderate, in the direction of such an assertion. He did so in the following way. He asked Critias whether "shortly before" it had not been said by him that nothing prevented the craftsmen from being moderate even though they make the things of others. Critias was thus led to think that it would be a question of defending his assertion that the craftsmen may be moderate. To that extent he was put on his guard and as result, perhaps, agreed all the more readily to Socrates' suggestions that a medical man, in making someone healthy, "makes" (i.e., does) what is beneficial to himself and the one he cures; that in doing these things he does what needs (or ought) to be done; and that in doing what needs or ought to be done he is moderate. Having agreed to these points, Critias was forced to grant that it isn't necessary for the medical man to know

---

28. *Plato's Charmides*, Cambridge Classical Studies (Amsterdam: Adolf M. Hakkert, 1968 [unchanged reprint of the 1951 edition]), p. 22.

29. Cf. Xenophon, *Memorabilia* I 1.6–8; *Charmides* 173c3–7.

when his curing is beneficial and when not, or for any other craftsman to know when he is to be benefited (cf. 164b8–9 with b1) from the work he does and when not. "But then sometimes the medical man, in acting [doing] beneficially or harmfully won't know himself, how he acts—yet in acting beneficially, according to your argument, he acts moderately. Or didn't you speak in this way?" Critias agreed. "Then, as it seems, sometimes, acting beneficially, he will act moderately and be moderate but not know himself, that he is moderate."

As we will see shortly, Critias cannot accept this result; he would rather give up his definition than grant that a human being is moderate while not knowing himself. If Socrates had had reason (drawn perhaps from his prior acquaintance with Critias)[30] to suppose that Critias would insist on the connection between moderation and self-knowledge, then he made it likely that Critias would abandon his definition of moderation as doing the good things when he chose, as *the* example of doing good, the practice of the arts. He thus brought it about that self-knowledge replaced rather than refined or modified the understanding of moderation as doing the good things. But he had also brought it about that "doing the good things" had replaced "doing one's own things" in Critias' definition, and he might as easily, it would seem, have led the discussion to self-knowledge from "doing one's own things" as from "doing the good things." (Cf. *Alcibiades* I 133c18–e3; cf. 131a5–b9.) It looks then as if Socrates introduced "doing the good things" into the discussion in order to have it rejected in this context.

How are we to understand that step? We must begin by raising the question of the link between "doing the good," self-knowledge, and moderation. Socrates seems to insist that an awareness of his moderation belongs to the moderate human being. As is pointed out by Tuckey, this is not yet to insist that the moderate human being (fully) knows himself.[31] It means, according to what is said in the present context, that the moderate human being is aware of or knows the goodness of his actions, for moderation is doing the good things. Tuckey was thus led to ask "how far the consciousness of the rightness of one's action demanded by Socrates' words in 164b coincides with self-knowledge."[32] This question points to the prior question of why Socrates "demanded," in the case of

---

30. Cf. Tuckey, p. 24.

31. Tuckey, p. 25.

32. Tuckey, p. 24.

moderation, an awareness of the goodness of one's actions.[33] Would he have demanded that such an awareness or knowledge be an ingredient (or necessary accompaniment) of the possession of the other virtues? Yet the other virtues too can be defined as "doing the good things": is not each of them, at any rate, believed to consist in or to cause the doing of good things? (Socrates said of Critias' revised definition, which made moderation to be the doing of the good things, and of no other definition in the dialogue, that nothing perhaps prevented Critias from speaking the truth [164a1].) To this extent then moderation is indistinguishable from the other virtues, or virtue is one. But in the case of the "other" virtues, the belief, unaccompanied by knowledge, that one possesses the virtue and is acting virtuously and doing good things is not thought to impugn one's possession of the virtue. If a courageous or just man believes that what he does is good without knowing it to be so, he may still be just or courageous. From the point of view of moderation, however, such a belief, unaccompanied by knowledge, must come to sight as boasting; and boasting, especially of such a character, seems to be incompatible with possession of moderation.[34] Moderation then, as distinguished from the other virtues, would require that one have knowledge of the goodness of one's actions, if it should prove to be true that—to restate an earlier suggestion—"by nature" no one fails to claim or believe to be virtuous or to do good things in this sense. But, to repeat with Tuckey, "how far [does] the consciousness of the rightness of one's action . . . [coincide] with self-knowledge?"

---

33. To this prior question, Tuckey's answer, repeated throughout his book, is as follows: "The question which Plato is asking himself is evidently this: 'if virtue is knowledge, and if, as this implies, no man can habitually and consistently do good without knowing that he is doing good, how is a man to know that he is doing good? . . .'" (p. 22; cf. p. 107). This answer, as Tuckey himself indicates, presupposes that Plato believed he knew what moderation or virtue is: satisfied as to this, the main point, he moved on to examine an implication of the understanding of virtue he had accepted. But this is to ignore the context in which Socrates' demand is made: an attempt to discover what moderation is. And more generally, how can one reasonably assume, prior to an examination of the *Charmides* itself—even on the basis of other Platonic dialogues or letters—that this great question was settled for Plato, and settled in a certain way?

34. Cf. *Republic* 560c5–d4; Aristotle, *Nicomachean Ethics* 1123b5. Cf., on the other hand, the ambiguous testimony of *Protagoras* 323a7–b7, which refers however to what one says rather than to what one thinks, and where Protagoras is the speaker.

Critias' response to Socrates' refutation (of the assertion that a moderate human being as Critias had defined him would not be unaware of his moderation) was in the form of his longest speech yet. He began by saying that what Socrates had suggested—that a human being might be moderate but not know himself, that he was moderate—would never occur. If Socrates thought that this was a necessary result of Critias' earlier agreements, Critias would rather alter something of them, and would not be ashamed to say that he had spoken incorrectly, rather than ever grant that a human being, while not knowing himself, is moderate. For this was just about the very thing that he asserts moderation to be: knowing oneself.

Seeking to compensate for this beginning, Critias then stated his agreement with the author of the famous inscription ("Know thyself") at Delphi. For it seemed to Critias that that writing was offered as a greeting by the god to those who entered the temple in place of *Chaire* (the traditional or usual form in which people greeted one another, the literal translation of which would be something like "Rejoice"), on the ground that this was not a correct greeting—"Rejoice"—nor ought human beings to recommend this to each other, but rather, "Be moderate." Thus, as it seemed to Critias that the author of the inscription thought, does the god address those entering the temple, in a way different from human beings: to know oneself is not to rejoice.[35] "He says to the one who enters nothing other than, 'Be moderate,' he says." (It is not clear that Critias' agreement with the author in question extends to both the correctness of the new greeting and its ascription to the god.) But he spoke like a prophet, in a riddling form; for "Know thyself" is the same as "Be moderate" as Critias and the inscription say, but one might perhaps think it to be something else. This, according to Critias, was what happened to the authors of the later inscriptions. Taking "Know thyself" to be a counsel rather than the god's greeting for the sake of those entering the temple, they added their own useful counsels. Had they understood that "Know thyself" stood for "Be moderate," Critias suggests, they would not have made that mistake: one would not have taken an exhortation to a virtue to be merely a matter of imparting some useful advice.

Having invoked not just Hesiod, but the most famous Delphic saying, and spoken of some errors of others, Critias returned to his point. All that he had said was said to indicate to Socrates that he gave up to him

---

35. Cf. Thales, DK I.71, as quoted in Tuckey, p. 9.

all that had gone before, "for perhaps in some respect you spoke more correctly about those things, perhaps I, but nothing of what we said was very clear." But now Critias was willing to give Socrates an argument if Socrates did not agree that moderation was knowing oneself.

Socrates took Critias' last remark to accuse him in effect of claiming to know concerning the things he raised questions about (cf. *Apology of Socrates* 22e6–23a5) and of being able, then, if he wanted, to agree with Critias. This was not the case: Socrates sought with Critias for what was at any time proposed because he himself did not know. (The word used for knowing in these two cases is *eidenai*, whereas the word used in the phrase "Know thyself," or oneself, was *gignōskein* [164c1, 6, d2, 4, e7, 165a4, b4; cf. 164a3, b7].) He was willing, after his examination, to say whether he agreed or not, and he asked for Critias' forbearance while he examined. Critias' response, too, indicated that the examination was to be Socrates'. Did Critias feel no need for such an examination? After the understanding of moderation as doing the good things had been replaced by self-knowledge, Socrates went beyond his former refusal to state his opinion (163e6–7: note however *pō*) both by his admission or profession of ignorance and by his promise to state later, after examination, whether he agreed with Critias or not: the latter promise balances or compensates for the former admission. The examination is apparently to remedy Socrates' ignorance of moderation sufficiently to enable him to determine whether he agrees. But was this the first time that Socrates had looked into the question of moderation? And was there any reason to have a greater expectation of this investigation than of former ones?

B. A Knowledge of What One Knows and Does Not Know

Socrates began his examination by asking Critias whether it was clear that if moderation is *gignōskein ti* (that is, knowing in some loose sense or recognizing something) it is *epistēmē tis kai tinos* (that is, some science and a science of something). "It is," Critias said, and he added, "of oneself." By collapsing, with Critias' agreement, the distinction between recognizing or knowing in some loose sense and science, Socrates prepared the way for treating any knowing with the strictness belonging to science, or for treating science with special looseness, or, at various times, for both these procedures.

Socrates now began by raising the question of the product of a "science of oneself" rather than by looking at that science, before making clear the precise character of that science. He asked whether medicine too was a science—of the healthful. Very much so. "If then you should ask me, 'Medicine, being a science of the healthful, is in what respect useful to us and what does it produce [*apergazesthai*]?' I would say that it produces not a small benefit, for it produces health, a beautiful [or noble] product [or work]—if you accept this." Critias did. "And if then you should ask me with respect to house-building, being a science of building houses, what product I say it produces, I would say that it produces houses. And so on for the other arts." The models chosen by Socrates for the elaboration of Critias' suggestion are productive arts, which as arts (*technai*) share with sciences the knowing of something, or are sciences; but they are distinguished more by what they produce or bring about than by what they know. Two arts, with their products and what they know, are mentioned; but they are not in every respect similar. The product of house-building is not called, like that of medicine, beautiful or noble.[36] Could this be due, paradoxically, to the fact that while the "product" of medicine is natural, that of house-building is not, so that although guided to some extent by natural needs—supplying the shelter we require next only to food—house-building is easily expanded to the building of beautiful (or noble) and great houses, to say nothing of temples? (Cf. *Republic* 369d1–4; 419a5–6; 394a4–5; consider Critias' calling, or wishing to call, his own things [*oikeia*] good or noble—163c3–6 and d2–3; cf. also 157e2.)

Socrates next said that it was therefore incumbent on Critias, since he said that moderation was a science of oneself, to be able to answer the question, "What beautiful work does it produce for us worthy of the name?" By assimilating, as we have seen, the sciences to productive arts, Socrates was able to proceed on the assumption that moderation too, as a science, has a work or product and perhaps also that the product is useful or beneficial. But the heterogeneity of his models precludes his asserting on their authority that the product of moderation is beautiful. That the product or work of moderation is beautiful (or noble) would seem to be guaranteed or promised by the name "moderation" (cf. p. 135f. above). Names are not so unimportant as, in an earlier exchange with Critias, Socrates seemed to suggest (163d1–e2). Their importance may be partially understood by comparing Socrates' reference here to the name "moderation" with a still earlier exchange, between Socrates and Charmides (158e6–159a10). In that passage, Socrates seemed to suggest

---

36. Critias' former insistence on the beauty of every work or product has been silently dropped without his noticing it, or at any rate without a murmur of protest on his part. Cf. 163b4–c4.

that such words as moderation merely label what we know from experience, what we have felt or can feel and know. If that were unambiguously true, a conversation about moderation would require, to be adequate, the participation of moderate men, as in the *Lysis* Socrates speaks about friendship with two boys who, as it appears at least, are friends But is this requirement fulfilled in the *Charmides*, where Socrates, who at times claims not even to know what moderation is, speaks with the future oligarchs Charmides and Critias? Is it fulfilled in any of the other dialogues devoted to a virtue (*Euthyphro, Laches, Republic, Theages*)? Its non-fulfillment could lead us to wonder whether the name "moderation" might not be as much an indication of what we seek or think to find in experience or in ourselves as it is of what we have found there. (Cf. 175b2–4.) But in question here is not moderation itself but its product. It is better then to ask of that product whether it is beautiful as health is beautiful or as a noble house or temple is beautiful. More precisely still, the question concerns the product of moderation understood as a "science of oneself." By pointing to a product of a science of oneself, Socrates perhaps meant to suggest that it is due to that science, or something like it (cf. 169e6–7; one must make allowance here for the fact that Socrates has collapsed the distinction between recognizing or knowing in a loose sense and science), that we can recognize our need for medicine on the one hand or that we conceive a need for "house-building" on the other (cf. *Alcibiades I* 133c21–24). (The medicine contrasted here with "house-building" is of course not "Thracian medicine.")

But in his reply, instead of seeking for some product, Critias found fault with Socrates' question. Socrates had based his inquiry on the assumption that the sciences are similar to one another (165d6); but "this one" (it is not clear whether Critias thinks of moderation or of a science of oneself) is not by nature similar to the other sciences nor they to each other. For example, Socrates would not be able to show such a work or product of the logistic art or geometry as there is of house-building and weaving and of many arts. (The sciences are not then totally dissimilar; they fall at least into certain classes.) Socrates granted that he was not able to show such a product of logistics or geometry. But he asserted that he was able to show what each of these sciences is "of," the object in question being something else than the science itself. For example, logistics is of the even and the odd, how they are in respect of multitude towards themselves and towards one another, the even and the odd being other than logistics itself; while the weighing art[37] is of the heavier and the lighter, the heavy and light being other than the weighing art itself. (We note that each of these two arts is "of" a pair of things, as is emphasized especially by the comparatives "heavier" and "lighter." We note also that logistics is distinguished not only or sufficiently by its being of distinct objects but also by its being of a certain aspect of them, their relations in respect of multitude toward themselves and one another: it seems to be rather logistics' unmentioned companion art arithmetic which is of the objects themselves in respect of multitude.)[38] When Critias had granted these points, Socrates asked him what moderation was a science "of," the object in question being other than moderation itself. In other words, a universal characteristic of the sciences having come to sight in otherness with relation to their objects (if not in production), even if moderation is like logistics, geometry and the weighing art rather than the productive arts, it must have an object other than itself, which Critias might reasonably be asked to state. But had he not already done so in saying that moderation is a science of "oneself"? (See 165c7 and Socrates' acknowledgment of this answer at 165e1.) Socrates' insistence that the object of moderation be other than the science itself comes despite the fact that the answer which has been given appears to satisfy that requirement.[39] Had Socrates forgotten that answer? Critias at any rate did not choose to remind him of it. It turned out, he explained, that Socrates, in seeking (again) for a non-existent similarity of moderation to the other sciences, had come to precisely that in which it differs from them. While the others are all sciences of something else, but not of themselves, moderation alone is a science of the other sciences and of itself.

The surprising development for which Critias thus took responsibility was explained or justified by him in no other way than to say that these things were far from escaping Socrates, "but I think that what you just now denied doing, this you do: for you attempt to refute me, neglecting that

---

37. Socrates speaks of the weighing art where Critias had spoken of geometry (165e6). Does he substitute, as more appropriate to Critias, an oligarchic art for an aristocratic—or perhaps democratic [Aristophanes, *Clouds* 202–205]—one?

38. Cf. *Gorgias* 451a–c and, for a more competent discussion of these references to logistics and arithmetic, Jacob Klein, *Greek Mathematical Thought and the Origin of Algebra* (Cambridge: The MIT Press, 1968), pp. 17–25.

39. Cf. Tuckey, pp. 33 and 38.

which the argument is about." In the statement which Critias apparently took to be a disavowal of the intention to refute, Socrates had denied knowing whether or not moderation is knowing oneself and had said that it was on account of his ignorance that he investigated with Critias what was at any time proposed (165b5–c2): he had not spoken of refutation. Accordingly, he now responded to Critias by denying that there is such a simple opposition between refuting and learning as Critias had implied: however much Socrates may refute Critias, he does it for no other purpose than that for which Socrates would search himself as to what he says, fearing that it might escape him that he thinks he knows something but does not know. Does this mean that Socrates' refutation of Critias is to aid Critias in this way or that it, together with Socrates' self-examination, belongs to Socrates' attempt to keep himself from such error? Is it perhaps necessary to Socrates that he refute others? Now then as well, Socrates continued, he claimed to do this, to examine the argument especially for the sake of himself but perhaps also for the others who are suitable (or friends)—or did not Critias think it to be a common good for just about all humans, that it become clear, with regard to each of the beings, how it is? (After stating the concern not to think he knew what he did not know, Socrates spoke of the "common good" for just about all humans that there come to be clarity about each of the beings. Not to think one knows what one does not know is to be prepared to that extent to strive for clarity about the beings. Is it to be prepared also in the sense that it is especially when one is so disposed that such clarity comes to sight as, or becomes, preeminently good?) In response to Socrates' question, Critias could not fail to say that he did indeed consider such clarity to be good. Socrates thereupon exhorted him to be bold in answering what was asked in the way it appeared to him: let it go whether Critias or Socrates is the one being refuted, but applying the mind to the argument itself, see how it will turn out, being refuted. I will do so, Critias said, for you seem to me to speak with measure. Critias obviously did not share Socrates' concern for discovering what he might think he knew but not know—at least, not so far as to welcome a public discovery. Socrates was therefore forced, in order to secure his continued cooperation in the discussion, to direct his attention away from his possible refutation and toward the examination or refutation of the argument. That cooperation was still necessary, it seems to me, because Critias had entered the discussion as more or less of an authority for Charmides: Charmides might well regard his own refutation as indecisive, so long as he could continue to look up to one who remained unrefuted.[40] As we may already suspect then, and the sequel confirms, the argument to which Critias' attention is directed, will be the vehicle for his refutation. But as we will also begin to see in this context, "refutation"—and therefore Socrates' deed in refuting Charmides/Critias—is connected with the themes with which the argument is concerned: self-knowledge and moderation. Nor is Socrates prevented by his intention to refute from conducting a discussion which, while refuting, will illuminate (for the companion, e.g., and others) that connection and those themes.

Having brought the discussion to this point and having somewhat conciliated Critias, Socrates asked him to state (again) his position regarding moderation. Critias said that it alone is a science of itself and the other sciences. Socrates asked whether it was not then a science also of non-science (non-knowing [*anepistēmosunē*]), if it was of science. Critias readily accepted this addition, although he had spoken of a science of the other sciences and itself rather than of science. Socrates then made the following statement:

> The moderate man alone, then, will himself know [*gignōskein*] himself and will be able to put to test what he happens to know [*eidenai*] and what not, and will in like manner have the power to examine in the others what one knows and thinks—if he knows—and what he himself [mss. BT at 167a4] thinks he knows but does not know. No one else. And it is this, to be moderate and moderation as well as to know oneself: to know what one knows and what one does not know.—Is this what you say?

Critias accepted Socrates' statement as his own. The statement makes clear that the next or altered definition was not meant to imply an abandonment of the identification of moderation with self-knowledge. But while it appears from its beginning that in possessing a science of science one is moderate and knows oneself, it appears from its end that to know oneself and to be moderate is to know what one knows and does not know. A science of science might prepare a knowledge of what one knows and does not know. But is Critias' acceptance of Socrates' statement sufficient indication that this was the purpose for which he introduced a science of

---

40. Cf. *Theaetetus* 162a5–6, 166a6–b1, and 169d10–e3.

the other sciences and itself? (Cf. 169d9–e5.) Does that statement itself point unambiguously to this solution to the difficulty it poses? The possessor of a science of science will know himself but *be able* to examine himself as to what he knows and does not know; but to know what one knows and does not know is to know oneself (cf. 169d6–8 with 169e6–8).

A science of the other sciences and itself replaces or explains Critias' suggestion of a science of "oneself." When Critias, after accepting Socrates' identification of recognizing or knowing in some loose sense and science, had gone so far as to speak of a science of oneself, but had denied in effect that that "science" has a product, Socrates raised the question of the otherness of various sciences with regard to their objects. He seemed to imply that that otherness is everywhere where there is science. Thereupon Critias ceased to speak of a science of oneself and began to speak of a science of the other sciences and itself. The reason may have to be traced to the following considerations: if a science is always other than its objects, the objects will be known as other; but "oneself" is an object which cannot be known as other—indeed, speaking strictly, it is an "object" whose being depends on the recognition of something as not being other by the act of knowing or thinking, or which comes to be in that act.[41] It may be true then that wherever there is knowing, *something* knows which is not just knowing: it does not necessarily follow that that something can know or think itself as itself. As for the significance of this, it is sufficient to begin with to remember that self-knowledge, in the sense in which we usually understand the term, is knowledge of or about ourselves. It presupposes therefore the grasp or recognition of oneself which it seeks to clarify or deepen. When we ask, What am I, we already grasp something to which we give the name "I." What Socrates has pointed to, is the difficulty of understanding how such a grasp (and hence such a question) is possible.

He did so in response to Critias' denial that there is a product of knowing oneself. It is as if Socrates had replied, "Perhaps then one cannot know oneself in this sense." Then Critias made a suggestion as to how this is possible, a suggestion which Socrates saw fit, for the time being, to accept: one who has the science which Critias described will know himself. But Socrates in turn on his own initiative immediately pointed out—changing somewhat the description of Critias' science for this purpose—that possession of that science will enable one to examine

---

41. In other words, one cannot speak even of "oneself" as merely an object of a science of oneself, any more than of a house as merely an object of a house-building science.

himself and others[42] as to what one knows and does not know. And he indicated (contradicting himself in the manner we have observed) that it is a knowledge of what one knows and does not know, rather than a science of science or of the other sciences and itself, that is self-knowledge. The contradiction may be explained or justified if the sort of self-knowledge whose possibility Critias has attempted to explain is more the basis or prerequisite of self-knowledge as we usually understand the term than that very knowledge. It would be in need then of a supplement. It would need a supplement all the more if it gave rise to such a product as tended to obstruct our view of our true condition, i.e., if we had such a reaction to knowing ourselves in this sense as led us to hide from ourselves that condition. That Socrates has referred to the product of knowing oneself as noble (165d8–e2) does not necessarily contradict this suggestion.

A further hint as to the basis of the claim of a knowledge of what one knows and does not know to be, or rather to be necessary for, the full or fuller self-knowledge is supplied by what Socrates next said: "Back then—the third to the Savior [Zeus]—as if from the beginning, let us examine first if it is possible or not for this to be, to know what one knows and what one does not know, that one does not know; then if it is granted to be possible, what would be the benefit for us in knowing it?" The words, "back . . . as if from the beginning," together with the number "three," link the new theme to a prior new beginning; they point to 163d7, where the words, "back from the beginning," are also to be found. There a new beginning was necessary because Critias wished to call one's own things good, or only good things one's own, so that his definition of moderation became "doing the good things" rather than "doing one's own things." They were to begin the examination of that revised or new definition. The first new beginning failed to find satisfactory the definition it considered because, as it seemed to Critias, one may do the good things without knowing them to be good, but a moderate man would not be ignorant of his moderation. As a result "doing the good things" was replaced by self-knowledge. We believed to be able to follow that step to this extent: we saw that a moderate man, given the universality of the pretension to virtue, would have to know the goodness of what he did. But what is the connection or relation between that knowledge and self-knowledge simply? Here a new beginning has become necessary, a

---

42. We will consider later why the primary self-examination is at a later stage supplemented by examination of others, as the mss. at 167a4 indicate. Cf. 166c7–d4.

final new beginning as Socrates' reference to the final libation at a feast indicates, because self-knowledge has been said to be knowledge of what one knows and does not know. A knowledge of what one knows and does not know may be as close as one can come to knowing the goodness of what one does, in the required sense. In speaking then, at the end of the section marked out by references to new beginnings (163d7–167b1), of a knowledge of what one knows and does not know, Socrates may be returning to the point, or almost to the point, he reached toward its beginning. But will a self-knowledge linked to a knowledge of what one knows and does not know have as strong a claim to the name "moderation" (of whose demands Socrates has just reminded us) as a self-knowledge linked to a knowledge of the goodness of what one does would have had?

V. Self-Knowledge and Moderation

No longer concerned to change or modify Critias' definition of moderation, Socrates turned to the examination of the definition which had been reached. A knowledge of what one knows and does not know must be possible as well as beneficial or good—sufficiently good [cf. 158b4, 176a1, and the reference in the present context to savior Zeus]—if it is to be accepted as moderation. (Cf. 169b1–5.)

When Critias agreed that an examination was required, it looked for a moment as if Socrates would turn that task over to him, the reason being that Socrates, as he professed, was at a loss. But without waiting for Critias to respond to this invitation or command, Socrates offered to tell Critias where he was at a loss. Charmides was thus given the opportunity to see whether Critias was able to solve the difficulties Socrates raises, i.e., to see whether Critias was any the less at a loss than Socrates.

Socrates first secured Critias' agreement to the proposition that "all these things would be, if there exists what you just now were saying, some one science which is not a science of anything else than of itself and of the other sciences as well as—this same one—of non-science." That is, following the plan indicated in the opening remark of this section, Socrates turned first to the question of the possibility of knowing what one knows and does not know. More precisely, he speaks of the condition for the being of "all these things": he has not forgotten the question of that primary self-knowledge which constitutes our first knowledge or thought of ourselves; the ensuing remarks treat that question as well as the other, if with a certain reserve or reticence.

Socrates then asked Critias to observe how strange was the thing they attempted to say. If Critias would examine the same thing in other cases, it would seem to him, as Socrates thought, to be impossible:

"For consider whether there seems to you to be some seeing which is not a seeing of the things of which the other seeings are seeings but is a seeing of itself and of the other seeings, and likewise of non-seeings; and even though it is a seeing, it sees no color but [sees] itself and the other seeings. Does there seem to you to be some such seeing?"

"No, by Zeus, not to me at least."

"But what about a hearing, which hears no sound but hears itself and the other hearings and non-hearings?"

"Not even this."

"Examine collectively concerning all the perceptions whether there seems to you to be some perception of perceptions and itself, which perceives nothing of what the other perceptions perceive?"

"Not to me, at least."

"But there seems to you to be some desire which is a desire of no pleasure but which is [a desire] of itself and of the other desires?"

"No indeed."

"Nor a wanting, as I think, which wants nothing good, but wants itself and the other wantings."

"Certainly not."

"Some love, you'd say there is of this sort, [a love] which happens to be love of nothing beautiful, but of itself and of the other loves?"

"Not I," he said.

"Some fear you've observed before now, which fears itself and the other fears, but fears not even one of the terrible things."

"I haven't observed one," he said.

"An opinion, which is an opinion of opinions and itself but opines nothing of what the others opine?"

"Not at all."

"But, as it looks, we say there is some science of this sort,
which is a science of no learning matter, but a science of itself
and the other sciences."

"We do say so."

As these exchanges suggest, seeing and hearing, as well as the perceptions generally, and desiring, wanting, loving, fearing and opining are directed to objects other than those motions themselves. Socrates spoke first of seeing and hearing (and the perceptions collectively), then of some of what we call the passions, then of opinion. In a partial repetition (168d3 ff.), he speaks of hearing and seeing, and then of a motion which moves itself and a heat which kindles itself. At least the former of the new items may refer to soul.[43] If so, soul replaces in the enumeration the passions and opinion: soul is above all the passions and opinion (we remain what we are without the ability to see and hear, but not without the ability to desire, want, love, fear and think). It is better to say that soul is the common source of the passions and opinion, of feeling and thinking: but it is a source which, it could seem, manifests itself only as the motions in which it issues. There is at any rate no sense or perception of soul. How then can the soul have feelings toward itself? Moreover, the motions in which it issues are severally directed outward toward objects which are other rather than toward themselves; and the otherness of the objects remains even where the motions have each other as objects. The question whether a soul can know itself at all could seem to rest then on the question whether knowing, as opposed to the other motions in which the soul issues, can be directed toward itself. We come back then to Critias' suggestion.

According to that suggestion, it is by possession of a science which knows itself that one knows oneself (see 169d9–e5). The list of motions which has been offered by Socrates as analogues to that science suggests that it is to be understood in this context as a knowing, an act of knowing, which knows itself, i.e., the very knowing that it is (as well as other acts of knowing). If the analogy holds, as there is reason to suspect, there is no such knowing; knowing, like the other motions, is such as always to be

---

43. See Jacob Klein, *A Commentary on Plato's Meno* (Chapel Hill: The University of North Carolina Press, 1965), p. 25.

called forth by or in relation to something other; knowing or awareness is always of something other as other.[44]

Nevertheless, a human soul may come to know, and in a sense experience itself, in a manner indicated by an unobtrusive correction which Socrates, on a suitable occasion, makes of Critias' suggestion. According to the new formulation, one will know oneself when one possesses what knows itself, or, perhaps, something knowing the self or selfness (169e6–8; cf. mss. at 170a1; cf. *Alcibiades I* 129a7–b3, 130c5–d6). The meaning of this suggestion, so far as I can understand it, is as follows. As we have to some extent already seen, we may mean by the term "self-knowledge" two related but different things. We may mean the knowledge of a being which knows, more or less fully, the very being that it is; or we may mean the knowledge of a being which knows itself as some being, which knows that *it* is some being. In the latter case, we might call what the being knows its selfness, its possession of the characteristic or character of being a self. Selfness in this sense is nothing but being other from other things; it does not differ from otherness.[45] Let us grant that a human soul is such a being as possesses the character of selfness, and moreover that, as human, it knows somehow that character or knows somehow what it is to be a self. How will it know that character as its own, or know *its* selfness in that character? Showing itself, as it seems, only as motions which are severally directed outward from themselves, the soul knows what it knows as other. The other, however, as an exchange in this vicinity might remind us (168b2 ff.), is always other than or from another. If the objects of knowing are known as other, a sense of otherness from those objects must accompany or be an ingredient of the act of knowing: by that sense of otherness, the soul which thinks manifests itself in, and not just as, the act of thinking. Now in the case before us, the object of thought is selfness, i.e., otherness; as an object it is and will be known as other; a sense or feeling of otherness from it will be present. But it is

---

44. Nor is there, as Robert R. Wellman suggests, an awareness of knowing, or of the fact that "we" know, that accompanies knowing. "The Question Posed at *Charmides* 165a–166c," *Phronesis*, IX (1964), 112. In our ordinary experience of knowing, there is awareness only of the object as other. Cf. Nietzsche, *Beyond Good and Evil*, nos. 16 and 17.

45. The significance of this is suggested by a remark which Socrates makes in this context: "will not whatever has its own power [the power of itself] toward itself have the being toward which its power is?" (168d1–3).

the articulation, it is the character of that very sense. It will not then be known simply as other; in knowing selfness, i.e., otherness, a human soul will know itself, or will know its selfness.

It is thus through such a thought, by this account, that a human soul comes to know itself in the indicated sense and indeed to experience itself, that it becomes capable of saying and thinking "I." However that may be, it is this capacity which enables all of us not only to wonder about ourselves but more generally to become objects of our cares, wants and fears, open to experiences or passions to which we would otherwise be closed—for example, a fear of fear, i.e., a concern for "our" future, and corresponding wants, hopes and wishes. Other passions, love for example, are perhaps transformed. Because we know ourselves in this sense, that is, we are different selves than we would otherwise have been. This, it seems, is the necessary background for the consideration of a knowledge of what one knows and does not know, to which we now return.

Socrates had reminded Critias of what he was "just now saying"—that there is some one science which is not a science of anything else than of itself and of the other sciences as well as, this same one, of non-science—above all in order to suggest that this science is the condition for the being of a knowledge of what one knows and does not know. This is perhaps the reason why in repeating Critias' words, Socrates altered them. Where Critias had spoken of a science which is "itself of itself" (166c3, e6; cf. 169e1, e4; cf. 165b4; cf. also 167a1 and 169e7; cf. on the other hand 164d4, e7 and 169d7; 167a6 is disputed in the mss.), Socrates spoke of a science which is "of itself" (167c1, 168a7; cf. 167c2; cf. however 168d6, d9, e9, and 169a4–5 as well as 168d1 and e5); Socrates added, as he had before (166e7, just before the introduction of a knowledge of what one knows and does not know), that the science in question is also of "non-science"; and he required, as Critias had not, that the science be of nothing else than itself, the other sciences, and non-science (cf. 168a7). The consequence of a science's knowing itself (that it would become "itself" or a self that is known by itself) is not in this context at issue; but the science must have some access to non-science. The meaning of the last mentioned change is not yet clear.

In the meantime we have seen that Critias' science, understood in a certain way, appears to be impossible. But there may be another way to understand it, a way suggested by the very terms in which Critias first described his science. This alternative comes to sight if we have recourse to kinds or classes of sciences—that is, if we consider whether there are, not only particular sciences, knowings by a particular being of one or more objects, but also kinds of sciences, or classes of sciences comprising all knowings of a particular kind: "medicine," for example, as opposed to the particular knowledge of a particular doctor. If there are kinds of sciences, there might be a knowing of those kinds, or a science which has as its objects the kinds of sciences—which they are, how they are distinguished from one another—the kind that it is among others. But for a science of the kinds of sciences to be as such a sufficient condition of a knowledge of what one knows and does not know, it would seem to be required that there be exhaustive knowledge of all the possible kinds of sciences (and therefore of what are not sciences) and that the pretensions most requiring discovery be those to fake or non-sciences. Such exhaustive knowledge is not likely to be available. It might be more helpful then to turn to a science which would be akin to that science and indeed a prerequisite of it: the possessor of a science of the kinds of sciences, if he is to know which are sciences and which not, would have to know to begin with what science or knowing is, just as a doctor must know somehow what "the healthful" is in order to know the healthful things.[46] It is a science of science (and of its opposite) which would seem to be required if we are to test ourselves, or others, as to what we know and do not know.

Socrates had already spoken once of a science of science and non-science (166e7–8); and he has again added non-science to the objects of Critias' science (167b10–c2). He further draws our attention to a science of science by a slight variation in his treatment of the cases which are supposed to cast light on Critias' science. When speaking of the particular perceptions and of the passions, he frames his questions in this manner: is there some seeing, for example, which sees (or is of) itself and the other seeings . . . ? But in the cases of the perceptions generally and opinion, he asks about some perception of perceptions and itself, an opinion of opinions and itself. That is, he reverses the order of the objects and drops the article and the qualification "other." (Cf. also 168b10–11 with c4–6.) He thus seems to point to an act of knowing which knows the class comprising all knowings or sciences, or the character that makes them a class, and hence knows in a sense the acts of knowing and itself, since it too is an act of knowing. This science too, as we see, is in a sense a science of the sciences (170c6; cf. 174d4–5 and 9). It is a question then whether it is to be taken

---

46. Cf. 171b4–5 with 170e7 and 171a9.

as an alternative to Critias' science or a new way of understanding that science. (At 168a6–8, Socrates still speaks of a science of itself and the other sciences.) However that may be, so gradually does Socrates lead us and Critias to accept it as the science Critias meant, that it comes to the point where, dropping the formula "a science of the other sciences and itself," he can speak exclusively of a science of science or of the sciences without ever seeming to have departed from a consideration of Critias' suggestion (see especially 169b5–7). In this way, science comes to be a theme of the latter part of the dialogue. It comes up in the course of the consideration of what is necessary to a knowledge of what one knows and does not know; it thus seems to be wholly subordinate to that theme.

Continuation of the investigation as to the being of Critias' science having been agreed to (168a10–b1), Socrates now turned to the question of a science of science in particular. He has dropped, for some reason, his insistence that Critias' science be also of non-science. (This requirement is dropped, as far as the above illustrative cases are concerned, after the first two, and is not brought back otherwise until 169b7; cf. 168a6–8 and 169b1.) On the other hand, to judge again partly from the illustrative cases, the requirement that Critias' science be of nothing but itself and the other sciences is retained (cf. 168a7).

Socrates began by asking whether "this science" is a science of something and has some such power as to be of something. He speaks of "this science," as he had spoken before of some science (168a6) and even of "some one science" (167b11). But by way of illustration, he spoke next of "the bigger." The bigger too has some such power as to be bigger than (or of) something, something smaller, if it will be bigger. "If therefore we should find something bigger, which is bigger than [or of] the bigger things and itself, but bigger than none of the things the other bigger things are [bigger than or] of, by all means, surely, this would belong to it, if it would be bigger than itself, to be also smaller than itself." The example suggests that the character of "the bigger" is controlling as to what is possible or necessary with regard to a particular bigger thing: it is because "the bigger" must always be bigger than something smaller, that a bigger thing cannot be bigger than itself. But this would mean that there is a bigger which is of the other bigger things (whether or not it is also of itself) without—except incidentally, insofar as they are also bigger things—being of any of the things which they are bigger than. This is "the bigger," or the class comprising all bigger things, or the character which makes them a class.[47] In the same way, "science," or the class comprising all sciences or knowings, would be of those sciences or knowings, including those of which, according to our supposition, it is the object; for it was to such a science that we looked as the object of a science of science.

In the succeeding examples, however, Socrates ceased referring, even obliquely, to the relation between kinds or classes of things and the things comprising those classes. This proves to have the consequence that the class "science" can no longer be conceived of as merely an object. Socrates spoke, it is true, of some double, which is of the other doubles and itself; but he failed to add the requirement that this double not be of any of the things the other doubles are doubles of, and he did not refer to "the double." "Double is not, surely, of anything else than half" (168c6–7; this is more emphatic than the corresponding statement about bigger at 168b8). He then spoke of (a) more than itself, (a) heavier (than itself) and (an) older (than itself), without referring to the other mores, the other heaviers, and so on. This prepared the consideration of the following rule: will not whatever has its own power (literally, the power of itself) toward itself also have the being toward which its power is? Applying this to the science with which we are concerned, we come first to the thought that a science, if it is really to know something, must know something that is; a science "has its power toward" things which are. "Science," then, or the class comprising the sciences, which we supposed as the object of a science of science, must *be*. But according to Socrates' rule, it is that which has its power toward itself which must be; or what is (in this case) must have the power which is directed toward it. "Science," the class "science," must know.

In this way, Socrates directs our thoughts to the difficulty underlying the notion of a science of science, to what must be if there is to be such a science. "Science," or the class "science," if it is to be the object of a science,

---

47. ". . . There is in the earliest dialogues nothing whatever which Socrates' audience (or even we, with the *Republic* before us) could reasonably interpret as implying any belief in transcendental Forms . . . . A good example of the early approach is the *Charmides*. . . . Not a word, not a hint about Ideas. The same absence of compromising expressions . . . . " G. M. A. Grube, *Plato's Thought* (Boston: Beacon Press, 1968), p. 7. We may grant that Socrates does not use the term "form" (*eidos*) or "idea" (*idea*) in the technical sense (but cf. 154d5, e6, 158b1, 175d7) without being forced to grant that the thoughts which lead to the introduction of these terms are altogether absent from the *Charmides*.

must be; but if it is to be science, it seems, it must know. Can the class "science" (can classes of sciences)[48] know? It is at this point that Socrates speaks, by way of illustration of the proposed rule, of hearing and seeing. "The hearing, we say, is not hearing of anything else than sound . . . ." "The seeing," if it will itself see itself, must have some color, for seeing never sees anything colorless. Seeing and hearing, it seems, are always of things which have color or sound, i.e., of particular bodily things. Are not they too always particular and linked to body? Socrates' use of the article (at 168d3 and 9; cf. d10) seems to emphasize this point: "the seeing," in other words, being always of color, is always *a* seeing or *this* seeing. If this is correct, we have example of motions always particular and linked to body which are of what is particular and bodily. On the other hand, in "the bigger," which is related to "the smaller" and also to the bodily biggers, we have something neither particular nor bodily which is of both what is and what is not particular and bodily. Is there something—a motion—always particular and linked to body, which is of both what is and what is not particular and bodily? We have been led to wonder whether this is not the case of science (Consider 169a8–b1 [*genesthai . . . einai*] as well as 169d3–4; cf. the earlier 167b10 [*estin*].) If so, the only science is that which we, or thinking beings, have. This would be a more important conclusion than the denial that a science of science, as it is understood here, is possible: there might still be some understanding of science or of what it means to know something which is sufficient for the purpose of a knowledge of what one knows and does not know. It would point to the importance of accounting for the coming to be of science in us.

Having cast doubt on the possibility of a science of science but not proved that it is impossible, Socrates now prepared to call upon Critias, whom he addressed here by name (168e3), to defend "his" suggestion. (The spirit in which Socrates approached Critias here is best indicated by his injunction to him to show not so much the possibility of a science of science as the possibility of his demonstrating—i.e., his capacity to demonstrate—that possibility. [Socrates plays on the ambiguity of

---

48. This is not meant to rule out that the kinds or classes of sciences, e.g., medicine, which we once supposed as objects of Critias' science, might have a somewhat better claim to being than the class "science." If there is no "science" or "knowing" by itself, must not knowing or science be all the more inseparable from its various objects? Cf. 171a5–b5 and *Theaetetus* 146c7–d2.

dunatos—169b7 and b8—as one sees if one retains the words excluded by Burnet at the suggestion of Heindorf.] Or, as Socrates indicates in the next sentence, the issue is also, if not primarily, the correctness of what Critias says [169c1–2; cf. 166c5–6, d8–e2].) If our suspicion is correct, a science of science is not absolutely necessary for a knowledge of what one knows and does not know: when Socrates professes in this context not to know whether a science of science is possible, he does not seem to doubt that he knows that he doesn't know this. On the other hand, some understanding of science, of what it is to know something, does seem to be required. And, given the deliberate looseness which Socrates has been permitting himself in the use of the term "science," the name "science of science" might well be applied to such an understanding if, for other reasons (e.g., the discomfiture of Critias), it served Socrates' purpose to do so.

This explanation is however to an extent premature, since Socrates did not at once speak here of a knowledge of what one knows and does not know. By forgetting about that knowledge for a moment, he was able to take a "science of science" as the definition of moderation (169a6–7 and b5–7). This in turn enabled him to raise the question of the goodness, as well as the possibility, of such a science. In this connection, by way of preparing to ask Critias to speak to both of these questions, Socrates made the following statement:

> I don't trust myself to be adequate to determine these things;
> therefore neither am I able to insist as to whether it is possible
> for this to come to be, that there be science of science, nor—if
> it is granted that it is possible [or exists]—do I accept that it
> is moderation before I examine whether it would benefit us
> in some way, being of such a sort, or not. For I divine that
> moderation is something beneficial and good.

He was thus enabled to call attention to the contrast between his doubts as to the existence of a science of science and his confidence, not to say faith, in the goodness of moderation, as well as to the related contrast between his distrust of his ability to settle the question of possibility and his apparent confidence in his ability to examine the question of benefit.[49]

---

49. George Grote points out, regarding an earlier passage, that it is inconsistent for "Plato" to insist on the beauty of moderation before determining what moderation is,

In a similar statement (regarding a knowledge of what one knows and does not know) in an earlier context, Socrates had not spoken of divination and he had left it open whether his difficulties did not extend equally to the examination of both questions—goodness as well as possibility. (167a9–b7; cf. however b7–c4.)

Socrates began by pointing out that in some of the cases they had gone through it appeared impossible, in others doubtful, that they had their own powers toward themselves. Magnitudes and multitudes and such things belonged to the impossible cases; hearing, seeing, motion, heat, and presumably also the passions and opinion, to the doubtful, or perhaps not so doubtful, ones. "It requires some great man, friend, to determine this adequately in all cases, whether none of the beings is of a nature to have its own power itself toward itself—except science—but towards another, or some are and some not; and again, if there are those which themselves have it [or are] toward themselves, is science, which we say is moderation, among these?" The word we translated "determine" has a primary meaning of "divide." Socrates calls in effect for a division, in particular of the doubtful cases, into two classes according to their natures: those, if any, which have their powers toward themselves, and those which do not. The determination of the possibility of a science of science is said to depend on such a division (and the subsequent placing of science in the proper class): "I don't trust myself to be adequate to determine [or divide] these things; therefore neither am I able to insist as to whether it is possible for this to come to be, that there be a science of science . . . ." And yet Socrates has indicated, in a somewhat awkward way—suited however to his purposes—that both the possibility and impossibility of a science of science are compatible with either outcome of such a division. For either (1) none of the beings has its power, or is directed, toward itself, except science (retaining the words at 169a4 excluded by Burnet at the suggestion of Schleiermacher); or, (2) some of the beings have this, including science; or, (3) some of the beings have this, but not science; or, we can therefore

---

"for we shall come to other dialogues wherein he professes himself incompetent to say whether a thing be beautiful or not until it be determined what the thing is. . . ." *Plato and the Other Companions of Socrates* (London: J. Murray, 1865), I, 496. This is true as well of Socrates' confidence here that moderation is good; but that confidence has the special function in the *Charmides* of demonstrating the common failing Grote speaks of at I, 495–96 as well as in his Preface (I, v ff.). Grote's failure to consider this possibility may be related to his view that "the dramatic art and variety of Plato [is] charming to read, but not bearing upon him as a philosopher," (I, 484, n. 1; cf. I, 492).

add, (4) none of the beings—not excepting science—have this. How then does the division called for by Socrates help to settle the question? It could seem that Socrates intended to lead his "great man" on a wild goose chase of considerable proportions. This uncharitable suggestion however would not be entirely correct.

The division which Socrates calls for presupposes, and thus calls our attention to, a more elementary division which consists in our dividing the disputed cases or motions from one another in the first place. For we cannot deliberate as to where seeing, for example, belongs, until we have to an extent separated seeing from the other motions so as to be able to focus our attention upon it. But among the motions from which it is separated or divided in this way, and which is in its turn set apart from the others, is science. And to separate science from the other motions is in a sense to know it. By speaking of "dividing" then, Socrates calls our attention to an elementary "science" of science (and non-science) which seems to be both possible and more accessible than the one he gives the appearance of looking for.

We can now see that the suggestion of this science of science was already contained in his listing of various motions, including science, which we are capable of (see p. 145f. above). That list was constructed with exceeding care. It begins, as we have seen, with seeing and hearing and the perceptions generally, goes on to what we call the passions, or some of them, and ends with opinion and science. Our attention had been called on an earlier occasion to the close relation between perception and opinion (159a1–3); here, as we see, the passions intervene. The relations among the motions listed are further indicated by differences and similarities of grammatical details in their presentation, which have no apparent direct relation to the sense. For example, in six of the nine cases, Socrates spoke of some seeing, some desire, etc.; but in three cases—*hearing, wanting* and *opinion*—he omitted "some." These happen also to be the only three cases where his questions omitted a main verb. In three cases again—*perception, fear* and *opinion*—what the motion is to be of is mentioned before what it must not be of. In another three—*love, fear* and *opinion*—the name of the motion begins the sentence (and is in the accusative case). In two—*desire* and *science*—the name of the motion is the second word in the sentence, while the first is "But" (*alla*). In three cases—seeing, as it is first presented, perception and opinion—the usual object of the motion is not specified. But this variation seems to be meaningful in itself: it seems to point to the comparative comprehensiveness of the motions in question as to objects, as is perhaps confirmed by the fact that Socrates repeated his question about seeing and then specified an object (color), seeing being the least comprehensive of the three motions. A verb from the same root as opinion (*dokei*) is used to form questions regarding *seeing, perception* and *desire*, which points to the fact that some of the motions may have other motions as objects. We should also note that different motions may in some cases share an object—for example, a wanting and an opinion of a good thing. There are other linkings of the motions—for example, only *hearing* and *opinion* are used three times as substantives, twice as verbs and only *wanting* and *fear* twice as substantives, twice as verbs—but the ones we have mentioned above are perhaps the most obvious, and at any rate are sufficient to indicate the frequency with which they involve opinion, together with the motions which directly or indirectly affect it.

The problem of opinion seems to be called to our attention because, for one reason or another, it is the most difficult of the motions to separate from science. For while we seem to separate opining from knowing at times, there are cases where we fail to do this. There are, it seems, certain opinions which are so precious to us that we wish to, and come to, regard them as knowledge, or perhaps divinations of the truth (169b4–5; cf. *Republic* 505d11–e3), where we do not employ the awareness of the difference between knowing and opining which seems, otherwise, to be available to us. In those cases, apparently, we are not simply open to the truth or the question of our openness to the truth may be raised. It would be wrong however to conclude that this is because the truth is of no concern to us there: there could be no temptation to conceal what is of no concern to us. Rather it is in just those cases that the truth is most obviously of concern to us—so much so, that one is led to wonder about the other cases, where (to begin with at least) we are indifferent or merely curious. How does knowing in those cases (cases which seem to include most comprehensive truths), a knowing whose pleasure seems always to coexist with sadness, a knowing in which we seem somehow to die (*Phaedo* 64a4–6)—how does knowing there come to be of such concern to some that they want or desire above all to engage in it?

But this understanding of the problem of opinion, in tracing that problem to the failure to apply a "science of science" which is in our possession, presupposes that such a "science" is generally possessed or available. Is there evidence that this is so? When this question comes up again (p. 164 below), the development of the argument will have cast new light on its significance.

Socrates' confession that he was at a loss regarding the question of the possibility of a science of science was not designed to point unambiguously to such a simple suggestion as we have made. It was designed primarily to place a most imposing task on Critias, "son of Kallaischros," as Socrates now addressed him (169b5)—and yet a task which it would be difficult for Critias in particular to refuse. (The name of Critias' father means something like beautiful-ugly or ugly-beautiful one. Critias himself is beautiful insofar as his speech is enriched by his association with Socrates; he is ugly in that he doesn't know what he says. Taken together with his self-assertiveness, these two characteristics make him a most fitting interlocutor of Socrates in a dialogue in which secrets are to be spilled cautiously: he can't follow up properly what he proposes, and Socrates can hold him at arm's length, appearing to take no responsibility for "Critias'" proposals, even where, those proposals not having gone far enough, the finishing touch is openly applied by Socrates himself [167a1–7; cf. however 169d7, as well as 171d2–5, 172c8–9 and 175d3–4, with 169b5–7]. But as this also suggests, in referring to Critias as "son of Kallaischros," the beautiful-ugly Socrates may be referring to himself.) When Critias heard what Socrates said and saw that Socrates was perplexed, he, too, like those who yawn because they see others yawning, seemed to Socrates to be forced by Socrates' perplexity to be himself taken by perplexity. As Socrates intimates to the companion, Critias' experience or consciousness of perplexity did not go very deep; he did not see a problem; he had merely been made to feel flustered. Inasmuch, then, as he had a reputation to uphold, he felt shame before those present; and he was unwilling to concede to Socrates that he was not able to determine (divide) those things Socrates had challenged him to, and he said something not at all clear, covering over his perplexity.

Socrates does not report to the companion the unclear things that Critias said: bad or unclear arguments of Critias are not as fruitful as bad or unclear arguments of Socrates, for they do not disguise and therefore point to an underlying clarity.[50] He says: "And I, so that the argument would proceed for us, said, 'But, if this is the decision, Critias, now let us concede this, that it is possible for a science of science to come to be; but hereafter we will examine whether it is so or not.'" It seems that Socrates had paused

---

50. This suggestion should not be taken to imply that we look for a meaning above or beneath the text. For we share Grote's disinclination to ascribe to "Plato any purpose exceeding what he himself intimates," (I, x)—in particular, to try "to divine an ulterior affirmative beyond what the text reveals," (I, ix; cf. I, 270–71)—as well as his intention to study each dialogue "as it stands written," (I, x). But having readily granted this much, we must be allowed to pay the closest attention we can to what is written, in all its complexity: for example, to Socrates' very ambiguous statement of the results of the investigation. (Cf. our Conclusion below with Grote, I, 491–92.)

to confront Critias where he did, not because the argument had reached a climax, but because the place was convenient for purposes of refutation; for in proceeding, he emphasizes to the companion the unfinished character of the argument. We do not know whether the refutation of Critias had now been completed to Socrates' satisfaction—that is, whether Charmides had been able to see through Critias' efforts to cover his perplexity. The argument, which is in the service of Socrates' deed, is also to an extent independent of it. This will enable the argument in the present case to explain that deed, while the deed in turn illustrates the argument.[51]

"Come then," Socrates continued, "if it is granted that this [i.e., a science of science] is possible, how is it [or one] more able to know what one knows and what not? For this, surely, we said to be knowing oneself and being moderate, did we not?" At an earlier stage of the argument (167b10–c2), Socrates himself had brought forward the suggestion that a science of itself and the other sciences as well as non-science is the condition for a knowledge of what one knows and what one does not know. He now seems to call into question whether a science of science (and non-science) is even useful in that regard. Intervening developments have prepared us to doubt whether a science of science is a sufficient condition for a knowledge of what one knows and does not know, by leading us to question whether it is always applied for that purpose—Socrates' questioning of what he had appeared to grant would seem to give some confirmation to that doubt. Nor are we surprised to see that it was in this context that Socrates, taking advantage of an opening given to him by Critias, chose to correct Critias' understanding of how one comes to know oneself (in the first place). For Critias, who had not objected to Socrates' identification of a science of science with moderation (169b1–2 and 5–7), now easily overlooked Socrates' reintroduction of a knowledge of what one knows and does not know. Replying to Socrates as if he had asked how a science of science brings it about that one knows oneself, he said: "Certainly, and so it happens, surely, Socrates. For if one has a science which itself knows [*gignōskein*] itself, he would be of such a sort as what he has is. Just as whenever one has swiftness, he is swift, and whenever one has beauty, he is beautiful, and whenever one has knowledge [*gnōsis*], he is knowing; and whenever one has knowledge [*gnōsis*] itself of

---

51. One might consider here Socrates' different purposes in conversing with Charmides (and Critias) on the one hand, and in narrating that encounter to the companion on the other.

itself, surely he will then be himself knowing [*gignōskōn*] himself." (Note that whereas Critias spoke of oneself knowing oneself, Socrates, who was referring to a different kind of self-knowledge, spoke of knowing oneself.) But Socrates has questioned not just the sufficiency of a science of science to bring about a knowledge of what one knows and does not know, but even its usefulness in that regard. When he had appeared to grant that some such science is sufficient for this purpose, he had spoken of a science of itself and the other sciences (167b10–c2; cf. 166e7–167a5, where it is not a question of a sufficient condition). Has the evolution, so to speak, of that science into a science of science deprived it of all usefulness for a knowledge of what one knows and does not know?[52]

Socrates' response to Critias' statement was as follows: "It is not this I dispute, that whenever one has what knows itself [or, something knowing the self or selfness], one will oneself know oneself—but what necessity is there for the one having this to know what he knows and what he does not know?" The second "this" is ambiguous: the immediate context suggests that it means a knowledge of oneself, or a knowledge which leads to this knowledge; while the broader argument (which has been interrupted to an extent by Critias' misunderstanding) suggests that it means a science of science (see 169d2–7 and what follows here). Both meanings make sense: it is doubted on the one hand whether possession of a knowledge of oneself (in the primary sense), and on the other whether possession of a science of science, leads necessarily to a knowledge of what one knows and does not know (which is or prepares a knowledge of oneself in a fuller sense [167a5–7, 169d6–8]). According to the second meaning, Socrates restates the question he had raised prior to Critias' statement, the question which

---

52. The question which Critias believed to have been asked but was not asked, is never explicitly raised by any participant in the dialogue either about a science of science or about a knowledge of what one knows and does not know. Perhaps Critias' slip was due in part to the fact that—to his credit—he was somehow aware that it very much needs to be asked (in both cases). For, if the *Charmides* is worth studying at all, it will not do to say that, " 'Knowledge of oneself' can readily be expanded as 'knowing what one knows and what one does not know' . . . which is relatively simple and sounds Socratic . . . ." M. Dyson, "Some Problems Concerning Knowledge in Plato's *Charmides*," *Phronesis*, XIX (1974), 104. As it turns out, we may get some help, regarding the relation of a knowledge of what one knows and does not know to self-knowledge, from following Socrates' treatment of the question he did ask: the relation of a science of science to a knowledge of what one knows and does not know.

Critias had failed to grasp. But he confines himself now to questioning the necessity that a science of science bring about a knowledge of what one knows and does not know. Does this mean that the usefulness of that science is no longer at issue? One gets the impression from the subsequent argument that this is not the case; that argument deals with usefulness more obviously than it does with necessity. To what connection between the question of usefulness, which (explicitly at least) he raised first, and the question of necessity, which he now puts in its place, does Socrates point?

Critias made this reply to Socrates' question: "Because, Socrates, this [or the self or selfness, if one reads *to auto* at 170a1 with mss. BT instead of *touto* with Cornarius] is the same as that." He seems to mean that knowing oneself is the same as knowing what one knows and does not know, or that one's self is nothing but the sum, so to speak, of one's knowledge and ignorance—as his understanding of self-knowledge as it developed in this conversation may well have implied. "Perhaps," Socrates said, "but I run the risk of being always of a similar sort: for I don't understand how it is the same to know what one knows and to know what someone does not know." Socrates' response can be understood as an explicit denial of Critias' suggestion. It is more easily read and understood as a denial that knowing what one does not know is the same as knowing what one knows. This however requires in turn that one understand Critias' remark to have suggested that they are the same (which is perhaps a possible reading of his remark; Cornarius' *touto* makes it easier). Or does it? (Note Critias' puzzlement at Socrates' response.) By ascribing to Critias the suggestion that possession of a science of science will necessarily lead to a knowledge of what one knows and does not know, providing that to know what one does not know is the same thing so to speak as to know what one knows, Socrates is enabled to explain his denial of that necessity by a denial that these things are the same, by an assertion, that is, of the uniqueness (of the unique difficulty, as it will prove) of knowing what one does not know.

Critias was so puzzled by Socrates' remark—which, as Socrates indicates, he must have heard one or twice before—that he said, "What do you mean?" It was especially the meaning of the remark in the context which puzzled him. Socrates began his reply with, "The following . . . ." What follows most manifestly does not explain the difference between knowing what one does not know and knowing what one knows (cf. 175c4–8). It is rather the light cast by that difference that enables one to make sense of what follows. It is in this way that "the following" makes clear the meaning of Socrates' remark in the context.

The first part of Socrates' argument went like this. A science which is of science would be able to determine (divide) no more than that "of these things," this is science, that not science. But sciences and non-sciences of different objects are themselves different. The examples Socrates uses are science and non-science of what is healthful, science and non-science of what is just: one is medicine, one politics, one nothing but science. (Socrates seems to mean by the last, the science whose object is science.) Now if one doesn't know in addition the healthful and the just, but only science, having a science only of this, one would likely know, "both regarding oneself and regarding the others," that one has some science. But one will not know "by this science," what one knows. For it is by medicine, not moderation (i.e., a science of science), that one knows the healthful; by music and not moderation that one knows the harmonic; by house-building and not moderation that one knows what pertains to house-building, and so on in all cases. "By moderation," if indeed it is only a science of "sciences," one will not know that one knows the healthful or that one knows what pertains to house-building. (Socrates thus completes his return to the use of technical examples, examples belonging to the generally accepted arts or disciplines, from which he had made what is for this dialogue a very rare departure by the introduction of politics and the just if not also music [cf. 165c–d and 161e6–13, 164a9, 173b1–c2, as well as 173c3–7]. This is not to deny that, in this dialogue at least, the example of medicine is not always a purely technical one.) Then the one who is ignorant of "this" will not know what he knows but only that he knows—and being moderate as well as moderation is reduced from knowing what one knows and what one does not know to knowing that one knows and that one does not know only (170a6–d4).

The cause of this reduction appears to be the reduction of Critias' science of the sciences, i.e., of the kinds of sciences (which Socrates' occasional use here of the plural in science of "sciences" [170c6] reminds us of), to a science of science (cf. 171a3–9 and 175b7–c3). A science which knows only what science is would no more be able to identify or separate from one another the particular sciences than a science of "the bigger" would be able to tell us anything further, about the objects it identifies as bigger, than that they are bigger. But granting this, let us see on a closer look whether it has the consequence which has been laid to it.

The first part of Socrates' argument concluded as follows: nor then will this one (i.e., the moderate person) be able to examine "another," who asserts he knows something, as to whether he knows what he says he knows or does not know it; but, as it looks, he will know this much only, that he (the other) has some science; as to what it is of, at any rate, moderation will not make him knowledgeable. This conclusion serves most pointedly to remind us that Socrates had been speaking of what the possessor of a science of science might know "both regarding himself and regarding the others" (170b9–10). Indeed, it indicates that the emphasis, in the portion of the argument just prior to the conclusion, is on what such a one might know of himself. Socrates was asserting there that he will not know what, but only that he knows. The crucial step in the argument (as one might perhaps see also from Critias' response [cf. 170c11 with c5]) occurred when Socrates, dropping the qualification "by this science" (170b12) or "by moderation" (170c6), said, "Then the one who is ignorant of this will not know what he knows but only that he knows." The statement is on the whole clear enough; there is only a little darkness regarding "this": to what does it refer? If, as seems likely (cf. 170b6–8), it refers to the healthful or to what pertains to house-building, we have the argument that the one who does not know the healthful, or what pertains to house-building, will not know that these are the things he knows—which is true, but his ignorance is not due to the fact that a science of the sciences has been reduced to a science of science. If, on the other hand, it refers to the knowledge (on the part of one who does know these things) that one knows the healthful or what pertains to house-building, it is true that one who lacks such knowledge will not know what he knows: but the argument has not shown that a moderate man (who knows these things) will suffer this lack. It has shown at most only that he will not know "by moderation" that these are the things he knows; but he will know that by medicine and house-building (which of course he possesses too), while by moderation, according to this argument, he will know that his medical and house-building knowledge is *knowledge*.[53] But

---

53. For a helpful discussion of this and other difficulties of this passage, see Tuckey, pp. 54 ff. (esp. p. 57). Cf. also Findlay, p. 94. Dyson (p. 108) attempts to avoid this difficulty by reading 170b6–10 as if Socrates were speaking of what a science of science knows, instead of, as the words clearly indicate, what a man who possesses only such a science knows. (Note the phrase "having a science," where "science" is in the accusative case; cf. also 170b12 and c6, where Socrates speaks of what one knows "by this science" or "by moderation"—not of what this science "by this science" knows.) Dyson wished to show that "Plato is not guilty of this rather obvious contradiction," (p. 108). Apparently convinced on the one hand that Plato would not contradict himself in an obvious way, even intentionally, and on the other that Plato was either uninterested in (". . . Plato's cavalier attitude towards precise formulae, nowhere demonstrated more clearly than in this dialogue . . . ," p. 107 n.) or perhaps incapable

this means that a "science of science" is essential to a knowledge of what one knows and does not know. Without such a "science," one would be unable to determine that "of these things" (170a7), i.e., of these opinions, this one is science, this one is *not* science; one might regard all one's opinions as true; one would not know any of them to be true.

But the significance of a science of science does not become clear with regard to the generally accepted disciplines, and as it confirms for us that we know what we know. It becomes clear if one applies it to such a controversial science and subject as politics and the just (or indeed, moderation) and becomes aware thereby of what one does not know—that one does not know it (167b2–3). According to our contention, the *Charmides* is nothing but a gloss on the experience which follows when this application and the inquiry it demands are made. For as we cannot help thinking, that experience is of unrivalled significance for the ordering of one's life—becoming, so to speak, the touchstone of our pleasures and concerns, admitting, elevating those that retain their power in its hard light. But perhaps we deceive ourselves, and the strength of the experience derives not so much from the experience itself as from our interpretation of it. In ascribing to it such strength, do we not think to know what we do not know? (See 167a4–5—reading *autos* with mss. BT—and preceding context.) Moreover, it could not maintain its strength if it were not necessary, nor perhaps maintain it steadily if it were not known to be necessary; but this too, we do not know. One is thus forced to seek confirmation for one's experience, and one's understanding of it, in the experience of others. Some confirmation might be found if it could be shown that all men, or perhaps all men of a certain type, take certain fundamental things for granted, that they are convinced of the truth of certain opinions, without knowing them to be true, and that the direction of their lives depends on that conviction. This could be shown, to the extent possible, if one could shake such opinions in as many as one found occasion to converse with in this way—that is, if one could (partially) "strip" them—and if their reaction to such stripping were such as to reveal the importance those opinions had for them, if, for example, even young men like Alcibiades, who thought that they cared very little about justice, discovered as the result of a conversation with Socrates that they cared above all about it.[54] Socrates would have been forced then, if this argument is correct, even in

---

of truly tight argument, Dyson is satisfied to find flaws which are compatible in his view with the argument's "undoubted brilliance," (p. 111).

54. Cf. *Alcibiades I* 105a6 ff. and 113d1–8 with 135d7–e5.

the absence of other inducements, to conduct political conversations or refutations of this type, having first engaged in a sort of political inquiry himself (*Apology of Socrates* 21b).[55] But to show that such opinions are so to speak universally held, is not yet to show that it is necessary that they be called into question. Does not the experience of many of Socrates' interlocutors show to the contrary that it is not necessary, that one can avoid that questioning to begin with, that it can be rather easily forgotten? However that may be, such questioning would be necessary in effect if possession of a science of science led necessarily to its being applied in this way. It was the question of this necessity that Socrates raised when he asked whether possession of a science of science leads necessarily to a knowledge of what one knows and does not know (169e6–8).

If possession of a science of science leads necessarily to its being applied in this way, i.e., against all our opinions or the most important of them, it will be so applied wherever possessed. The question of the necessity of its application could be clarified then if the question of its possession could be clarified. Socrates has been speaking, despite some hints to the contrary (above, p. 155, p. 156), as if that possession were rather limited, and this manner of speaking reaches its peak in the second part of his argument in this subsection (170e1–171c10). Not only does he say that "we gave" understanding of science to moderation alone (170e9–10), without ever having indicated that moderation is widely possessed, but he speaks of the moderate man as an artisan, a craftsman (171c8–9): to possess a science of science is to be an expert, to have an area of competence like the other experts, but different from theirs as theirs are different from each other. The rarity of knowledge of what one knows and does not know (*Apology of Socrates* 23c6–7) might plausibly be traced then to the rarity of the possession of this type of expertise—a science of science—which however, when acquired, must necessarily be applied to that end. Yet it is in just this part of his argument that Socrates leads us to question this understanding of how widely a science of science is possessed.[56]

Elaborating on the insufficiency of moderation, as a science of science, for testing others, Socrates is concerned to show that the moderate man will be unable to distinguish (separate) one who "pretends" to be,

---

55. Cf. *Gorgias* 521d6–8, Xenophon, *Oeconomicus* 6.12–17.

56. That it is the question of such possession which is at issue here may be indicated also by the one explicitly positive result of Socrates' otherwise negative argument: the possessor of a science of science is given the capacity to determine of others only this—whether or not they possess a science of science (171c8–9).

but is not, a medical man from a true medical man. (Does Socrates wish to show incidentally how easy it is to pretend to be a medical man, even or especially a Thracian medical man?) He makes the very sensible point that it will be necessary for the moderate man, or any one else who wishes to know the true medical man from the false, to converse with (*dialeges-thai* [170e6]) him not about "medicine" but about the healthful and its opposite. But he gives two different reasons for this. The first is that the medical man knows nothing about medicine, which as a science is the province of moderation alone (170e6–171a2); the second is that medicine is "in" the healthful and its opposite (171a11–b6). A shift in the purpose of conversing and in the role of the moderate man goes along with this. At first it is said that the moderate man will know of the individual to be tested that he has some science (the alternative, that he has no science at all, being forgotten about); but he will need to inquire about the objects of that science to test which science it is (171a3–10). But then it develops that it cannot be ascertained whether the alleged medical man has any science until it is ascertained whether in the healthful things and their opposites he speaks truly and acts correctly: that is, this cannot be ascertained without medicine or by anyone else than a medical man (171a11–c3). As a result, the role of the moderate man—except insofar as he is himself the possessor of an art—is reduced to nothing in distinguishing (separating) a medical man or any other knower who knows his art from someone who does not know, "whether professing or thinking" to know; while the role of the arts is correspondingly raised (171c4–10).

Now the latter part of this conclusion corresponds to our ordinary experience, for it is especially to artisans or experts that we look to test the competence of their fellow experts. (It suggests incidentally that Socrates would have been unable to test others regarding political matters, if he had not become a sort of political expert himself [cf. 172b6–7].)[57] But is

---

57. Tuckey doubts whether this was necessary for Socrates, to enable him to discover the ignorance of others. "Socrates knew . . . that Euthyphro did not know *to hosion*, but he made no profession of knowing it himself. It was his ability to detect logical inconsistency which enabled him to find out that men did not know what they professed to know, irrespective of the objects of their supposed knowledge. His knowledge . . . of ignorance was based therefore on his ability to think clearly and consistently" (p. 67; cf. p. 69). Something of this sort may well be true in many cases, but is it true in all? And does not clear thinking, especially as it is applied to the testing of others, require some knowledge of the matters thought? Tuckey's citation (p. 69) of *Apology of Socrates* 21d3–4 does not necessarily prove that Socrates was not an "expert" in the manner indicated at the end of the paragraph in our text to which this note is attached.

it true, as might seem to be implied (cf. 172b7–8), that the experts can do this without themselves possessing a science of science, at least in the sense that we have been speaking of it? The movement of the argument forces us at least to raise this question. In testing others, the experts make use of their particular expertise, examining the alleged fellow experts as to whether they speak truly and act correctly in matters of the art in question. In order to apply the standards of true speech and correct action, they must know them; they must themselves possess the art. But one does not truly possess an art without knowing its limits: we expect a medical man to be able to tell us when he cannot cure us; a shoemaker who is competent in all other respects but believes he knows how to make shoes that will last forever or that will enable the wearer to fly, is not a shoemaker, nor can he be relied upon to test another's possession of that art. The artisan as artisan must somehow know then what it is not to know, as well as what it is to know something. Moreover, he is protected from exclusive reliance on words or teaching by the necessity, here alluded to, to test the dogmas of his art against the deeds it is supposed to perform. The artisan as artisan then possesses a science of science of some sort. (If what has been suggested earlier about the class "science" is true, one could not know "science" without first possessing some particular science or without first knowing some [other] thing.) This is not to say however that he is enabled by this science (together with his particular expertise) to tell of another with certainty that the other possesses the science he claims to possess (cf. 171a3–4). One can at best make the inference that such true speech and correct action as the other shows are unlikely to result from opinion and lucky guessing alone. One can more surely tell of another that he does not possess a particular science, not least in the case where he claims to know as true what is not or claims to know more than can be known. (If there should be an area of alleged expertise which admits of no expertise, it might be said of one who has examined that area that he knows only that he knows nothing, or that his expertise consists in a science of science alone [cf. 171b1–2]. In that case at least, Socrates would seem to be justified in speaking of the possessor of a science of science as a particular artisan or craftsman different from the others.)

The artisans then who are truly artisans both possess a "science of science" and apply it as a matter of course in the practice as well as the acquisition and development of their arts.[58] They apply it as a matter of

____

58. If moderation is a science of science alone, the artisans are moderate by virtue of possession of their particular arts.

course to what they know, so to speak. Its application is not limited in principle however to what they know. For while it may require expertise to confirm or deny the possession of similar expertise in another, it requires no expertise but only a "science of science" and a suitable application of it to tell us, regarding our own opinions which are mere opinions, that they are not knowledge—whether or not they admit of being transformed into knowledge. (In the case of the artisans, this requires only that they draw the appropriate conclusion from the contrast between the solidity of their technical competence and the lack of solidity of other things.) Possession of a science of science should lead necessarily then to a knowledge of what one knows and does not know. It would do so if to know what one did not know were the same as to know what one knows, if, that is, application of a "science of science" to all one's opinions were as "morally" easy as that application is in technical matters and others of that kind. That it is not so easy, the case of the artisans, above all others, shows. For since, in the practice of their arts, they show in a particularly impressive way that they know something and know what it is to know, and not to know, something, when they too prove to "think" they know what they do not know (*Apology of Socrates* 22c9–e1),[59] it can be concluded that this results from a failure to apply the "science of science" which is available to them. It is not in this way then that the questioning we are concerned with can be shown to be necessary, and Socrates' doubt that possession of a science of science leads necessarily to a knowledge of what one knows and does not know appears to be justified.

But "necessity," as Socrates used it in expressing that doubt, is ambiguous. There may be necessities which admit of evasion but work their will by exacting a price for it, as well as those which are more simply inexorable. Socrates' words may also be taken then to have raised the question whether some necessity of this kind does not impel those who possess a science of science as well as a knowledge of oneself toward the kind of questioning which has been indicated.

The kind of questioning which leads to a knowledge of what one knows and does not know would be necessary for us if that knowledge were good, or *the* good for us. Socrates is able to consider the goodness of a knowledge of what one knows and does not know because, as we perhaps need to be reminded at this point, that knowledge has been asserted to be moderation; and Socrates turns now to an examination of the benefit to be derived for us from moderation as the discussion has presented it (a

---

59. Cf. *Charmides* 171c7 with 170e1.

science of science or a knowledge of what one knows and does not know).
This is more or less in accordance with the explicit plan of the section,
which called for an examination first of the possibility of knowing what
one knows and does not know, and then of the benefit for us in knowing
it (167a9–b4). The question of benefit, we recall, was raised because Socrates, divining that moderation is something beneficial and good, would
not accept as moderation anything which did not benefit us (169b1–5)—a
position consistent with the point of view expressed throughout the dialogue not only by Socrates, but by Charmides and Critias as well (e.g., at
157a3–b1, 158b2–4, 160e6–13, 162a4–6, 163c3–8 and 163e1–164a1). But
Socrates' consideration of the goodness of a knowledge of what one knows
and does not know compels him to deny that it is good. This conclusion
would not be different if in his consideration here he had been more open
about what he means by a knowledge of what one knows and does not
know: while it is necessary to assert that moderation is a knowledge of
what one knows and does not know (above pp. 133–34, 144), it is equally
necessary—from the point of view indicated—to deny that a knowledge
of what one knows and does not know is moderation (p. 144 above).
This would seem to leave open however that such knowledge might be
good in a lesser degree than is required of a virtue (cf. 172b1–c4). But,
as it seems to me at least, Socrates hesitates to assert that this is so. His
hesitancy may have to be traced to the fact that what we can perhaps call
immoderation appears, in some form or other, to be inevitable for us: we
must either take certain fundamental things for granted, or, impelled by
the experience which follows the knowledge of our ignorance of them, seek
clarity "about each of the beings" (166c7–d6) above all things; a simple
acceptance of our limits appears to be impossible, our nature refusing, as
it seems, to allow us to be unconcerned by those limits. But doesn't this
mean that a knowledge of what one knows and does not know is good
at least for Socrates and those like him (*Apology of Socrates* 22e1–5)? The
answer to this difficult question may perhaps be somewhat clearer after a
consideration of why the questioning which leads toward that knowledge
is necessary. As it turns out, in considering the goodness of moderation as
the discussion has presented it, Socrates gives us a demonstration which
illuminates that necessity.

(This development was foreshadowed by a departure which Socrates
made earlier from the explicit section plan he here reminds us of. The
question of the possibility of a knowledge of what one knows and does
not know was to be considered on the basis of the agreement that such

knowledge would exist if a science of itself and the other sciences exists [167b10–c3; cf. 166e7–167a5]. The first part of the examination focused therefore on that science. When its possibility was conceded—if only that the argument might proceed—the examination should have turned to the question of the benefit for us from a knowledge of what one knows and does not know. Instead, Socrates made an issue of what he had appeared to grant—the relation of a science of science to a knowledge of what one knows and does not know—asking first whether that science is able to contribute to or bring about such knowledge, and then whether there is any necessity that it bring it about [169d2–e8]. The ensuing discussion led us to the thought that a science of science would be unable to contribute to or bring about the knowledge if there were not some necessity that it be applied in questioning of this kind. It was the consideration of the goodness of a knowledge of what one knows and does not know that Socrates displaced to bring this difficulty to our attention.)

Addressing Critias by name, as he will do frequently in this context,[60] Socrates first asked what benefit there would be for us from moderation as the argument has presented it. Since the argument had ostensibly reached the conclusion that there is little or no connection between a science of science and a knowledge of what one knows and does not know, and since Socrates had chosen to understand this as meaning that moderation was said to be a science of science (170c6, d1–3, 171c4–5; cf. 172b1–3), the question concerned the benefit from moderation as a science of science. But instead of waiting for Critias to answer it, Socrates went on to describe how greatly beneficial "we say" it would be for us to be moderate if, "as we posited from the beginning," the moderate man knew both what he knew and what he did not know—of the former that he knows it, of the latter that he does not know it—and was able to examine another who was similarly placed:

> For both we ourselves and those who have moderation and
> all the others, as many as were ruled by us, would go through
> life without error. For neither would we ourselves attempt to
> do what we did not know [*epistasthai*]—but finding out the
> knowers [*epistamenoi*] we would give it over to them—nor

---

60. 171d1, 172a4, d5, 173d5, 174c3, c9, 175a9. Cf. 172b8 and 174b11. Cf. the absence of such addresses between 167b6 and 168e3 (cf. 167c4 and 168d9) and between 169d3 and 171d1.

would we permit the others, whom we ruled, to do anything else than what, in doing, they would be likely to do correctly; and this would be what they had a science [*epistēmē*] of. And in this way a household managed by moderation would be likely to be nobly managed, and a city governed, and everything else moderation should rule. For when error is taken away and correctness is guiding, it is necessary for those so disposed to do nobly and well in every doing and for those who do well to be happy.

Critias readily, eagerly agreed that this was what they meant or said when they said what a good it would be to know what someone knows and what he does not know. Moderation secures an error-free life—a life, that is, in which the sciences, whether our own or others', guide all the doings which affect our lives as well and the lives of those who are ruled by us. Thus understood, moderation comes into its own as a ruling art: the working of its full benefit presupposes that knowers in all fields are at its disposal, if not also that non-knowers are prevented from acting. One might therefore conclude that the need for political reform to bring about the rule of moderation (which is not necessarily the rule of moderate men) is at least as pressing as the need to acquire moderation oneself.

Their hopes from moderation thus understood appeared to be checked, at least temporarily, by the fact that, as Critias must admit, no such "science" has anywhere appeared. Socrates therefore asked whether "what we now find moderation to be, to know science and non-science," might not have some lesser good:

> . . . that the one having this [*tautēn*, feminine, to agree with moderation or perhaps science] whatever else he learns, will learn it more easily and everything will appear to him clearer, inasmuch as he will be seeing science in addition to each thing that he learns; and he will examine the others more nobly with regard to whatever he himself should learn, while those examining without this [*toutou*, neuter or masculine, antecedent ambiguous] will do this more weakly and poorly?

(He thus indicated in passing why a science, of the sort he had just supposed a knowledge of what one knows and does not know to be, had nowhere appeared: it will not appear before an expertise which enables one to examine other experts in their fields without knowing their fields, appears.) These benefits from a science of science require more clearly than those claimed for a knowledge of what one knows and does not know that one possess that science oneself (note Socrates' switch here to the third person). On the other hand, they may apparently be enjoyed in full by one who leads a private life in a poorly governed city (which does not necessarily mean that they can be enjoyed only in such a city). However that may be, the decisive consideration is, as Socrates indicates, their limited character: "Are such things as these, friend, what we will enjoy from moderation, but we look to something bigger, and seek that it be something bigger than it is?" "It might be so," Critias replied. As his response indicates, he hesitates to give up all hope of the greater benefits they had ascribed to the greater, so to speak, moderation.

Was it this that induced Socrates to suggest another look at those benefits? He seems to have already taken such a look himself: he wonders whether they sought or searched for nothing good; strange things appear to him regarding moderation if it is of such a sort. The question was apparently not moot, for though they had been unable, as Socrates reminds us here, to show that they knew even a science of science to be possible, they had also, as it appears, failed to show that a knowledge of what one knows and does not know, as it is now understood, is impossible. Socrates therefore had ground for suggesting that they grant the possibility of a science of science and grant that it (cf. 175b7ff.), or moderation, knows what one knows and what one does not know, in order that they might examine "still better" whether, being of such a sort, it helps us in any way. "For," as he adds, "what we were just now saying, that moderation would be a great good if it were of this sort, guiding the management of household and city—we don't seem to me to have nobly [i.e., properly] agreed to this, Critias."

It was difficult for Critias to see how their agreement could have failed to be noble (172d6, e1, e3). Socrates appears to have meant by this that they had agreed *too easily* that it was some great good for human beings, if each of us should do what they know and give over what they don't know to others who know (172d7–10), as well as that the substance of the agreement was not correct (172e6–173a1). For Socrates, "by the dog," (he used his characteristic oath here) must have shared Critias' attachment to that agreement if (ms. B at 172e4) he said that when he looked at it then and now *strange* things appeared to him and that he *feared* that they did not examine correctly (172e4–6). But that very attachment would have prevented him from taking the agreement too lightly, from accepting it too easily, without a close look, so to speak. And when he took such a look, it "truly" did not seem to him at all clear that moderation, if it is granted to be this sort of thing, produces a good for us. Socrates became aware, that is, at the same time, that he did not know it to be such a good as they thought, and that there was some reason for doubting that it was. "How?" Critias asked. "Speak so that we too may know what you mean." So far as we have observed, Critias had never before in the dialogue shown this sort of interest in what Socrates was saying. "I think I am being foolish," Socrates replied, "nevertheless, it is necessary to examine what has appeared, and not pass idly by, if someone cares for himself even a little." "You speak nobly," Critias said.

The necessity which drives us to apply such a science of science as we possess in questioning our cherished opinions is our very self-concern, coupled with the importance we place on those opinions. To treat those opinions with the seriousness demanded by our reliance on them is on the one hand to take the question of their *truth* seriously: to wish them to be true, to wish to know their truth or to be convinced of it—wishes indeed that for the most part induce us to think or believe we know what we do not know. But it is on the other hand to wish *certain things* to be true. The more seriously we take the opinions in question, the more strictly will we insist on these things. But we can't help, then, becoming aware, at some time or other, of difficulties regarding these things. In becoming aware of these difficulties, we become aware that we did not know what we thought we knew. It becomes as urgent matter to seek to transform our opinions into knowledge. We must follow up the difficulties. In the course of the investigation, we may become aware of other problems: these too must be followed up and investigated, "if one cares for oneself even a little." There is no necessity, perhaps for more than one reason, that such investigations lead to complete wakefulness. We may perhaps again and again believe we know what we do not know. But to take those beliefs seriously is to come up necessarily, again and again, against the same difficulties, to be compelled again and again toward the same questioning. The necessity in question then, however it may fall short of guaranteeing wakefulness, is sufficient, at least for some, to prevent a peaceful sleep. And given this fact, if there is an activity which makes a life of wakefulness bearable, some might prefer its austere joys, even if they don't completely make up for the loss of an apparent bliss, to any available alternative.

The difficulty, to continue, which Socrates had discerned regarding the rule of moderation, as it is now defined, was as follows. That rule would bring about nothing else than that everything would be done for (or by) us in accordance with science or art. Socrates referred to three or four arts in particular—first to piloting, medicine, and generalship: ". . . and neither would someone asserting to be, but not being, a pilot, deceive us, nor would a doctor, nor a general, nor anyone else, pretending to know what he did not know, escape our notice. Would anything else result for us from these things, then, than to be healthy in our bodies more than now, and to be saved on the sea and in war [more than now] . . . ?" Moderation is, after all, the key to health—but not in the Thracian manner. As a result, no more is claimed for it than that it leads to our being *more* healthy, *more* saved than now: one can't be of perfect health, or be saved forever. Socrates next spoke of prophecy: "If you wish, let us grant that the prophetic art too exists, a science of what is to come to be, and that moderation, ruling it, turns away the boasters and establishes the true prophets as foretellers for us of the things to come." Were it not for this concession, they might have been forced to take a different view of how far boasting extends. Socrates at any rate thus found occasion to confirm our impression that moderation is to be understood as an antidote to (conscious or unconscious) boasting. But if we leave things at this fairly sober view of sobriety, if moderation is to be understood as no more than this, can it still, given what we expect of virtue, be understood as a virtue? (Cf. *Apology of Socrates* 41c8–d2.) "When the human race is so equipped," Socrates concluded, "I follow that it would do and live scientifically—for moderation, being on guard, would not let non-science creep in to be our fellow worker—but that in doing scientifically we would do well and be happy, this we are not yet able to learn, friend Critias."

Critias attempted to raise an objection to Socrates' conclusion; but his words, at least as interpreted by Socrates, contained the germ of a new suggestion regarding doing well, if not happiness, which may be particularly fitting in light of the development that has taken place. "But, indeed, you will not easily find some other end of doing well if you dishonor 'scientifically.'" As Socrates easily discovered or demonstrated, Critias did not mean either that the practice of any art or science (as opposed to the enjoyment of the products of the arts and sciences) or that knowing or science as such makes one happy. But in the process, Socrates put on record the not easy question of the scientific life and happiness (173e6–7, 174a4–11).

Pressed, in order to defend the thesis that Socrates was ascribing to him, to find a particular science which makes the knower of it happy, Critias said it was especially that by which one knows the good and the bad. (Cf. *Republic* 505b5–c5.) "Wretch," Socrates said (cf. 161b8), "from long ago you have been dragging me around in a circle, hiding the fact that it wasn't 'living scientifically' that made one do well and be happy—not as to all the other sciences—but as to this one only [or alone], the science regarding the good and bad. . . ." Socrates then "proved" by use of the science or art of good and bad that there is no benefit whatsoever from the other arts and sciences when this science is taken away from them. This is an exaggeration—defensible perhaps by reference to the blinding effect which looking toward happiness may have on our capacity to see lesser goods—of the fact that the thesis, that only a science of good and bad makes one happy, is equivalent to the thesis, that all other arts and sciences, alone or together, are insufficient to make us happy. In this way, moderation is shown to be non-beneficial: "How then will moderation be beneficial, being craftsman of no benefit?" "In no way, Socrates, as it seems at least." In other words, it is not simply non-beneficial. In calling into question such goods as moderation had seemed to be, a science of good and bad bears a curious resemblance to a knowledge of what one knows and does not know.

VI. Conclusion

Socrates now chose to summarize and conclude the discussion. In the course of a single long speech, he addressed first Critias and then Charmides. He first drew back for a moment from the suggestion that moderation is not beneficial. The conclusion they had reached is evidence rather of his inability as an examiner:

> You see, then, Critias, that plausibly did I fear from long ago, and justly did I blame myself for conducting an examination of no worth regarding moderation: for surely, what at any rate is agreed to be most noble [beautiful] of all—this would not have appeared to us non-beneficial [or non-beneficial for us] if there were some benefit from me in regard to searching nobly. But now—for we have been beaten in every direction, and we are not able to discover on whichever of the beings the lawgiver placed this name, "moderation" . . . .

Moderation, as is generally agreed, is most noble of all: hence it must be beneficial (cf. 160e6–161b2). What we call "moderation" is one of the beings, i.e., something natural, not due to any human making or convention. But it owes its name to the "lawgiver." Does the agreement as to its nobility stem from its being or from its name? (Cf. 158e7–159a7, 165d8–e2 and pp. 120 and 137–38 above.) This is not to say that the lawgiver could ascribe to the being in question something our nature did not in some way divine or want or long for (cf. 169b4–5 and pp. 143, 148, and 153f. above). This mixed character of "moderation" may explain the mixed character of the investigation as to what it is. That investigation is not unmindful of perception or experience; but it also, and even primarily, is conducted through arguments which are not simply attempts to describe accurately some perception or experience (cf. 176a3–4). Virtue, one can perhaps say, is not simply the perfection or health of the soul; but that perfection wishes to be understood in the light of virtue.[61]

By accepting responsibility for the failure of the investigation, Socrates seemed to imply that Critias could not have been expected to make a serious contribution to it. This was as close as he came to stating the lesson which his examination of Critias was meant to convey to Charmides, and which Charmides, as we will soon see, has not failed to appreciate (see 176a6–b4, noting Charmides' switch to the second person singular). Socrates suggested two views of the failure, each of which is compatible with deference to the position of the lawgiver and/or general agreement: they have found moderation, but have been unable to understand its genuine beneficence; or what they have found, which is truly non-beneficial, cannot be moderation. Each view, incidentally, makes some concession to the validity of the investigation and hence to Socrates' ability as an examiner.

Socrates seemed to be on the point of adopting the latter view but to be checked by an unlikely consideration: the many concessions they had made, beyond what the argument strictly permitted, to reach that view of moderation. (He had in mind their conceding that a science of science exists, their conceding to this science the knowing [*gignōskein*] of the works of the other sciences—so that the moderate man would become for us a knower [*epistēmōn*] of what he knows, that he knows, and of what he does not know, that he does not know—and above all, in connection with this, their failure to investigate the impossibility of knowing [*eidenai*] somehow what one does not know at all. It would be difficult to see how this last problem could be as serious as Socrates suggests, if a knowledge of what one did not know amounted to no more than knowing which

---

61. Cf. Leo Strauss, *Natural Right and History* (Chicago: University of Chicago Press, 1953), pp. 145–46.

of the generally accepted arts and sciences one did not know.) Socrates seemed to regard these concessions as reason for concluding that they had found moderation. The difficulty must then lie in their failure to understand its genuine beneficence. But while perhaps alluding to this alternative, Socrates did not now return to it; the considerations which would seem to demand such a return were apparently not conclusive for him. He said that what they had posited to be moderation had "very hubristically" appeared as non-beneficial. Since the immediate sequel at least seems to show that Socrates regarded that appearance as true, the hubris which Socrates ascribes here to moderation itself does not seem to consist in the untruthfulness of its present appearance. However that may be, the reason for these steps may be found in the fact that Socrates was about to address Charmides directly once more. He wished him to feel that the argument had not prevented them from understanding moderation as they wished—so that he might feel all the more the argument's failure to find the goodness of what they took moderation to be.

"For my part, I am less indignant; but on your behalf Charmides," Socrates said, turning to him, "I am very indignant, if you, being of such a sort in your form, and in addition to this most moderate in your soul, will not be helped from this moderation, nor will it in any way benefit you in your life, being present." Socrates almost seemed to accept Charmides' moderation as a fact; he no longer doubted that Critias' definition of moderation was correct. He only insisted that this moderation did not appear to be beneficial. But if one accepts this, and if the thought that moderation is not good is unbearable, one will be forced to reject Critias' suggestion (a step which Critias' embarrassment at the hands of Socrates has made easier than it would otherwise have been). And, as Socrates delicately suggests, the fall of Critias' authority regarding moderation undermines, to say the least, his credibility as witness to Charmides' moderation, which is less obvious and therefore in greater need of such testimony than his beautiful form. (Cf. 158a7–b6.) "Still more," Socrates went on, "am I indignant on behalf of the song which I learned from the Thracian, if, though it pertained to a matter of no worth, I learned it with much seriousness."[62] As this remark indicates, it was not a deficiency of self-concern which caused Socrates to be less indignant in his own case than in that of Charmides about the worthlessness of moderation: did

---

62. Cf. 155b9–c4 and p. 112 above. The seriousness, of which we were forced to make so much, is in a sense not Socrates' last word.

he not believe to know that Charmides would be deeply moved if his confidence that he was moderate was shaken? (Cf. pp. 163–64 above.) It was this question at any rate that Socrates now attempted to resolve.

He did so by suggesting that he did not very much think this account of these things to be so—but rather that he is a poor searcher, since he thinks moderation to be "some great good" and Charmides, if indeed he has it, to be blessedly happy. "But see if you have it and are in no need of the song: for if you have it, I would rather advise you to consider me to be foolish and unable to search for anything through speech, but yourself, the more moderate you are, the more happy." For if Charmides regards moderation as a great good, as the key to happiness, this advice of Socrates to be unconcerned by such a challenge to moderation's goodness as has been made, is just what he will be unable to accept. He must take that challenge to mean—contrary to what Socrates has been saying—that they have not found moderation. But if they have not found moderation, how can he know that he is moderate? (The premise of Socrates' initial procedure in testing Charmides, according to which a failure to know, or have an opinion about, moderation is indicative of a failure to possess it, is a deliberate exaggeration of this conclusion, to which a Socratic refutation is meant to lead.) On the other hand, Socrates would not raise such questions unless he knew or was able to discover—contrary to other of his assertions—what moderation is (*Apology of Socrates* 23a3–5, *Charmides* 165b5–7): is not his Thracian story, with its offer of the application of a song to make one moderate, serious at least to this extent? It becomes of the utmost importance then to associate with Socrates, for the purpose of acquiring moderation or at least learning what it is, for as long as Socrates considers it to be necessary. And this is, in fact, the gist of Charmides' response, which is strengthened by an oath. (Cf. 158c7–d6.)

Critias then seconded Charmides' intention: he will take it as a sign that Charmides is moderate if he submits to Socrates' singing and does not leave Socrates for even a little. Charmides in turn promised to obey his guardian: he will begin his association with Socrates from this very day (cf. *Alcibiades I* 135d9–10, e4–5). But Socrates did not, as he had when Alcibiades had expressed a similar intention, express the wish that the intention in question would be carried out to its conclusion. This did not now deter Charmides, as it might have earlier.[63] The combination Critias-Charmides, which foreshadowed their association in the rule of

______

63. Cf. 156a4, 158d1–4 and 162b9–11.

the thirty tyrants, threatened to force Socrates somehow to continue in (as Critias had forced him to adopt) his Thracian role, beyond what he would otherwise have wished, beyond perhaps what he was capable of. But it is not clear whether what was threatened came to pass. In the *Theages*, Socrates reports that he once warned Charmides on the authority of the *daimonion*, not to undertake a course of training (which involved stripping) for a certain race. Charmides disobeyed that advice, apparently to his sorrow; but there is no indication that Socrates was involved in that training. Charmides is mentioned also in the *Symposium*, by Alcibiades in his speech about Socrates. According to Alcibiades, Charmides too was treated hubristically by Socrates—that is, deceived into thinking that Socrates was in love with him, while Socrates rather made himself the beloved. Charmides is the first of the two individuals mentioned by name in that connection. Charmides appears again in the *Protagoras* (where Alcibiades and Critias also appear); he is mentioned as being in the train of Protagoras; he is not with Critias.[64] Plato is much more reticent than Xenophon as to Socrates' association with Charmides, or he makes less of it.[65]

However that may be, Socrates responded here to the playful threat of force by saying that if Charmides—whose attractions he has just successfully withstood—attempts to do something using force, no human being will be able to withstand him. This graceful, if hubristic, allusion to Socrates' almost inhuman continence brings the *Charmides* to a fitting close.

---

64. *Theages* 128d8–129a1; *Symposium* 222a7–b4; *Protagoras* 314e3–315a2 and 316a3–5.

65. Xenophon, *Memorabilia* III 6.1, III 7 (cf. *Hellenika* II 4.19) and *Symposium* 1.3, 2.15–19, 3.1–2, 3.9, 4.8, 4.27–28, 4.32, 8.2.

6

On the Original Meaning
of Political Philosophy

An Interpretation of Plato's *Lovers*

The question posed by my title is a historical question, and therefore my hope is to uncover Plato's view. But the answer to a historical question may be of more than historical interest. The place of political philosophy within the discipline of political science has for some time been a matter of uncertainty or dispute. Political philosophy as we know it is concerned with "values," claiming to be able to provide rational guidance as to what is good and just in politics. Since Max Weber, however (see his essay "Science as a Vocation"), many political scientists have held that reason, or science, cannot, by itself, supply such guidance and that, insofar as political philosophy seeks to supply guidance as to what is good and just, it is not as rational or scientific as it claims. Others within the profession, students of political philosophy especially, refuse to accept this conclusion. Moved by awareness of the need for "normative" political guidance as well as by respect for science as the only unquestioned authority of our age, they insist that science must and can supply this guidance in the form of a political philosophy that is at once normative and scientific. But they have been unable to establish to general satisfaction either that such a political philosophy already exists (whether in the work of contemporary students or past masters) or that it is possible for it to be developed in the future. As a result, the study of political philosophy within our discipline remains something of an embarrassment as well as an anomaly: it reminds us of the shortcomings of a value-free political science without, apparently, being able to show how they might be remedied.

The premise of the study that follows is that the uncertainty as to the place and worth of political philosophy must be understood in the light of a crucial change in its character that emerged in the course of its history. If we are to understand this change and its significance, we must first see what political philosophy was prior to it or originally; we must return to the origin of political philosophy in the thought of Socrates. I argue that this origin is most clearly and directly presented in the *Lovers*, a dialogue that has been generally neglected or despised—so much so that doubts have been raised as to whether it is a genuinely Platonic work. Since these doubts appear to be based on a judgment as to the merits of the dialogue rather than on any hard external evidence (see, for example, the Introduction of Schleiermacher), a secondary aim of the study is to help lay them to rest.

The *Lovers* is one of only four dialogues narrated from beginning to end by Socrates, the others being the *Republic, Charmides*, and *Lysis*. This fact may tell us something as to the place of these dialogues within the Platonic corpus. When he was obliged to defend himself publicly against charges of impiety and corrupting the young, Socrates gave the Athenians an account of his way of life as a whole. However memorable that account is, its adequacy—that is, its truthfulness and completeness (*Apology of Socrates* 17b8)—may have been adversely affected by the circumstances in which Socrates was forced to present it: his audience was of questionable friendliness and openness, and he was allowed to speak for only a legally prescribed period of time (*Ap. Soc.* 37a6–b2). At any rate, Socrates himself suggested that his account had struck some of his hearers—perhaps not the least discerning—as ironical (*Ap. Soc.* 38a1). The dialogues just mentioned, on the other hand, present occasions on which Socrates, without apparent compulsion, provides accounts of his life, or of significant episodes in it, to companions who are familiar with philosophy and friendly to it—to judge at least from hints supplied in two of the cases.[1] Thus the defects of circumstance that may have inhibited Socrates in his public defense are not present there or are not present in the same degree.[2]

---

1. The person or persons to whom the *Lovers* is narrated are familiar not only with Anaxagoras but also with Oinopides. The one to whom the *Charmides* is narrated is more familiar with Socrates' companion Chairephon than with Critias.

2. The *Phaedo* could not have been narrated by Socrates, but its audience (both that to which the dialogue is narrated and that present at the original conversation) would

In the *Lovers*, Socrates recounts to one or more people a conversation in which he successfully defended philosophizing against the assertion of a young athlete that it is frivolous or ridiculous, if not also shameful. Socrates had entered a grammar school full of those among the young considered to be most decent in appearance (and to come from noted fathers) and the lovers of these boys. Two of the boys were disputing—about what Socrates was not very able to hear. But as he tells whomever he is narrating the encounter to, he conjectured that it was about Anaxagoras or Oinopides, for the boys appeared to draw circles and to imitate certain slopes with their hands. The athlete was a lover of one of the two boys. By asking him what the boys had become so serious about—"surely some great and noble thing"—Socrates innocently or deliberately provoked the attack on philosophizing. In putting his question to the athlete, Socrates had, not so innocently, withheld from him the fact that he had already formed a conjecture as to what the dispute was about, as to the identity of that which he called "great and noble."

Socrates' defense of philosophizing took the form of a refutation of the athlete's rival in love, a culture vulture who regards himself as a philosopher. This "philosopher" asserted, in response to the athlete's attack, that philosophizing is noble, but he proved unable to back up his assertion. The encounter of Socrates with the two lovers took place in the presence of the two boys, who broke off their philosophical-astronomical dispute in order to listen to it; the boys as well as the others accepted the results of the argument directed by Socrates.

Most of Socrates' account is taken up by his narration of this argument. In the course of describing how the discussion began and how it came to take the form that it did, Socrates appears to allude to his famous turn in philosophy (from concentration on things or deeds to concentration on speeches: cf. *Phaedo* 99d4–100a7 with *Lovers* 132d4–5), and he calls attention to his notoriously erotic nature (133a; cf., e.g., *Protagoras*

---

qualify it for inclusion in this group; moreover, the *Phaedo* culminates in Socrates' narration, to the companions present, of most significant experiences of his youth (96a1–100a8). In the *Theaetetus*, one of those reported as present at the original conversation in the *Phaedo* reads, to a companion also reported as present there, a record of a conversation that he claims was narrated to him by Socrates. In the *Republic*, as in the narrative portions of the *Protagoras* and *Euthydemus*, Socrates recounts an experience that he has just had, and may have wished to fix in his memory by reliving it. The episodes recounted in the *Charmides*, *Lysis*, and *Lovers*, on the other hand, occurred at some unspecified time in the past. Cf. *Charmides* 153a1 with *Republic* 327a1, *Protagoras* 309d3–310a8, and *Euthydemus* 271a1, 272d4–e7.

309a). These facts, together with the inconclusive character of pre-Socratic natural philosophy (reflected, perhaps, in the boys' dispute), appear to form the background against which the argument of the *Lovers*, which is more narrowly the topic of this essay, must ultimately be understood. The argument itself went as follows.

The Argument

I. Socrates asked the "philosopher" whether it was his opinion that it is possible to know with regard to anything at all whether it is noble or shameful if one doesn't know to begin with what it is. When the "philosopher" said it was not, Socrates asked him whether he knew what philosophizing is. "Certainly." "What is it then?" According to Socrates' interpretation of the "philosopher's" response, which the "philosopher" accepts, philosophy is *polymathia* (the knowledge which consists in having learned, and thus knowing, many things).

In recounting this last exchange, Socrates as narrator indicates that he had some doubt as to the adequacy of such a view of philosophy. This alerts us to a shift that had just taken place or was about to take place in the course of the argument. Socrates' next questions, which appear designed, as we might have expected, to examine the nobility of philosophy as polymathia, were in fact designed to test the adequacy of this view of philosophy: to test it by seeing whether philosophy as polymathia would be noble. (What permitted or required this shift was the fact that the "philosopher," despite his agreement that one must know what a thing is before one can know whether or not it is noble, had greater confidence in the nobility of philosophy than in any particular view as to what it is. If he came to believe, then, that philosophy, according to his view, would not be noble, he would more readily modify or abandon his view than agree that philosophy itself is truly not noble.) More precisely, the view in question was to be tested by examining the goodness of philosophy as polymathia. But the question of goodness is linked to that of nobility in the following way. The noble things appear to us to be also good. If the nobility of something is believed to imply its goodness, we can ultimately accept as noble (or high or serious) only what can be established as good. The meaning to be given here to "goodness" will be clarified as the argument proceeds.

Socrates began by asking whether the "philosopher" held that philosophy is only noble or also good. "Also good, certainly." Did the "philosopher" see this in philosophy alone, or was he of the opinion that it is the case in other things too? For example, did he hold that love of athletics (*philogymnastia*) is not only noble but also good? When the "philosopher" agreed that he did, Socrates asked him whether he held, in athletics, that love of athletics is the performance of many exercises (*polyponia*). The "philosopher" was quite ready to see the situation in athletics as parallel to the one he had claimed to see in philosophizing. Socrates thereupon asked him whether the lovers of athletics desire anything other than what will make their bodily condition a good one. He replied that this is what they desire. "Do the many exercises then make one's bodily condition good?" How could this come about from few exercises? the "philosopher" responded.

At this point, Socrates appealed to the experience of the athlete (or, as he is called here, the lover of athletics) to establish the fact that human beings achieve good bodily condition not through many exercises, nor indeed through few, but through a "measured" amount. (Socrates' appeal is perhaps not as superfluous as it might appear to be. "Measured" [*metrios*] is indeed so flexible a term as to be applicable to any quantity that is beneficial, but for that very reason it might be applicable to a very large or even to the largest possible number of exercises as long as that number is beneficial. That is, a "measured" amount might not be different from many. That it is different—or indeed the same—could not perhaps be established without the assistance of the relevant experience.) The "philosopher" yielded the point to Socrates and the athlete. He agreed also that the case with food was the same, and beyond that he was forced by Socrates to agree that, with all other things having to do with the body, "measured" rather than great or small amounts are most beneficial. What then about the things having to do with the soul? Is it the measured things, or those without measure, that, when administered, are beneficial? Whether because a question phrased in this way admits of only one answer, or because he accepted the suggestion that Socrates' procedure conveys—that what holds true for the body holds true for the soul—the "philosopher" answered, "The measured things." He then agreed that one of the things administered to a soul is *mathēmata* (things learned or to be learned). It followed that, of these, too, a "measured" amount, and not many, is beneficial.

Philosophy, then—if, being noble, it must be good, indeed good for a soul—must be learning, or having learned and thus knowing, a "measured" amount of things. But what things? Without waiting for the amended view of philosophy to be stated or expressly agreed to, Socrates went on to ask a series of questions designed to uncover the expert to be consulted concerning mathēmata, as to the amounts and kinds that are "measured." "Whom would we justly ask which exercises and foods—with regard to the body—are measured?" The three interlocutors agreed that this was a doctor or trainer. "Whom concerning the sowing of seed—how much is a measured amount?" Here again they agreed (on the farmer). "Whom would we justly ask, concerning the planting and sowing of mathēmata in a soul, how many and which are measured?" Here, according to Socrates account, the interlocutors were all at a loss. Apparently, they didn't know of any such expert or expertise. It seems to be clear, then, if this was the case, that they didn't know what mathēmata are good for a soul or that any are good for a soul.

Nevertheless, Socrates was able to keep the conversation going by asking the others more directly which "we guess" to be the mathēmata the one philosophizing must learn, since these are neither all nor many. The "philosopher" replied to this question without characterizing his reply as a guess. In asking it, Socrates was asking which mathēmata they guessed to be "measured," beneficial to a soul. That is, a distinction was implicitly made here, or rather was confirmed, between a philosopher and the expert they had been seeking. A philosopher is taken to be something other, at any rate something more than the possessor of an expertise. He is closer to the lovers of athletics spoken of earlier than to a doctor or trainer. While a lover of athletics was indeed consulted regarding exercises, such lovers were said to desire only what will make their bodily condition a good one. What forms these lovers, we can say, is a desire to benefit from, rather than to exercise or even to possess, the expertise regarding exercises. Similarly, a philosopher, it was now implied, must learn the mathēmata that are "measured," must acquire the learning that benefits a soul.

The "philosopher's" reply, however, spoke of the mathēmata that would be noblest and fitting and referred to reputation (what they make one seem to be) rather than benefit to a soul (what they make one to be truly) as their goal and fruit. He didn't appear to think of benefit. But this would be simply true only if he now separated the noble things from the good things, only if he had dropped his insistence that the noble things be also good, good for us.

According to his reply, the mathēmata from which one would have most reputation for philosophy would be noblest and fitting, and one would have most reputation if one were reputed to be experienced in all of the arts,[3] or in as many as possible and especially in the noteworthy ones, through having learned the portions of those arts that are fitting for the free to learn—the portions that belong to the understanding rather than to manual work. Socrates forced the "philosopher" to reformulate his suggestion by raising a difficulty that would apply especially to the great or noteworthy arts that he had in mind: is it not impossible for the same person to learn in the indicated way two such arts, let alone many?[4] What he requires of the one philosophizing, the "philosopher" now said, is not precise knowledge of each of the arts, like the one who possesses the art, but rather what is to be expected of a free and educated man: superior ability to follow things said by a craftsman and to express a judgment himself, so as to be reputed most refined and most wise of those who happen to be present whenever there are words or deeds concerning the arts.

This answer still left open the possibility that the "philosopher" required of one who is philosophizing knowledge of a different and higher kind than that belonging to the arts: for example, knowledge deriving from reflection on the ends of the arts and their importance to us. (See Socrates' remark at 135d8 that he was still uncertain as to the "philosopher's" meaning.) Socrates' next inquiry, however, and the response it elicited made it clear that the "philosopher" did not have any such knowledge in mind. Philosophizing proved in his view to make those who engage or, rather, who have engaged in it something like pentathletes of the arts—inferior, concerning the arts, to those who excel in the relevant understanding but, as second-raters, superior to the others. But what Socrates saw as mediocrity or deficiency our "philosopher" saw as strength. It is the very failure of the philosopher to be a slave to any one matter or to have labored at anything to the point of precision that has made it possible for him, as opposed to the craftsmen, to have—to a "measured" degree—laid hold of all.

---

3. *Technai*, which, in the Greek usage, include such diverse "arts" as medicine, farming, piloting, shoemaking, and poetry.

4. Charles H. Fairbanks, in his valuable work on the *Lovers* ("Reason, Technique, and Morality in Plato's *Lovers*," a paper presented at the Annual Meeting of the American Political Science Association, San Francisco, August 28–31, 1975), has explained Socrates' stratagem here. Socrates took as his example a most difficult art, architecture, which is exercised almost entirely with the understanding. According to the "philosopher's" first formulation, the one who is philosophizing would be required to have learned all of this art together with many others. See Fairbanks, "Reason, Technique," pp. 23–25.

Our "philosopher's" view of the mathēmata required of a philosopher was thus clarified. They had recommended themselves to him, as we saw, for what he took to be their nobility. It remained to be seen whether he still required of noble mathēmata, as of noble things in general, that they also be good—indeed good for the souls of those who have learned them. (See Socrates' mention at 136b3–4 of his "being eager," after this last answer, to know "with certainty"[5] what the "philosopher" would say.) Socrates ascertained that the "philosopher" took it that those who are good are useful (useful to others: 136c4, c7–e2) and that those who are wicked are useless. Socrates then asked him whether he held that philosophic men are useful or not. In asking this question, Socrates was asking about the goodness of philosophers. For if the good in every case are useful, the useful may be good, while the useless are surely not. Our "philosopher" agreed that philosophers are useful and added that he held them to be most useful. We infer from this response that he still expected the noble mathēmata to benefit the philosopher, that he expected them indeed to benefit him in such a way as to make him good—and hence useful. But to infer is not yet to know "with certainty."

If our "philosopher" still required noble mathēmata to benefit the philosopher (and to benefit him in the manner or to the extent now indicated), Socrates should be able to impugn in his eyes the nobility of the mathēmata under discussion by showing that they do not make one who has learned them useful, as they would unfailingly do, according to our "philosopher," if they made him good. Socrates showed this by stressing the inferiority of the philosopher, as dabbler or second-rater in the arts, to the possessor of each of the arts. This inferiority is most striking where dependence on art is greatest, where one's life or the life of a friend or relative for whom one cares in a serious way is at stake. In such cases, our "philosopher" himself would choose to rely on a doctor or pilot, for example, rather than on a philosopher. It thus became clear that a philosopher is not useful whenever a craftsman—possessor of an art—is available. But given the general availability of craftsmen, this conclusion seems to mean, as our "philosopher" was forced to agree, that the philosopher is useless simply. And since the good have been agreed to be useful, what follows?

Having indicated the direction that an examination of our "philosopher" should take, Socrates broke off to summarize the argument to

---

5. On this translation of *saphos*, see Burnet's edition of the *Phaedo* (Oxford, 1959), notes at 57b1, 61d8, and 85c3. Cf. *Gorgias* 453b5–c1, 454b8–c5, and 489d1–3.

this point in a manner authorized by the anticipated but not supplied completion of the examination: "We agreed that philosophy is noble and that we ourselves are philosophers; that philosophers are good, the good are useful and the wicked useless; again, we agreed that philosophers are useless so long as there are craftsmen, but that there are always craftsmen. Have not these things been agreed upon?" The "summary," admittedly rough (*pōs* at 137a1), included points that had not been stated previously: that "we" are philosophers, that philosophers are good. By granting that he had agreed to these points, the "philosopher" now showed that, as far as he was concerned, these previously unstated points had always been understood. In suggesting that the goodness of philosophers had been taken to follow from the nobility of philosophy, and their usefulness from their goodness, the summary brings to light what the examination was expected to help confirm.

Socrates then stated the argument's conclusion as follows: "We were agreeing then, as it looks, according to your argument at least, that if philosophizing consists in their being knowledgeable about the arts in the way you say, they are wicked and useless so long as there are arts among human beings." Anticipating, however, the "philosopher's" reaction to such a conclusion concerning philosophizing or the mathēmata that constitute it, Socrates offered at once another interpretation of the outcome of the argument: philosophers may not be wicked and useless, because philosophizing may not consist in having become serious about the arts, in poking about, becoming involved in many matters (being a busybody), any more than it consists in having learned many things—but may rather consist in something else. From the latter part of the argument (the agreement that the good are useful and the emphasis on the usefulness of the arts), we might wonder whether philosophizing does not consist in having become serious enough about some one art to learn it well, whether it does not consist in being or becoming useful through the acquisition of such expertise. This possibility seems to be ruled out by an apparently casual remark that Socrates added here, without objection on the part of the "philosopher." He thought, he said, that seriousness about the arts was a matter of reproach and that those who have become serious about the arts are called "banausic." Indeed the reproach in question, if applied to dabblers in many arts, was no doubt applied still more strongly to the craftsmen or experts proper. It thus reminds us of the "philosopher's" earlier rejection of the precise knowledge belonging to craftsmen as inappropriate to a philosopher. In other words, despite the recognition that has been given in the meantime to the fact that the mathēmata with which craftsmen are concerned confer usefulness, these are still not held to be noble mathēmata. (If the implication is that they are not held to confer the benefit expected of noble mathēmata—that is, to make us good—then we have an indication that the usefulness of craftsmen, at any rate, is not held to be human goodness, whatever may be the case with any other sort of usefulness.)

The argument still remained, then, in the impasse it had reached when it became clear that Socrates' interlocutors, if not also Socrates himself, did not know what mathēmata are good for a soul, or whether any are good for a soul. The reason is in part the fact that a single set of assumptions has governed the argument throughout. The "argument" in fact has been nothing so much as the gradual, just-completed uncovering of these assumptions. What is noble is held to be also good—that is, is held to benefit us. Good human beings—that is, those who have been benefited in a fundamental way—are taken to be also useful (to others). But it is not clear that all useful human beings are held to be good: perhaps only those useful in a certain way are held to be (also) good; perhaps human goodness is held to be something more than usefulness. Philosophy is held to be noble and therefore also good—that is, it is believed to benefit us. And since it consists in mathēmata, which affect the soul, it is believed to benefit our souls, indeed to make us good. From the perspective determined by these assumptions or expectations, what philosophy or philosophizing is will be unknown as long as mathēmata that so profoundly benefit a soul are unknown.

II. In suggesting that philosophizing may consist in something other than what has already been proposed, Socrates now implied that *he* knew, or had an opinion about, what philosophizing is. He had withheld this suggestion, which had the effect of shifting the initiative in the argument entirely to him, not only until the "philosopher" had been chastised for presuming to know what philosophizing is, but also until the assumptions or expectations of the "philosopher" regarding philosophy had been brought to light. Socrates thus did his best to ensure that his own "proposal" would be greeted and later examined with these expectations in mind.

The elaboration of Socrates' proposal took place in two stages. First he called attention to the links among three kinds of knowledge for dealing with (punishing, improving, judging) animals of concern to human beings (horses, dogs, human beings)—identifying them, for each kind of animal, as a single art. The art or science applying to human beings he further identified with justice and moderation as well as with the science or art by which a city or household is managed correctly. Then Socrates suggested that, in part to avoid what is shameful, the philosopher must master this art. His argument went as follows.

Those—only those—who know how to improve beings of a certain kind ("make them better" or "best") know how to punish those beings (horses, dogs, or human beings) correctly. (The implication is that punishment is a necessary means to improvement and that improvement is the only correct end or purpose of punishment, that punishment for any other end is incorrect, not to say tyrannical or despotic. If punishment were not necessary to improvement, one might have knowledge of improvement without knowledge of correct punishment; if there were correct ends of punishment other than improvement, one might have knowledge of improvement without the whole knowledge of correct punishment.) And this twofold art of improvement and correct punishment and no other is that which judges (*gignōskein*) of the beings it is set over, which are good and which evil, or distinguishes (*diagignōskein*) the ones from the others—whether it is a question of one such being or many. (Such judging is more clearly necessary to an improving-punishing art than to any other.)

The science that correctly punishes the unrestrained and unlawful in the cities is the judicial science, also called justice. And the science by which they punish correctly is the one by which they judge which are the good human beings and which the evil, whether it is a question of one or of many. If, then, as is the case, judging (*gignōskein*) which are the good and evil human beings is necessary to human beings who are not to be ignorant of themselves, of whether they are good or evil; and if, as is also asserted to be the case, to know (*gignōskein*) oneself is to be moderate, since to be ignorant of oneself is to be immoderate, the writing in Delphi ("Know thyself") is apparently an exhortation to practice moderation and justice. Justice, the science by which we know how to punish correctly, is the same as moderation, the science by which we know how to judge (*diagignōskein*) both oneself and others. (Knowing whether one is good or evil, in other words, which requires the ability to judge others too in this respect, is not merely necessary to self-knowledge but is its core. Cf. *Charmides* 167a1–7.)

Moreover, cities are well managed whenever those doing injustice pay the penalty: the science we are considering is then a political one, too. And when one man manages a city correctly, he does so by the kingly and tyrannic art: these arts, too, then, are the same as those others. And the arts by which one man manages a household correctly are apparently the economic (household) and despotic (master) arts; since by justice and no other art he, too, manages the household well, we can conclude that this one art is at once kingly, tyrannic, political, despotic, economic, and justice and moderation.

Our "philosopher" had implied earlier that it would be shameful for the philosopher to be able neither to follow when a doctor says something concerning the sick nor to make a contribution of his own concerning the words or deeds of a doctor or any other of the craftsmen. Is it not shameful, then, for him to be able neither to follow nor to contribute when the speaker (or doer) in question is a judge or king or one of the others just mentioned? Must the philosopher here be a pentathlete and second-rater, useless as long as one of those is available? Or rather is it for him, first, not to turn his own household over to another but, sitting in judgment himself, to punish correctly, if his household is to be well managed? Next, if his friends turn over to him matters for arbitration, or the city orders him to decide or give judgment on something, is it shameful to come to light as a second or third-rater in these matters rather than to lead?

When our "philosopher" had conceded these points, Socrates drew the conclusion that philosophizing is far from being polymathia or preoccupation with the arts. This statement reduced our "philosopher," who was ashamed at what he had said earlier, to silence, while the athlete declared it was so, and the others (that is, the boys) praised what had been said.

Discussion

The search for the mathēmata that constitute philosophy was thus brought to an apparently successful end. Socrates had pointed in a direction in which, he suggested, lie mathēmata that the philosopher must master, and his words had met with approval—especially on the part of the boys, for there is no reason to suppose that "what had been said" refers to Socrates' concluding statement alone. But several clouds darken this picture, among them the concluding statement itself. Why did Socrates choose to leave his listeners and interlocutors with a merely negative statement? Moreover, what basis do we have for supposing that the mathēmata to which he had pointed, even if they truly exist, are noble in the sense indicated in the first (or destructive) part of the argument, that they fill the great bill of expectations regarding philosophy that was uncovered there with such care? Surely the fact that the mastery of such mathēmata would make the philosopher useful can by now be dismissed in advance as conclusive evidence of their being noble. Nor is the fact that they are not open to the other objections advanced against our "philosopher's" suggestions positive evidence of their adequacy. Indeed, lacking as we do any explicit Socratic assertion to this effect, what basis do we have for supposing that Socrates himself, the philosopher of ignorance (*Ap. Soc.* 21d4), regarded them as noble in the indicated sense?

It will be argued on the other side, I suspect, that, as I have admitted and even stressed, the most important audience of Socrates on the spot, those who have shown by deed their potential for philosophy, that is, the boys (consider 135a1–5), must have understood him to be recommending these mathēmata as noble. To admit the possibility of what I have tentatively suggested is, then, to admit the possibility that Socrates left the boys with what he regarded as a false impression. This objection can be regarded as conclusive only as long as one regards it as certain that Socrates had no reason for leaving the boys, even temporarily, with a false impression. For purposes of indicating what such a reason might be, I will assume that what I have tentatively suggested is true: that Socrates did not regard the political mathēmata as noble, that indeed, as he once in the dialogue went so far as to indicate, he didn't know of any mathēmata that are noble in the required sense.

It must be recalled that, at the outset of the dialogue, the boys were seriously engaged in an astronomical-philosophical dispute. Socrates conjectured, at any rate, that their quarrel concerned Anaxagoras or Oinopides—that is, he linked their concerns to those of pre-Socratic, nonpolitical philosophy (see also 132b9). Socrates seemed to have conjectured as well, on the basis of their manifest seriousness or earnestness, that they regarded the object of their concern as noble. It is not very significant for our purposes that our "philosopher" acknowledged openly his opinion that philosophizing is noble; it is much more significant that Socrates' questioning of the "philosopher" on this point silenced the boys and drew their attention to the Socratic discussion. Their attitude toward philosophizing may not have been very different from that of the young Socrates himself, in whose opinion the wisdom called "inquiry into nature"—to know the causes of each thing—was a "splendid" thing (*Phaedo* 96a5–10, cf. *Lysis* 215e1–216a2). That is, the seriousness of the boys is due to the fact that they regard the object of their concern, the wisdom or learning they strive for, as serious or high or noble. But the question "What is noble?" was not, as far as we can tell, a part of their inquiries.

In these circumstances, Socrates' examination of our "philosopher" must have begun to awaken in the boys this question, or the question of what is implied in our holding something to be noble. Moreover, it must have aroused in them some doubt as to the adequacy of their own activity in terms of the standard being brought to light: is astronomy, or philosophy as they have been pursuing it, good for the soul? They were thus prepared to greet Socrates' proposal toward the end with the enthusiasm with which they apparently did greet it. If their praise is sincere, they are about to turn from astronomy or natural philosophy to political philosophy. Socrates will have brought about in them the very change in philosophic orientation that he apparently underwent himself. But this statement is not quite correct. The enterprise that must have been embraced by Socrates in full awareness of its character and possible limits will be embarked on by the boys as the result of a false impression as to its worth for which Socrates is in some sense responsible.

We are back to our original dilemma. The boys will have changed the object of their studies but not their expectations from them. But this very fact may now begin to suggest a solution. For what the boys expected earlier—without being aware of it—from their natural studies, may, to repeat, not differ greatly from what was always expected from philosophizing as long as philosophizing was regarded as a way of life. The choice to philosophize, to give one's life to philosophizing, is after all a human choice, made for human reasons, on the basis of some human concerns—among which the concern to know is not likely to have played the sole, perhaps not even the leading, part. The thought that philosophy or wisdom or the knowledge of the causes of all things is noble or high or serious may always have had great weight in this choice. (Consider, regarding the objects of philosophy, *Laws* 889e6 and a4–5; cf. Aristotle, *N. Ethics* 1141a18–22 and 34–b3.) But if this is the case, the unique significance of political philosophy is immediately apparent. What is, at the outset at least, the unexamined assumption prompting philosophizing of every sort becomes a necessary object of critical examination in philosophizing of only one sort, political philosophy. This, at least, is the suggestion of Plato's *Lovers*, where the nobility of anything is first shown to imply its goodness—that it makes us good—and where political science is then equated with knowledge of what makes us good. By putting the boys on the path to political philosophy Socrates was putting them, then, on the path to self-knowledge.[6] (Among other things, the attempt to acquire knowledge of what makes us good will require us to consider whether the punishing done "in the cities" accomplishes this goal. The goodness of horses and dogs is clear because we understand by that goodness their usefulness to us. Clear too, then, is the role of punishment in making them "good," that is, in molding them in accordance with our needs or desires. But we saw that, by the goodness of human beings, we may mean more than our usefulness to one another. We must wonder, then, whether the standards imposed by the punishing done "in the cities" are ultimately different from usefulness or whether the art of improvement is there, as is proper, setting the standards of good and evil for the punishing art to follow or vice versa.)[7]

If Socrates put the boys on the path to self-knowledge, he must have regarded self-knowledge as good. He was, then, not as unaware of mathēmata that are good for a soul, not as innocent of expertise in that respect, as he occasionally suggested and I supposed. Only two "virtues" are mentioned in the *Lovers* by name: justice and moderation. Since justice, the art of punishing correctly, has to do principally with the improvement of others and is, at any rate, only what *brings* a soul into good condition, I surmise that moderation, that is, self-knowledge, is this good condition itself. Moreover, if human goodness is or presupposes self-knowledge, we can understand why punishment is necessary to improvement: becoming aware of what one thought one knew but did not know cannot be so free from pain as to make it unreasonable to speak of it as punishment.

But in what sense is self-knowledge the good condition of a soul? Does it render one perfect and free from needs or rather good *for* something? (This question is justified by the fact that self-knowledge was said here

---

6. That Socrates should make a proposal with one thing in mind while giving part of his audience the impression that he has something else in mind, is wholly consistent with the definition of irony suggested by his remark at 133d8: saying two things at the same time with a view to the differences among one's addresses. Cf. Fairbanks, "Reason, Technique," p. 11. In other words, Socratic irony is not totally absent from the *Lovers*.

7. Once "the cities" have been mentioned by Socrates, he ceases to refer by name to the improving art. Note also the improper conversion—the wicked are useless, therefore the useless are wicked—at 136b7–8 and e3 and 137a10–b1, which may have the function of calling our attention to a kindred and more important improper conversion. This difficulty may also lie behind the association of the political art with tyranny and despotism. Note the coordination of justice and despotism at 138c7–10 (the items that advance a place in the second list).

to be moderation, i.e., a virtue, only on the basis of a false conversion.) In the exchange on experts, it was clear that a doctor or trainer is to be consulted, as to exercise and foods, for the sake of the body and its good condition. But it was unclear whether the farmer is to be consulted, as to the sowing of seed, for the sake of the crop or for the sake of the land and its good condition, or for both (cf. Xenophon, *Oeconomicus* 17.1–11). What, then, about the planting of mathēmata or seeds of mathēmata in a soul—in particular the political mathēmata whose seeds Socrates planted in the boys toward the end? In what sense will they, or the self-knowledge to which they may lead, make the boys better?

It is unlikely that a single dialogue, especially one as short as the *Lovers*, will supply a definitive answer to such a question. Each dialogue presents only a part of Plato's view and must eventually be put together with all the others, beginning with those most closely associated with it in one way or another. If we are to confine ourselves here then to what can be established on the basis of the *Lovers* alone, we must rest satisfied with certain indications of what the answer might be. While mentions of "philosophizing," "philosophy," and "philosopher(s)" abound in the dialogue, as we would expect, given its theme, Socrates and our "philosopher" use these terms in somewhat different ways. Socrates speaks first of "philosophizing" (132c2), the "philosopher" of "philosophy" (132c7). The "philosopher" speaks of what must be learned by "the one who is going to philosophize" (133c7–8) and again of what must be known, though not with precision, by "the one who is philosophizing" (135c8–d7 and also 135b5; cf. 136a6–b2, the three uses of the perfect tense). Socrates, when not absolutely prevented by the need to present the "philosopher's" view, speaks of what "the one who is philosophizing" must learn (135a8–9) or of what philosophizing does for those who are engaging in it (135e6–7; cf. 136a3 and 137a9–b6). Socrates appears to understand by "philosophy" (or "philosophizing") a process of learning, while our "philosopher" takes it to be possession of a body of knowledge. (Consider also Socrates' initial approval and subsequent rejection of the "philosopher's" first definition, at 133c4–11.) Once we have observed this difference in usage, we are likely to be surprised by Socrates' apparent insistence toward the end of the dialogue that the political mathēmata must be mastered by the philosopher. But the difficulty disappears once we remember that the political mathēmata are never identified as philosophy. If we are cautious and do not go beyond what Socrates suggests, we can only take them, or rather "political philosophy," to be a needed preliminary to philosophizing. This is the most important meaning of the purely negative ending of the dialogue. Every explicit definition of philosophizing suggested is rejected. The only definition that has not been rejected, that remains, is the one supplied by the boys at the beginning by their deed.[8] We can expect, then, that there will be a vindication, within the Platonic *corpus*, of astronomy and its kindred sciences. This expectation is borne out by the *Laws* (especially 966d6–968a1 and 888a7–d2). Socrates' advice in the *Lovers* to two unnamed boys to turn from astronomy to political science is answered there by a demonstration of the importance of astronomy given to two old citizens by an unnamed Athenian.

The foregoing suggestions admittedly leave many questions unanswered. For example, in what context, at what stage of reflections, does the return to "astronomy" first take place? Is political philosophy only preliminary to philosophizing proper, or is this its primary or most important, rather than its sole, function? But, to repeat, these questions may not be answerable within the limits of a consideration of the *Lovers*. Even the question posed by the title considered in the light of Socrates' description of the opening scene of the dialogue—was Socrates himself one of the "lovers," or what is the connection between philosophizing and love?—may be posed but not answered by the dialogue. And this question in turn may be linked to that of the *way* in which political philosophy or self-knowledge is a necessary preliminary to philosophizing, the question of its bearing on the capacity to philosophize.

There is a parallel in the *Charmides* (155b9–156d3) to the scene at the beginning of the *Lovers* (133a), and the *Charmides* seems to be more intensely and narrowly concerned with its importance and meaning. In addition, with regard to all these questions, we should never forget the suggestion conveyed by Socrates' question to the athlete regarding exercise: to answer some questions we must first acquire the relevant experience.

Conclusion

As we can see with the help of the *Lovers*, political philosophy emerged in a situation that was in many significant respects, though not in all, the

---

8. Cf. Fairbanks, "Reason, Technique," p. 9. On the investigation of political or human affairs as a necessary preliminary to the investigation of heavenly or divine things, cf. Xenophon, *Memorabilia* I 1.11–12. This is a part of the passage in which Xenophon presents Socrates' critique of his philosophic predecessors.

opposite of ours. Philosophy or science, far from being the only universally respected authority, was suspect in the eyes of many citizens of ordinary decency (represented in the *Lovers* by the athlete), who would not think of looking to it for guidance as to what is good and just even if they felt the need for such guidance. What evidence or authority the political and moral values of the time had did not stem from their being put forward or confirmed by any allegedly scientific or rational teaching. Science had not yet had a widespread impact on ordinary moral-political life; rather, the values respected by ordinary citizens were likely and even bound to exercise on scientists—on those citizens who undertook to engage in philosophy or science—an influence that had not yet learned to disguise itself in professions of scientific objectivity or neutrality. In that situation, it was somewhat more obvious than it is now that, if philosophy or science is to have clarity about itself, its first task is to come to grips with its own motivations.

According to the *Lovers*, Socrates turned to political philosophy to meet this challenge. That is, the only "value" that political philosophy originally intended to put on a rational basis, or to prove, was the value of philosophy or science as a way of life. Only in this respect was it originally concerned to establish a rational set of values. It is true that, as the *Lovers* also shows, political philosophy seemed from the beginning, inevitably, to promise more—to promise to provide general guidance for political life. Nor could it count on never being asked, or never needing, to deliver on the broader promise it apparently held forth. But it is not perfectly clear that Socrates considered political philosophy, as he originated it, to be capable of providing such guidance: it is at least conceivable that the studies to which he directed the boys in the *Lovers*, which he himself must have undertaken previously, achieve their primary goal without ever equipping one to accomplish this additional task. (Cf. *Laches* 186b8–c5.) More precisely, it is not clear that Socrates regarded the truths discovered by political philosophy as *directly* relevant to the guidance of political life. And indeed, the first philosopher in the Socratic tradition who seriously attempted the broader task found it necessary to borrow certain fundamental assumptions from decent political life that, for the purpose at hand, were simply accepted as the starting points of discussion (Aristotle, *Ethics* 1095a30–b8 and 1098a33–b4). Only with their help—in respectfully clarifying, modifying, and applying these, the very assumptions whose questioning and challenging had been necessary to its primary task—was Socratic political philosophy able to fulfill its secondary but politically most important task, which, accepted by all subsequent political philosophy, eventually came to be regarded as the primary task. In the process, there took place the crucial change in the way the task was approached to which I referred at the beginning of this chapter. It came to be believed that scientific truth (e.g., the truth uncovered by investigation of the state of nature) is directly relevant, without such mediation as Aristotle had relied on, to the guidance of political life. As a result, the claim to scientific validity was raised much more loudly or boldly on behalf of certain modern doctrines than it had been by Aristotle. (Cf., e.g., the conclusion of the second part of Hobbes' *Leviathan* with *Ethics* 1094b11–27 and 1098a26–b8.) And this claim in turn was forcefully rejected by Weber, who thus helped to bring about or call attention to our present predicament.

If the foregoing analysis is correct, it may be possible, by reflecting again on the reasons for Aristotle's procedure and for his caution, to see more clearly both the basis of the difficulty that concerned Max Weber and the solution to it. But to do so, it will be necessary first to come to grips, as I have tried to begin to do, with political philosophy as Aristotle himself first knew it, as it was bequeathed to him by Socrates and Plato, with the original meaning of political philosophy.

Part III

Writings on Strauss

7

Strauss on Xenophon's Socrates

*Xenophon's Socratic Discourse: An Interpretation of the
Oeconomicus. By Leo Strauss.
(Ithaca: Cornell University Press, 1970).*

The following study of Professor Leo Strauss's writings on Xenophon's presentation of Socrates will be devoted chiefly to a discussion of his interpretation of the *Oeconomicus*. A word is therefore in order about this choice and about the form the discussion will take.

In *On Tyranny*, his study of Xenophon's *Hiero*, Strauss wrote, "The charm produced by Xenophon's unobtrusive art is destroyed, at least for a moment, if that art is made obtrusive by the interpretation. . . . One can only hope that the time will again come when Xenophon's art will be understood by a generation which, properly trained in their youth, will no longer need cumbersome introductions like the present study" (27, revised edition). Strauss did not say that in the hoped for time introductions as such would no longer be needed: after all, training is not everything. The words we have quoted first appeared in 1948. Twenty-two years later, Strauss published his *Xenophon's Socratic Discourse: An Interpretation of the Oeconomicus* and, two years after that, *Xenophon's Socrates* (Ithaca: Cornell University Press), the work with which, "I complete my interpretation of Xenophon's Socratic writings" (Preface). Perhaps these two books, the last books which Strauss published in his lifetime, are his gift to the generation for whose training he is in some sense responsible.

Certainly they present unusual difficulties to the reader, trained or untrained. The manner in which they are written may be illustrated by reference to a one-sentence paragraph occurring in *Xenophon's Socrates*, in the course of the discussion of Xenophon's *Symposium*: "Xenophon claims to have been present at the banquet" (144). In the last sentence of the preceding paragraph, Strauss had asserted that the *Symposium* is "devoted not merely to Socrates' playful deeds but simply to his deeds: his deed, as distinguished from his speech and his thought, is nothing but playful." Why did Strauss choose to place, right after this sentence, the one-sentence paragraph which concerns us rather than to convey elsewhere the information it contains, as he easily could have done? As it turns out, the connection is explained in his article "Xenophon's *Anabasis*" (*Interpretation*, Volume 4, Number 3, 117–47), which may have been intended as a sort of appendix to the two books on Xenophon's presentation of Socrates. There Strauss says, referring to the very page of *Xenophon's Socrates* that we have been considering, "Surely, Xenophon (does not equal Plato) presents himself in his difference from Socrates" (140; cf. 124: "Xenophon was a man of action: he did the political things in the common sense of the term, whereas Socrates did not. . . ."). In other words, Xenophon's presence at the banquet which is described in the *Symposium* is meant as a silent suggestion of an alternative to the Socrates who is celebrated there. Now, not to mention the many difficulties which are not thus explained, Strauss could not have known, when he wrote *Xenophon's Socrates*, that he would live to write "Xenophon's *Anabasis*." It is true that the explanation supplied in the *Anabasis* article is confirmed by hints occurring in *Xenophon's Socrates*, hints which may begin on the very page in question. But, for the moment at least, the enigmatic sentence-paragraph is allowed to stand. From this, we draw the following conclusion regarding Strauss's manner of writing in the two books on Xenophon's presentation of Socrates: if point A, considered together with point B, yields conclusion C, Strauss does not always regard it as necessary or appropriate for him to state conclusion C, or even to acknowledge that points A and B are related; he leaves it in these cases at mentioning points A and B in the same vicinity and relies on the reader to do the rest.

This places of course a very great burden on Strauss's reader or interpreter and makes it unlikely that an interpretation will carry conviction or be of much use unless it makes clear the tracks, so to speak, that it has followed. Now it would be impossible, within the limits of the present review, to do this for both of the books before us; and, given the necessity to choose one book to concentrate on, it is easy to show that the first, that on the *Oeconomicus*, is the more fundamental one. Not only is this acknowledged in the preface to the second book; but the second book (as well as the article on the *Anabasis*) is preoccupied with the theme of the defense of Socrates before the city and the characteristics or limitations of Socrates which rendered that defense so difficult, and this theme is a secondary one from the point of view of the *Oeconomicus* itself (*Xenophon's Socratic Discourse* 176–77).[1]

We may have given the impression that the interpretation of Strauss's work is primarily a technical affair. Technical matters of interpretation can never be more than subordinate to the task of uncovering the question or questions which moved Strauss and by which he found his way back to a forgotten world and showed it to be still fit for habitation. It is, of course, more than likely that the question has been revealed in the great body of Strauss's prior writings on ancient, medieval and modern political philosophy. But, even if his chief concern has been sufficiently revealed in that work, have we grasped it? Besides, may not the last two books on Xenophon, as constituting Strauss's final statement on Socrates[2] and to that extent the culmination of his life's work, have been shaped by his guiding question or concern more fully and deeply than his earlier work? This would be an additional reason for that apparent heightening of his habitual reticence which makes these books so difficult.

On the Introduction

In his Introduction to *Xenophon's Socratic Discourse*, Strauss says that the "Great Tradition of Political Philosophy was originated by Socrates" (83); he explains why Xenophon ought to be regarded as a preeminent source for "our precise knowledge of Socrates' thought" (83–84); and he discusses the different purposes or themes of Xenophon's writings on Socrates (84–86). He does not ask why we should be concerned with political philosophy nor why, given that concern, we should be concerned with its origin. As for the first question, Strauss may indicate the answer he expects his reader to have supplied already, and to be moved

---

1. The question of the difference between Xenophon and Socrates belongs to the treatment of this theme.

2. In this respect, the last two books on Xenophon were prepared by *Socrates and Aristophanes* (New York: Basic Books, 1966). Funds made available to Boston College by the Mellon Foundation have enabled me to confirm this by a study of that work and have assisted me in the present study.

by, in a remark regarding Socrates' alleged total disregard of "the whole of nature . . . in order to devote himself entirely to the study of ethical things": "His reason seems to have been that while man is not necessarily in need of knowledge of the nature of all things, he must of necessity be concerned with how he should live individually and collectively" (83). Now, Strauss himself does not vouch for the truth of this suggestion as to why Socrates' investigations took the direction they are said to have taken, any more than he indicates whether he is himself satisfied with the accuracy of the report of that direction which he conveys. In other words, we cannot assume that Strauss is satisfied that the true character and purpose of the Socratic concern with ethical-political matters has been brought out here. If he is not, this would be an early indication of the gulf which he expects to exist at the outset (though he does not call attention to it—cf. 94) between himself and his reader.

Given that we are concerned, for the reason indicated, with political philosophy, why should we be concerned with its origin and with Socrates? Readers of Strauss's earlier writings—*Natural Right and History*, in particular—might find that the reason has to do with, or should have to do with, the crisis of political philosophy brought on by those views (positivism and historicism) still powerful in our time which question the existence of natural right or of a rational, objective answer to the question "how one should live individually and collectively." However, Strauss makes no reference to that crisis now. The reader he is primarily concerned with here may, rightly or wrongly, not be so troubled by those views as to fear that it is futile to search for an answer to the question of how one should live. Such a reader would look to Socrates, then, simply as one who may have found that answer, the answer still valid today because it is valid for human beings as such. Now, it is just such a reader who is most likely to be troubled by a suggestion which emerges from Strauss's apparently low-key discussion of the different purposes or themes of the Socratic writings. (Hence Strauss's immediate, if half-hearted, effort to downplay the significance of that suggestion.) The *Memorabilia*, according to Strauss's argument, is devoted "as a whole . . . to proving Socrates' justice" (85). But this may well mean, he continues, "that the other three Socratic writings are not devoted to Socrates' justice" but are devoted "to Socrates even if he transcends justice" (86). The concern to know how one "should live individually and collectively," the concern which animates the reader's interest in Socrates, is difficult—to say the least—to distinguish from the concern for justice: how else should we live, individually and collectively, than justly? What can it mean then that Socrates, however just he may be, "transcends justice"?

ON THE TITLE AND THE OPENING

The reader has seen that, in Strauss's view, the *Oeconomicus* is "Xenophon's Socratic *logos* or discourse par excellence" (86). Now Strauss asserts that, "The *Oeconomicus* teaches the art of the manager of the household (*oikonomos*)" (87). Why should Xenophon devote his Socratic discourse par excellence to "Socrates' teaching the art of managing the household"? To this question, which Strauss raises himself, he claims to have given a "provisional answer" (89). According to this answer, the reason must be traced to the high rank Socrates accorded to the art of household management (it hardly differs from "the political or royal art" and "is not inferior to the art of generalship" (87) but perhaps even more to Xenophon's wish to indicate that Socrates preferred teaching this peaceful art to teaching the warlike art of generalship, which he could also have taught. This is in accord with Xenophon's downplaying of Socrates' military exploits and with his tacit denial that Socrates possessed the virtue of manliness (88–89). If, in Xenophon's presentation, Socrates transcends justice, it is not because he is manly as well as just.

While the "provisional answer" may explain why Socrates preferred teaching household management to generalship, it fails to explain why he taught this or any art at all. One might easily find that the answer to this question is conveyed by Strauss's treatment of the opening of the work. On the basis partly of a look at related portions of the *Memorabilia*, Strauss urges us to "keep in mind the question whether there is a connection between the themes 'management of the household' and 'friendship.'" (91) Among other things, it turns out that Kritoboulos, to whom Socrates teaches the art of household management in the *Oeconomicus*, was the son of Socrates' friend Kriton. Socrates' teaching of that art here could well be an act of friendship (cf. 101). Moreover, this would supply as well the solution to our earlier and graver difficulty, for an act of friendship would as such "transcend justice" by going beyond anything Socrates may have owed to Kritoboulos or his father. And Strauss refers in this context to "the profound difference between the *Memorabilia*, the work devoted to Socrates' justice" and the *Oeconomicus* (90), a difference which, as we recall from Strauss's earlier remark, implied according to him that Socrates "transcends justice." But if it is simply in the direction of friendship that

Socrates "transcends justice," why would Xenophon have been anxious, as Strauss also emphasizes here, to "conceal" the profound difference between the two works (and therewith what this difference implies)?

Whatever may be the case, then, with this explanation of why Socrates teaches an art, the fundamental difficulty of understanding the manner in which he "transcends justice" remains unsolved. This may be connected with the fact that Strauss goes out of his way at this point to show that Xenophon was aware of Aristophanes' treatment of Socrates in the *Clouds*: that treatment too was based on the premise (see the debate between the Just Speech and the Unjust Speech) that Socrates "transcends justice."

ON CHAPTER ONE

Toward the beginning of his discussion of Chapter I, Strauss raises the question, as one still unanswered, "why Xenophon chose Kritoboulos as the interlocutor of Socrates in *the* Socratic discourse" (92). Kritoboulos's being the son of a friend is not then a sufficient answer to this question. Perhaps it is not in any simple way the answer to the related question of why Socrates would teach or attempt to teach him. This suspicion is confirmed by the fact that it is Socrates, as Strauss emphasizes, who leads the discussion of Chapter I toward the conclusion "that for a man who knows how to use his friends for his benefit, the friends are money . . ." (95). It seems that we were correct in resisting the temptation to conclude that it is in the direction of friendship that Socrates allegedly transcends justice. But how then does he "transcend justice" and how is the suggestion that "friends are money" intelligible as a Socratic suggestion, as a thought belonging to or compatible with the Socratic life?

It surely cannot mean that excessive concern with wealth is a characteristic of the philosophic life: Kritoboulos, not Socrates, suggests that the aim of household management should be increase of wealth (93); "according to Socrates, the wise man needs very little for himself" (97), a view to which Socrates' whole life bears witness. Its meaning must be indicated, rather, by the reflection (on the relation between knowledge and possession) of which it is a part, a reflection on the basis of which Strauss suggests that Socrates transcended justice in the sense of legality. In particular, Socrates disregarded in principle, if not in practice, the legal definition of property, or the distinction between mine and thine as that is established by law: to this extent, he "looked at things from the point of view of the good as distinguished from that of justice" (96–97).

The reflection we are concerned with began with the observation that one cannot learn how to manage well one's own household without learning at the same time how to manage well that of one's neighbor. The knowledge or art of managing the household is "transferable to what is not one's own" (93) or is indifferent to the distinction between mine and thine. To understand Socrates' indifference to that distinction however this observation must be supplemented by a line of reasoning based on the further observation that we mean by possession or property something good. This means that only those of our possessions which are good or useful to us really belong to us. Furthermore, it is especially knowledge which makes things useful. This would seem to mean that only a knower can truly possess anything. For example, if there are things legally mine which I do not know how to use, they are not truly mine; they may even be the property of another, one who knows how to use them and who would, therefore, have a perfect right to make whatever use he might choose of those things, which are, after all, his property. But what use should he make of them? That is, this line of reasoning is still insufficient or incomplete because it fails to indicate for whose benefit the knower should use "his" property. But in fact this is already settled once one recognizes the necessity of looking at things "from the point of view of the good as distinguished from that of justice." Lest there be any doubt on this point, Strauss makes it clear that the thought that a wise man would "make use of his property, i.e., of all things, by distributing it properly according to the needs or merits of his fellow men" is unacceptable—unacceptable because the choice of such a troublesome and even miserable life would, as such, be an unwise choice (97). It is only for this reason (to avoid unnecessary trouble and misery), Strauss gives us to understand (and because he needs for himself not indeed nothing, but very little) that the wise man or philosopher is a respecter of law and property as ordinarily understood.

It is likely to be some time before these thoughts—which Strauss arrives at "by thinking through Socrates' argument with Kritoboulos" (97) and which he all but "fully states" though Socrates had left matters at merely suggesting them (96)—sink in, in their deep and troubling import. In the meantime, we cannot help being struck by the fact that Strauss, who expresses only a prudential reservation regarding Socrates' "silence" on justice or legality (96–97), appears to regard Socrates' related "silence" on piety as detracting from the truthfulness of the account of household management which is given in Chapter I. Or rather, his serious reservation as to the "abstraction . . . from justice or legality" seems to be only that it leads to the silence on piety. Piety is "an indispensable ingredient of the management of the household" (99), as Socrates later grants to Kritoboulos, insofar as success in that enterprise depends on the gods. Socrates' silence on piety in Chapter I is manifested in his appearing "too eager to maintain by hook or by crook that possession of a household, knowledge of how to increase it, and willingness to work hard and shrewdly to this effect are the complete conditions for the increase of one's household" (98).[3] Strauss does not explain why Socrates temporarily adopts this untenable position, as he easily could have explained it, by referring here to Socrates' need in the circumstances to leave the lazy Kritoboulos no excuse for failing to get down to learning how to manage his own affairs (cf. 100–02). He explains the silence on piety "provisionally . . . as a consequence of the abstraction . . . from justice or legality, for piety depends on law" (99). What makes it necessary to take piety seriously, Strauss seems to suggest, is the weakness of our knowledge (which only a dogmatic faith in the omnipotence or completeness, actual or potential, of our knowledge can blind us to)[4]; and what makes it possible for us to be pious is our respect for justice or law, which leads to and sanctions worship. But where does this leave us if the law itself, in accord with Strauss's earlier suggestion (never, explicitly at least, withdrawn), proves to be less than completely respectable? The importance of this issue for Strauss may be confirmed by reference to his two earlier studies of Xenophon. In "The Spirit of Sparta or the Taste of Xenophon," in speaking of "the ultimate reason why political life and philosophic life . . . are incompatible in the last analysis," he says, "philosophy is the denial of the gods of the city" (532). And in *On Tyranny* (where he is already somewhat more reticent), in the last paragraph of the last chapter of the original study, a chapter entitled "Piety and Law," he suggests that, "One's manner of understanding and evaluating the man-made law depends . . . on one's manner of understanding the order which is not man-made" *and vice versa*; and he raises the question, as one to be determined by "a comprehensive and detailed analysis of Xenophon's Socratic writings," whether Socrates shared the respectful attitude (and all that that attitude implies) of the gentleman Ischomachos toward law.

---

3. Even this position would be a step back from a suggestion "that virtue is knowledge and nothing but knowledge, or that knowledge overcomes everything obstructing it" (97).

4. See *Memorabilia* I.1.15 as well as *Xenophon's Socrates*, 83.

On Chapter Two

In his discussion of Chapter II, Strauss deals more fully—and with only mock reluctance—with the delicate matter of Socrates' true relationship with Kritoboulos and Kriton. Socrates, he suggests, began the conversation on household management in order to remind Kritoboulos "of his neglect of his duties" relating to the management of his household (101). Socrates may have done this at the request of Kriton and thus as an act of friendship—if an act the need for which may have arisen because Socrates had caused Kritoboulos to admire him more than he admires his own father (101). Looking a bit deeper, we see that Socrates' act of friendship was not wholly unselfish: "part of Socrates' wealth consists of Kritoboulos and Kriton. Friends are supposed to help one another: Socrates helps Kriton and Kritoboulos with speeches, while Kriton helps Socrates with more tangible things if and when he needs them" (103). Moreover, as this implies, Socrates' willingness to help Kritoboulos (and presumably Kriton) had strict limits. For example, he was not willing to take over or to assist in the running of Kritoboulos's estate. In defense of his refusal to do so, he gave the excuse that he lacked altogether the art of household management, although, "The sequel will indeed show that Socrates possesses, in a manner, the art of household management, at least that part of it which Kritoboulos most urgently needs" (105).

This discussion obviously has some bearing on the question of Socrates' justice. In the course of his remarks to Kritoboulos, Socrates "speaks of his income-producing possessions. He asserts that he has no such possessions . . ." (104). Now this means "that Socrates has no income whatever—no visible or invisible means of support" (104). No wonder then that he claimed earlier to Kritoboulos that his present wealth was altogether adequate to his needs (101). Strauss calls attention to Socrates' claim in this connection that he resisted the attempt of Kritoboulos "to bring to light the truth about Socrates' life" (104). But Socrates has admitted in the meantime "that what he possesses might not altogether be sufficient for his needs, i.e., that he might be compelled from time to time to increase his possessions" (102–03). Socrates must then, if he possesses no income-producing possessions, "be a parasite, a beggar—in a word, an unjust man" (104).

But "Socrates was in truth of course not unjust but thoroughly just . . ." (104; cf. 102). The view that Socrates was a beggar or parasite and hence unjust is (at least potentially) the view of the gentlemen like

Ischomachos, an ultimately untrue view (104–05). Socrates had to conceal the truth about his way of life (cf. 110) no doubt because of how that truth would be interpreted by the gentlemen "in the common meaning of the term," the moral and civic-minded men. This introduction to the treatment of the contrast or conflict between Socrates and the gentleman (whether the actual gentleman Ischomachos, here named for the first time, or the would-be gentleman Kritoboulos) is probably the most important task which Strauss set for this chapter. It would be difficult to imagine a more fundamental issue than this, concerning as it does the point of view from which all of life, including economics, is to be understood. For just as Socrates appears in a certain light when looked at from the point of view of a gentleman, so can the gentleman be looked at from Socrates' point of view. From that point of view, the gentleman's need for increase of wealth (cf. *Oeconomicus* XI.8 and VII.15) "bespeaks a defect" (101–02). Even more important, from Socrates' point of view, Strauss implies, the gentleman's freedom from what Strauss calls "prejudices" comes to light as less than complete.[5] It appears that Socrates' justice—referred to by Strauss for the first time in the commentary proper on 102—went together with freedom from "prejudices," while the justice of the gentleman did not. This makes us all the more eager to understand Socrates' justice. What was it that it could come to sight, or permit Socrates to come to sight, as "transcending justice" in the manner indicated in the first two chapters, or how is it related to justice as commonly understood?

On Chapter Three

In his discussion of Chapter III, Strauss no longer speaks explicitly of Socrates' justice or transcendence of justice; but the title which he gives to his discussion ("Socrates' promises"), alone, would show that this question is not forgotten. Socrates' willingness to help Kritoboulos out of the economic difficulties which he had called to Kritoboulos's attention had yielded no more, in Chapter II at least, or had been limited to the promise to show Kritoboulos "the best masters of the economic art, so that

---

5. Cf. 102 top—which refers to 98—with what is suggested by Socrates' attitude toward sacrifices (102 toward the middle). Kritoboulos's frivolity (102 toward the bottom), or his sharing to some extent in Socrates' frivolity, was no doubt one of the reasons why Socrates found his company pleasant (cf. 109 and also Socrates' comments about Hermogenes in *Symposium* 6.1–4 and 4.46–50).

he could learn from them" (107). In his discussion of Chapter III, Strauss stresses Socrates' clarification so to speak, not to say quasi-abandonment, of this promise:

> . . . Socrates renders his promise more precise by speaking of some of the parts of the economic art (107);

> He will, then, not simply take Kritoboulos to the masters . . . but will make him discover those masters by himself; or, more cautiously, he will show him both the masters and the bunglers (108);

> In the literal sense of the word, Socrates does not 'take' Kritoboulos anywhere in the *Oeconomicus*. (108)

This may mean, Strauss suggests, that "the present conversation of Socrates with Kritoboulos is only the first stage in Kritoboulos's learning under Socrates' guidance the complete art of household management," i.e., that Socrates took Kritoboulos to the masters (and bunglers) later on (108–09). But Strauss continues, "It is almost equally possible . . . that Kritoboulos's learning of the art is completed in the present conversation" (109); "surely not all promises [made by Socrates to Kritoboulos in Chapter III] are kept in the *Oeconomicus*" (111); as to the promise to introduce Kritoboulos to Aspasia, "This promise at any rate is not kept in the *Oeconomicus*; we are permitted to wonder whether it was kept at all" (111).

Strauss also brings out and reflects here on another fact relevant to the evaluation of Socrates' dealings with Kritoboulos: his willingness to be persuaded by Kritoboulos to join him in going to look at comedies, the very activity which he himself singles out as keeping Kritoboulos from more urgent things. "We might feel that Socrates, who knows all the time that Kritoboulos neglected his duties, should never have given in to Kritoboulos's importunities. But perhaps he indulged Kritoboulos's wish in order to gain his confidence or his affection and thus increase the likelihood that the young man would listen to him when he would see fit to remind him of his duties" (109). Only by the "perhaps" does Strauss permit himself to indicate the alternative he considers—that Socrates' action is better explained by his own love of comedies and his being more concerned with what he could learn from them than with alleviating the economic difficulties of Kritoboulos—though Strauss has certainly prepared us for the reception of this thought.[6]

The shape of Strauss's discussion of Chapter III is perhaps most affected by his wish to demonstrate the strong link between the *Oeconomicus* and the *Clouds*. Xenophon refers to the *Clouds* in Chapter III, according to Strauss's suggestion, not only by explicit references to comedy, especially, as well as to tragedy, and by bringing out the somewhat less than serious nature of Socrates' instruction of Kritoboulos in economics.[7] He refers to it also by dwelling on subjects crucial to the *Clouds*: horses, farming and wives (108–11). The very lack of clarity of the order of subjects treated in Chapter III is a pointer to the *Clouds*, since the darkness disappears once one thinks of the *Clouds* (111–12). Strauss concludes that the *Oeconomicus*, "*the* Socratic discourse" of Xenophon, is a response to "*the* Socratic comedy," the *Clouds*, "a response not altogether without comical traits" (112). Here too, in speaking of the link between the *Oeconomicus* and the *Clouds*, Strauss continues his treatment of Socrates' alleged transcendence of justice, since that transcendence, as we noted before, is a fundamental premise of the *Clouds*.

Strauss calls our attention to the fact that Chapters I–III appear to form a section insofar as each indicates something that must be considered in order to understand the *Oeconomicus*: "not only the subject matter strictly and narrowly understood (household management) and the qualities of the two interlocutors (Socrates and Kritoboulos), but the *Clouds* as well . . ." (112; cf. also the beginning of his discussion of Chapter IV: it reads like a new beginning to the whole discussion). Strauss, who believes that what is most important and controversial in carefully written books is often hidden, and at the same time indicated, by being mentioned in the central place, speaks explicitly of Socrates' justice only in his discussion of Chapter II, while speaking of his alleged transcendence of justice in the discussion of Chapter I and of his (broken) promises in the discussion of Chapter

---

6. The discussion of this chapter affords another example of Strauss's reticence: his surprising suggestion on 110 that Socrates (whose wife was the notoriously difficult Xanthippe) as opposed to Kritoboulos and Ischomachos, among others, is to be understood as a master rather than a bungler in dealing with his wife—this suggestion is explained only on 158. Cf. also "with smithing in the center" on 92 with 115, and the references to animals on 117 and 124 with 196.

7. In a rare instance of self-awareness or prescience in this conversation, one of whose witnesses was Xenophon, Kritoboulos "wonders whether he, the lover of comedy, will not himself be a subject of comedy . . ." (109; cf. 107).

III. Is it possible that Socrates' justice is in some way more in need of being hidden, in Strauss's view, than his alleged transcendence of justice?

On Chapters Four and Five

Toward the end of his discussion of Chapter III, Strauss raises the question of "the connection between household management in general and farming . . . in particular" (112). That connection is the primary theme of Chapters IV and V; and Strauss's discussions of those chapters, as the titles he gives them and the many comparisons he draws between the chapters show, must be considered together. For example, toward the beginning of his discussion of Chapter IV, Strauss reminds us that the art of household management, as Socrates possesses and practices it, would exclude the art of war (113–14; cf. 87–89). Toward the end of the discussion of Chapter V, Strauss speaks again of war. Farming is akin to warfare—"a kinship which induces Socrates to abstain from calling the art of farming a peaceable art" (123)—not only for the reason Strauss indicates in the immediate context of this observation, but also in being more dependent on the gods or piety than the other arts are (124). Nevertheless, the practice of farming is less dependent on the gods than the practice of warfare: whereas "prior to warlike actions men appease the gods *and consult them* by means of sacrifices and omens as to what men should do or forbear to do," it is necessary merely to "appease and worship the gods in regard to agricultural actions" (124, my emphasis). These facts must be taken into account, Strauss implies, when one weighs the implications of Socrates' willingness to praise farming rather than the art of war and of his abstaining from the practice of farming: Socrates resisted such reliance on the gods (cf. "The Spirit of Sparta or the Taste of Xenophon," 534: "In Xenophon's view of the dignity of war as compared with the dignity of peace and leisure and education, his judgment on piety is implied."). By pointing to this resistance, Strauss supplies in advance an important gloss on his remark that Socrates "proves" in Chapter V that "piety is good" or necessary (124; cf. 114). In the same context, Strauss may have gone even further by suggesting that Socrates regarded the earth, which he called "a goddess" (123), as "something natural" (124). But we are concerned not merely with Socrates' views, but with how he established or proved those views, the views that he held as distinguished from those he presented to Kritoboulos. Having heard that Socrates' "method" is "dialectics" (148; cf. *The City and Man* 20, *Natural Right and History* 124), we are drawn especially to the following remark of Strauss on the two chapters before us: "The case for farming that Socrates makes without any regard to the Persian king is more didactic or rhetorical and less *dialogical* than the case he makes with regard to the Persian king" (121, my emphasis). Our consideration of Strauss's discussion of Chapters IV and V must be devoted then to trying to understand this remark.

The connection between household management and farming which is established in Chapters IV and V is not established on the basis of a concern with money-making "regardless of the quality of the pursuit or pursuits through which . . . [one] makes his money" (113). (Cf. 121: ". . . 'increase of the household' is now flanked and hence limited by two other ends. The qualification of increase of the household by another consideration was begun in the preceding chapter . . . .") Nor is the basis for the choice of farming the Socratic life: Socrates praises farming in the strongest terms in these chapters without ever having engaged in farming and without having the slightest intention of engaging in it. The principles or concerns which qualify money-making here and thus lay a basis for a commitment to farming are supplied by, or with a view to, Kritoboulos. They cast no direct light, therefore, on Socrates (but cf. 121); our attention must be directed rather to Socrates' willingness to adapt himself or bow to them or to the way in which he develops arguments which, while in themselves defective, are impressive to Kritoboulos. (See, for example, especially 117.)

Kritoboulos's concern with "the noble, in the sense of the resplendent, vulgarly famous or of high repute, or the pompous," leads Socrates to suggest in Chapter IV that "they" should imitate the Persian king (116). But the example of the Persian king does not speak clearly in favor of the dignity of farming. Hence, Strauss points out at one point, "the reader ought to wonder whether the way in which Socrates proves that the king devotes himself vigorously to farming is not equally serviceable for proving that the king devotes himself vigorously to the arts of smithing or shoemaking" (116). And he stresses Lysander's incredulity at the suggestion "that Cyrus, most beautifully and splendidly attired as he was, could have planted anything with his almost royal hands," i.e., he points to the inherent implausibility of Cyrus's assertion (118; cf. 120). Moreover, as the full Lysander story shows, the praise of Persia implies the rejection of the authority of the most respected Greek city and the abandonment of gentlemanship (cf. VI.12). "We conclude that Socrates' first attempt to make a case for farming was not altogether satisfactory. Let us then turn to his second attempt" (119).

The second attempt (that of Chapter V) is presumably free from these defects of the first. "The pursuit of farming" is now praised as "some soft pleasure" and "a training of the bodies so that they can do whatever befits a free man" as well as for being "an increase of the household" (120). The substitution of concern with pleasure for concern with nobility is intelligible insofar as concern with nobility had led away from the city and gentlemanship without leading toward farming (though Strauss goes out of his way here to indicate an interest of Socrates himself in that substitution, 121). "Yet it is obvious that a man striving for pleasure without any qualification whatever would not choose farming; the central argument in Socrates' long speech indicates the price one has to pay for the pleasures derived from farming . . ." (121–22). "The concern with nobility as distinguished from pleasure is to some extent preserved," Strauss suggests, "in the concern with the 'training of the bodies so that they can do whatever befits a free man'" (122). This chapter accordingly extols the farmer-soldier or the citizen-soldier but "the reasonable praise of peasant soldiers must not make us oblivious of the [superior] virtues of professional soldiers" (123).

The second attempt to make a case for farming is then in itself not much more successful than the first. Yet it manages, as the first (which went "beyond 'the cities' toward the king of Persia," 122) did not, to remain within and thus sketch or outline a certain horizon, the horizon to which we have already been introduced in Chapter II as that of the free man or gentleman. (See especially 102 and 104–05.) Whereas Socrates now speaks of freedom, "he had not even mentioned freedom or free human beings, let alone free men," in the Persian chapter (122). "The free man as presented in the present chapter is both a farmer and a warrior" (122); in accord with his praise of this farmer-soldier or citizen-soldier, Socrates now speaks of justice, "whereas he had been completely silent on justice in the 'Persian' chapter: transcending the city means transcending justice" (123). Moreover, "Given the connection between justice and piety, we ought not to be surprised to observe that the 'Persian' chapter, which is silent on justice, is silent also on piety or the gods, while the present chapter, which mentions justice, speaks more than once of the gods" (123). Indeed, in the most extensive statement on a god in the chapter (which Strauss quotes in this context) the earth is said, being a goddess, to teach justice (123).

The "free man" whose horizon is sketched here is of course a believer in the city's gods: part of "the price one has to pay for the pleasures derived from farming" is "sacrifices" (121–22).

In calling the case for farming which Socrates makes in the Persian chapter more "dialogical" and less "didactic or rhetorical" than the case which he makes in Chapter V, Strauss has in mind primarily that Socrates' remarks in Chapter IV called forth four responses by Kritoboulos, whereas "He does not once interrupt Socrates' long speech" in Chapter V (121). Now three of those four responses were occasioned by references to what Socrates "knew from hearsay" about the Persian king (121–22); and references "to what is generally thought to be, to what people say, to opinions, reputation, rumor, hearsay, or authority . . . abounded" in the Persian chapter, while "they are absent from Socrates' long speech" in Chapter V (120). Perhaps then what Strauss means in the second place by the dialogical character of Chapter IV is that "Socrates adapts himself" there "to the needs, or the tastes, of Kritoboulos" (115) or to the opinions held and represented by Kritoboulos. But such adaptation would seem to characterize still more Chapter V, the very turn to which was caused in part by Socrates' wish to beat a tactical retreat from the position which had been reached by "going beyond" the cities. Indeed, why should such a procedure be called dialogical, rather than didactic or rhetorical? Moreover, this suggestion takes no account of Socrates' concern, which Strauss goes out of his way to mention in this vicinity, to find a standard "independent of opinion and reputation" (121).

Perhaps then what Strauss has in mind in his characterization of Chapter IV is this very movement "beyond 'the cities' " which distinguishes it from Chapter V—a movement based on, made possible and even necessary by, an initial bowing to the opinions prevalent in the cities or to the authority of the city. For Socrates was "compelled" to go beyond the cities once he adopted as his guiding consideration, in accordance with Kritoboulos's wishes, "the noble" (122). Or, what he does in Chapter IV is no more than to spell out the sort of thing that is implied if "one looks at things from the point of view of the noble, in the sense of the resplendent, vulgarly famous or of high repute or the pompous" (116). And, as Strauss points out in his discussion of Chapter V, the "concern with nobility . . . is to some extent preserved" in the concern with freedom, i.e., it is an element of the horizon of the free man which Strauss sketches there (122). In other words, the seed of the transcendence of the city and its opinions, of its justice and piety, is contained within those opinions; or the civic horizon is constituted by elements which contradict one another. For this reason, the critique of Sparta, the most impressive city known to the Greeks, can be largely entrusted or ascribed to the Spartan Lysander. (Sparta was the only Greek city which made the virtue or gentlemanship of its citizens a matter of public concern [201; cf. *Constitution of the Lacedaimonians* x, 4, and 7. Strauss speaks on 119 of Lykourgos]. Yet the most outstanding contemporary Spartan was so far from being fully devoted to virtue and gentlemanship that he implied that one can be happy without being a gentleman and even without being good [119; cf. 160: the story of Cyrus is characteristic of Lysander].) And for this reason, Socrates' transcending of the city's justice, based as it is on an initial bowing to or conformity with that justice, can be said to be authorized by it, or to be itself just. Socrates seems to point to this aspect of the procedure being described by his comic attempt to prove his assertion about the king's devotion to farming "by starting from the universally held view according to which the king devotes himself vigorously to actions connected with war," i.e., by suggesting that from a universally held view one may be led to a highly paradoxical one (116; cf. 128 with 105; cf. *What Is Political Philosophy?* 90–91). Still, this explanation of what Strauss means by "dialogical" seems to me incomplete: the significance of what Strauss himself stresses in so describing Chapter IV, its conversational character, remains to be accounted for.

In speaking of Lysander's conscious or unconscious critique of Sparta, Strauss refers to "the critique of Sparta that is implicit in the *Oeconomicus* as a whole" (119) without spelling out what he understands this critique to be. He seems to distinguish it from Lysander's critique, though the Lysander critique would seem to be a significant part of it. To begin with what Strauss mentions in this context, the *Oeconomicus* as a whole praises money-making generally (not just farming), while "the authority of original Sparta or of Sparta as a city spoke against money-making in any form . . ." (119). But beyond this, "money-making" may masquerade as "the art of arts" or be "an image of the art of conversing or reasoning," i.e., of philosophy (106 and 126). What Strauss may mean then is that an adequate praise of philosophy necessarily implies, or requires, a critique of "Sparta" or the city.

On Chapter Six

Strauss's discussion of Chapter VI confirms in two ways the impression conveyed by his discussion of the earlier chapters that the issue of piety or the gods is of paramount importance for him. First he stresses Kritoboulos's expansion of Socrates' statement on the need for piety—i.e., he stresses the limited character of Socrates' own statement, of even Socrates' explicit statement (cf. 125 with 124). Secondly, he reflects on the different claims of the art of divination, on the one hand, and the art of conversing or reasoning, on the other, to be the art universally needed, the art of arts (125 and 126). This may be as close as Strauss comes in this work to stating outright what he regards as the fundamental issue: in the last resort must our reliance be on the divine or on our own reasoning (cf. *Natural Right and History*, 74)? Strauss considers the possibility that "the art of money-making is an image of the art of conversing or reasoning": if this is so, "it would not be surprising that *the* Socratic discourse is devoted to the art of increasing one's wealth" (126). But precisely in Chapter VI, "Socrates . . . brings about a shift from 'household management' to 'perfect gentlemanship'; the question is no longer what the work of household management is but what the work of the perfect gentleman is" (128). Moreover, according to Strauss, "After Socrates has made perfect gentlemanship the theme, we understand better than before why the *Oeconomicus* is *the* Socratic dialogue" (129). Is it philosophy then (the art of conversing or reasoning) or gentlemanship which is the theme of *the* Socratic dialogue? Or to what connection between the two themes does Strauss wish to call our attention?

Perfect gentlemanship had been mentioned without being discussed or explained in the discussion of Chapters IV–V (as well as in that of Chapter II). In remedying that deficiency now (128–29), Strauss seems to supply also the answer to our question of the connection between the themes of philosophy and gentlemanship: "For, as we know, Socrates was exclusively concerned with ethics and politics, with virtue and the city, and 'perfect gentlemanship' includes in a manner all ethical and political themes" (129; cf. 83). But in the immediate sequel, Strauss indicates the difficulty with this answer and with the premise (as to Socrates' exclusive concern) on which it is based. In the *Oeconomicus* at least, perfect gentlemanship is approached or looked at from a rather ungentlemanly point of view, "from a point of view which is rather low: from the point of view of the question of how the perfect gentleman earns his living . . ." (129). It is true that interest in this question is not likely to have been the true or deepest reason for Socrates' own concern with the perfect gentleman. But Strauss's remark leads us to wonder whether Socrates' reason was any the less ungentlemanly than (if not as "low" as) the economic one. Surely the dialogue as a whole makes clear that Socrates had and has no intention of becoming a perfect gentleman (160–61, 185, 202–03). But if Socrates' concern with ethics and politics, with perfect gentlemanship, was not motivated by the desire to *become* a perfect gentleman, we must be open to the possibility that his ethical/political concerns do not exhaust or close the circle of his philosophic concerns, that his ethical/political concerns must be understood in the light of concerns which are trans-political.[8] To be open to this possibility is not necessarily to doubt the significance, for Socrates and the philosophic life generally, of that "unique event of his past" which was "his discovery of what perfect gentlemanship is" (129), but only to wonder about its character. Strauss underlines that significance here, while reminding us of his discussion of Chapters IV–V, by the remark already quoted: "After Socrates has made perfect gentlemanship the theme, we understand better than before why the *Oeconomicus* is *the* Socratic dialogue" (129; cf. 121). So far as I observed, this is the first time Strauss uses the word "dialogue" to refer to the *Oeconomicus*, having referred to it previously always as a "discourse" (89, 90, 92, 112, 126; cf. 130).

Part of Chapter VI is devoted to summarizing the results of the previous conversation. Strauss points out that "the recapitulation . . . differs strikingly from the conversation it is meant to summarize" (125). For example, Socrates "restates the case for farming with scrupulous omission of anything reminding one of the Persian king . . . . Above all—and this in a way compensates for the silence on Persia—he claims that they had agreed about farming being a work and a science very fit for a perfect gentleman . . . In a word, in the recapitulation, Socrates . . . introduces the theme 'the perfect gentleman' . . . ." (127). The connection between "Persia" and "perfect gentleman" (which permits the introduction of the latter to compensate for silence on the former) is clarified in Strauss's remark that the shift from "household management" to "perfect gentlemanship" "was prepared by Kritoboulos's desire to hear [only] of the lucrative science which is reputed to be most noble or beautiful" (128–29), i.e., by the same desire which had led Socrates in Chapter IV to speak of the Persian king. That is, the concerns or opinions which lead ultimately to "Persia," lead before that to perfect gentlemanship; or, as we saw in the discussion of Chapters IV–V, it is concerns or opinions belonging to the horizon of the

---

8. Since perfect gentlemanship is not something visible or perceptible to the senses, its discovery became possible only when Socrates turned away from the evidence of sight to "take his bearings . . . by hearing, by reputation" or by what is "universally" said (128; cf. 116; cf. Plato, *Phaedo* 99d4ff).

perfect gentleman (free man, farmer-soldier, citizen-soldier: cf. 161) and those who aspire to gentlemanship which, when properly followed up, lead to "Persia" or to what that stood for according to Strauss's suggestion in his discussion of Chapters IV–V.

As a result of what Socrates had said in Chapters IV, V, and VI, Kritoboulos had become "eager to hear the causes why some farmers are highly successful and others fail altogether . . ." (127). Socrates had promised him something of this sort in Chapter III: "That promise was the only one accompanied by Socrates' rebuke of Kritoboulos for his deplorable propensity to prefer comedies to farming" (128). Now, however, instead of providing the promised economic demonstration, Socrates narrates for Kritoboulos (and the others present) his first encounter with a perfect gentleman, only a smallish part of which involves a discussion of farming. Socrates' narration, or his treatment of the perfect gentleman Ischomachos, is "not altogether without comical traits" (112; cf., e.g., 158, 161; even in the present chapter farming is recommended as "a science very fit for a perfect gentleman" because, in part, "farming seems to be the science most easy to learn" (127). In view of this, Strauss seems to suggest, we are free to regard Socrates' substitution of this narration for the promised economic demonstration as a further indulgence of Kritoboulos's "propensity to prefer comedies to farming" (cf. 109). Perhaps Socrates doubted whether Kritoboulos was likely to improve much as a money-maker in any case (126; cf. 130).

On Chapters Seven Through Ten (Part One)

The remainder of the *Oeconomicus* consists of Socrates' narration, to Kritoboulos and the others, of his meeting with the perfect gentleman Ischomachos. Socrates had sought such a meeting apparently in order to find out what a perfect gentleman is, but it is not until the fifth chapter of this section that we hear Ischomachos tell of his own activity. (Strauss gives to this chapter or his discussion of it the title "*Andrologia*.") The first four chapters, VII–X, are devoted at Socrates' request to Ischomachos's account of his educating his wife. That account by itself would justify the advance billing of the Ischomachos section as a comedy.[9] But it is difficult

---

9. See Strauss's reference to comedy on 132, as well as, among other places, 133, 136, 137–39, 144, 155, and above all 156–58, which was prepared by 131, 134 and 151 in particular.

to see why Socrates should have found this subject so compelling as to have brought it about that, in Strauss's words, "in the *Oeconomicus* the *gynaikologia* precedes the *andrologia*" (147). Strauss raises this difficulty early in his discussion of the section on the wife (132–33) without providing an acceptable answer to it in that place.

The high point of his discussion appears to be his treatment of Chapters VIII–IX, which are devoted to the theme "order," and above all his statement (in the discussion of Chapter IX) on dialectics, Socrates' " 'method' " or "the peculiarly Socratic philosophizing" (148). What occasions this statement is Xenophon's or Ischomachos's description of the latter's "separating his indoor things according to tribes in order to establish order within his house" (147). This "reminds us" according to Strauss, "of Socrates' separating the beings according to races or kinds in order to discover the order of the whole. According to Xenophon, Socrates 'never ceased considering with his companions what each of the beings is,' i.e., what each kind of the beings is. He called this activity or art 'dialectics,' which means literally the art of conversation. He asserted that the activity is called *dialegesthai* with a view to the fact that men coming together for joint deliberation pick or select (*dialegein*) things according to races or kinds" (147–48). The statement on dialectics (from which the quoted portion is drawn) is unusually full and helpful. It is not what we were led to expect however by Strauss's singular use of "dialogical" in his discussion of Chapters IV–V (121), a usage which he resumes most conspicuously in his discussion of the section on the wife (138, 140, 153; cf. also 129 in the discussion of Chapter VI). Perhaps then the explicit statement on dialectics is not meant to be complete.

With a view to the similarity pointed out between Ischomachos's activity and Socrates' separating the beings according to kinds, Strauss raises the question "whether Ischomachos's separating his indoor things according to tribes is not the model for the peculiarly Socratic philosophizing" (148). In raising this question, Strauss underlines the link between the question of the completeness of the account of Socratic philosophizing he explicitly provides here and the question of what Socrates learned from Ischomachos: if Socrates learned from Ischomachos something more or other than "order," then precisely if his meeting with Ischomachos was of fundamental importance to him, if it "made an epoch in his life" (161), there must be more to the "peculiarly Socratic philosophizing" than dialectics in this sense. Now the whole subject of order arose without any doing on Socrates' part (140): it was not then the knowledge or information he was looking for from Ischomachos in seeking a meeting with him. In addition, while Ischomachos apparently intended his discussion of order "to educate even Socrates" (142 and 148), Socrates, who on the whole remains silent during that discussion (152 and 142–43), shows almost no sign of interest in it (153). What he does show interest in consistently, in this discussion and throughout the whole section on the wife, is Ischomachos's education of his wife and the wife's reaction to that education! (146, 152, 140, 153–54, 156).

In a roundabout way, Strauss brings out the problematic character of the suggestion that "Ischomachos's separating his indoor things according to tribes is . . . the model for the peculiarly Socratic philosophizing" in his very defense of it. He begins by speaking of the "human things": "We recall that Socrates approached Ischomachos in order to learn from him what perfect gentlemanship is . . . The question regarding the perfect gentleman may be said to comprise all the questions regarding human things which Socrates was always raising, like What is pious? What is impious? What is noble? What is base? and so on; these questions call for separating, for instance, what is pious from what is noble" (148). In the discussion of an earlier chapter, Strauss had said, "as we know, Socrates was exclusively concerned with ethics and politics, with virtue and the city, and 'perfect gentlemanship' includes in a manner all ethical and political themes" (129; cf. 83). But now Strauss admits and even stresses that "Socrates' most comprehensive teaching . . . transcends the human things" (148), that "Socrates did not limit his inquiry to the human things" (150), that he was concerned indeed with "the nature of all things" (150). If Ischomachos's activity was the model for Socratic philosophizing, it must have been the model for this aspect of that philosophizing as well; and Strauss seemed to have this aspect in mind when he first called attention to the resemblance between Ischomachos's activity and Socrates' (147—"the order of the whole"). In defending his suggestion, however, Strauss stresses the kinship of the activity of the "model economist" Ischomachos not with Socrates' asking of his "What is . . ." questions (i.e., with his "separating the beings according to races or kinds in order to discover the order of the whole") but with a Socratic teaching to the effect that "the order of the whole cosmos . . . serves the benefit of men and is due to the god's *oikonomein*" (148). Strauss makes it clear that he regards this teaching—which he generally calls a "teleo-theology"—as something different from the teaching which might emerge from Socrates' "What is . . ." questions by saying that its connection with those questions "is not clear" (148–49). In fact, he suggests the following possible connection. The "teleotheology is exposed to difficulties" (148; cf. 150—"however precarious that teaching might be"); moreover, remarks of Socrates indicate that he was well aware of this fact (148–49). Perhaps then "the Xenophontic Socrates was . . . , like the Platonic Socrates, dissatisfied with the simple teleology—anthropocentric or not—which at first glance seems to supply the most rational solution to all difficulties, and turned for this reason to the 'What is . . .' questions or to 'the separating of the beings according to kinds'" (149). In other words, the Socratic physics which Strauss sketches in this context (150) is not to be understood as teleological. Or, to state this in terms of Ischomachos's ordering activity, whereas Ischomachos separates his possessions according to kinds in order to bring each of those kinds to its proper place, a place established in accordance with the hierarchy of his needs or with his purpose, Socrates can see no more order in the whole than its articulation into kinds or classes of beings (146–47; cf. III.2–3 and 108; cf. 141).

Ischomachos's activity could then have been the model for this aspect of Socratic philosophizing only to a limited extent, as Strauss seems to grant by now calling his suggestion "a deliberate exaggeration" (149). But one must go further. By pointing out Socrates' indication that the interest of Ischomachos's wife in order did not antedate Ischomachos's lecture on order (146), Strauss suggests that Socrates indicates that his own interest in order did antedate that lecture: what Socrates learned of ordering from activity of the Ischomachean sort (148), he is not likely to have learned from Ischomachos. Accordingly, in his final statement here on the "Ischomachean" origin of the philosophizing peculiar to Socrates, Strauss puts "Ischomachean" in quotation marks. (150)

It seems then that Strauss has led us on a wild goose chase or in a great circle. But that circle has the merit of describing a large hole or gap in our knowledge or of pointing to a question. If it was not dialectics in this sense that Socrates learned from Ischomachos, what *did* he learn from him that was of such importance that their conversation could be said to have "made an epoch in his life"? (161) Strauss's procedure has the additional merit, which we have already seen, of indicating that the answer to his question must be used to modify or supplement the explicit account of Socratic philosophizing or dialectics that has been given. The answer to it still clearly available in Strauss's discussion of the section on the wife—the "human things"—is insufficient or incomplete for the following reason. It fails to make clear *why*—in the context of what consideration, to answer what question—Socrates turned to the human things (cf. 164). For, as we have seen, Strauss rules out early on and repeatedly the most obvious reason for Socrates' seeking out Ischomachos, a reason Socrates himself suggests: that he wished to learn what he must do in order to become a perfect gentleman.[10]

Toward the beginning of his discussion of the last chapter of the section (i.e., shortly after his discussion of "dialectics"), Strauss suggests that "Xenophon regarded his reproduction of Socrates' virtue for more than one reason as inferior to that virtue itself, one reason being that in publicly presenting Socrates' virtue he could not assume that he was speaking only to friends" (154). In a footnote to this reference to Xenophon's reticence, to the incompleteness of Xenophon's account of Socrates, Strauss calls upon us to compare a passage in the *Memorabilia*, which speaks of Socrates' adapting the expression of his thought to the different natures of his interlocutors (cf. *Xenophon's Socrates* 122–23 and 92–93), with the passage in the *Oeconomicus* in which Socrates states to Kritoboulos in the presence of the others his reason for seeking out Ischomachos. Strauss calls upon us, that is, to read the latter passage in the light of the former. He thus underlines the insufficiency of Socrates' explanation of his seeking out Ischomachos, as well as of his own treatment of that explanation.[11] He points to the very problem which his whole discussion of the section on the wife is designed to bring out, a problem we are entitled to call *the* problem of the dialogue, the problem of Socrates' reason for seeking out Ischomachos. No passage more than this one (text and note together) shows Strauss's simultaneous desire to reveal and conceal. He points to the concealment *here* because the reason for Socrates' seeking out Ischomachos is the most important thing concealed. He *points* to what is concealed here because he wishes also to reveal it. As to a reason for his procedure other than the one already mentioned, a reason applying even to "friends," one might consider the comparison he draws in *Xenophon's Socrates* between Socrates and Theodote. Since Theodote lived by means of her friends, as Socrates did, her way of life may be considered "a caricature of Socrates'" (87), or there is a "resemblance between 'Socrates and his friends' and 'Theodote and her friends.'" (89) But Theodote was ignorant as to how

---

10. 132, 160–61, 163, 165, 185; cf. 129. Socrates suggests this to Ischomachos (XI.6; but cf. XI.7).

11. It is similarly only in a footnote that Strauss refers to Socrates' use of the "What is . . ." questions "regarding human things" in *refutations* (148 n.4).

to attract friends, while Socrates, who "surpasses Theodote by far in the erotic art . . . is the true *erotikos* who can make others long passionately to be together with him in speech" (89). Strauss gives one example from Socrates' instruction of Theodote in how to "approach a friend according to nature": "she must not obtrude her favors when the friend has no hunger for them" (88). According to the text Strauss refers to at this point, one of the means of arousing this hunger or of bringing it to its highest pitch is to flee after showing oneself willing to oblige (*Memorabilia* III.11.14).

The result of Socrates' seeking out Ischomachos was a "conversation" or a dialogue in the sense that Strauss calls our attention to especially in his discussion of the section on the wife (cf. 138, 140 and 153 with 129 and 121). It was that "conversation" which made an epoch in Socrates' life (161; cf. 129). For the discovery of Strauss's view of what Socrates sought to learn and did learn from it, we must rely, for the most part, on Strauss's observations regarding the course of the conversation itself, keeping in mind Socrates' incomplete explanation of his reason for seeking out Ischomachos—especially the fact that nobility or beauty as an ingredient of gentlemanship, or a concern of gentlemen, is not something perceptible through sight but only through hearing. Occasionally, somewhat extraneous or irregular remarks of Strauss provide further hints. Toward the end of the first chapter of his discussion of the section on the wife, he contrasts or distinguishes "dialogical" from "theological" teaching (138). In discussing Socrates' teaching about "the god's *oikonomein*," Strauss generally, as we have seen, refers to that teaching as a "teleotheology" (148, 149, 150). But when he raises the question of its connection (or non-connection) with the "What is . . ." questions, Strauss refers to it as "Socrates' theology" (149). Then, shortly afterwards, when referring to Socrates' dissatisfaction with and possible rejection of it, he refers to it as a "teleology" (149). He thus forces us to wonder whether the rejection of teleology and the turn, which according to Strauss is coeval with it, to the "What is . . ." questions, to "dialectics" as explicitly discussed, also disposes of all "theology." (According to an indication he gives in this context, it is possible to regard "the gods as at least as much disturbers of the philanthropic order as its supporters" [149].) In other words, Strauss wishes us to wonder whether the Socratic physics sketched here (150) as compatible with "dialectics" is more than hypothetical, or whether "dialectics" as explicitly discussed is perhaps incapable of settling theoretically all questions regarding the gods and for that reason incapable even of establishing the very possibility of a physics (account of a fixed, unalterable nature). Surely in his discussion of this section, Strauss goes beyond his previous account of Socrates by admitting and stressing Socrates' concern with "the nature of all things" and thus raising the question of the connection of this concern with his interest in the "human things."

On Chapters Seven Through Ten (Part Two)

We have seen that according to Strauss what interests Socrates most, in the section on the wife and even in the *Oeconomicus* as a whole (132), is Ischomachos's education of his wife. Toward the end of his discussion of this section, Strauss admits "that Socrates is at least as much interested in Ischomachos's *report* about his wife's virtue as in that virtue itself" (154, my emphasis), and he points out that the reason is not likely to be that Ischomachos is a particularly good interpreter of his wife's virtue. In fact, Ischomachos is deficient not only as an interpreter of his wife's virtue, but also as educator of his wife to virtue or her duties. It is possible—Xenophon does not let us know for sure—that Ischomachos's wife turned out quite badly (cf. 131 with 157–58). Even if she did not, "what Xenophon's Socrates reports about Ischomachos and his wife," i.e., what Ischomachos was led by Socrates to tell him on this subject, "is perfectly compatible" with such a result (158). And Socrates' awareness of this fact, even at the time of their conversation, is shown by his frequent questions to Ischomachos regarding his wife's reactions to his instructions. Now, if Ischomachos's deficiencies as an educator were merely private or particular failings on his part, having nothing to do with his being the model of a perfect gentleman, they would not have merited the attention given to them by Socrates, Xenophon and Strauss.

In the context of the *Oeconomicus*, perhaps the most striking manifestation of Ischomachos's gentlemanliness is his being interested in increasing his wealth by noble and just means alone (134). Shortly after he has made this clear, he urges his wife "to do as well as she can what the gods have enabled her to do by bringing her forth, and what in addition the law praises" (134–35). According to Strauss, "It is not surprising that immediately after the limitation of the increase of wealth to its noble and just increase, the law should make its first appearance in the *Oeconomicus*" (135). In expecting such an appearance, Strauss does not have in mind the law's undoubted concern to regulate or limit the pursuit of gain. (See the passage referred to on 135 n.12.) The law which Ischomachos refers to is that which "puts the stamp of the noble" on certain actions (137).

It is not "merely the law laid down by the Athenian legislator" but "an unwritten law, traces of which are found in a variety of codes" (135). It is the law which establishes what is noble and base in the sense that the gentleman recognizes nobility and baseness; it is thus a comprehensive code which regulates the life of the gentleman and forms his outlook. (One can say that what is in question here is the noble or base by law, the conventionally noble and base, so long as one keeps in mind that Ischomachos is far from looking at law with the critical eye of a pre-Socratic philosopher. The nobility in question is compatible with—whether or not its demands can be reduced to—the requirements of life as a free man, citizen of a free commonwealth [131, 161].) Among other things, it forms his outlook on marriage, the proper relation between man and wife and the proper role of the wife. It prescribes, for example, that marriage have more to do with the mutual management of a household (its noble and just increase) and of children than with eros or "sleeping together" (133–34; 137; cf. 155). But a doubt may arise as to whether this view of marriage is completely in accord with human nature and especially with the nature of such a spirited woman as Ischomachos's wife (153, 155; cf. 152). Such a doubt certainly had arisen in Socrates' mind; but apparently it did not arise with sufficient force in Ischomachos's mind. In this and also in other respects, he was too sanguine (145 n.6; 158; 167–68). What is the cause of his hopefulness?

Given the status in his eyes of the noble and the law which establishes it Ischomachos expects that there must be some support for that. (This already implies, it is true, some awareness of the problem on his part, of the fact that the law is in need of support.) In order to grasp his thought, one must give proper weight to the fact that "Ischomachos does not ascribe divine origin to the law" (135; cf. 148). He distinguishes between the law and what the gods are responsible for: "What the gods have generated, what owes its being to the gods, is 'nature' as distinguished in particular from law" (135). His primary and fundamental concern is for law (or the noble) not the gods or nature. Nevertheless, this primary concern forces him to extend his concern beyond it: therefore, " 'Nature' and 'law' make their first appearance in the *Oeconomicus* in the same context, in the same chapter" (135; cf. *On Tyranny* 109; cf. the references on 135 and 137 to praise and blame). Another formulation of the problem is suggested by Strauss's observations on 156 and 152: while Ischomachos could have admitted that the other sorts of order he discusses are improvements on nature, he cannot afford to admit that the law is an improvement on—i.e., deviation from—nature, precisely because it is only a qualified improvement. In accord with this, Ischomachos stresses to his wife the "perfect agreement between nature [i.e., divinely originated nature] and law" regarding the role of the two sexes in marriage: "the law puts the stamp of the noble on the specific actions for which the god has designed the two sexes . . ." (137). It is true that Ischomachos's accounts of the gods' provision for marriage (135–36) and of the gods' fashioning the nature of the woman for her part of the couple's work (137) are less than convincing, and that Ischomachos seems to be aware of this (137), just as he is aware that the noble is in need of support. More generally, "Ischomachos indicates some doubts regarding the teleotheology" which he puts forward here (149). For example, since he regards the drone bees as useless, he "does not see why, and even whether, the god has fashioned them" (138). Moreover, he believes that "if a man acts against the divine or natural order by neglecting his work or doing that of the wife, his disorderly conduct is *perhaps* noticed by the gods and he is punished for it" (137, my emphasis). And he reports to Socrates (without objecting to them) remarks made by the boatswain of a Phoenician ship which imply a doubt "about evil befalling only the bad, i.e., about whether one can speak in strict parlance of divine punishment" and in which "the gods are mentioned only as disturbers of order" (143; cf. 162). (The absence of any sign that he also reported these remarks to his wife, when he recounted to her what he had learned from his visit to the Phoenician ship, tends to confirm that his lectures to her reflect an "improved" version of his true views [144].) But whatever Ischomachos's doubts may have been, either about nature or the gods, they remained within certain limits and thus left a basis for his hopefulness (cf. 133, 161–62). Strauss points this out by contrasting the conclusion which Socrates would have drawn—from the observation that some of those who act against "the divine or natural order," i.e., the order on which the law has put the stamp of the noble, are not punished by the gods—with the conclusion which, as we have seen, Ischomachos draws. Socrates would not have balked at the thought that the gods are aware of the actions which they fail to punish (137; cf. Herakleitos B 102).

If this difference were a purely theological one, if it rested on nothing but differing assessments or experiences of the divine, it might well be unresolvable. There would be no ground common to Ischomachos and Socrates on which to base a reasonable decision. Each could continue to maintain his position indefinitely, in what would amount to a mere test of wills. But the situation is altogether different if their disagreement regarding the gods rests on differing assessments of that which the law declares to be noble, and if the question of the truth or genuineness of this nobility is open to discussion. Ischomachos's vulnerability on that score becomes clear when one puts together his strong disapproval of cosmetics or "spurious beauty," of boasting or deception as opposed to truth (X as a whole, also XI.25 and 166), with the indication given in Chapter XI (165–66) that he, as opposed to Socrates, has not investigated what justice is. Given the intimate connection of the just and the noble (cf. 134), we can assume that the same holds for nobility, as far as he is concerned. Indeed, this is already suggested by his deference, regarding the noble, to the law. The situation is altogether different that is if the "evidence" for the gods (as Ischomachos conceives them to be) consists in his concern for what the law declares to be noble (in all its dignity but also in its need of support to secure the deference it claims as its due but does not sufficiently elicit on its own), if it is such concern which calls forth belief and which sustains it, in however modified a form, through the all but inevitable disappointments. (See again 99 and 123.) In that case, a conversation which led "Ischomachos" to a different, more adequate view of the noble (a conversation made possible by Socrates' learning through "hearing" Ischomachos's original view) would change the basis on which evidence bearing on the question of the gods is assessed by him.

It is not clear that Socrates ever had such a conversation with Ischomachos. If he did, it surely is not the conversation presented in the *Oeconomicus*, where Socrates may have wished only to confirm its possibility in principle—which would not mean that it is in fact possible to have such a conversation in every particular case (cf. *What Is Political Philosophy?* 94). The course it might take is indicated to some extent by the discussion of Chapter VIII. The subject of that chapter seems to be especially the beauty of order (cf. 146), i.e., its subject is beauty (nobility) as well as order. Ischomachos had seen a particularly beautiful example of order aboard the Phoenician merchant ship. After discussing Ischomachos's account of this example, Strauss compares it with the story of Cyrus and his pleasure garden, which Lysander had so admired for its beauty (118), a beauty consisting in no small part in its orderliness (IV.21–22):

> In both cases barbarians are presented as models in regard to order. In both cases the order is of human origin. Yet in the Persian story the ordered thing is the pleasure garden, and the

orderer is a man who was almost a king; in the Phoenician story the ordered thing is a merchantman, and the orderer is a nameless boatswain. In the Persian story the order belongs together with Cyrus' resplendent adornments of all kinds; in the Phoenician story the splendor is altogether replaced by utility. (143)[12]

An earlier remark of Strauss's seems to suggest that the noble (beautiful) is that which one can be concerned with "for its own sake," as well as for one's own sake (117). Ischomachos seems to hold this to be true of that which the law declares to be noble. His limitation of increase of wealth to noble or just increase (134) is not for the sake of greater gain in the future; "he cannot plead his cause well if it is useful for him to say the untruth" (166); he forgoes for a day supervision of his estate (163) in order to keep his part of an appointment in town "with strangers who stood him up" (131; 145; XII.1–2). Yet, as has been suggested, the intrinsic choiceworthiness of the noble as he understands it is not beyond question; if it were, the noble would not be in need of support. Lurking beside the noble but also somehow within it, as roots or ingredients, are two other ends: utility and splendor. The role, for example, which Ischomachos finds noble for his wife to fill is certainly also not without utility for them both—to say nothing of the arrangement of their pots and pans which he finds beautiful (144). And the noble life, as he understands it, seeks honor in the city and culminates in adornment of the city (162–63). Utility and splendor do not appear to be open to question to the same extent or in the same way as the noble. (The relationship of pleasure to the noble is considered on 121—cf. 162—and, in *Xenophon's Socrates*, especially on 77.) Given this state of affairs, it is difficult to avoid the question whether it would not be better to pursue exclusively either or both of these ends and to forget about the noble insofar as it is not reducible to them. One may object that, as the Phoenician and Cyrus stories suggest, the radical pursuit of these ends amounts to barbarism; that Greekness, or cultivated

---

12. This opposition is clearly not identical to that developed in the discussion of Chapters IV–V, for the point of view of the free man and gentleman farmer (IV) cannot be identified with that of the boatswain (but cf. 160 and 201). Also "Persia" seems to have had a richer or more symbolic meaning in the earlier discussion than it does here or in Chapter XI (161)—it was twice put in quotation marks on 123. Strauss does remark here however that, "The Persian story is silent on the gods . . ." (144).

freedom, depends upon the resistance to such a course, on the refusal to see the noble as no more than such roots. Hence the appropriateness of Socrates coming upon Ischomachos as he is "sitting in the colonnade of Zeus the Deliverer—the deliverer of the Greeks in particular from the Persian danger" (131; cf. *Xenophon's Socrates*, 167—"what is good for the city, is frequently noble rather than good for the individual . . . ."). But, not to mention the possibility that a certain case might be made for "barbarism" ("Xenophon's *Anabasis*," 134), if the choiceworthiness of the noble as Ischomachos understands it is questionable and he cannot give an account of its superiority to utility and/or splendor pursued by themselves, he will be vulnerable to their temptation—as Chapter XX, especially, shows (200–01; cf. 208). This alone would show the need, the legitimacy of searching for the true nobility or beauty which would be truly choiceworthy for its own sake and our own sake. And, according to Strauss, "true human virtue is not in need of conventions"[13] (while its possessor "is as remote from Barbarians, from barbarism, as possible") (160).

On Chapter Eleven

It is only in Chapter XI, it seems, that Socrates, putting "a stop to Ischomachos's report about his wife's doings by asking him to tell him of his own doings . . . turns . . . to the subject for the sake of whose understanding he had approached Ischomachos in the first place" (159). It seems, in other words, as if Chapter XI is devoted to "the account of the perfect gentleman" (165). In fact, it is devoted to "the profound difference" between Socrates and the perfect gentleman (159), to "the serious difference between Ischomachos's virtue or gentlemanship, which Socrates lacks—and whose lack he does not even deplore—and Socrates' virtue or gentlemanship, which both antedated and survived his conversation with Ischomachos" (161), or to "the confrontation of the two incompatible ways of life" (165). The reason may be that much has already been revealed of Ischomachos's outlook—and of the reasons why Socrates found it important to understand that outlook—through Ischomachos's account of his education of his wife. The question which this background prepares, and which despite clear indications already given might still be thought

---

13. It is apparently in this light that Strauss's interest in the two forms of virtue or gentlemanship, or in the comparative "rank" of Ischomachos, Cyrus and Socrates, is to be understood (144 and 161).

to await a definitive answer, is whether Socrates accepted Ischomachos's outlook (on the noble) and the views associated with it. Such an answer is provided, according to Strauss, in Chapter XI.

"The most massive difference between the two kinds of virtue [that of Ischomachos and that of Socrates] is that the former presupposes and the latter does not presuppose the possession of considerable wealth" (161; cf. 159 f.). This difference might have been thought to be a trivial one if it were not elaborated on in the sequel. (The elaboration serves also to indicate the connection between the lesson which Socrates explicitly draws from his horse story—true human virtue does not require wealth—and the lesson which Strauss says that he draws—"true human virtue is not in need of conventions" [160].)

"Ischomachos's full account of his activity begins with his serving the gods" (161–62). Among the aims of the activity begun in this way, and the aim apparently making the biggest impression on Socrates, is the noble increase of wealth: "Socrates, who is poor and satisfied with being poor, is apparently struck most by Ischomachos's concern with being wealthy and his willingness to undergo the many troubles which accompany the possession of wealth" (162). But to Ischomachos, wealth is pleasant: "wealth is pleasant because it enables a man to honor the gods magnificently, to assist his friends in their need, and to contribute toward the adornment of the city. These purposes for which wealth is to be used and which justify the concern with the acquisition of wealth are not selfish; this is perhaps sufficient reason for Socrates to call them, not indeed pleasant, but noble; to this extent the pupil Socrates has become convinced by Ischomachos's defense of the perfect gentleman's way of life" (162). But Socrates' deed did not accord well with these words. We have already heard that his lacking Ischomachos's virtue or gentlemanship is something "he does not even deplore" (161). Now we hear that, "He certainly makes it clear that he belongs to the many who are able to praise the perfect gentleman's pursuit and use of wealth but unable to imitate them" (163). In the light of the first statement, we are entitled to conclude that the core of the inability referred to in the second, as far as Socrates was concerned, was unwillingness. Either he did not regard nobility and the pursuit of noble objects as the most important concern and pursuit, or he did not regard the objects he had just called noble as truly noble (see the "perhaps"), or he knew of things still more noble, or he was moved by some combination of these reasons. However that may be, if he did not deplore his failure to use wealth as Ischomachos used it, he did not deplore his failure to honor the gods magnificently, among other things. (In leaving us to draw this conclusion here, Strauss does not refer to Xenophon's defense of Socrates on this point in *Memorabilia* I.3.3—presumably because that defense is not unanswerable.)

We heard earlier that the rule, "that one ought to begin every work with appeasing the gods," belongs to Kritoboulos (125) and Ischomachos (133) rather than to Socrates, at least the Socrates of the *Oeconomicus*, "the most revealing . . . of Xenophon's Socratic writings. It is the most revealing because in its central chapter Socrates is directly contrasted with a perfect gentleman" (*Xenophon's Socrates*, Preface). In the discussion of Chapter XI, "the economist Ischomachos" is described as a "freeman who is a member of a republic, a commonwealth, and who minds his own business" (161). Earlier we had been told that "the successful practitioner" of economics "seemed to be the free man, the man in no way enslaved by low desires, not to say by prejudices of any kind" (102). But we were also told that this assessment was made before such a man was compared with Socrates. As we suspected even then, when compared with Socrates or looked at from Socrates' perspective, the gentleman's freedom from prejudices comes to light as less than complete. In Chapter XI, Socrates seems to go so far as to understand "honoring the gods magnificently . . . as part of adorning [or strengthening—cf. XI.13 with .10] the city" (163), i.e., as serving an essentially political function. (Among other things, it supports the gentleman's way of life, a way of life so conducive to citizenship in a republic.)

Having delved thus far into these matters, Strauss turns to a comparison of the *Oeconomicus* with Aristophanes' *Clouds* (the occasion for which is provided by a line of Chapter XI which is almost literally a quotation from the *Clouds*):

> The Aristophanean Socrates corrupted completely a youth who was already half-corrupted by horsemanship and who was the son of a farmer; the Xenophontic Socrates leads a young man who is the son of a gentleman-farmer, and who is in danger of losing himself in frivolities, back to farming or saves him from corruption by teaching him, among other things, the rudiments of farming. In contradistinction to the Aristophanean Socrates, who is nothing but a teacher, the Xenophontic Socrates is in the first place a pupil, not of idle talkers, i.e., of alien sophists or students of nature, but of the most perfect gentleman in Athens. (163–64)

This comparison must strike us as very strange. To say nothing of the question of the seriousness or earnestness of Socrates' attempt to reform Kritoboulos (cf. 169, 191), Xenophon's Socrates has been transformed from the critic of Ischomachos into his pupil (cf. 130, 162). What is the meaning of this change? Strauss concludes his comparison as follows: "The *Oeconomicus* is then in a properly subdued manner a comical reply to Aristophanes' comical attack on Socrates. More precisely, the *Oeconomicus* describes Socrates' famous turning away from his earlier pursuit, which brought him the reputation of being an idle talker and a man who measures the air and which left him wholly unaware of what perfect gentlemanship is, toward the study of only the human things and the things useful to human beings" (164). Apparently Strauss wished to speak so emphatically of Socrates' turn to the human things only after having cast it in the most innocent possible light. He does this toward the close of a portion of his book in which he seems to have gone far toward revealing the true intent and meaning of that turn; what he does here is needed by way of compensating for that openness. For, as Strauss has already stressed, even after his turn to the human things, Socrates "did *not* limit his inquiry to the human things" (150, my emphasis), i.e., his turn to the human things must be understood in the light of his continuing concern with "the nature of all things" (150). And there were, and may be again even if there are not now, "those who condemn the study of nature as wicked" (164, cf. 154).[14] Insofar then as the *Oeconomicus* is a reply, in the manner indicated by Strauss's comparison, to Aristophanes' attack on Socrates in the *Clouds*, it is only a "comical reply." But behind or informing the comedy is the serious need to protect a pursuit which was made not less, but perhaps even more hazardous by Socrates' turn to the human things. Aristophanes' play may have helped draw Socrates' or Xenophon's attention to this need (cf. *Xenophon's Socrates*, 169).

The final subject of Chapter XI and the one Strauss appropriately takes up next in his discussion is rhetoric. (In order to achieve this order, Strauss had to make his summarizing statement before "the account of the perfect gentleman or the confrontation of the two incompatible ways of life" had been completed [165].) The most important points brought

---

14. Cf. the observation, made for another purpose by David Bolotin in his review of Strauss's book on Plato's *Laws*, that Strauss's work shows his "exceptional freedom from vestiges of the secular faith in progress" (*American Political Science Review*, Vol. 71, 1977, 669).

out appear to be these. Socrates, who spent "his life considering the just and unjust things," "was not in any way concerned with accusing others" (165–66); the opposite is shown to be true of Ischomachos, of whose concern with punishment we saw some evidence earlier (137 and 142–43; cf. 151). Ischomachos says that "he cannot plead his cause well if it is useful to him to say the untruth; swearing by Zeus, he says that he cannot make the weaker argument the stronger one" (166; cf. *Clouds* 893–95). In his reply, Socrates "corrects" Ischomachos, according to Strauss, i.e., disagrees with him, though he does so unobtrusively. The need to defend or protect the Socratic way of life from those who would misunderstand it (cf., e.g., 104–05) may make it impossible for Socratic rhetoric to abide by such a limitation.

On Chapters Twelve Through Fourteen

According to Strauss, "The mere fact that the discussion of stewardship [Chapters XII–XIV] follows immediately the confrontation [in Chapter XI] of the two ways of life (the Ischomachean and the Socratic) could induce one to consider the possibility that the discussion of stewardship continues and deepens that confrontation" (176). In making this suggestion, Strauss seems to have in mind first the following reflection: "the account of the stewards is an account of Ischomachos's educating his stewards, just as the account of the wife was an account of Ischomachos's educating his wife" (167); the emphasis on Ischomachos's activity as an educator appears to point to that activity as "an important link" between Ischomachos and Socrates, who "regarded himself later as an expert on education and only on education" (167); yet, "This is not to assert" that Socrates "was an expert on the education of wives and stewards" (167); indeed, "It is obvious that Socrates is in no way engaged in educating human beings to stewardship" (176). Ischomachos's educating activity establishes in this case then a link not with Socrates, but with his own stewards (167), i.e., with slaves (173). The depth of this link is suggested by the fact that, "The perfect gentleman Ischomachos is able to educate at least some of his stewards so that they become perfect gentlemen" (175). In other words, freedom is not an essential ingredient of gentlemanship "in the Ischomachean sense." But Ischomachos himself was of course free: therefore, "One would go too far were one to assert that there is no difference whatever between the perfect gentleman in Ischomachos's sense and the perfect steward. It suffices to remember Ischomachos's account of his activity as the citizen of a commonwealth" (176; cf. 161). Or does Strauss intend us to remember this together with his observation on the fact that the chapters on the education of stewards are "silent on piety as an objective or ingredient" of that education (170): "The powerful presence of the human master makes the recourse to divine masters less necessary *than it otherwise would be*"? (170, my emphasis; cf. 123 on the difference between Chapters IV and V). Ischomachos's freedom, as citizen of a commonwealth, consisted precisely in the (relative) absence of human masters. In the course of stressing the kinship between Ischomachos and his stewards, Strauss finds occasion to say that "a perfect gentleman in the Ischomachean sense differs profoundly from the perfect gentleman in the Socratic sense. A perfect gentleman in the Socratic sense is a man who knows through thinking what is pious, what is impious, what is noble, what is base, and so on, or who considers thoroughly the just and unjust things" (175–76).

But this is merely another way of expressing the point—regarding Ischomachos's expectations or hopes of support for the noble way of life—which has already been made in the section on the wife. In speaking of a *deepening* of the confrontation between the two ways of life, Strauss must have in mind then the second point that he makes in this context: "Socrates differs from Ischomachos . . . by the fact that he is not a man capable of ruling" (177; cf. 166, on Socrates' powers in argument, with the repetition on 176). Since this fact emerged from a consideration of what it takes to rule slaves (see especially 172 as well as 169) and means primarily that Socrates is unable to rule slaves, we are unlikely to see its significance—why should Socrates even wish to rule slaves?—unless we connect it with Strauss's first point: the similarity between Ischomachos and his stewards (cf. 102). Strauss also reminds us here of Socrates' "accusers and condemners" (176), who were of course free men (only) in the Ischomachean sense. (Cf. 104–05. Cf. the references on 171 and 174 to "Socrates' view that there is no essential difference between despotic rule and rule over free men." The central paragraph of Strauss's discussion of the stewardship section deals with what is required for the ruling of slaves. The following paragraph calls attention to the fact that the stewards, too, are slaves; while the next two paragraphs bring out the similarity between Ischomachos and some of his stewards.)

Socrates' inability to rule slaves stemmed from his inability or unwillingness to use coercion (177 n. 10; cf. 172). One can say that his ruling was limited to teaching, provided that one adds that teaching, without coercion, may be ineffective in many cases: "Teaching not accompanied by coercion or, more precisely, by despotic power is insufficient for the education of stewards" (169). The need for coercion or despotic power stems in part from the limited teachability of diligence, which may be assumed to be "at least an indispensable ingredient of every virtue" (168); and the limited teachability of diligence is due at least in part to the fact that the one who is to learn it must already possess various sorts of continence (168; cf. 169–70, 172–73). Not even Ischomachos suggests that continence is teachable. Strauss's treatment of the theme "continence" is perhaps the strangest feature of his discussion of the chapters on stewardship. After calling attention (in a paragraph he contrives to make the central one in his discussion of the first chapter of the section) to the incompleteness of Ischomachos's enumeration of the kinds of continence required of stewards, he says, "Perhaps Xenophon merely indicates by this that something of importance is consciously omitted by him but unconsciously omitted by Ischomachos" (170). In other words, Ischomachos forgot about a kind of continence that is necessary. In his discussion of the next chapter, how-ever, Strauss points out that the workers' *possession* of continence of the omitted kind would make it more difficult to secure their obedience, while he adds that the treatment of stewards does not differ much from that of workers. Here then is the solution to Ischomachos's omission, a solution which suggests that the omission does him credit. Yet Strauss says merely, "Perhaps this explains his silence in the preceding chapter on continence regarding the belly," the kind of continence in question (172–73).

Only in the context of the larger problem of the section do these hints begin to make sense. If Socrates' inability to rule stems ultimately from the unteachability of continence, that inability would appear to have nothing to do with any difficulty Socrates might have in dealing with Ischomachos and his kind: can not Ischomachos be presumed to be a model of continence and therefore, as far as that goes (cf. 176), of teachability with respect to virtue? Or is this presumption precisely what Strauss wishes to call into question? Is it perhaps characteristic of Ischomachos to forget to some extent about continence? (Cf. 193 n.2, on Socrates' relative avoidance of mention of "the vine and its fruit," with 198 n.3 and context. Regarding continence of the belly in particular, cf. VII.6 and, for Strauss's understanding of this passage, 151.) The central paragraph in Strauss's discussion of the first chapter of the stewardship section has one other theme in addition to continence: piety or the gods. These themes seem to be linked in Strauss's work on the *Oeconomicus* as early as his treatment of Chapter I. Socrates, apparently wishing to avoid an admission that piety is necessary to the successful management of the household, gives the impression that he maintains that "possession of a household, knowledge of how to increase it, and willingness to work hard and shrewdly to this effect are the complete conditions" for such success (98). In this context, he identifies a sort of man, whom we would be likely to call incontinent, as a slave. Strauss renders his explanation as follows: "a man who wishes to be rich and does not wish to work toward that end is irrational; his thought is obscured by beings whose slave he is or who rule him" (98). Kritoboulos, not implausibly, assumes that Socrates refers to invisible rulers. Yet Socrates denies this, saying that he means, among other things, vices "like softness of the soul" (98). The incontinent, then, are slaves, however well-born or conventionally free they may be (which is not to say that all slaves are incontinent). Can Strauss, who has already referred in this context to praying, be suggesting that in many cases piety is supported by incontinence in the form of softness of soul? (Cf., with 102, *Thoughts on Machiavelli*, 211.) Incontinence in general, perhaps more than anything else (cf. 176), limits the teachability of virtue in either sense of the term (113–14, 161, 175–76). Yet, as we have seen in the case of the stewards, and as we suspect in the case of Ischomachos himself, virtue of the Ischomachean variety is compatible with some incontinence. This may not be the case, however, with that "true human virtue" which, according to Strauss, "is not in the need of conventions" (160). Incontinence in a form compatible and more than compatible with Ischomachean virtue may well be an irremovable barrier to the acquisition and therefore the teaching of Socratic virtue.

At the very outset of his discussion of the stewardship chapters, Strauss observes, on the basis of a remark of Socrates, that "Socrates seems to have learned everything about perfect gentlemanship that he wished to learn," by the time the discussion of stewards begins (167). In all likelihood then, he already knew, prior to his conversation with Ischomachos, of the limited teachability of virtue (see especially 168–69) or of the limits of his power of speaking (177). Very frequently in these chapters, Socrates is "surprised" by claims of Ischomachos to be able to teach things which Socrates doubts can be taught (167, 168, 171, 174); but those claims tend not to receive very impressive support. Or, as Strauss puts it, "prior to his conversation with Ischomachos, Socrates already possessed a better understanding of education than did the perfect gentleman" (168–69). That his power to teach through speaking was limited—it was not to learn this that Socrates sought a conversation with Ischomachos, which is no doubt one of the reasons why this limitation does not "become the theme in the *Oeconomicus*" (177). Nevertheless, as brought to light and examined in the stewardship section, this limitation tells us something about the conversation he did seek, about the constraints which in most cases place limits on its progress and about its hazards. One can perhaps put the difficulty this way. The philosopher as philosopher can never rule the majority of human beings—to do so even for a time, he would have to cease for that time to be a philosopher. Partly for this reason, i.e., partly because the rule over free men in this sense is no different from the rule over slaves (171, 174), he has no wish to rule (cf. 97). But this means that he must accept the rule of others, who can be expected to be unalterably opposed to what he stands for; and the necessary accommodation to those others will also require that he modify in some way his philosophic activity, i.e., cease to that extent to be a philosopher. To judge from remarks he makes elsewhere, Strauss seems to have suspected that Xenophon was critical of Socrates for not complying sufficiently with this necessity.[15]

On Chapters Fifteen Through Nineteen

Strauss begins his discussion of "the section on farming (Chs. XV–XIX)" (197) by observing of the chapter which introduces it that it is, apart from Chapter VI, "the only one devoted to the transition from one part of the work to another" (178). He goes on to suggest that "the division of the Ischomachos section into a part devoted to gentlemanship and a part devoted to farming is as incisive as the division of the work as a whole into the Kritoboulos section and the Ischomachos section" (178). This suggestion is tacitly modified however toward the end of the discussion of the farming section, when Strauss raises the question "whether Chapter XII is not the beginning, and Chapter XIX the end, of one and the same section, the section on stewards. After all, the art of farming is practiced, and taught, by the stewards rather than by the master himself . . ." (195). The difference which had impressed Strauss between the Ischomachos chapters prior to Chapter XV and those including and after it was that only the latter are devoted to an art, "a kind of knowledge" (179). "Diligence and the other qualities discussed in the three preceding chapters are not arts" (179; cf. 195). The chapters prior to Chapter VI, too, were devoted to an

---

15. See "Xenophon's *Anabasis*" 124, 131, 138, 139–40, 146, and *Xenophon's Socrates*, 50, 126, 140 (cf. 144, 177, 178, 3, 21).

art, "the knowledge of how to manage one's household" (179), an art which was, at least in one of its forms, possessed by Socrates (113). Farming, on the other hand, whether or not he leaves its teaching and practice to his stewards, is the art possessed by Ischomachos (cf. XII.4); indeed, it is "the apparently most important cognitive ingredient of his whole life" (180; cf. 204). By his treatment of the divisions of the work, Strauss seems to suggest that however fundamental in itself is the distinction between art (or knowledge) and what is not art (or knowledge), Ischomachos's art, or his manner of possessing that knowledge, is compatible with stewardship, with being a steward or slave.

The chapters on farming, like those preceding them on stewardship, belong to the part of the discussion between Ischomachos and Socrates which takes place after Socrates has indicated that he has "learned everything about perfect gentlemanship that he wished to learn" (167). But Strauss does not suggest regarding the farming chapters what he had suggested regarding the stewardship discussion proper, that it "continues and deepens" the confrontation between "the two ways of life" (176). He does not lead us to expect from these chapters, or his treatment of them, any extension, any deepening, of what has already been brought out. Their significance—understandable only in light of the extreme terseness and difficulty of Xenophon's text (and Strauss's commentary) thus far—may consist then chiefly in this: that what is brought out here, in some ways more fully than before, is only what we are already supposed to have learned. Strauss may indirectly refer to the indirectness of his procedure as well as Xenophon's when he says that "it appears that Socrates knew more about casting the seed than this philosopher might be thought to know . . ." (189). Shortly before, he had called attention to the care or economy with which the term "philosopher" is used by Xenophon (185). His own use of the term here may be explained by his later remark that "the art of farming in particular may well be used as a likeness of the art of rhetoric" (192), an art exercised by Socrates (191). A speaker or writer who understands his task to be the casting of seeds does not feel obliged, perhaps not even entitled, to elaborate his thought fully (cf. *Xenophon's Socrates*, Preface); he does or must content himself with letting the hints which he has planted, or their juxtaposition or order, lead the listener or reader to that elaboration on his own.

In the first paragraph of the first chapter of his discussion of the farming section, Strauss had called attention to "the division of the Ischomachos section into a part devoted to gentlemanship and a part devoted to farming" (178). Only in the second paragraph does he tell how Socrates leads Ischomachos to speak of farming. Strauss emphasizes two points. First, while Socrates had "learned" from Ischomachos that the steward must be (among other things) "just," when speaking of the quality in question in his summary of the stewardship section, Socrates refrains from using the term "just": he was reluctant, apparently, to accept as justice "abstaining from another man's property" (178; cf. 95–97). Second, Ischomachos has some difficulty in understanding what Socrates is after, because "he did not think that Socrates could be interested in farming" (179). The third paragraph returns to the theme of the first, the distinction between art as a kind of knowledge and what is not art. The question is raised whether Ischomachos's "knowledge" of how to produce in his stewards (among other things) "justice" is not an art (179). Knowledge of how to produce justice in someone would, however, necessarily include knowledge of what justice is. We are not surprised therefore to learn in this same paragraph that it is the art of farming which is "the apparently most important cognitive ingredient" of Ischomachos's life (180)—which could hardly be the case if he *knew* also how to make someone just. In this paragraph Strauss also alludes again to the fact or probability that Socrates is reluctant to farm. His reluctance is still more emphasized in the fourth paragraph: Socrates refuses to accept the suggestion that farming is philanthropic (cf. 121–22). Nevertheless, in repeating his summary of the stewardship section, Socrates indicates a greater interest than before in taking up farming. Strauss links this to another change in Socrates' summary: "he says now that the steward must be just" (180). If one accepts Ischomachos's view of what justice is, it is difficult to avoid the conclusion that Socrates must take up farming: "Surely a man circumstanced like Socrates can now no longer avoid desiring to learn the art of farming" (181; cf. 104). Just as the third paragraph alluded to Socrates' reluctance to farm, the fourth alludes to the theme of knowledge, in particular to Ischomachos's view of what constitutes knowledge. According to Ischomachos, farming can be understood in part "by watching men doing farm work" and in part "by hearing" (180).

The first paragraph of the next chapter begins with the declaration, "This much is clear: Socrates will not be a farmer, i.e., a practicing farmer, a farmer 'in deed.'" (182) The preparation Strauss has laid in the preceding chapter insures that this declaration will have the proper impact, although Strauss softens the blow for the time being by holding out the possibility that Socrates "may very well become an outstanding teacher of farming, a man who teaches farming through and through, most precisely, 'in speech.'" (182; cf. 191) He thus at the same time brings in the theme of precision, or speech, or knowledge, or "theory." Strauss treats in this paragraph Ischomachos's attack on those who treat farming too "theoretically"; Ischomachos's attack on the theorists forces him in the direction of adopting certain of their positions—in particular, their distrust of "hearsay" and their "emancipation from 'one's own.'" (183; cf. 95–97) It is safe to assume that Ischomachos adopts these positions only to a very limited extent. (For example, Ischomachos's "emancipation from 'one's own' . . . might remind us" of that achieved by Socrates (183)—it is surely not identical to it.) The next paragraph deals with Ischomachos's view that in teaching Socrates farming, "he is not likely to teach Socrates anything new to him; his teaching will rather consist of reminding Socrates of what he knows already" (184). Strauss has already suggested by his references to "hearing" and "hearsay," that Ischomachos's understanding of what constitutes knowledge is rather loose; it would therefore be wrong here to accept Ischomachos's view of the state of Socrates' knowledge of farming without further consideration. And as for Ischomachos's contribution to Socrates' later view of teaching and learning—that view is, at most, the outcome of Socrates' "meditation on a thought first suggested to him by the practice of the perfect gentleman par excellence" (184). The final paragraph of this chapter, like the first, deals implicitly with justice (or Ischomachos's view of justice, or Socrates' non-acceptance of that view) as well as with knowledge. Strauss interprets a remark of Socrates to mean that, "The philosopher . . . is a man characterized by a conditional or qualified love of lucre. This love might induce him under certain conditions not specified by Socrates to strive to get the greatest possible harvest of crops; . . . under no circumstances does he wish to become a perfect gentleman, in the ordinary meaning of that expression." Socrates "is more concerned with lucre than with perfect gentlemanship" (185). Strauss then speaks of two points regarding farming which Socrates proves to know, of a somewhat questionable inference drawn by Ischomachos from one of these points, and of the "similar" way in which Ischomachos and Socrates reach "full agreement" on the other points pertaining to the topic under discussion. (186). The connection between the themes justice and knowledge would appear to be this: if Ischomachos's view of what constitutes knowledge is loose, he may regard as knowledge of justice what is not knowledge or be blind to the need to investigate the adequacy of his understanding of justice (cf. 165–66).

The first paragraph of Strauss's next chapter (which treats Chapters XVII and XVIII of the text), the central paragraph on the farming section, introduces a new theme into the discussion of that section: theology, or Socrates' interest in theology. At the same time, the treatment of the theme knowledge continues, so that there are two themes to this paragraph too; theology takes the place of justice. The nature of the connection between theology and justice is indicated by Strauss's treatment of a Socratic reference to divine punishment. By thinking through just punishment, we see that the bad consequences of an action men are compelled to take cannot be regarded as divine punishment. Further reflection on justice would no doubt bring out this connection more fully; but in order to be able to undertake that reflection, one would have had to become aware of the inadequacy of one's knowledge of justice. The theme knowledge is treated here in connection with the question of agreement. Strauss raises the question whether the agreement between Ischomachos and Socrates, reached at the end of the previous chapter, "is based in all points on the fact that both possess the required knowledge; perhaps on some points they only happen to have the same opinion" (187). Later on in the paragraph, Strauss refers to Socrates' tracing universal agreement to the teaching of the god and to his tracing disagreement as well to the god's action. Strauss then asks whether "all universal agreement, as well as the lack of it," must "be traced to the god or the gods" (188). This question is answered by the suggestion which Strauss ventures to include in the next paragraph, "that Socrates and Ischomachos genuinely agree only if they are not taught by the god or if their wisdom is only wisdom concerning human things, or human wisdom" (188). As can be seen in the case of justice, agreement regarding human things is not without bearing on agreement regarding divine things. Each of the following three paragraphs indicates that a connection may exist between ignorance and knowledge, that one may have knowledge of one's ignorance and that this presupposes that one has some knowledge of other things as well (cf. also 193). Is human wisdom, at least in part, such knowledge of ignorance? More precisely, these paragraphs show Socrates' awareness of his ignorance regarding crucial elements of farming,[16] while leaving it uncertain whether Ischomachos is

____

16. The central one of these paragraphs seems to show this less clearly than the two which surround it—"he does not even raise the question" (190). On the other hand, it may contain a reference to the "right of the stronger" and thus remind us of the issue of justice (189–90; cf. 123).

equally aware of Socrates' ignorance or takes it sufficiently to heart when he speaks of "reminding" Socrates of farming (184) or ascribes to Socrates knowledge of farming. Strauss puts great emphasis here on the spurious character of this knowledge:

> Is not the 'knowledge' of the art of farming that he acquires through his conversation with Ischomachos shot through with ignorance? (189)

> Ischomachos leads him to understand the reason . . . by appealing partly to facts Socrates knows and partly to plausibilities. Socrates comes into possession of the correct answer through 'hearing' . . . rather than through having seen. He knows the whole art of farming partly from having seen . . . and partly from having heard explanations . . . . But, as we have seen, this knowledge is not genuine knowledge of the art of farming. (190)

The third of these paragraphs speaks also of Socrates' interest in the art of rhetoric. "Socrates exercised that art not only prior to his meeting with Ischomachos but also after it . . ." (191). For example, "His teaching of the art of farming, his exhorting Kritoboulos to exercise that art, is an act of rhetoric" (190–91). This use of rhetoric, in particular, is traceable to Socrates' meeting with Ischomachos: "after this fateful meeting his rhetoric serves the purpose, for instance, of making a gentleman farmer out of a gentleman farmer's son" (191). Yet Socrates' teaching Kritoboulos farming is "not altogether serious" (191; cf. 182), i.e., in this respect at least, the change ascribed to his meeting with Ischomachos is not so great as first appears.[17] Beyond that, rhetoric itself is not "altogether serious" (192). What is serious, as we are told here, indeed "the most serious of all arts or sciences," is "theology" (192). The theme casting its shadow on this chapter and the whole treatment of this section is Socrates' approach to "theology," an approach which, we take it, was based on his strictness regarding what is and what is not knowledge. This strictness made him

---

17. As the discussion of the section on farming confirms, Strauss views the pursuits of the younger and older Socrates in other respects, too, as essentially continuous. (Consider especially 196.) In the passage discussed above in the text, Socrates' reputation as an "idle chatterer" is ascribed to his post-Ischomachos activity (191); earlier, it had been ascribed to his pre-Ischomachos pursuit (164).

aware of what he did not know and enabled him to remedy that ignorance where possible (cf. 165). At the same time, it made him aware of others' not yet possessing such awareness or of the looseness in their view of what constitutes knowledge, and thus of the potential (if the looseness should be removed) for coming to "genuine agreement" with them, regarding important matters, based on merely human wisdom. In the sixth and last paragraph of this chapter, Strauss again treats Socrates' knowledge of farming—its spurious as well as genuine elements.

Strauss's treatment of the final chapter of the farming section, Chapter XIX, consists of only two paragraphs. In the first, he mentions "dialectics" for the first time in the discussion of this section: "Socrates learns from Ischomachos's practice that teaching is questioning and is thus brought on the way toward his discovery of dialectics in the twofold meaning of the term" (194). Strauss had said something very similar in the course of his discussion of Chapter XVI: "Socrates' later view of teaching and learning is the outcome of his meditation on a thought first suggested to him by the practice of the perfect gentleman par excellence" (184).[18] In his earlier remark however he did not mention "dialectics" by name. Apparently he wished to introduce "dialectics" as a theme of the farming section not in the discussion of Chapter XVI but in that of Chapter XIX. His combined discussion of the two intervening chapters had emphasized Socrates' interest in theology (188, 192). Theology is prominently mentioned in the discussion of Chapter XIX too—in the second paragraph. After calling attention to the large number of oaths in Chapter XIX as well as Chapter XII, Strauss observes, "Just as Chapter XII is silent on piety, Chapter XIX is silent on theology" (195). The silence on piety in Chapter XII was remarkable because there was a reason to speak of piety there: piety might have been thought to be an important ingredient of the education of stewards, which was the topic under discussion (170). But what reason was there to bring theology into Chapter XIX? It is not sufficient to say that it had been brought into other chapters of the farming section: it was not included in Chapter XVIII and that absence occasioned no comment by Strauss. We suspect that what makes the similar silence of Chapter XIX worth noting is that dialectics, according to Strauss, has become a theme there. Strauss's remark on dialectics speaks of Socrates'

---

18. The earlier statement taken as a whole (see the last sentence on 184) is more obviously hesitant about assigning any responsibility for Socrates' discovery to Ischomachos. Cf. however the use of "Ischomachean" on 194 with its use on 150.

discovery of dialectics "in the twofold meaning of the term" (194). A footnote to this remark refers us to *Memorabilia* IV.6.13–15, a passage which explains the difference between Socratic conversations which lead toward the truth and those intended merely to produce agreement. This distinction is related to distinctions called attention to by Strauss in the farming section: between Ischomachos's teaching Socrates "by appealing . . . to facts Socrates knows" and his teaching Socrates by appealing "to plausibilities" (190); between what Socrates knows of farming "from having seen" and what he "knows" "from having heard" (190; cf. 180); and between agreement of Socrates and Ischomachos based on their both possessing the required knowledge and their agreement based on shared opinion (187; cf. 188). Strauss casts further light on his remark on dialectics by reminding us in its vicinity of Socrates' having called attention to the rhetorical character of Ischomachos's teaching in one of its aspects (194; cf. 190). In his discussion of the earlier passage, Strauss spoke of Socrates' interest in rhetoric; shortly before he had spoken of Socrates' interest in theology (188; cf. 192). Strauss was to speak again of rhetoric in his discussion of the *Memorabilia* passage he refers to in his footnote here: "It makes sense to call the Odyssean dialectics [those intended to produce mere agreement] rhetoric"; but this rhetoric, or the Odyssean dialectics, must then be distinguished from "dialectics strictly understood" (*Xenophon's Socrates*, 123). There appears to be a correspondence between the twofold character of dialectics and the twofold character of Socrates' interests (in rhetoric and "theology"). In other words, the "dialectics strictly understood" would appear to be the Socratic approach to "theology" (which we recall was a conversational approach), or the Socratic replacement for theology. In the second paragraph of his discussion of Chapter XIX, Strauss speaks not only of theology but of what underlies Socrates' concern with it: his life-long interest in nature or *physiologia* (cf. *Natural Right and History*, 82–84). If the dialectics strictly understood are the Socratic approach to "theology," "theology" would constitute the link between dialectics and *physiologia*;[19] moreover, one would be able to

---

19. A very different account of this link, and of dialectics generally, was given on 147–48. Strauss refers to that passage too in the footnote to his remark on dialectics which has already been mentioned. (He does so in a very unusual way; he says "see" these pages: his merely corroborative references, so far as I have observed in this book, always have the form "cf.") The remark here seems to support the hesitancy I felt when reading the account on 147–48 at accepting it as the whole of Strauss's treatment of dialectics. Cf. also "Plato," 43–44 in *History of Political Philosophy* (second edition).

understand on this basis how political philosophy—in the form of the dialectics strictly understood—can be at the same time both "the political introduction to philosophy" and "the core of philosophy, or rather 'the first philosophy.' "[20]

ON CHAPTERS TWENTY AND TWENTY-ONE

In Chapter XX, Ischomachos explains why, despite the fact that "all men know equally well the things pertaining to farming," "some farmers are very wealthy and others are very poor" (197). On the basis of an earlier passage (V.18–20), Strauss suggests as one of the reasons for this state of affairs "divine dispensation"; he then calls attention to the fact that "Ischomachos does not have recourse to that reason" (197). He does this in the first paragraph of his discussion of Chapter XX. In the next paragraph (indeed in the next sentence), he points out that for the most part Chapters XX and XXI, "the two last chapters of the *Oeconomicus*," in contrast to those making up the immediately preceding section on farming, are not in the form of a "dialogue between Ischomachos and Socrates" (197). Strauss points this out here although he could have done so elsewhere in his discussion of the two chapters—for example, after he discusses the suggestion (of Ischomachos) "that ruling over willing subjects is clearly something divine" (207; cf. 208). Apparently, he wished to link the non-dialogical character of these chapters with the absence of the question of the gods rather than with its presence.

As Strauss's remark on the form of Chapters XX and XXI indicates, he does not understand them to comprise part of the section on farming. Since they pursue questions which arise out of the farming section, directly or indirectly, they could be said to constitute a kind of appendix to it; but they serve also to conclude the *Oeconomicus* as a whole. In this capacity, they convey the teaching of the work in the most public, if not the most revealing, manner. Strauss's discussion, which relies heavily on comparisons with the *Hiero* for this purpose (203–04, 205, 209), is designed to explain the meaning of this conclusion as much as to follow the questions immediately at issue. For example, while the last paragraph of his discussion of Chapter XX explains, in terms of the particular question at issue in Chapter XX, why the argument of Chapter XXI is needed, the

---

20. The quotations are from *What is Political Philosophy?* (93–94; cf. "The Spirit of Sparta or the Taste of Xenophon," 532) and *The City and Man* (20).

preceding paragraph has already explained this in terms of the teaching of Chapter XX taken as a part of the conclusion to the whole work. We will concentrate on this aspect of his discussion.

The *Oeconomicus* concludes, in Chapter XXI, with Ischomachos's praise of rule over willing subjects as "something divine that is given to those who have been truly initiated into the mysteries of moderation" (207) and with his blame of "tyrannical rule over unwilling subjects," which he regards as "no less a divine gift than ruling over willing subjects" but a gift which "is given by the gods . . . to those whom they regard as worthy to live the life of Tantalus in Hades . . ." (208). This final teaching (among other things) would appear to place the *Oeconomicus* in sharp contrast to the *Hiero*, which "ends with strongly worded praise of the tyrant who rules over willing subjects" (209). To put the teaching of the *Hiero* in the terms used by Ischomachos in the *Oeconomicus*, there is nothing in principle to prevent rule over willing subjects from being given to a tyrant who, as "a man who has in the past committed innumerable crimes" (209), is not likely to have been "truly initiated into the mysteries of moderation." In accord with this difference between the two works, the teaching of the *Hiero* is entrusted not to Socrates but to Simonides, a wise man of a very different stripe than Socrates and in particular a man "who can always find refuge with a tyrant, since he is not attached to his fatherland" (209).

The appearance of opposition between the two works is to some extent misleading however. "Both dialogues are narrated by Xenophon" (209), i.e., to that extent he takes responsibility for them, for bringing them to our attention: Xenophon's "instincts," as we were told earlier, are "controlled by his admiration for Socrates" (203). Socrates, for his part, "remains altogether silent" in response to the speech of Ischomachos which conflicts with the teaching of the *Hiero* (205). Moreover, a somewhat different view of the relation between *Hiero* and *Oeconomicus* has been presented in the discussion of Chapter XX. Strauss took up again there a remark of Ischomachos which carried an implicit criticism of Socrates: "Precisely because the knowledge required for farming is easily available to everyone and therefore what makes the difference between the good and the bad farmer is not knowledge but diligence, farming, or rather the earth which in its justice treats well those who treat it well, is the reliable accuser, not only of a bad farmer, but of a bad soul" (198–99; cf. 104). But in examining the question "what it is that makes human beings diligent" (199), Strauss reached the conclusion that the motive of Ischomachos himself, or at least of his father whose practice he continues, "proves to be love of gain" (201). Since the motive of a perfect gentleman "is not so much gain as what is noble, what is becoming, what is conducive to the common good" (201), Ischomachos thus "comes close to abandoning perfect gentlemanship" (201).[21] Yet Socrates does not for this reason disapprove of him. One may even say "that he goes further than Ischomachos or his father" in this direction (202). It was in this context that Strauss offered his first and deeper statement of the relation between the *Oeconomicus* and "the parallel work, the *Hiero*," which is at the same time an explanation of why Chapter XXI exaggerates the tension between the two works: "in both works Xenophon experiments with extreme possibilities . . . . It goes without saying that Xenophon did not wish to experiment with both extreme possibilities in one and the same work. If any proof for this were needed, it would be supplied by the last chapter of the *Oeconomicus*" (203–04). Chapter XXI then is meant to compensate for the approval which Socrates has given, most recently in Chapter XX, to love of gain.

Strauss may have intended to indicate the perspective from which that approval is given by referring to a passage in the *Eudemian Ethics* (203 n.18). (He does so after he has likened Ischomachos's quasi-abandonment of perfect gentlemanship to the "change effected by Xenophon's Cyrus" when he persuaded the Persian nobility "that virtue ought not to be practiced as it was hitherto practiced in Persia, for its own sake, but for the sake of great wealth, great happiness, and great honors" [203].) The continuation of that passage, at any rate, speaks of "the contemplation of god" as the goal or target which ought to govern our actions. Someone who made all of his actions serve "the contemplation of god" would look upon some of them—those which a gentleman would view as choice-worthy in themselves—differently than the gentleman; in this respect, he would be closer to the Ischomachos of Chapter XX or to the Persians "corrupted" by Cyrus than to such a gentleman. An uncertainty remains as to whether this means that the theoretical man abandons altogether the concern for the noble as such.

It may help to look briefly at some of the many places in *Xenophon's Socrates*, the sequel to *Xenophon's Socratic Discourse*, where Strauss appears to take up this question.

On page 74, he says, "wisdom for which the philosophers long is obviously something noble . . . ." Shortly afterwards however he raises the

---

21. The mention of Sparta in this context reminds us of Lysander's earlier step in the same direction (119).

question, as one yet to be answered, whether "the good, the noble, and the pleasant are the same, if not simply, at least in the most important case" (77–78). By "the most important case," Strauss almost surely means wisdom (cf. 125, "on the highest level"). What this question means, as applied to wisdom, appears from the immediate context. Strauss has just come close to identifying the "beautiful" (a term he appears to use interchangeably with "noble"—119, 167; cf. *Xenophon's Socratic Discourse*, 121), insofar as it is something solid, with the pleasant or reducing the beautiful to the pleasant (77 and the reference on 120 to the textual passage discussed on 77; cf. 85, 167); with this tentative identification in mind, he asks whether it is necessary to retain the beautiful or noble as a distinct category or characteristic in the case of wisdom, or whether wisdom cannot be understood adequately in terms of the good and pleasant alone. The promised or half-promised answer to this question is never given as such, although it may be implied in Strauss's account of the coincidence, in wisdom and its pursuit, of "the greatest good" and "the greatest pleasure" (125; cf. 114, 115), an account which is silent on the beautiful. Later on, Strauss treats more or less disparagingly a reference to Socrates' nobility (139); and he insists that Socrates' losing a beauty contest to Kritoboulos is not to be taken as due to a lack of bodily beauty alone (167); on the other hand, he says that Xenophon, a man of "light-heartedness, grace, and flexibility," was a lover of Socrates (171).

There are several passages—the one on pages 80–81 standing out—in which Strauss appears to suggest that the *objects* of wisdom are or belong to the beautiful or noble things (cf. 85 and 167; 104, 103; consider the repeated references to *Memorabilia* II.2.3). A later statement, however, which is his most extensive and explicit one on the subject, distinguishes the objects of wisdom from the beautiful or noble (as well as the good) things (118–20). Still, it is not completely clear how definitive this statement is meant to be, or how far it is meant to go. The difficulty which strikes us first is that Strauss calls here the objects of wisdom "the most excellent things" (119). In an earlier passage, where he had called things akin to the examples now given of objects of wisdom "the best things," he spoke of them as being higher "in rank" than likenesses of things which can only be seen (83; cf. "Plato" in *History of Political Philosophy*, ed. Strauss and Cropsey, 2nd edition, 51). We are reminded by this of the fact that although he remains silent on the beautiful, in his account of the coincidence in wisdom of the greatest good and the greatest pleasure, Strauss speaks there of what the good and the pleasant are "on the highest level"

(125; cf. 81). Moreover, on a closer look at the statement now before us, we see that while he says in one part of it that the good and noble things "are" not the objects of wisdom (119–20), he says in a slightly earlier part merely that "it would seem that wisdom is not concerned with the good and beautiful things as such" (119).

To try to find a way through these difficulties, we turn to the context of the remarks, in the two passages we have been looking at (80–81 and 118–20), bearing on the question of the objects of wisdom. This means that we turn to the question that Strauss was concerned with in making those remarks. According to the later statement, "The good and noble things are the objects, not of *sophia* (wisdom), but of *phronesis* (good sense) (cf. IV.8.11). The Socrates of the bulk of the *Memorabilia* is *phronimos* but not *sophos*: the concealment of Socrates' *sophia* is *the* defense of Socrates" (119–20). As it happens, the reference to the concealment of Socrates' wisdom picks up and makes more explicit a comment in the first of our passages: "The use of 'reasonable' here may remind us of the fact, deliberately left obscure in the preceding discussion, that the wisdom (*sophia*) spoken of there is in fact reasonableness (*phronesis*) (cf. IV.8.11). The Socratic denial of the difference between reasonableness and wisdom follows from the denial of the difference between the good and the beautiful or noble things, among the latter the objects of sight standing out (II.2.3)" (80–81). This earlier comment suggests that the denial of the difference between the good and the beautiful or noble things deprives wisdom of its proper objects—which are the beautiful or noble things. By depriving wisdom of its proper objects, that denial deprives it of its distinct existence and in this way contributes to its concealment. Wisdom becomes indistinguishable from *phronesis*, reasonableness or good sense, which looks at everything, including the beautiful, from the perspective of utility, or reduces the beautiful to the useful (74–77, 119–20). Now, when it is asserted in the later statement that wisdom is *not* concerned with the noble (or the good) things, the identification of the beautiful with the useful is in fact tacitly understood (cf. 120). The contradiction between the two statements is thus only apparent: the later statement does no more than reaffirm the conclusion of the earlier one, that wisdom is not concerned with the noble or beautiful things *in the same way* that *phronesis* is (that is, only insofar as they are useful). As it does not deny, wisdom emerges from behind the screen of *phronesis*, or comes into its own, as the non-utilitarian character of its concern with the beautiful or noble is recognized, or only when we see that it is concerned with the beautiful or noble insofar as the beautiful or noble transcends utility.

Two considerations prevent me from being completely satisfied with this solution to our difficulties. First, why would such a wisdom ever have been in need of concealment? Second, as Strauss indicates most clearly later on, there is more than one way in which the beautiful or noble transcends utility or more than one sort of the beautiful or noble (167). With which sort, and with which sort of transcendence, is wisdom primarily concerned, and in what way? Perhaps by failing to make this clear, Strauss's statements distinguishing wisdom from *phronesis* leave wisdom as much in concealment as does Socrates' practice of identifying the two. It has obviously become necessary to take up more directly the question of the character of this concealment and the need for it.

On page 117, Strauss begins a paragraph as follows: "Since Socrates considered what each of the beings is, Xenophon cannot well present the results of these considerations without defeating the purpose of the *Memorabilia*," that is, the defense of Socrates. The sentence which concludes this paragraph suggests that Xenophon refrains in particular from presenting Socrates raising the question, "What is a god?" (118) Strauss had noted earlier in the book that Xenophon refrains from presenting Socrates raising the question, "What is law?" (15; cf. 17) In a later article on the *Anabasis*, he was to indicate comparatively openly his view that these two questions are intimately related.[22] In *Xenophon's Socrates*, he limits himself to suggesting that the appearance of wisdom in its distinct character goes together with acknowledgement of the philosopher's concern with "the laws" (121). But he has already indicated that the appearance of wisdom in its distinct character requires or is indistinguishable from acknowledgement of the philosopher's concern with the question of the gods. (For another indication that the concealment of Socrates' wisdom serves the purpose of presenting him as pious or more pious than he would otherwise appear as being, consider on page 126 the implication of "On the other hand . . . .") Now, as we learned from *Xenophon's Socratic Discourse* (137 and 135), the law is intimately related to the noble. We should expect to find then for this reason alone, whatever may be the case with any other reason, a philosophic concern with the noble.

The character of that concern is pointed to by Strauss's fuller treatment of the way the denial of a philosophic concern with the noble contributes

---

22. "Xenophon's *Anabasis*," 133.

to the concealment of wisdom, and we are now in a somewhat better position to try to follow his discussion. As we saw, Socrates in effect denies that philosophy is concerned with the noble, by identifying the noble with the good. Strauss says that this identification "stems from the attempt to reject the excess of the noble over the good as irrational . . ." (76). Shortly afterwards, referring to Socrates' discussion of "the most becoming location of temples and altars," he says, "Socrates does not speak here of the beautiful or of the good; but if anything can illustrate the excess of the beautiful over the good (useful), this example can" (77). The point is pursued in the case of "the denial of the essential difference between the city and the household." Strauss traces this, too, to "the attempt to reject the excess of the noble over the good as irrational" (76); it in turn has some responsibility for "the assertion that knowledge, and not election, makes a man a ruler" (63); and that assertion amounts to denying the need for prayer and for sacrifices (83). "Socrates abstracts from the specific dignity, grandeur, and splendor of the political and military . . ." (63). He ignores the fact that "what is good for the city, is frequently noble rather than good for the individual" (167; cf. 68, 59, 60–61). In abstracting from the noble in this sense, he seeks to dismiss ("to reject as irrational") what is, perhaps inevitably, called upon *in support of* this sort of nobility. For the good things "are more fundamental" than the noble ones (98), or "all choose what they believe to be most advantageous to themselves" (121), or "the noble is more problematical than the good" (76). (Consider also 5, and the repetition on 16, "the most important thing" in one's exercise for example of the strategic art is "whether the exercise of that art will benefit" one.) But prior to investigation, nothing can be dismissed as irrational by an open-minded person. We must assume then that Socrates undertook an investigation of the support for this sort of nobility, as in fact *Xenophon's Socratic Discourse* is devoted to showing, an investigation which, for reasons developed more fully there, required that he pay the greatest attention to the noble in this sense. As for the other sort of the noble or beautiful, that which Strauss openly characterizes as "good only to be looked at" (85 and 167; cf. 60), the philosophers' concern with or expectations from it are bound to be affected by what they learn from their investigation of the nobility which is linked to law.

Socrates' identification of the noble and the good served to hide this investigation, and therewith his wisdom, from those he wished to hide it from, while pointing in the direction of its result. As to why an investigation would be more in need of being hidden than its result—it is only in thinking through the reasons for a position that we make it, provided they be sufficient reasons, so thoroughly our own that we are inescapably possessed by a thought we would otherwise be able to dismiss almost at will.

8

A Return to Classical Political Philosophy and the Understanding of the American Founding

I.

What is the significance for the understanding of the American Founding of Leo Strauss's efforts toward the recovery of classical political philosophy? That this is a legitimate question to address to Strauss's work is suggested by the claims which he made in the introductions to a number of his most famous books (among other things). He opened his study on *Natural Right and History*, for example, by raising the question whether our nation "in its maturity still cherish[es] the faith in which it was conceived and raised," that is, whether it still holds the fundamental proposition of the Declaration of Independence to be true. In doing so, he gave warrant to the expectation that that study, which may be said to culminate in a treatment of classical natural right and make a case for its superiority to all alternatives, would contribute to the strengthening or restoration of our Founding faith. In

This is a corrected version of a paper prepared for a conference on Classical Theory and Practice and the American Founding, John M. Olin Center for Inquiry into the Theory and Practice of Democracy, the University of Chicago, 16–18 June 1988. I've received invaluable help in thinking about the themes of the paper from several friends: Tom Pangle, Nathan Tarcov and especially David Bolotin whose questions, insights and judgment have drawn me back from many errors and set me again upon the track. I wish also to thank my research assistants, In Ha Jang and Michael Grenke, for their help in perfecting the manuscript and preparing it for publication.

similar fashion, the opening of *The City and Man* presents that work's turn "toward the political thought of classical antiquity" as dictated by "the crisis of our time, the crisis of the West," a crisis which it locates "in the West's having become uncertain of its purpose." The purpose spoken of in *The City and Man* is not identical to the Founding faith appealed to in *Natural Right and History*; but it is not hard to see the close kinship between the two. And, again, warrant is given for the expectation that the outcome of a successful return to classical political thought will be a recovery of the West's certainty as to its purpose. Indeed, the clear and powerful meaning which Strauss thus attached to his efforts toward the recovery of classical political philosophy helps explain both the widespread influence his work has had on students concerned with the health of American politics and also the fact that it has inspired in many of them, as Gordon Wood has pointed out in a recent article,[1] a deepened interest in the American Founding. But clear and powerful as the bearing of Strauss's work may be on our most urgent concerns, that is, clear as it may be that his work has an important bearing on those concerns, the precise character of its bearing is a matter of some ambiguity. These ambiguities, moreover, are bound to affect students who have undergone its influence. That this is the case with those who have turned to the study of the American Founding has also been pointed out by Wood. It is on these ambiguities, then, insofar as they affect the study of the American Founding, that we must concentrate our attention if we are to answer the question with which we began.

"The crisis of the West," as Strauss saw it and as he led many others to see it, is constituted in large measure by the collapse of modern political philosophy or modern natural right—which had supplied to the West its universal purpose—into "historicism," the view that all doctrines are tied fundamentally to a particular time and place, that there can be no universal purposes or timeless truths. This philosophic doctrine, which denies to philosophy the possibility of reaching its essential goal, was characterized by Strauss as "the self-destruction of reason"; and he came to understand it as "the inevitable outcome of modern rationalism as distinguished from pre-modern rationalism."[2] A return to premodern rationalism (which meant ultimately to classical political philosophy) represented, then, the

---

1. "The Fundamentalists and the Constitution," *The New York Review of Books*, 18 February 1988, pp. 33–40.

2. "Preface to the English Translation," *Spinoza's Critique of Religion*, trans. E. M. Sinclair (New York: Schocken, 1965), p. 31.

soundest hope for a recovery of rationalism, simply, as a "science" that, according to the formulation of Husserl which Strauss had recourse to, "would satisfy the highest theoretical needs and in regard to ethics and religion render possible a life regulated by pure rational norms."[3] Those who saw in Strauss's work the achievement of such a return might well believe themselves entitled, therefore, to entertain, with respect to the American Founding, a possibility which many of their contemporaries had all but abandoned and consequently rarely permitted themselves to dwell on: the possibility, namely, of holding the guiding principles of the Founding to be simply true, as indeed they had been claimed to be, true not merely for "a decade or two" or for "several cultures at the same time,"[4] but everywhere and always. At the same time and in the same way, it became possible once again to take seriously the Founders' own understanding of what they were trying to accomplish.

But though Strauss's efforts supported and were no doubt intended to support these possibilities, though, for example, they truly vouched for the legitimacy of the *question* of the truth of the Founding principles, they were far from suggesting a simply positive answer to that question. The rationalism whose recovery Strauss aimed at or achieved was "premodern": his efforts conceded and indeed sought to confirm the inadequacies of modern rationalism. It was to modern rationalism, however, in its earlier forms, that he himself traced "the theory of liberal democracy,"[5] if not all aspects[6] of the political order established by the Founders. The "undeniable fact" of the link between liberal democracy and early modern thought did not permit us, then, to return to that thought: "the critique of modern rationalism or of the modern belief in reason by Nietzsche cannot be dismissed or forgotten."[7] Or, as Strauss

---

3. "Philosophy as Rigorous Science and Political Philosophy," *Studies in Platonic Political Philosophy* (Chicago: University of Chicago Press, 1983), p. 34.

4. Cf. Wood, "Fundamentalists and the Constitution," p. 34.

5. "The Three Waves of Modernity," typescript, p. 19 (published in *An Introduction to Political Philosophy: Ten Essays by Leo Strauss*, ed. H. Gildin ([Detroit: Wayne State Press], p. 98); cf. "On a New Interpretation of Plato's Political Philosophy," *Social Research* 13 (1946): p. 357.

6. Cf. "Liberal Education and Responsibility," *Liberalism Ancient and Modern* (New York: Basic Books, 1968), pp. 15–19.

7. "The Three Waves of Modernity," p. 20 (*An Introduction to Political Philosophy: Ten Essays by Leo Strauss*, p. 98).

put it on another occasion, "All rationalistic liberal philosophic positions have lost their significance and power. One may deplore this [as, on a practical level, Strauss surely did], but I for one cannot bring myself to clinging to philosophic positions which have been shown to be inadequate."[8] (It is perhaps worth noting that both of the statements just quoted occurred in lectures, only one of which Strauss permitted to be published in his lifetime.) When Strauss claimed, therefore, that "liberal democracy . . . derives powerful support from . . . the pre-modern thought of our western tradition,"[9] he cannot have meant by this such support as derives from a demonstration of the universal truth of the Founding principles as originally understood. The reason is not only that liberal democracy (whether or not the premodern thinkers would have preferred it to all currently available alternatives) is not the sort of political order considered best by premodern thought in general or classical political philosophy in particular. More important still is the fact that classical political philosophy did not intend to provide, or believe it possible to provide, a simply rational basis for *any* sort of political order, even the best: "it asserts that every political society that ever has been or ever will be rests on a particular fundamental opinion which cannot be replaced by knowledge and hence is of necessity a particular or particularist society."[10] It is in philosophy rather than politics that, according to classical political thought, true universalism is to be sought.[11]

We can sum up this point, then, by saying that Strauss's efforts toward the recovery of classical political philosophy—insofar as they raised again, in the face of the most powerful currents of modern thought, the question of the possibility of a genuine and viable rationalism—helped students of the American political order take seriously the Founders' claim as to the universal truth of the Founding principles; but those efforts did not thereby guarantee that that claim would be found valid in the final analysis.

---

8. "Existentialism," typescript (probably from a tape and unedited), 4 (edited and published as "An Introduction to Heideggerian Existentialism," in *The Rebirth of Classical Political Rationalism*, ed. T. Pangle [Chicago: University of Chicago Press, 1989], p. 29).

9. "The Three Waves of Modernity," p. 20 (*An Introduction to Political Philosophy: Ten Essays by Leo Strauss*, p. 98).

10. *Liberalism Ancient and Modern*, p. viii.

11. *The City and Man* (Chicago: University of Chicago Press, 1977), pp. 226–31; cf. "Philosophy as Rigorous Science and Political Philosophy," p. 29.

The bearing of Strauss's work on the understanding of the Founding is ambiguous for a second reason, which has already been touched on in the discussion of the first reason. The classical political philosophers were not democrats, and still less liberal democrats. Strauss never sought to hide this fact: "I do not believe that the premises—democracy is good and Aristotle is good—lead validly to the conclusion that Aristotle was a democrat."[12] More than that, the acceptance of the premise that Aristotle is good calls into some question the premise that democracy is good. The recovery of classical political philosophy is at the same time a recovery of the classical critique of the democracy known to the classics; and, although ancient democracy was very different from our own, the classical critique is not without its contemporary applications. To put this point in another way, the crisis of liberal democracy, as Strauss understood it, is not due entirely to the loss of confidence in the truth of its Founding principles; nor can the aspects of contemporary America which are open to reasonable criticism all be traced to a falling away from those principles. In his analyses of the thought of the modern political philosophers, Strauss exposed the tendency of the principles in question with almost ruthless thoroughness; and he indicated his view of their contemporary consequences in occasional but telling remarks: "If we look . . . at what is peculiar to our age or characteristic of our age, we see hardly more than the interplay of mass taste with high-grade but strictly speaking unprincipled efficiency."[13] And, again, appropriating and explicating a remark of Nietzsche, in order to bring out the "dangers threatening democracy . . . from within":

> The reading of the morning prayer [has] been replaced by the reading of the morning paper: not every day the same thing, the same reminder of men's absolute duty and exalted destiny, but every day something new with no reminder of duty and exalted destiny. Specialization, knowing more and more about less and less, practical impossibility of concentration upon the very few essential things upon which man's wholeness entirely depends—the specialization compensated by sham universality by the stimulation of all kinds of interests and curiosities

---

12. "The Crisis of Political Philosophy," *The Predicament of Modern Politics*, ed. Harold J. Spaeth (Detroit: University of Detroit Press, 1964), pp. 93–94; cf. *The City and Man*, pp. 35–41.

13. "Liberal Education and Responsibility," p. 23.

without true passion, the danger of universal philistinism and creeping conformism.[14]

Such remarks, together with his critique of the modern political philosophers, might seem to lend some weight to the suspicion that Strauss's return to classical political philosophy was politically motivated. He did, indeed, oppose to contemporary liberalism classical liberality,[15] and he wrote that "True liberals today have no more pressing duty than to counteract the perverted liberalism which contends 'that just to live, securely and happily, and protected but otherwise unregulated, is man's simple but supreme goal' and which forgets quality, excellence, or virtue."[16] In opposing the new political science which had come to dominate the political science departments of major universities, he drew attention to its more or less unconscious harmony with "a certain version of liberal democracy," something he designated "its democratism";[17] his call for a restoration of the older political science was at the same time, therefore, a call to re-open the examination of "the very complex pros and cons regarding liberal democracy."[18] He approved of "setting up outposts which may come to be regarded by many citizens as salutary to the republic and as deserving of giving to it its tone."[19] But what Strauss meant by this, as the context of the last remark makes clear, was no more than that we should take advantage of the freedom democracy affords to all to "cultivate our garden"—that is, to pursue excellence on our own, so far as we are capable of doing so, while, if we are teachers (especially in political science departments or law schools), encouraging "whatever broadens and deepens the understanding" rather than "what in the best case cannot as such produce more than narrow and unprincipled efficiency."[20]

The deepest reason for this restraint is pointed to by the fact that the classical political philosophy to which Strauss would have us return—on

---

14. "Existentialism," p. 7 (*The Rebirth of Classical Political Rationalism*, p. 31).

15. "The Liberalism of Classical Political Philosophy," *Liberalism Ancient and Modern*, pp. 28ff.

16. Ibid., p. 64.

17. "An Epilogue," *Liberalism Ancient and Modern*, p. 222 and context.

18. Ibid., pp. 223, 222, and 205ff.

19. "Liberal Education and Responsibility," p. 24.

20. Ibid., pp. 24 and 19.

the ground, among others, that its analysis of political life is superior to that of its modern alternatives[21]—is ultimately as harsh in its criticism of aristocracy as it is in its criticism of democracy. At most, the harshness of these criticisms differs only in degree. Aristocracy in its ideal (say, Platonic) form is devoted to the pursuit of excellence or virtue; but the adequate investigation of the question "What is virtue?" leads to the conclusion "that the ultimate aim of political life cannot be reached by political life, but only by a life devoted to contemplation, to philosophy."[22] Some of those who believe that they discern a political motivation behind Strauss's efforts toward the recovery of classical political philosophy are aware that, in Strauss's understanding of it, that philosophy is so far from calling for political action that it is concerned with bringing to light "the limits set to political life, to all political action and all political planning."[23] Yet they regard this fact as a confirmation rather than the definitive refutation of their thesis. They see in it or through it the conservatism of one who appealed to Plato's *Republic* as a critique of political idealism,[24] and attempted thereby to purge the best of contemporary youth of their longing for political action and political reform.[25] But the remarks quoted in the preceding paragraph are sufficient indication of Strauss's dissatisfaction with the present political situation in the West, however preferable it remained, in his view, to that in the East. Moreover, not given himself to undue despair, he was not inclined to encourage it in others, with regard to politics or anything else. For, since the outcome of serious conflicts is, generally speaking, unpredictable, " 'men can always hope and never need to give up, in whatever fortunes and in whatever travail they find themselves.' "[26]

Still, it was not to political hopes of any sort that Strauss ultimately wished to address himself. Or, to return to our original question, it was neither reverence for the Founders' work—which he encouraged by opening up the prospect of recovering a genuine and viable rationalism—nor

---

21. See, for example, "An Epilogue," pp. 209–210, as well as *The City and Man*, pp. 10–11.

22. "On Classical Political Philosophy," *What Is Political Philosophy?* (New York: Free Press, 1959), pp. 90–91.

23. Ibid., p. 91; *The City and Man*, p. 138.

24. *The City and Man*, p. 127.

25. Cf. M. F. Burnyeat, "Sphinx Without a Secret," *The New York Review of Books*, 30 May 1985, pp. 30–36.

26. "An Epilogue," p. 209; and "Liberal Education and Responsibility," p. 24.

dissatisfaction with their work—a dissatisfaction bound to be deepened by the recovery of premodern thought—that was intended to be the final result of Strauss's return. These may well, however, have been intended to be way stations on a journey individuals as individuals were to be encouraged to make to solve a problem that only individuals can solve. The individuals in question were likely to be distinguished by the strength and purity of their devotion to liberal democracy as well as by the depth of their concern, or potential concern, with its plight; for the hope to which he ultimately addressed himself is all but certain to find its first expression, to make its first appearance in a more or less political guise.

II.

Which hope, then, did he wish to address, after having first responded to it himself? The hope of an individual, in whatever circumstances he may find himself, to guide his life by a rational or natural standard, or by reason. Considered in this light, the return to classical political philosophy reveals itself eventually as a return to a philosophy that attempted "to lead the qualified citizens, or rather their qualified sons, from the political life to the philosophic life."[27] Or, as he put it in an early article on Lessing which was published only after his death, "freemasonry," that is, philosophy, "came into being, when someone who originally had planned a scientific society which should make the speculative truths useful for practical and political life, conceived of a 'society which should raise itself from the practice of civil life to speculation,'" which is the same thing as to say that "the intention of the good works of the freemasons is to make good works superfluous."[28] Yet the difficulties or ambiguities attending Strauss's return, when it is understood in this way, are scarcely less massive than those we encountered in considering its significance for the understanding of the American Founding. One example will probably suffice for showing that this is the case. While Strauss gave frequent expression to the view that the human or political science of the ancients is superior to the modern alternatives, he was much more hesitant to assert the superiority of their

---

27. "On Classical Political Philosophy," pp. 93–94. This is one reason, though not the only one, why it remains a return to *political* philosophy. Cf. "Exoteric Teaching," *Interpretation* 14 (1984): p. 53 at the end of the first paragraph, as well as note 47 below.
28. "Exoteric Teaching," pp. 52–53.

natural science or metaphysics. Indeed, as he indicated on one occasion, "who can dare to say that Plato's doctrine of ideas as he intimated it, or Aristotle's doctrine of the *nous* that does nothing but think itself and is essentially related to the eternal visible universe, is the true teaching?" But does this not mean, he continued, that "those like myself who are inclined to sit at the feet of the old philosophers [are] exposed to the danger of a weak-kneed eclecticism which will not withstand a single blow on the part of those who are competent enough to remind them of the singleness of purpose and of inspiration that characterizes every thinker who deserves to be called great?"[29] Strauss could not ultimately have accepted, in other words, as he may sometimes seem to have come close to doing,[30] what he called, in *Natural Right and History* "a fundamental, typically modern, dualism of a nonteleological natural science and a teleological science of man . . . a position which presupposes a break with the comprehensive view of Aristotle . . . ." He traced "the fundamental dilemma, in whose grip we are," to "the victory of modern natural science." And he asserted that, "An adequate solution to the problem of natural right cannot be found before this basic problem has been solved."[31] Since he seems to have had little to say about such a solution, we might appear to be justified in concluding that he regarded the return to classical political philosophy as merely tentative; some of his remarks, moreover, seem to lend support to this view.[32] But other remarks leave no doubt that, at a relatively young age, he had already reached the conclusion that the decisive difficulties had been overcome, at least in principle.[33] We are thus forced to consider the question of how that conclusion was reached.

In order even to begin to approach this question, we must first try to see more clearly what exactly it was that led Strauss to regard a return to premodern philosophy as *desirable*—and this is the only aspect of the question which will be discussed here. In what context, in other words,

---

29. "Existentialism," p. 11 (*The Rebirth of Classical Political Rationalism*, p. 34).

30. Cf. *What Is Political Philosophy?* pp. 38–39; and Stanley Rothman, "The Revival of Classical Political Philosophy: A Critique," *APSR* 56 (1962): p. 350. Cf. "On the Intention of Rousseau," *Social Research* 14 (1947): p. 487.

31. *Natural Right and History* (Chicago: University of Chicago Press, 1953), p. 8.

32. See, for example, *The City and Man*, p. 11. Cf. "On a New Interpretation of Plato's Political Philosophy," pp. 338–39.

33. *Philosophy and Law*, trans. Fred Baumann (Philadelphia: Jewish Publication Society of America, 1987), pp. 3, 11–16, 111–12; "Preface to the English Translation," p. 31.

did the thought of such a return present itself to him? His first book, *Spinoza's Critique of Religion*, "was based on the premise, sanctioned by powerful prejudice, that a return to premodern philosophy is impossible."[34] His second book, *Philosophy and Law*, which has the subtitle, "Essays Toward the Understanding of Maimonides and His Predecessors," all but begins with the assertion that "Maimonides' rationalism is the truly natural model, the standard that must be carefully guarded against every counterfeit, and the touchstone that puts modern rationalism to shame," or, more generally, that "medieval rationalism" is "the standard against which modern rationalism proves to be only apparent rationalism."[35] (The ground or grounds which sustain so harsh a judgment against modern rationalism are apparently sufficient to dispose also of " 'irrationalism,' " which "is only a variety of modern rationalism."[36]) The return to premodern philosophy takes place, then, in the course of Strauss's investigation of the problem to which each of these two books is devoted—what he called "the theological-political problem." It is true that the return in question here is a return to *medieval* philosophy and that the preeminence of Strauss's concern with classical philosophy becomes more visible in his work at a later stage, just as his concern with "the theological-political problem" becomes less visible there. But apart from the fact that he understood medieval philosophy from the beginning—that is, from the period to which *Philosophy and Law* belongs—in the light of "its classical (Aristotelian and Platonic) foundation,"[37] Strauss confirmed as late as 1965 that since his early work on Spinoza, "the theological-political problem has remained *the* theme of my investigations."[38] We must thus conclude that his mature concern with classical philosophy, too, grew out of and was sustained by his preoccupation with that problem.

---

34. "Preface to the English Translation," p. 31.

35. "Introduction," p. 3.

36. Note 1 to "Introduction," p. 111.

37. "Preface to the English Translation," p. 31; and, among other places, *Philosophy and Law*, pp. 103ff.; "Quelques Remarques sur la Science Politique de Maimonide et de Farabi," *Revue des études juives* 100 (1936): pp. 2–6.

38. Preface to the German edition of his Hobbes book, *Interpretation* 8 (1979): I; cf. the remark of Avicenna which he prefixed to the last book he completed before his death, *The Argument and the Action of Plato's "Laws"* (Chicago: University of Chicago Press, 1975); cf. on the importance of that remark for Strauss, "A Giving of Accounts," *The College* 25 (1970): p. 3.

In the 1962 "Preface to the English Translation" of his Spinoza book, by way of explanation of the context out of which the book emerged, Strauss has given us an account of the theological-political problem as he understood it and had confronted it. (The "Preface" may be supplemented by the "Introduction" to *Philosophy and Law*—a much earlier document from which it borrows whole passages virtually *verbatim*—as well as by a number of other statements, such as "A Giving of Accounts," the 1965 preface to the German edition of Strauss's Hobbes book, and "The Mutual Influence of Theology and Philosophy.") The problem has a "social or political" aspect (p. 6), as well as an aspect which concerns individuals as individuals. In his discussion of the latter aspect, Strauss begins from the case "of the Western Jewish individual who or whose parents severed his connection with the Jewish community." The individuals Strauss is concerned with admit that "their deepest problem would be solved" by "return to the Jewish community, the community established by the Jewish faith and the Jewish way of life," but "believe such a return to be altogether impossible because they believe that the Jewish faith has been overthrown once and for all, not by blind rebellion, but by evident refutation . . . they assert that intellectual probity forbids them to sacrifice intellect in order to satisfy even the most vital need" (p. 7).

On the basis of an analysis of the alleged obstacles to return, as they were understood by his contemporaries and their predecessors, the young Strauss had apparently been tempted to draw the opposite conclusion: "Considerations like those sketched in the preceding paragraphs made one wonder whether an unqualified return to Jewish orthodoxy was not both possible and necessary—was not at the same time the solution to the problem of the Jew lost in the non-Jewish modern world and the only course compatible with sheer consistency or intellectual probity" (p. 15). Yet, "Vague difficulties remained like small faraway clouds on a beautiful summer sky. They soon took the shape of Spinoza . . ." (p. 15). Some light is shed on this rather enigmatic remark by what Strauss says—more clearly, perhaps in the "Introduction" to *Philosophy and Law* than in the "Preface"—about "the most significant representatives" of "the movement of return," Hermann Cohen and Franz Rosenzweig. These men "did not unreservedly undertake the return to tradition"; in other words, they did not return to an undiluted orthodoxy ("Introduction," pp. 8ff.; cf. "Preface," pp. 13–15 and 27). Their reservations could be traced back to the Enlightenment (to Spinoza among others), to a philosophy, that is, which had in the meantime allegedly been "overcome." These facts—the alleged overcoming of Spinoza or of Enlightenment thought, together with the continued reliance on that thought—made it necessary to re-open the question of whether Spinoza or the Enlightenment "had in fact refuted orthodoxy" ("Preface," pp. 27–28, "Introduction," pp. 9–10).[39] "Orthodoxy could be returned to only if Spinoza was wrong in every respect" ("Preface," p. 15).

Strauss summarized the results of his early examination of Spinoza—the examination which produced *Spinoza's Critique of Religion*—in both the "Preface" and the "Introduction." It appears from these summaries that he reached the conclusion that Spinoza was wrong, if not in every respect, in the decisive respect or that he had not refuted orthodoxy ("Preface," pp. 28–29, "Introduction," pp. 10–11). Yet, while this appearance is ultimately not misleading, it must be qualified. This is shown most simply by the fact that Strauss fails to present himself as having taken the step which only Spinoza's opposition, now apparently disposed of, had hitherto prevented.

As he indicates most clearly in the "Introduction," "even though the attack of the Enlightenment upon orthodoxy failed, the battle of the two hostile powers still had a highly consequential and positive result for the Enlightenment" (p. 11).[40] He even goes so far as to speak of what "justifies" the Enlightenment ("Introduction," pp. 13, 15, 16, 18, 19, and "Preface," p. 30). According to Strauss, "The quarrel between Enlightenment and Orthodoxy made clearer and better known than before that the presuppositions of Orthodoxy (the reality of Creation, Miracles, and Revelation) are not known (philosophically or historically) but are only believed and thus lack the peculiarly obligatory character of the known" ("Introduction," p. 12).[41] From this conclusion, accepted by Strauss, there is only a step to "the view . . . that the assertion of miracles is relative to the prescientific state of mankind and thus has no dignity whatsoever" ("Introduction," p. 15).[42] As we learn from the Spinoza book itself, the additional step was taken by "the positive mind" which "finds itself . . . unmovable by all reports

---

39. Cf. Preface to the German edition of Hobbes book, p. 1, and "A Giving of Accounts," p. 3.

40. Cf. "A Giving of Accounts," p. 3.

41. Cf. "Preface," p. 28: Spinoza's refutation is therefore a failure only so long as orthodoxy "limits itself to asserting that it believes" the fundamental points.

42. Cf. "The Mutual Influence of Theology and Philosophy," *The Independent Journal of Philosophy* 3 (1979): p. 115.

on miracles, and therefore by all experience of miracles" because to it "it is plain that the prophets and the apostles did not view and analyze the events which they report with the same sobriety and severity which that mind brings to bear on events observed" (pp. 134–35); "miracles . . . are seen as occurring for a state of consciousness which is not capable of strict scientific investigation of experience" (p. 136). Comparing itself to such a state of consciousness, the positive mind, or "positive consciousness," which is "self-conscious of empirical awareness" (p. 126), regarded itself as having achieved a pure and decisive progress in openness to the world as it is. Abstaining from the more ambitious but flawed attempt to prove that miracles are impossible, it demanded only that they be "indubitably established" as such by being submitted to its own "precise observation and stringent analysis" (pp. 213, 134). But Strauss came to see that that very demand or "the will to 'establish'" destroys the possibility of experience of miracles (pp. 213–14); and he therefore wondered whether that demand or will was "itself something to be taken for granted" (p. 214; cf. 145). Doubts on that score led him to see the issue as one "between the unbelieving and the believing manner of experiencing the world" (p. 198); and he drew the conclusion that "Just as the assertion of miracles is called in question by the positive mind, positive critique of miracles is called in question by the mind that waits in faith or in doubt for the coming of the miracles" (p. 214).[43] The openness to which the positive mind laid claim thus revealed itself to him as less than complete.[44]

Having reached this point, Strauss concluded at this stage that "the antagonism between Spinoza and Judaism, between unbelief and belief, is ultimately not theoretical but moral" ("Preface," p. 29; cf. "Introduction," pp. 15–16). His examination of that antagonism over the course of its history led him to the view that "The last word and the ultimate

---

43. Cf. ibid., p. 116; and especially "Introduction," p. 15.

44. It was on its way to becoming "probity," something which Strauss was to distinguish from "attentiveness" or "love of truth," from genuine openness to the world as it is. (Note 12 to the "Introduction," *Philosophy and Law*, pp. 113–14)—It is possible and even probable that Strauss was helped, in coming to understand this limitation of the positive critique of religion, by historicism, which "understands modern natural science as a historically conditioned form of 'world interpretation' along with others" ("Introduction," p. 14; cf. note 2 to the "Introduction," ibid., p. 112). However that may be, his insight into this limitation of the positive critique must have confirmed for him the (limited) truth of the historicist critique of modern natural science ("Introduction," p. 15; cf. "On a New Interpretation of Plato's Political Philosophy," pp. 338f.).

justification of Spinoza's critique is the atheism from intellectual probity which overcomes orthodoxy radically by understanding it radically . . ." ("Preface," p. 30, "Introduction," p. 19). But this solution to his problem, too, failed to satisfy him: "its basis is an act of will, of belief, and, being based on belief, is fatal to any philosophy" ("Preface," p. 30).[45] Just after speaking, therefore, of the overcoming of orthodoxy by "the atheism from intellectual probity," he refers to the same development as "the victory of orthodoxy through the self-destruction of rational philosophy" (p. 30).[46] Yet, as he goes on to point out, neither Jewish orthodoxy nor Nietzsche can dispense entirely with an appeal to reason or objective truth. Moreover, "Other observations and experiences confirmed the suspicion that it would be unwise to say farewell to reason." It was at this point that Strauss "began therefore to wonder whether the self-destruction of reason was not the inevitable outcome of modern rationalism as distinguished from pre-modern rationalism, especially Jewish-medieval rationalism and its classical (Aristotelian and Platonic) foundation" (p. 31).[47]

---

45. The most recent assessment of Strauss's work ("Truth for philosophers alone?" by Stephen Holmes, *Times Literary Supplement*, 1–7 December 1989, pp. 1319–24) gives no evidence that its author is aware of this dissatisfaction or, more generally, of Strauss's critique of probity. It thus in effect ascribes to Strauss a position—"dogmatic atheism"—whose denunciation by him had aroused the ire of an earlier generation of critics (see Strauss's "reply" to Schaar and Wolin in *American Political Science Review* 57 (1963): p. 153).

46. Cf., again, *Philosophy and Law*, p. 111 (note 1 to "Introduction"): " 'Irrationalism' is only a variety of modern rationalism"; cf. also *Natural Right and History*, pp. 74–76, as well as "The Mutual Influence of Theology and Philosophy," pp. 117–18.

47. In the "Preface" itself, Strauss gives one hint as to what may have permitted "the change of orientation" that consisted in his coming to regard a return to premodern philosophy as not only desirable but also possible: he says that that change "found its first expression" in the article on Carl Schmitt reprinted at the end of the volume. In that article, Strauss says that, "In order to launch the radical critique" of modern political philosophy that Schmitt had in mind, he "must first eliminate the conception of human evil as animal evil, and therefore as 'innocent evil,' and find his way back to the conception of human evil as moral depravity" (p. 345). For the import of this remark, cf. the Spinoza book proper, when Strauss was still proceeding on the basis of the premise "that a return to pre-modern philosophy is impossible," p. 204, with *The City and Man*, pp. 38–40 and "On a New Interpretation of Plato's Political Philosophy," p. 344. Cf. *Natural Right and History*, p. 78.

9

"True Esotericism"

The work of Ernest Fortin suffices by itself to call our attention to a number of important themes and to further our understanding of them. It would be impossible, however, to discuss the particular theme on which I have been asked to speak without taking up another figure and considering, at least briefly, Ernest's relation to him. Leo Strauss was not a Catholic, nor even a Christian, and therefore his thought and work belong from the outset to a wholly different world than that to which the thought and work of Ernest belong. Yet, according to Peter Augustine Lawler in his recent review of Ernest's *Collected Essays*, "In our time, classical philosophy, as presented by Strauss, is the natural ally of revealed religion."[1] Lawler's appreciation of this natural alliance and of its basis underlies his suggestion that Ernest "shows how it is possible to be a Catholic Straussian." Indeed, the review goes so far as to suggest that "Strauss is surely responsible for much of" what Lawler calls Ernest's "unparalleled moral and political judgment on the Church's behalf." For all of that, Lawler is not unaware of the fact that Ernest's stance is disturbing to some Catholics as well as to some, or (as Lawler thinks) even more, Straussians. We can only add that this is likely to be even more true of many scholars who, to paraphrase Gulliver, would gladly excuse the compliment of inclusion within either of these worthy, and partially overlapping, circles.

Now Ernest himself, as I assume is well-known, is not given to dwelling on the reaction to his work—be it favorable or otherwise—on the part of those who may at any given time wield influence in academia.

---

1. *Crisis* (May 1997), pp. 44–45.

269

But he could not help noticing that one suggestion that he took over from Strauss and adapted and used in his own way was particularly "offensive to reigning academic taste": what Ernest calls "the notorious issue of esoteric writing."[2] In the face of this taste, Ernest sought to show, in a series of beautifully written studies (many of which are available in the *Collected Essays*), that a number of outstanding Christian writers, among them Fathers of the church, have made an exemplary use of esoteric writing on behalf of that faith and of its thoughtful acceptance. And in the retrospective foreword to the first volume of the *Collected Essays*, he offered an explication of the understanding of "true esotericism" (as he calls it) that may underlie those studies, an explication which presents esotericism as "something less ominous and more rational" than it is often today taken to be. "In essence," according to Ernest, "it consists in observing a prudent reserve in the public expression of truths that could easily be misunderstood and thus prove harmful to the speaker, the listener, or the truth itself."[3] For the understanding of this remark, it is helpful, I believe, to consider Ernest's reformulation of the Platonic distinction between genuine and political or vulgar virtue: "Differently and more clearly stated, the highest moral principles are seldom if ever directly applicable to concrete situations and must be diluted in order to become operative."[4] However that may be, since Ernest's explication, if not also every detail of his studies themselves, could lead someone to wonder how "the notorious issue" ever achieved the notoriety to which he has called our attention, it might be of use to devote the remainder of these brief remarks to a preliminary consideration of the esotericism thesis itself, with special attention to its original presentation and reception.

The volume in which Strauss presented that thesis to the scholarly world, *Persecution and the Art of Writing*, appeared in 1952. With the exception of the introduction, which "made free use" of an earlier article, all of the essays contained in the volume had been published before. Indeed, two of them, the title essay and an essay on Maimonides entitled "The Literary Character of the *Guide for the Perplexed*," had already appeared in print more than a decade earlier. As Strauss later reported, when his friend Jacob Klein had read in manuscript the latter essay, he declared,

---

2. *CE* 1: p. xv.

3. *CE* 1: p. xv.

4. *CE* 2: p. 186.

"We have rediscovered exotericism."[5] Klein's comment, if meant as a forecast of scholarly reaction to the exotericism–esotericism thesis, proved to be premature. According to an essay originally published by Strauss in 1954—that is, more than a dozen years after the original publication of the two essays already mentioned, and several years after their republication in *Persecution and the Art of Writing*—only four or five scholars of his generation had become interested in the thesis. And since, as Strauss points out in the same 1954 essay, the questions that the thesis raises "are obviously of importance" and are so far from being "trivial in the sense that they are discussed in every textbook . . . that it is a considerable time since they have been discussed at all,"[6] we can safely conclude that the indifference that Strauss referred to was not unrelated to the hostility to which Ernest would refer later on. Rather than denoting a genuine lack of interest, it was but that hostility's silent and hence more effective twin. What was it then, to come back to our question, that led Strauss's contemporaries to wish to bury his thesis beneath a silence broken only occasionally by more or less intemperate denunciations?

It probably goes too far to ascribe to them the sort of perspicacity that led the contemporaries of an early critic of Dante—who, not long after the death of the great poet, had leveled against him the charge of Averroism—to ignore and reject that thesis: "The reason, paradoxical as it may sound, is probably not that he was wrong but [their awareness] that he may have been right."[7] But many of Strauss's contemporaries may have recoiled instinctively from giving fair consideration to an understanding of the great writers of our tradition that would tend in more than one way to alienate them from us. Strauss himself had acknowledged that, "Every decent modern reader is bound to be shocked by the mere suggestion that a great man might have deliberately deceived the large majority of his readers."[8] And that observation or prediction received some confirmation from a no doubt un-self-consciously revealing remark that Strauss quotes

---

5. "A Giving of Accounts," *The College* (April 1970), p. 4.

6. "On a Forgotten Kind of Writing," as republished in *What is Political Philosophy?*, pp. 222–23.

7. This according to "Dante and Averroism," in *Actas del V Congreso Internacional de Filosofía Medieval*, vol. 2 (Madrid: Editora Nacional, 1979), pp. 1–3, 9—a paper of Ernest's that, for some reason, did not find its way into the *Collected Essays*: compare *Persecution and the Art of Writing*, p.17.

8. "Persecution and the Art of Writing," as republished in the volume of that name, p. 35.

in his 1954 essay from a review of *Persecution and the Art of Writing* by one of those contemporaries who did venture to criticize its thesis publicly: he "should have preferred," the critic said, "to believe that Spinoza was quite honest," in making a certain statement whose complete frankness had been disputed by Strauss.[9] But we cannot be reasonably confident that we have understood the reaction to the exotericism thesis, before we are reasonably confident that we have understood the thesis itself (so that, having peered into all of its corners, so to speak, we can be sure that nothing that might be intrinsically objectionable in it has escaped our notice). And in this case, as in the case of every other thesis put forward by Leo Strauss, it is far safer to assume that we still lack such an understanding than that we have already achieved it. We would perhaps do better, then, to let the hostile reaction to the exotericism thesis on the part of Strauss's contemporaries and others, even or precisely if we are not inclined to share it, serve to raise a doubt in our minds as to whether the critics might not have discerned or divined something in the thesis that we have missed. We would do better, that is, to postpone the attempt to understand or to answer the critics until after we have undertaken and completed the reexamination of the thesis itself that becomes a genuine possibility only on the basis of some such doubt.

Let me try to suggest, therefore, one place where such a reexamination might begin. If there is something intrinsically objectionable (as I have put it) in the thesis itself, we can reasonably assume that Strauss's way of presenting it will reflect his awareness of this fact. Let us look briefly, then, at the two programmatic essays—"Persecution and the Art of Writing" and the 1954 restatement "On a Forgotten Kind of Writing"—to see whether we can detect any sign or signs of such awareness on his part. The first of these essays, which had appeared initially in 1941, took as its point of departure the fact that "In a considerable number of countries which, for about a hundred years, have enjoyed a practically complete freedom of public discussion, that freedom is now suppressed and replaced by a compulsion to coordinate speech with such views as the government believes to be expedient, or holds in all seriousness" (p. 22). Despite this beginning, or in accord with it, the essay leaves little doubt that its first concern is with the thought of the past. The short paragraph that opens its central section reads as follows:

---

9. "On a Forgotten Kind of Writing," p. 226.

> Suppression of independent thought has occurred fairly frequently in the past. It is reasonable to assume that earlier ages produced proportionately as many men capable of independent thought as we find today, and that at least some of these men combined understanding with caution. Thus, one may wonder whether some of the greatest writers of the past have not adapted their literary technique to the requirements of persecution, by presenting their views on all the then crucial questions exclusively between the lines. (p. 26)

To this, one can add that in summing up, at the end of the second essay, the (intended) effect of his presentation of the exotericism thesis, Strauss lays a peculiar stress on its bearing for historical studies: "At the very least the observations I have made will force historians sooner or later to abandon the complacency with which they claim to know what the great thinkers thought, to admit that the thought of the past is much more enigmatic than it is generally held to be, and to begin to wonder whether the historical truth is not as difficult of access as the philosophic truth" (p. 232). Indeed, in the central section of the first essay, he had addressed himself particularly to "the historian" and his "more modest duty" as distinct from "the philosopher" (p. 29), and he had attempted to develop criteria that would enable or help historians to carry out that duty, that is, to continue "the tradition of historical exactness" (p. 29) when dealing with the sort of writings and authors with which the essay is concerned. He recalls that attempt in the second essay ("seven sentences which are meant to indicate some rules of reading," p. 223) in responding to the critic already mentioned, whom he accuses of evading "the question of the criteria which would allow us to distinguish between guessing at and knowing what an author indicates between the lines" (p. 224); and he also notes there, of another critic whom he praises for his "open-mindedness," that the latter "realizes above all that my suggestion is not incompatible with compliance with the demands of historical exactness" (p. 228). Now, the required criteria would have to enable us not only "to distinguish between guessing at and knowing what an author indicates between the lines," but also to determine to begin with whether a text with which we have to deal is one in which the author can be expected to have ventured such indications. And in this connection Strauss had suggested toward the end of the central section of the first essay not only a positive criterion, which we can disregard for our present purpose, but also this negative one:

"If it is true that there is a necessary correlation between persecution and writing between the lines, then there is a necessary negative criterion: that the book in question must have been composed in an era of persecution, that is, at a time when some political or other orthodoxy was enforced by law or custom" (p. 32). By putting this negative criterion in conditional form—"If it is true . . ."—Strauss at the same time called into question the "correlation" (proclaimed already by its title) on which the essay had appeared to be based.

The correlation thus called into question had attempted to consign or confine exoteric writing exclusively to the past, or to such modern societies as have the misfortune to experience a recurrence of some of the most regrettable phenomena of the past.[10] Yet, as he indicates in the second essay, Strauss could hardly have refrained from calling that attempt into question—that is, from admitting that his thesis raised a "philosophic" question as well as a "historical" one (p. 222)—even if his own concern had been exclusively with (furthering the search for) the historical truth or with the past.[11] For our understanding of the bearing or extent of the exotericism practiced by writers of the past will obviously be affected by the way in which we answer the question whether everything they may have refrained from saying can, safely as well as properly, be said now, at least in any well-ordered (modern) society. This question is all but identical to the question whether "opinion" is the "element" of all societies or only "of all non-liberal societies" (p. 222). Strauss claimed to know of societies of the recent past—that is, modern societies—in which men could "attack in writings accessible to all both the established social or political order and the beliefs on which it is based" (p. 224); but he could not help raising the question of "the wisdom of such extreme liberalism."[12] And it is reasonable to assume that a writer who doubted of the wisdom of the freedom accorded by such liberalism might hesitate to take full advantage of it.

In the final section of the first essay, Strauss pursued the *question* whether there is "a necessary correlation between persecution and writing

---

10. Pp. 22ff.; compare p. 21 of the same volume.

11. Compare p. 225 top.

12. P. 224; compare p. 230, where he says, regarding "the factual recognition of a given philosophy, or even of all philosophies, by certain societies," that "that recognition may be based on capital errors": compare also "Persecution and the Art of Writing," p. 34 n. 14.

between the lines"—the question which, as I say, he was compelled to raise and which he raised apparently with some reluctance—in this, perhaps more trenchant, manner. He drew a distinction between modern philosophers, who "believed that suppression of free inquiry, and of publication of the results of free inquiry, was accidental, an outcome of the faulty construction of the body politic" (p. 33), and premodern philosophers or, to speak more broadly (compare p. 35), "an earlier type of writers," who had "been driven to the conclusion that public communication of the philosophic or scientific truth was impossible or undesirable, not only for the time being but for all times" (p. 34). Now, Strauss had made no secret of his view that premodern philosophy is superior to modern philosophy in the decisive respect. He was himself therefore driven to say in this same context that "Exoteric literature presupposes that there are basic truths which would not be pronounced in public by any decent man, because they would do harm to many people . . . ." (p. 36; compare p. 34 top). For the understanding of this remark, it is necessary to recall that the premodern philosophers included the "falāsifa," who, according to Strauss, "implied that the principles of morality are not rational, but 'probable' or 'generally accepted.' "[13] It is true that Strauss goes on to treat his assertion about the presupposition of exoteric literature as if it had been equivalent to the assertion that "This literature is . . . essentially related to a society which is not liberal" (p. 36). But even if one disregards the fact that his reformulation of it does not prevent him from speaking immediately afterwards of some use of such literature "in a truly liberal society" (pp. 36 bottom–37 top), one cannot exclude the possibility that the reformulation's modification of the view of the matter that he had just articulated is but another sign of the reserve that marks his discussion throughout. This is not to deny that reserve may serve also to underline the intrinsic boldness of a discussion and of a thesis.

Someone may be troubled by the fact that I have refrained from asserting (or denying, for that matter) the correctness of the exoteric thesis. It would be easy for me to excuse this failure by recourse to the necessity of understanding what a thesis contends before we can venture any such assertion of it. But let me close instead by tipping my hat to the two individuals whose understandings of the thesis were the subject of my talk and who did, each in his own way, venture to assert its correctness.

---

13. *Persecution and the Art of Writing*, p. 11.

10

On the Place of the Treatment of Classical Philosophy in the Plan of *Natural Right and History* as a Whole

The interpreter must make explicit what the author merely presupposes, especially if it is something which we do not presuppose.

> —Letter to Gadamer, February 26, 1961,
> *The Independent Journal of Philosophy*, Vol. II, 1978, p. 6

. . . in our present-day perspective the most important things are almost invisible.

> —Six lectures on natural right and history,
> delivered at The University of Chicago, Autumn 1949, V, p. 1

The following remarks are meant to prepare a discussion of chapters three and four of *Natural Right and History* (NRH), the chapters entitled "The Origin of the Idea of Natural Right" and "Classic Natural Right," by considering the place of these chapters in the plan of the work as a whole.

Natural Right and History is widely taken to be, and reasonably taken to be, a defense of natural right. But, like Aristotle's defense of slavery, it is a defense of an unusual kind. It all but begins with a warning not to let the keenness of our awareness of the need for natural right hasten us to the conclusion "that the need can be satisfied" (NRH p. 6; cf. p. 150n24). And it is unsparing in its criticism of natural right teachings (like the one to which our nation was dedicated) that in its judgment

277

fall short of meeting that need (cf. NRH pp. 249–51, for example, with p. 1). Indeed, the book goes so far as to suggest that the only defensible natural right teaching is the classic one. This suggestion—made explicitly in the lectures on which the book was based (I p. 6)—is conveyed in the book itself by a remark to the effect that "an adequate solution to the problem of natural right cannot be found" before the problem "caused by the victory of modern natural science . . . has been solved": that victory "would seem to have . . . destroyed" the "teleological view of the universe"; and it is natural right "in its classic form" which is "connected with a teleological view of the universe" (NRH pp. 7–8). (Classic natural right is connected with that view through its apparent dependence on a "teleological view of man": cf. NRH pp. 7 and 126–27 with pp. 145–46.) If only one form of natural right is defensible, the defense of natural right offered in or constituted by *Natural Right and History* is, of necessity, a defense of that form of it. Yet, as a discussion that limits itself to "that aspect of the problem of natural right which can be clarified within the confines of the social sciences," the book explicitly declines to take up the problem whose solution it has declared to be required for an adequate defense of natural right in that form. The problem in question was caused, to repeat, "by the victory of modern natural science," a victory the book nowhere suggests can be reversed. (In the same context, the transcript of the lectures contains this additional sentence: "Naturally, there is no scarcity of elegant solutions to that problem, but the experience of some centuries has shown that modern natural science always survives the elegant solutions of the problems created by and coeval with modern natural science." I p. 7) In this situation, one might well be tempted to turn to a natural right teaching which is not undermined by the victory of modern natural science, but rather even presupposes it. And the book grants that there is such a teaching. Its originator, Hobbes, was the first man "to draw the consequences for natural right from this momentous change" from a teleological to a nonteleological natural science; Hobbes held "the conviction that a teleological cosmology is impossible"; and he shared with "his most illustrious contemporaries . . . a sense of the complete failure of traditional philosophy" (NRH pp. 166, 176, 170). But, not to mention now other difficulties, natural right in its modern form, the natural right teaching inaugurated by Hobbes, culminates according to *Natural Right and History* in a "crisis" whose "ultimate outcome" is historicism, that is, a type of thought that rejects natural right in any form (NRH pp. 34, 8). And it is against historicism, as the title of the book confirms, that its defense of natural right is above all directed. Yet in criticizing, as it therefore necessarily does, the path embarked on by Hobbes and his contemporaries—for "it is necessary to state not only the truth but also the cause of the error" (Aristotle *Nicomachean Ethics* 1154a22–26, as quoted in a letter to Helmut Kuhn regarding his review of *Natural Right and History* [which had just appeared in German translation], *The Independent Journal of Philosophy*, Vol. II, 1978, p. 23)—the book nowhere denies that their starting point reflected genuine awareness on their part of a difficulty in "traditional philosophy," that is, in classical philosophy as it had been transmitted to them or as they had come to understand it.

We thus seem to have involved ourselves, if not the argument we are trying to follow, in a contradiction. The natural right that the book attempts to defend is, as we have seen, classic natural right. Yet the thinkers who turned away from classic natural right, to elaborate eventually a new natural right teaching, were motivated in part by awareness of a genuine difficulty in the philosophy to which the classic natural right teaching belongs. Or, to put the matter somewhat more adequately, the book's defense of natural right is directed, as we have also seen, above all against historicism. Now, historicism's rejection of natural right is based on a rejection of philosophy as such "in the full sense of the term" (NRH p. 35; cf. p. 12). The intended defense of natural right requires, therefore, a vindication of philosophy as such, even though "the possibility of philosophy is only the necessary and not the sufficient condition of natural right" (NRH p. 35; cf. p. 93). But this has proven to mean that that defense requires a vindication (as against historicism) of classical philosophy, "which is nonhistoricist thought in its pure form" (NRH p. 33). And it is, in fact, to this (narrower or broader, at any rate preliminary) task that the argument of the book as a whole is explicitly devoted (NRH pp. 33–34; cf. pp. 31–32; cf., further, Helmut Kuhn, "Naturrecht und Historismus," *The Independent Journal of Philosophy*, Vol. II, 1978, p. 14). (As for the distinction between classical philosophy and classic natural right, consider NRH p. 11: "Conventionalism is a particular form of classical philosophy.") But it approaches this task having conceded at the outset, so-to-speak, that the moderns' dissatisfaction with classical philosophy—a dissatisfaction that extends indeed to classical philosophy in all of its forms (compare NRH p. 109 with pp. 172 and 174)—was not entirely without ground.

What it would seem to object to, then, is not their identification of the problem with which they were grappling, but rather the manner in which they were doing so or the path which the moderns chose to embark upon when they were confronted with that problem as one which remained, as they thought, unsolved. And this suggests that the way out of the impasse into which we have stumbled—if there is a way out—or at least its first step may lie in a full and frank elucidation of the problem in question. But nowhere in the book does Strauss provide such an elucidation.—This provisional conclusion is based on a premise that could well be questioned: that chapter two, "Natural Right and the Distinction Between Facts and Values," is not intended to supply the elucidation we seek. Compare, in particular, the remark toward the beginning of the chapter to the effect that "the perennial conflict between the Socratic and the anti-Socratic answer [to "the question of how man ought to live"] creates the impression that the Socratic answer is as arbitrary as its opposite, or that the perennial conflict is insoluble" (NRH p. 36) and the parallel remark, toward its end, that "If we take a bird's-eye view of the secular struggle between philosophy and theology, we can hardly avoid the impression that neither of the two antagonists has ever succeeded in really refuting the other" (NRH p. 75 and context) with NRH pp. 170–71.—Among the reasons for his silence on the matter, however, may have been a wish to indicate by it that, in the study of authors who are also philosophers, there is something which can be presupposed (because it *must* be presupposed): namely, their preoccupation with the problem in question. According to remarks he made elsewhere in criticism of intellectual probity, such probity differs from love of truth insofar as it consists (merely) in readiness to admit that one is an atheist and to draw all of the consequences that follow from this admission—insofar, that is, as it amounts to making an admittedly unprovable assumption into the dogmatic basis of one's position (*Philosophie und Gesetz* p. 26n1; GS II p. 25n13). Now, in order to appreciate the full bearing of these remarks, which (so far as I have been able to observe) tend to be somewhat misunderstood, we must not, like King David when he was confronted by the prophet Nathan, fail to apply them to ourselves: we who, at least in many cases today, are content to be "irreligious because fate forces us to be irreligious and for no other reason" (NRH p. 73). What Strauss suggests, in other words, by his remarks as to the *insufficiency* of intellectual probity (of which, incidentally, there can never be too much), is that philosophers as philosophers are constitutionally unable to content themselves in this way. It is only because we (as scholars of the history of philosophy) are not philosophers (as of course we readily grant) that a problem has been able to be rendered almost invisible to us, that was for them always at the center of their concerns.

What the argument of the book would seem then to object to, to repeat, is not the moderns' preoccupation with this problem but the path they took when they were forced, as they thought, to conclude that the philosophy which the tradition had transmitted to them had failed to solve it. The book's two last chapters, "Modern Natural Right" and "The Crisis of Modern Natural Right," consisting, each of them, of two parts and constituting together nearly half of the work as a whole, are devoted to the critique of that path. They are devoted, in particular, to showing why it had to lead to the result that, according to Strauss, it did lead to. Now, in this connection, one point—to which our attention had already been drawn at least as early as the end of chapter one—is especially noteworthy. Although the moderns had developed a distinctive natural philosophy (NRH pp. 169–77, 201, 248–49, 263–66, 272, 281, 311–12), as well as a distinctive political philosophy, the argument is concerned much more with the latter strand of their thought than with the former. And this choice can be regarded as (in every way) an obvious one, only so long as we allow ourselves to lose sight of the fact that the declared intent of the book, and of this last part of it particularly, is to vindicate classical philosophy and not yet classic natural right (paragraph three above). The most compelling reason for it was indicated early on in the remarks to which we have referred. According to what Strauss suggests there, it was the "crisis of modern natural right" that became a "crisis of philosophy as such" (NRH p. 34); historicism, in other words, which contends that "philosophy in the full sense of the term is impossible" (NRH p. 35) and which rests in part on "a critique of human thought as such" (NRH pp. 12, 20), is "the ultimate outcome" of a development that took place not within "philosophy in general" but rather within "political philosophy" (NRH p. 34). Now, a crisis in natural right need not, of itself, entail a crisis in philosophy as such, need not force one to question the very possibility of philosophy—any more than a crisis in a given natural right teaching forces one, in and of itself, to call into question even the philosophy to which that teaching belongs. Strauss acknowledges as much both in what he says about classical philosophy (NRH pp. 11–12, 81–93, 109–13, 145–52) and in a number of other passages scattered throughout the book (NRH pp. 23–24, 32, 35; 95–97, 118–19, 275–76; 26, 261–62). That the "crisis of modern natural right . . . could become a crisis of philosophy as such" requires therefore an explanation. And the explanation that he offers at the end of chapter one is that "in the modern centuries philosophy as such had become thoroughly politicized" (NRH p. 34). But this explanation is itself in need of some explaining: it does little more than to pose the question for which we must look to the last part of the work, the final two chapters, for an answer.

What development, then, did Strauss have in mind in referring to the thorough politicization of philosophy in modern times? The last part of the work yields its answer to this question somewhat grudgingly; but, for this very reason, at least one passage of startling clarity stands out (NRH pp. 169–79). Strauss admonishes us there, "in trying to understand Hobbes's political philosophy," not to "lose sight of his natural philosophy" (NRH p. 169). He does so by way of explaining a remark which he made after quoting Burke's description of a transformation that had taken place in atheists or atheism: " 'Boldness formerly was not the character of atheists as such. They were even of a character nearly the reverse; they were formerly like the old Epicureans, rather an unenterprising race. But of late they are grown active, designing, turbulent, and seditious.' " Strauss had commented (in part) as follows: "Political atheism is a distinctly modern phenomenon. No pre-modern atheist doubted that social life required belief in, and worship of, God or gods" (NRH p. 169). And, just before admonishing us, as we have seen, to keep in mind Hobbes's natural philosophy in trying to understand his political philosophy, he had ascribed this development to Hobbes (but cf. NRH pp. 177–79). Now, Hobbes's natural philosophy was of a sort to permit (or require) "an attitude of neutrality or indifference toward the secular conflict between materialism and spiritualism." But Hobbes was not entirely satisfied with a neutral stance in this regard: he "had the earnest desire to be a 'metaphysical' materialist. But he was forced to rest satisfied with a 'methodical' materialism" (NRH p. 174; cf. "On the Basis of Hobbes's Political Philosophy," WIPP p. 183). I am strengthened in my inclination to interpret these remarks as I do by what Strauss says, some hundred pages further on, about Rousseau. After directing us, for the understanding of "Rousseau's theoretical principles," to the *Second Discourse,* the *Discourse on the Origin of Inequality* (NRH p. 264), he observes that "The argument of the *Second Discourse* is meant to be acceptable to materialists as well as to others. It is meant to be neutral with regard to the conflict between materialism and antimaterialism, or to be 'scientific' in the present day sense of the term" (NRH pp. 265–66). Now, the *Second Discourse* presents a " 'history' of man" which is "modeled on the account of the fate of the human race which Lucretius gave in the fifth book of his poem" (a poem that Strauss had called, in his thematic treatment of it, the "greatest document of philosophic conventionalism" [NRH pp. 111ff.]). But Rousseau takes Lucretius' account "out of its Epicurean context and puts it into a context supplied by modern natural and social science" (cf. NRH p. 279 as well as p. 169); and this entails not only that, "at least at the outset, he follows Descartes rather than Epicurus," but also that, whereas Lucretius had sought the "remedies for the ills which he was forced to mention . . . in philosophic withdrawal from political life," Rousseau is concerned "to discover that political order which is in accordance with natural right" (NRH p. 264; cf. p. 179 as well as p. 273). Rousseau's "theoretical principles" or his "theoretical science" is of the same kind, then, as that of Hobbes, "namely, modern natural science" (NRH p. 263; in a footnote in the context regarding "the prehistory of this approach" [p. 266n29] Strauss refers us to the earlier passage). And his dissatisfaction with that science could not have been less than that of Hobbes (cf. NRH pp. 272, 281, and 265 with pp. 172–75; cf. also p. 312). In this situation, he was led to depart from a classical model in such a way as to place an emphasis on the discovery of the right political order than was absent from the original. (One might consider in this connection also Strauss's earlier observation that "Gassendi, the famous restorer of Epicureanism [in modern times], had stronger incentives that the ancient Epicureans for asserting the existence of natural right" [NRH p. 111n44].)

In speaking of the moderns' "sense" that traditional philosophy had been a "complete failure" (NRH p. 170), Strauss cannot have had in mind a rejection on their part of everything which the classical philosophers had said or thought, for he refers in many passages to what modern philosophers accepted or took over from classical teachings (for example, NRH pp. 167–69, 170, 172, 252, 261–62, 264, and 279, to say nothing of 164). He must have meant a sense, on the part of the moderns, that traditional philosophy had been a failure in the decisive respect. To put the matter in terms that he had used earlier in the book, traditional philosophy was thought to have failed to defend adequately "the most elementary premises whose validity is presupposed by philosophy" (NRH p. 31) or to have failed to respond adequately to the objection that philosophy, as "the life devoted to the quest for evident knowledge available to man as man," rests itself "on an unevident, arbitrary, or blind decision" (NRH p. 75; cf. pp. 30–31). It was this failure, then, that the moderns sought to remedy by developing a new natural philosophy to take the place of the discredited natural philosophy or natural philosophies of the classics (NRH pp.

170ff). But as we have seen in the cases of Hobbes and Rousseau, at least, the moderns were themselves not satisfied that the new natural science, which "is and will always remain fundamentally hypothetical" (NRH p. 174), fully answered their need. They turned therefore, in the train of Machiavelli (NRH pp. 177–79), to a new political philosophy which—by means of "a deliberate lowering of the ultimate goal" of political life (see, for example, in addition to NRH p. 178, pp. 182–83, 186, 191, 266–67, and 269)—promised to dispose on the practical plane of objections that could not be definitively disposed of theoretically (cf. NRH pp. 14–15 with p. 198). As for their own ultimate aim, it was nothing less than to give philosophy itself, or rationalism, a new breath of life. It is true, as can be seen already from the case of Rousseau, that the final result of their efforts was not very favorable to the cause of reason (NRH pp. 252, 262, 278–79, 293); but this would seem, according to Strauss's account, to be due to the fact that "In Rousseau's doctrine of the state of nature, the modern natural right teaching reaches its critical stage," or that "By thinking through that teaching, Rousseau was brought face to face with the necessity of abandoning it completely" (NRH pp. 273–74; consider also the contrast drawn between Rousseau and German idealism: NRH pp. 252–55 and 278–79 together with pp. 282 and 290). A rationalism which "rests ultimately," as Strauss had suggested of "Hobbes's rationalism" (cf. NRH p. 201 with p. 175), on political hopes is bound to be called into question, once those hopes no longer appear credible.

The distinctiveness of the intellectual position that Strauss, together perhaps with one or two others, occupied seems to be this: that he accepted the genuineness and gravity of the problem which preoccupied the moderns, while resisting their conclusions as to how it was to be dealt with. And the question to which this points is whether his resistance was not strengthened (at least) by his discovering, in the way that classical political philosophy had been brought by Socrates to complement a classical natural philosophy (NRH pp. 121–24), a path that the moderns had overlooked.

11

The Question of Nature and the Thought of Leo Strauss

My theme is the question—and questionableness—of nature: to what extent is it necessary to raise that question in order to come to grips with the thought of Leo Strauss, and what does raising it entail?

If not necessarily the thought itself, surely the expression of the thought of a genuine thinker is bound to be affected by his understanding of the situation in which he finds himself when he begins to speak out. The situation in which Strauss found himself—and in which we, to the extent that we remain unaffected by his thought, find ourselves still—was one in which philosophy had destroyed the credibility of religion for much of educated Europe. (According to an assessment that had been ventured already by Rousseau in one of his *Letters Written From the Mountain*, "Religion, discredited everywhere [in Europe] by philosophy, had lost its ascendancy even over the people" [*Collected Writings of Rousseau*, ed. Masters and Kelly, IX p. 227].) But the philosophy that had achieved this result—modern philosophy or the movement, which began according to Strauss with Machiavelli, known by the name of "the Enlightenment" (WIPP p. 46; TOM pp. 207f., 231)—had won its victory over philosophy's perennial antagonist without, in the end, being able to convince itself that that victory was deserved (*Philosophie und Gesetz* pp. 17f.).

Now, any doubts that it may have felt on this score had not at first imperiled the political dimension of the Enlightenment's effort (*Philosophie und Gesetz* pp. 20f.). We can perhaps approach the understanding of that effort required for our present purpose by beginning from the observation that the biblical religions had brought more fully to light than ever before certain fundamental human longings and demands. These longings and demands had, indeed, always been an element of pre-philosophic political life; but they had found a place within classical (Greek and Roman) politics, at least, without seriously threatening (that is, without more than sporadically threatening) the sway that political considerations proper and political forces strictly or narrowly understood exercised over those politics. (See, for example, what Thucydides indicates about the Spartans—*even the old-fashioned Spartans*—at V 70; and consider what Aristotle permits himself to say at *Politics* 1328b11–12.) To have posed or inspired such a threat, to have acquired a weight within political life comparable to that of the political necessities themselves, the longings and demands in question (for perfect justice, for example, or complete happiness) would probably have required a more explicit articulation than it was customary for them to receive. It is true that they were spelled out with considerable clarity and force by classical political philosophy—by Plato, above all, who then went on, as if unavoidably, to call for a true politics to replace the old and still actual politics. (Compare *Gorgias* 521d6–8 with 502d10–503d6; *Republic* 473c11–e2 and 592a5–b6.) But, whatever may have been Plato's ultimate intention, it was only the Christian teaching of "the truth and the true way" that succeeded in transforming political life root and branch, either by imposing upon politics the tasks that appeared—from the perspective of the demands and longings it gave voice to—to be the highest tasks, or by causing political life to be judged by a standard suggested by those longings and demands, or in both of these ways. (Machiavelli *Discourses* Bk II ch. 2 para. 2; Montesquieu *Spirit of the Laws* Bk IV ch. 4.) And the political achievement of the Enlightenment can therefore be said provisionally to consist in this: that it, in turn, succeeded in freeing politics from the tasks that Christianity had insisted upon—in part by diverting men from their pursuit (*Spirit of the Laws* Bk XX ch. 1, Bk XXV ch. 12), in part by assaulting the tasks directly with its rhetoric (*Spirit of the Laws* Bk XXIV ch. 11, for example).

Thus Enlightenment philosophy had apparently succeeded in returning politics to that form which they had had before they began to come under biblical influences, or to that form at its peak (NRH p. 164). But in doing so, this philosophy had demanded an all but explicit renunciation of tasks whose legitimacy had been recognized in principle even by the classical politics that had refused to permit their pursuit to set the direction of political life or in this way determine its character. (Compare, for example, *Spirit of the Laws* Bk XII ch. 4 with Aristotle *Ethics* 1129b14–25 and 1130b22–26, on the one hand, and *Politics* 1324b3–9, on the other.) The Enlightenment could therefore bring about no more than an approximation of such a return. The predominance within political life of political considerations proper—freedom and empire (Thucydides III 45.6)—and political forces strictly or narrowly understood was, indeed, restored. But the political order was at the same time stripped of something which even a tacit acknowledgment of the higher tasks had conferred upon it as a matter of course: a pretension to completeness, to being the whole within and through which human life might reach the utmost goal of its striving (*Ethics* 1160a20–23; Plato *Laws* 632c1–4, 817b1–c1, 887b5–c2). To many, therefore, the new or restored political order was bound to appear but a poor relation of its former self—and not just to those in whom the biblical claims, which had merely been discredited, that is to say weakened rather than definitely disposed of, continued to lead an underground life.

Now the dissatisfaction with modern politics flowing from these or other sources found powerful expression in modern philosophy itself, most notably in Rousseau. To the uneasiness that modern philosophy owed to its doubts as to the legitimacy of its victory over religion, there was thus added an uneasiness occasioned by the unsparing criticism that it proceeded to level at its own political program—if it was not this very criticism that first brought out or returned those doubts to active life within it (*Philosophie und Gesetz* p. 21; I would also refer in this context to the paper I gave at the MSU conference that opened this series [of conferences on the work of Leo Strauss]: in that paper I tried to answer the question whether the author of NRH still maintained the thesis which he had laid out in the "very daring" introduction to his second book [letter to Kojève of May 9, 1935, OT p. 230].) And the crisis in modern philosophy that begins with Rousseau (NRH p. 252)—and which is, among other things, a crisis in confidence—exacerbated, in its turn, the dissatisfaction with modern politics that had helped to set it in motion. For doubts as to the status of reason and its capacity to supply the guidance that we need both individually and collectively are, by that very fact, doubts about the soundness of any orientation or arrangement, either in politics or in life, that traces its origin to rational or philosophic endeavor. In the ensuing confusion, attempts were made to find an antidote in a return to supra-rational sources of light. But those attempts were undermined from within by lingering effects of the very victory of the Enlightenment whose legitimacy was now despaired of by the Enlightenment's own most proper heirs (*Philosophie und Gesetz* pp. 15–17; "Preface" to the English translation SCR pp. 13–15, 30).

The situation, in short, in which Strauss began his literary career could be summed up, and was in fact summed up by him at about this time, as follows: "unsere Situation ist gekennzeichnet durch die prinzipiell grenzenlose Anarchie, es gibt überhaupt keine allgemein-verbindliche Norm mehr . . . . Und es ist die *Frage*: ist diese Anarchie zu überwinden und wie ist sie zu überwinden?" (Strauss to Löwith #16 GS III pp. 630f.) And the works which he produced in its course can be said to have been addressed primarily to those with a capacity to *experience* the predicament thus summed up—a predicament that those works themselves make a comprehensive effort of matchless probity to clarify and to confront—to experience it *as their own*.

The question all but had to arise, therefore, as to what hope he gave us that this predicament, *the* crisis of our time, can be not only confronted but overcome. For many of those who have been attracted to Strauss, the answer to this question on the level of the individual—but not merely of the individual—is indicated by the terms "philosophy" and "the philosophic life." I do not entirely disagree with this view: I only wonder what it or these terms themselves entail. And I will attempt, in the balance of this paper, to approach its more particular theme by way of spelling out something of what seems to me to be worth puzzling about here.

To begin, then, at the very beginning: the predicament that we face is the absence of a norm or standard of universal validity by which to guide our lives both individually and collectively or, in other words, the omnipresent relativism, which is accepted with equanimity or even welcomed only by the most complacent or thoughtless among our contemporaries. And the solution, let us say, is philosophy or the philosophic life. But in what way is that which is designated by these terms the solution we seek? Does philosophy *discover* the norm or standard that we require? In that case, what is that norm or standard and by what arguments, appealing to what evidence, does philosophy establish its validity? These questions are the more necessary to raise here, since the crisis which, following Strauss's indications, we have tried to delineate (in some of its most massive features) has also been described by him as "the self-destruction of rational philosophy" ("Preface" to SCR p. 30). But the discovery and vindication of such a norm or standard would constitute, certainly, a rebirth of rational philosophy. What grounds, then, do we have for heralding such a rebirth?

Or is it the philosophic life itself that is to be seen, not so much as norm or standard, but rather as the end, or the peak of a hierarchy of ends, by and towards which we need to direct our lives? In this view, we are to look to philosophy not for an answer which it *gives*, but for that which it itself *constitutes*. But then in this case, too, we have to do with an answer to a question—indeed to *the* question, the question of how we are to live or of the right way of life—and therefore we remain, precisely as would-be philosophers, under the necessity of determining whether the answer (that which philosophy is said to constitute) is the correct one. The response will perhaps be made on philosophy's behalf that it, as we have just come close to conceding, is the very discipline that (in one or another of its forms) recognizes this necessity and undertakes the task of making the determination insisted upon. Well and good: but the undertaking of a task cannot be equated with its successful completion. Engaging in an inquiry cannot be taken to confer, by itself, a legitimacy or validity that the inquiry is admittedly in the process, merely, of seeking to establish. For—prior to its completion—if not all possibilities, at least some significant alternative or alternatives must remain open: what else can it mean that the inquiry has not yet been completed? And so long as there remains at least one significant alternative that has not been disposed of, we are so far from being able to anticipate our inquiry's successful conclusion, that we cannot exclude that an option for that alternative, based on what claims to be no more than a simple faith in its rightness, is superior to all of our striving. The task of determining the rightness of the answer that philosophy itself constitutes (to the question of how to live) must not only be undertaken, then, but also brought to completion, if we are to have a reasonable confidence in the rightness of this answer. And if that task has been completed, the same questions can and must be put to the answer that philosophy *is* as to any answers on this score that it merely *gives*: by what arguments, appealing to what evidence, is its validity established? Finally, if a part of that evidence should be said to be an experience or experiences which only philosophers as philosophers have, we ourselves would have to suspend judgment on the philosophic life until that time, not only when we will have had the experience or experiences in question, but when we are able to make clear to ourselves their character and significance.—The result of these and similar considerations could be expressed as follows: if philosophy itself, that is, the philosophic life, is to be regarded by us as the answer to the question of the right way of life, its claim to this effect must have been established by an inquiry that is, in principle, prior to our engaging in that life, or to our engaging in it from this point of view. And on other grounds, too, as it seems to me, the inquiry which establishes the desirability of philosophizing must precede philosophizing proper, in the strictest sense of the word. For it is difficult to see how the necessary inner freedom vis à vis philosophy's own most proper subject matter is otherwise to be won. (Cf. Strauss to Löwith #64 GS III p. 696.)

But what is, then, its proper subject matter? This is the question to which all of our previous reflections have been pointing, for—as the question of what philosophy is or of what philosophizing consists in—it lies behind, obviously, any question of what solutions philosophy may or may not supply to our fundamental predicament. And Strauss has given to it the following answer: "The discovery of nature is the work of philosophy. . . . The whole history of philosophy is nothing but the record of the ever repeated attempts to grasp fully what was implied in that crucial discovery which was made by some Greek twenty-six hundred years ago or before" (NRH pp. 81–82). Or again: "The first philosophers are called by Aristotle 'those who discourse on nature' . . . . The primary theme of philosophy . . . is 'nature.' What is nature?" ("Introduction" to HPP p. 2) Philosophy, then, is not simply deep or brilliant thinking, nor even deep and penetrating thinking. Strauss gave many indications to the effect that he regarded Heidegger as the greatest thinker, or even "the only great thinker," of our time ("Existentialism" *Interpretation* Vol. 22 Nr 3, p. 305; cf. Strauss to Löwith #41 GS III p. 674); but he gave indication also, at least occasionally, of a doubt as to whether Heidegger is properly called a philosopher (Strauss to Löwith #41 GS III p. 674; cf. "Philosophy as Rigorous Science and Political Philosophy" SPPP p. 34). The reason would seem to be that, as he put it in a lecture toward the end of his life, "Heidegger seems to have succeeded in getting rid of *phusis* without having left open a back door to a Thing-in-itself and without being in need of a philosophy of nature (Hegel)." ("The problem of Socrates" *Interpretation* Vol. 22 Nr 3, p. 330; cf. Strauss to Löwith #64 GS III p. 696.) As should go without saying, this same reason establishes not the irrelevance of Heidegger's thought to reflection on the meaning and possibility of philosophy, but the contrary; and the recently published correspondence (GS III pp. 377–772) adds to the evidence that we possess of Strauss's life-long engagement with it. We are compelled therefore, if we wish to uncover the subject matter of philosophy—that is, to see whether, strictly speaking, it has a subject matter—to try to get some grasp, however limited, of what is at issue in the confrontation of these two figures. And Strauss himself has encouraged us to do so by way of a remark which he graciously applied to his own case: "The scholar becomes possible through the fact that the great thinkers disagree. Their disagreement creates a possibility for us to reason about their differences—for wondering which of them is more likely to be right" ("Existentialism" p. 306).

He has helped us more materially by the remarks which from time to time he made about the character of the differences we are now concerned with. This, for example, from *Natural Right and History*: "Radical historicism," that is, Heidegger, "compels us . . . to realize the need for unbiased reconsideration of the most elementary premises whose validity is presupposed by philosophy" (p. 31). There are, then, such "premises" (whether or not they are precisely the ones pointed to in the context [pp. 30–31]): philosophy is not a presuppositionless activity. And Heidegger calls them into question. Another remark as to what philosophy "in the strict and classical sense" presupposes occurs in the concluding paragraph of Strauss's response to Kojève's critique of his first Xenophon book. (We should note that this paragraph was withheld by Strauss from subsequent printings of the response; it had appeared in the French version of their exchange and was restored to *On Tyranny* by Gourevitch and Roth: see the UC Press version of their edition for the authentic wording of the paragraph in question [pp. viii, 212–13].) And here, too, Strauss lays stress on the non-acceptance of the presupposition mentioned—in this case, on the part of Kojève, another contemporary for whom he had the highest regard: he had identified him earlier in the response as belonging "to the very few who know how to think and who love to think," that is, as "a philosopher and not an intellectual" (pp. 185f.) However that may be, philosophy "in the strict and classical sense," according to Strauss's remark in this paragraph, presupposes "that any 'realm of freedom' is no more than a dependent province within 'the realm of necessity.'" (p. 212; cf. NRH p. 90) Now what the primacy of "the realm of necessity" entails had been indicated by Leibniz's formulation of the "Satz vom Grunde" or "Principle of Sufficient Reason." And, when he made his response to Kojève, Strauss was aware of the fact that Heidegger had suggested that, "Die Freiheit ist der Ursprung des Satzes vom Grunde." (The remark of Heidegger occurs in "Vom Wesen des Grundes" [*Wegmarken* (1996) p. 172]; Strauss had referred to an earlier version of that treatise in a review essay that appeared in 1946 ["On a New Interpretation of Plato's Political Philosophy," *Social Research* 13, 3 September 1946, p. 336n]; cf. also

"The Problem of Socrates" p. 329.) But what is meant by nature, properly understood, is nothing other than necessity, or "the realm of necessity" in its primacy: Strauss refers in *Natural Right and History* to "knowledge of 'natures,' that is to say, of unchangeable and knowable necessity" (p. 90). Nature, then, is not merely philosophy's most proper subject matter. As we had to some extent foreseen, nature is also its fundamental presupposition, a presupposition that has come to appear to be radically questionable.

What is the source of the difficulty? Nature, as we can perhaps at least provisionally say, appears to presuppose man. According to one of Strauss's formulations, philosophy is "awareness of the fundamental problems and, therewith, of the fundamental alternatives regarding their solution that are coeval with human thought." (NRH p. 32; cf. WIPP p. 39; cf. also WIPP p. 249 where, bringing out apparently an unstated implication of Riezler's thought, Strauss says, "This implies that in order to be truly real, reality must be 'seen': if there are no human beings there cannot be concreteness.") Or, philosophy (at least in its Socratic form) is the attempt "to understand the unity that is revealed in the manifest articulation of the completed whole" (NRH p. 123); but the completed whole is "the given whole," that is, "the whole which is permanently given, as permanently as are human beings" ("On the Interpretation of Genesis," *L'Homme*, janv-mars 1981, XXI [I], p. 8). At the minimum, it would seem, one must raise the question "whether there can be a universe without man: is man's being accidental to the universe, to any universe?" (LAM p. 31; cf. Strauss to Löwith #53 GS III pp. 684–85; cf. Aristotle *Physics* 223a16–29) Now, so far as I am aware, Strauss's writings do not disclose his thought on the question of the permanence or impermanence of man. (Cf. the letter to Helmut Kuhn that was published in *The Independent Journal of Philosophy* Vol. II 1978, p. 24: "I am not an Aristotelian since I am not satisfied that the visible universe is eternal, to say nothing of other perhaps more important reasons.") He did not hesitate to stress, on the other hand, the centrality of the finiteness of man for Heidegger (NRH pp. 32, 176; "Existentialism" p. 312; "The Problem of Socrates" p. 327; cf. Strauss to Löwith #'s 53 and 62 GS III pp. 684 and 694). But the fact—if it is a fact—of man's finiteness would seem to cast a shadow on nature, and therewith on nature as we have seen that, according to Strauss, it must be understood. And for Heidegger, as the remark that we have quoted from "Vom Wesen des Grundes" would tend to indicate, this appears to have been the case.

Strauss himself quoted that remark in the late lecture to which we have referred ("The Problem of Socrates" p. 329). To understand the context in which he did so, we must return for a moment to the passage in *Natural Right and History* which contains his identification of "knowledge of 'natures'" with knowledge of "unchangeable and knowable necessity" (p. 90). The longer statement, of which this identification is a part and which concludes with the contention that "all freedom and indeterminacy presuppose a more fundamental necessity," is meant to "express the same fundamental premise" that, in its earlier formulation, had been said to hold "that no being emerges without a cause or that it is impossible that 'at first Chaos came to be,' i.e., that the first things jumped into being out of nothing and through nothing" (p. 89). Now, in the lecture, Strauss quoted the remark from "Vom Wesen des Grundes" after having referred to this same fundamental premise: "out of nothing nothing comes into being." As he had continued there, "This is apparently questioned by Heidegger: he says . . . out of nothing every being as being comes out." (The reference is apparently to "Was ist Metaphysik" [*Wegmarken* pp. 119–20]; cf. Strauss to Klein #116 GS III pp. 598f.) Strauss had then commented, in part, as follows: "This would suggest, things come into being out of nothing and through nothing . . . . This is of course not literally asserted nor literally denied by Heidegger. But *must* it not be considered in its literal meaning?" (p. 329). And the quotation from "Vom Wesen des Grundes," which follows shortly after this comment, appears to supply or to point to the response that Strauss thought Heidegger would have made to the question or challenge it put to him.

Strauss was clearly dissatisfied with this answer or non-answer on the part of Heidegger. It will perhaps be said that he had no need to take it seriously, since he has given no indication, in writing at least, that he accepted its Heideggerian basis: the finiteness of man. Still, given the darkness of the matter on which he has remained silent, it is worth considering how Strauss would have argued the question—that is, how he would have defended nature—precisely on that Heideggerian basis. And it may be that it is only in this way that we can approach the "true perplexity" in Strauss's position.

He would have argued, as it seems to me, that man's finiteness does not necessarily entail that he is also an historical being, in the radical sense that the fundamental problems themselves change from human epoch to human epoch: we have already recalled his contention that those problems are, rather, coeval with human thought. And he would have argued further, I think, that it is only the alleged historicity of man or human life—and not his finiteness as such—that can cast a shadow on the principle of causality and therewith on nature. In one of his last letters to Löwith, with reference to a statement of the latter on Heidegger, Strauss put the matter to him as follows: "Auf die Frage, ob der Mensch ein natürliches Wesen sei, antworten Sie mit einem *Ja und Nein* . . . ; wenn dem so ist, kann die Natur nicht *der* Grund alles Seienden sein und Heidegger, der diesen Grund in Sein findet, ist daher vorzuziehen" (#64 GS III pp. 695–96). The task, then, was to show that man is a natural being or, in other words, that he is not an historical being in the sense indicated. And this task Strauss undertook, not least by his historical studies of modern thought. What was urgently needed, in his view, was "an understanding of the genesis of historicism that does not take for granted the soundness of historicism" (NRH p. 33). Or, as he also put it, "An adequate discussion of historicism would be identical with a critical analysis of modern philosophy in general" (WIPP p. 60). In his own contributions to that analysis, he sought to demonstrate the part played in the genesis of historicism by dissatisfaction with the solutions that pre-historicist modern philosophy had found to the problems with which it was confronted. Now, since these problems were but variants of the perennial problems, Strauss's demonstration of their importance even or precisely to historicism served a two-fold purpose: on the one hand, it tended to confirm that they are indeed permanent problems, problems coeval with human thought; on the other, it brought out a certain superiority of historicist thought to its modern alternatives with respect to the understanding of what their adequate solution would require. And from this, we can perhaps begin to understand a remark which Strauss made in a letter to Klein written about the time when he was working on *Natural Right and History*, that is, when he was again attacking the problem of history. The remark is to the effect that it seemed to him that at the bottom of the whole affair lay "the problem of causality" and that Heidegger himself had at least pointed in this direction (#116 GS III p. 598). But, if this is the case, it was not simply the false lens of historicism or of the turn to history that had brought causality to sight as a problem. What truly has been gained, then, by showing that man's finiteness does not entail that he is also an historical being?

By way of elaboration of what he meant by the "problem of causality," Strauss had referred, in the letter to Klein, to Kant and "the unsolved

Humean problem" (Cf. "The Problem of Socrates" p. 329.) He had in mind, then, that problem as it had been understood and approached in modern philosophy. By showing the inadequacy of the modern approach (as he had begun to do already in his Spinoza book) as well as the unsoundness of the turn to history that was, in part, a reaction to that inadequacy, Strauss hoped to clear the way for an open-minded consideration of the ancient (Socratic) approach. The principle of causality had become the problem that it had for the moderns as a result of the challenge to it, unprecedented in its clarity and consistency, posed by the biblical doctrine of creation. (Cf. "Was ist Metaphysik?" p. 119, the passage in Heidegger apparently referred to in the letter to Klein.) Strauss turned to the ancient approach as to a sounder way of responding to such challenges. That ancient approach itself, then, could do no more than return the principle to the place that it could claim to occupy in the absence of such challenges. What place is that? According to one of the greatest heirs to the Socratic approach, it is ridiculous to attempt to demonstrate the existence of nature, for it is manifest that there are many natural beings and the attempt to demonstrate the existence of such beings would be an attempt to demonstrate the manifest by recourse to the immanifest (Aristotle *Physics* 193a3–6): this seems to me to fall short of a claim that the existence of nature is completely evident. (Cf. *Der Satz vom Grund* pp. 17–18.) Its existence can perhaps be said to approach such evidence; but everything depends, therefore, on how we must judge of the closeness of that approach. In the third chapter of *Natural Right and History*, after speaking of certain "presuppositions" which "follow from the fundamental premise that no being emerges without a cause," Strauss elaborates as follows: "In other words, the manifest changes would be impossible if there did not exist something permanent or eternal, or the manifest contingent beings require the existence of something necessary and therefore eternal" (p. 89). Now, if an evident premise or principle has as a necessary consequence something which itself lacks evidence, this fact must cast at least some shadow on the original principle. And, not to mention now other perhaps more familiar considerations, the very philosophy whose recovery is Strauss's lasting glory, Socratic philosophy, is constituted by the recognition of the elusiveness of that "necessary and therefore eternal" being (NRH pp. 122–23, Plato *Phaedo* 99d4–e6 and context; cf. Aristotle *Physics* 192b32–34).

In raising the difficulties or questions I have tried to raise—let me say in conclusion—my purpose has been only to indicate the character of the challenges which seem to me to confront any attempt to appropriate Strauss's thought for one's own. In the case of Strauss, as in that of any other thinker of his rank, these challenges are not the least of the good things that he has left to us.

Part IV

Xenophon, Plato, Aristotle

12

Xenophon

Of the companions of Socrates who wrote about him, only Plato and Xenophon left works which have come down to us more or less intact. But whereas Plato's writings are, so to speak, entirely Socratic, Xenophon's four Socratic writings (*Memorabilia*, *Oeconomicus*, *Symposium*, and *Apology of Socrates*) fill only one of the five volumes of the complete edition of his works. The reader is thus faced with the task, which has no counterpart in the study of Plato, of understanding the place of Xenophon's Socratic writings in the larger context of his work as a whole.

Xenophon's longest work by far, the *Cyropaedia* (Education of Cyrus), is a treatment of the education and career of the founder of the Persian empire, who is in Xenophon's presentation an exemplary practitioner of the royal art of ruling. His next longest work, the *Hellenica* (Greek Affairs), is devoted to the noteworthy political and military doings of the Greeks during Xenophon's lifetime. Beginning roughly where Thucydides' history breaks off, it is sometimes regarded in its early portions as a continuation and completion of that history. The *Cyroanabasis* (Ascent of Cyrus), or *Anabasis*, as it is generally called, is largely an account of the outstanding event of Xenophon's own political career, his leading back to Greece and safety of the bulk of the "ten thousand" Greek mercenaries who had accompanied a younger Cyrus into the heart of the Persian empire in support of his attempt to overthrow his brother, the Persian king. The Greeks had become isolated there after Cyrus was killed in battle and his other troops deserted to the king. The remaining non-Socratic works traditionally ascribed to Xenophon consist of shorter writings. They comprise a eulogy of Agesilaus, a Spartan king known personally to Xenophon; a dialogue on tyranny between the tyrant Hiero and the poet Simonides; and treaties on the Spartan and Athenian constitutions, on Athenian revenues, and on the arts of the cavalry commander, of horsemanship, and of hunting with dogs.

Xenophon, who lived himself for a time as lord of a country estate,[1] has told us something about the tastes and opinions of a Greek gentleman—for example, his admiration for the royal art of ruling on the one hand[2] and for the Spartan-style republicanism on the other[3]—as well as about the country or rural basis of many of the gentleman's activities, with its heavy demand for the use of horses and dogs.[4] It is tempting to conclude that his writings as a whole not only reflect such a taste but are intended to appeal to it, above all. This temptation may be strengthened when we observe, as we are bound to do, another difference between Xenophon's writings and Plato's. The solemn, moving, quasi-tragic tones of the Platonic dialogues are hardly to be found in Xenophon. In their place, we find an apparently lighthearted simplicity enlivened and graced often, if not always, by humor. Xenophon is a writer capable of presenting the problem of justice in the guise of a story of two boys, a large one with a small coat and a small one with a large coat.[5] He seems to have fled high seriousness as eagerly as, and more successfully than, Bertie Wooster (that latter-day gentleman of P. G. Wodehouse's invention) fled entanglements with women "steeped to the gills in serious purpose" and bent on improving his mind.

There may be some considerable truth to this first impression of what inspired Xenophon and of the audience he wished to address. But it fails to clarify the context in which his Socratic writings must be understood. Indeed, it leaves no place for those writings. For, as Xenophon demonstrates in his most extensive treatment of the gentlemanly life and character, the gentleman as such has no interest in Socrates,[6] while

---

1. *Anabasis* V 3.7–13.

2. *Oeconomicus* 21.10; 4.4; 13.5.

3. *Memorabilia* III 5.15–16. The testimony comes from the son of the great Pericles, author of Athens's anti-Spartan policy.

4. *Oeconomicus* 5 and 11.

5. *Cyropaedia* I 3.16–17.

6. The *Oeconomicus* includes the report of an extensive conversation between Socrates and a perfect gentleman, which culminates in a comparison of their two ways of life. The conversation is brought about by Socrates, and all of the questions which animate it proceed from him and serve his desire to learn about the gentleman.

Xenophon is preoccupied with him. This is shown not only by his Socratic writings proper but also by the appearance of Socrates and related themes in each of his other major works.[7] We come closer then to doing justice to both aspects of Xenophon's work—Socratic and non-Socratic—and to bringing to light their possible unity, by suggesting that Xenophon may have been one who pursued the Socratic *question* of the best way of life without ever coming to accept completely the Socratic *answer* that that way of life is the philosophic one.

This suggestion derives some support from the consideration that Xenophon—while calling frequent attention to his own relationship with Socrates, in sharp contrast to Plato, going so far as to call the chief of his Socratic writings "Memorabilia" or "Recollections," *his* recollections of Socrates—in the only two episodes he chooses to recount from their friendship gives more evidence of resistance to Socrates' teaching and advice than of acceptance.[8] If Xenophon's levity stands in the way of our adopting it, by causing us to wonder whether anyone who wrote in the way he did could have concerned himself with the question of the best way of life, we can recall Plato's own indications that the taste for tragedy, which he was so much more willing than Xenophon to indulge, is a questionable one.[9] But even if our suggestion will have to be revised or qualified on the basis of our study of Xenophon's works, it has the merit of permitting us to begin that study by helping us to discern the order in which the most important of them stand toward one another.

In the *Cyropaedia*, Xenophon presents his thoughts on the character of the perfect ruler and on the political way of life at its peak. The Socratic writings, led by the *Memorabilia*, are devoted to the philosopher par excellence and the philosophic way of life as Xenophon had observed it firsthand in the pursuits of Socrates. "Cyrus" and "Socrates" apparently represent the two alternatives which most impressed him, constituting the poles between which, he thought, all other human possibilities (for example, the quasi-public life of the gentleman) are to be found and by reference to which they are to be understood. In the *Anabasis*, the two poles are brought together as Xenophon, the student of Socrates, leaves

---

7. *Anabasis* III 1.4–8; *Hellenica* I 7.15 and context (compare *Memorabilia* I 1.17–18 and IV 4.1–2); *Cyropaedia* I 6.31–34; III 1.14, and 1.38–40; VII 2.15–25.

8. *Memorabilia* I 3.8–13; *Anabasis* III 1.4–8.

9. See, for example, *Laws* 658d2–4 and *Meno* 76e3–7. See Shaftesbury's *Characteristics*, I, 167 and 309 (Indianapolis: Bobbs-Merrill, 1964), for the view of one who preferred Xenophon to Plato on this ground.

Socrates against the latter's advice to join a campaign being organized by a new Cyrus.

Cyropaedia

The accomplishments of the elder Cyrus were due partly to his birth (family), partly to his nature, and partly to his education.[10] If he had not had a certain nature (outstanding natural abilities accompanied by the inclination to use them in a certain way),[11] he could not have conceived his great plans or carried them out. If he had not been born into two royal lines—his father was king of Persia, his mother's father king of Media—his opportunities would have been limited in such a way as to affect the character of his accomplishments.[12] But leaving these matters to one side for the moment, we will begin from a consideration of his education, as Xenophon's title bids us to do.

"He was educated in the Persian laws." Xenophon's account does not seriously claim to be historical. According to it, the Persia in which Cyrus was raised, the Persia whose armies he led to the conquest of Asia and in whose name he founded an empire, was a rather small republic or what we would call a constitutional monarchy. It was, moreover, a model republic along Spartan lines, an improved Sparta. If Xenophon admired Sparta, he must have admired still more this "Persia." Publicly educating its youth, as Sparta did, instilling in them continence and obedience as well as military skills, Persia suppressed Sparta's education to thievery in favor of an education to justice.[13] Like the cities praised by Plato and Aristotle, Xenophon's Persia regarded as its laws' most important task the formation of the character of its citizens: it wished to make them such as not even to desire to commit any wicked or shameful deed.[14] And, like those other highly regarded cities, it was an aristocracy, since the country's fidelity to its laws' high purpose depended on political authority remaining firmly

---

10. *Cyropaedia* I 1.6.

11. Ibid., I 2.1, 3.1–3, 4.24.

12. The comparative mildness of his rule depended in part on the claim to legitimacy, which he was always at pains to maintain, afforded by his birth. Consider especially VIII 5.17–20, 5.26, 5.28, and VII 5.37 ff.

13. Ibid., I 2.6 ff.; compare *Constitution of the Spartans* 2.6 ff. as well as *Anabasis* IV 6.14.

14. *Cyropaedia* I 2.2–3.

in the hands of those and only those who had completed the course of education thought to accomplish that purpose.[15] In other words, with the quasi-exception of his playful suggestion that the desirable political arrangements are not merely objects of future prayer or wish but actually existed at some time in the past, Xenophon's presentation of Persia follows the lines more familiar to us in Plato and Aristotle. And to the extent that Cyrus' success and that of his Persians was due to the formation they received from the Persian laws,[16] the *Cyropaedia* as a whole stands as a sort of tribute to those laws and to the Persian regime which maintained them.

But Cyrus' education in the broad sense of the term took place not just in Persia but also in Media at the court of his grandfather, a typical oriental despot presiding over a country of a very different sort from Persia.[17] In accord with this, Cyrus' success amounted to political change, indeed change on a vast scale, for Persia. The Persian empire he founded had little in common with the old Persia, which it effectively replaced, relegating it to the status of a smallish province—however much, for sound political reasons, Cyrus wished to stress the similarity between old and new orders rather than the differences.[18] And Xenophon appears to present Cyrus' transformation of Persia no less sympathetically than he presented the old Persia that Cyrus transformed. Moreover, the changes brought about by Cyrus could hardly have taken place, or been defended by him, if there had not been grave defects in old Persia. In presenting Cyrus' career, Xenophon could not help calling attention to those defects. This means, however, that he was forced to stress what Plato and Aristotle allowed themselves only to hint at: the defects of classical republicanism in its highest or most exalted form. He thus took an important step in the direction of Machiavelli's much less sympathetic critique, a favor Machiavelli acknowledged in many appreciative remarks.[19]

To return to Cyrus' Median education, he passed his thirteenth through fifteenth or sixteenth years at his grandfather's court, finding there things both to like and to dislike. For example, he was pleased with the

---

15. Ibid., I 2.15.

16. Consider, among other passages, ibid., I 1.6, 2.2, 3.1, 5.7–13; II 1.3; III 3.50–55, 3.70; IV 2.38–46, 5.1–4, 5.54; V 2.15–20; VII 5.70; VIII 8.15.

17. Compare ibid., I 2.2 with 3.1, 3.13–18, 4.1, 4.25, and 5.1.

18. Ibid., VII 5.85.

19. For reference to the *Cyropaedia* in particular, see *Prince* 14 and 16, and *Discourses* II 13; III 20, 22, and 39.

Median style of dress and adornment, which far surpassed the Persian in richness and splendor,[20] and he took extreme delight in learning horseback riding.[21] But he disliked the Median indulgence in fancy food—which made the process of satisfying hunger unnecessarily complicated and time-consuming[22]—and in intoxicating drink, if only because it made the king himself as well as his retainers forget the deference they owed him.[23] While Cyrus was highly critical of the conduct of the Median monarchs, at least in retrospect,[24] even as a boy he may have had some awareness that absolute monarchy is not without its advantages.[25] And at that time or later on, he formed the opinion that his comrades back in Persia would be attracted as he was by "Median" opportunities for wealth and distinction unavailable to them in the incomparably more austere Persian republic.

When Cyrus was probably still only in his middle to late twenties (but already considered in Persia one of the mature men), a combination of forces brought together and led by the king of Assyria began to threaten Media (now ruled by Cyrus' uncle Cyaxares). The threat to Media was at the same time a threat to Persia, since its alliance with its neighbor had surely been one of the rocks on which Persian independence had been maintained hitherto. The Persian government decided, therefore, in response to a request by Cyaxares, to send a force of thirty-one thousand Persians to help defend its ally. It also acceded to Cyaxares' wish in selecting Cyrus, who still had many friends in Media from his stay there of ten or more years before, to command this force. Cyrus was, as he said "not unwilling" to accept the assignment. This was the opening he must have been waiting for. But to see the forethought, daring, and inventiveness, the patience, determination, and perseverance which are among the elements of great political leadership, we have only to consider the distance between what Cyrus was authorized by this commission to do and what he intended to do, and between the resources it provided him with and those his larger project required.

---

20. *Cyropaedia* I 3.2–3; compare VIII 1.40–41 and 3.1–14.

21. Ibid., I 3.3, 3.15, 4.4–5; compare IV 3 and VIII 3.16 and 3.25.

22. Ibid., I 3.4; compare I 5.12; IV 2.38–47, 5.1–7; V 2.14–21, 3.34–35; VI 2.25–29; but also VIII 2.1–7.

23. Ibid., I 3.10–11; compare VIII 4.9–15.

24. Ibid., I 6.8; compare 3.18.

25. Consider ibid., I 3.16–18 with VIII 1.22, and Aristotle, *Politics* 1269a8–12, 1286a9–16.

Cyrus was indeed heir to the Persian throne; but even as king he would have had no independent authority other than to conduct sacrifices on the country's behalf.[26] His lawful authority consisted then entirely in the military command he had been appointed to. That is, it depended entirely on the (revocable) decision of the Persian government. Now, given the size and character of the force he was entrusted with and the occasion for its being sent, that government must have had in mind his engaging in nothing more than a limited and defensive war. And only such a war would have been truly compatible with the desire to maintain the unique Persian way of life, which required close mutual supervision on the part of citizens familiar with one another through daily contact.[27] Such a way of life would have been difficult, not to say impossible, to maintain in a "greater Persia" which might result from the attempt to absorb foreign conquests, and it would have been almost equally threatened by the multiple and prolonged absences from Persia which the governing of conquered territory as subject provinces would have required. Yet Cyrus intended not merely to help Persia's ally and thus contribute to the defense of Persia but to conquer all of the countries opposed to Persia and to incorporate them, together with others, into the greater Persia he envisioned. He had no intention, moreover, of turning these conquests over to the Persian government, whose limited kingship he would someday hold. Rather he was determined to govern them himself from the outset (that is, in his father's lifetime) as absolute, and not constitutionally limited, king.

While taking the steps necessary to accomplish these things, Cyrus would have to disregard the wishes, and perhaps even the orders,[28] of the Persian government until such time as he could present them with either an irresistible temptation[29] or a fait accompli[30] or some combination of the two. His military aims alone would require a vast army, of which his original Persian force could furnish at most the core—and even that only if he could assure himself of the army's assent to projects he was not entitled to require them to undertake. He would have to secure its assent as well to a very substantial reorganization aimed at compensating for deficiency

---

26. *Cyropaedia* VIII 5.26; compare I 3.18.

27. Ibid., I 2.3–5.

28. Consider ibid., VI 1.4.

29. Ibid., IV 5.16.

30. Ibid., VIII 5.

in numbers by increased capacity to fight. Allies, in addition to the Medes, would have to be found who would be willing, whether consciously or unconsciously, to toil and take risks for Persian supremacy and their own subordination; while the Medes themselves (not to mention Cyrus' uncle Cyaxares) would have to be brought to acknowledge the supremacy of their hitherto equal or even inferior ally. Finally, Cyrus' own Persian comrades-in-arms, many of whom were his political equals—collectively indeed his superiors—would have to be brought to recognize the desirability or necessity of granting him an unchecked authority, of bowing to him as Persians had never bowed to another human being.[31]

The army Cyrus had been given consisted of a thousand "peers"—that is, those who had completed the Persian education and were accordingly admitted to full citizenship rights—and thirty thousand commoners. (This was out of a total of one hundred and twenty thousand Persians.)[32] The strictly military significance of this proportion lay in the fact that only the peers were equipped and prepared for fighting at close quarters. This was the sort of fighting which generally Greeks rather than non-Greeks excelled in and which enabled numerically inferior armies to defeat considerably larger ones prepared only for skirmishing or fighting at a distance. But there was also a political significance to the division within Cyrus' army. At home in Persia, the whole class of the so-called peers was small in number, and yet it ruled over the much more numerous commoners, who had no share in civic rights.[33] Presumably, the peers' monopoly on the most effective sort of fighting contributed to the ease with which they were able to maintain their ascendancy; and we can assume therefore that in sending an army out of Persia the home authorities took care to maintain both within the army and among the Persians left at home a numerical ratio between the classes which they considered to be politically safe.[34] Even so, they must have considered the army they had given Cyrus equal to the (defensive) task that had been assigned to it. Or, if they had any doubts on that score, they had made the political decision to run a somewhat

---

31. Compare ibid., I 3.18 with VII 5.37 ff., VIII 1.1–5 and especially 3.13–14; compare *Anabasis* III 2.13.

32. *Cyropaedia* I 2.15.

33. Ibid., II 1.3.

34. Consider the fact that the additional force sent to Cyrus by the Persian authorities, when they decided to comply with his request for reinforcements, was composed of forty thousand commoners and no peers: V 5.3.

greater risk from their foreign foes rather than to put dangerous weapons into the hands of potential domestic ones.

Cyrus assessed his army's situation somewhat differently. He was unconcerned, to say the least, to preserve the political balance either within the army or at home, but very concerned that the small size of the army's most effective branch rendered it unfit for the tasks he had in mind for it. The obvious military solution was to give heavy weapons to the commoners (weapons to be paid for by the frightened Cyaxares)[35] and to induce them, by the promise of equal treatment in the future, to join the ranks of the fighters-at-close-quarters. The commoners could be counted on to jump at the chance to improve their status and lot in life; but opposition was to be expected from the peers within the army. Unlike the authorities at home, they were on the spot and would have to be informed immediately and even consulted as to any such change; and they would not be unaware of its domestic political implications. So before even broaching the subject of rearming the commoners, Cyrus addressed himself to the peers who had been chosen to accompany him.[36]

In this, the first of his many political speeches, he speaks to them of the practices they have inherited from their ancestors and of their own situation. According to Cyrus, they are now in a position to avoid their ancestors' mistake of failing to put those worthy practices to any use: "I have observed that our forefathers were no worse than we are: they too persevered in practicing what are held to be deeds of virtue. But what good thing they acquired through being men of this sort, either for the Persian commonwealth or themselves, this I am no longer able to see." Cyrus tacitly treats the preservation of the Persian regime and the Persian way of life as worthless. The good things he has in mind are precisely those which Persia does not provide: "much wealth, much happiness, and great honors" for oneself and one's country. This is the reason why the war, which was seen by the Persian authorities only as a threat to be put down as quickly as possible, is seen by Cyrus as an opportunity—an opportunity to make use of the qualities so long cultivated by the Persians which equip them in body and prepare them in soul for military supremacy:

> Since we know of ourselves that, starting from childhood, we
> have been practitioners of the noble and good deeds, let us

---

35. *Cyropaedia* II 1.2–10.

36. Ibid., I 5.7–14.

> proceed against the enemies, whom I know with certainty to be like amateurs in a contest against us. . . . Let us then set out boldly, also because the reputation of unjustly desiring things belonging to others is removed from us. For it is the enemies who are now advancing and initiating unjust blows, while our friends call on us as allies. What is more just than defending oneself, or more noble than helping one's friends?

Xenophon has no need to indicate here the reaction of the peers who heard this speech: the whole rest of the book is the indication. The peers, with perhaps an occasional exception,[37] acquiesced not only in Cyrus' rearming of the commoners but in his many other steps, and they did so despite the grave political consequences of each step by itself and all of them taken together. The reason is not that they were so foolish as to have no awareness of those consequences. It is to be found in the effect on them of Cyrus' speech. Their hearts, and therefore also their minds, were no longer set on a return home, to their ancestral way of life, but on partaking of the great prospects Cyrus' words had opened their eyes to.

The rearming of the commoners followed in short order. Having prepared the peers in advance in the manner shown, Cyrus had merely to point out to them the advisability of such a step from a strictly military point of view.[38] In order to understand the way in which he[39] put the proposal to the commoners however, we must revert to an earlier passage, where Xenophon casts light on "the whole regime of the Persians."[40] It turns out that none of the Persians is excluded by law from a share in honors and offices or what we have called civic rights; rather, all are permitted to send their children to the public schools of justice. But only those parents who can afford to support their children without requiring them to work do in fact send them. And only those men who have been educated in

---

37. Consider the remarks of Aglaitadas (a man of whom we hear nothing further) at II 2.11–16.

38. *Cyropaedia* II 1.10–12.

39. It was due to the suggestion of a helpful peer, apparently acting on his own initiative, that Cyrus himself was the one who presented the arms to the commoners: II 1.12–14. This is the first of many such "helps" Cyrus received in the course of his rise. Needless to say, those who showed such initiative were not forgotten: see VIII 4.11 and context.

40. *Cyropaedia* I 2.15.

the public schools and have passed successfully on to and through the other stages of training (these too requiring leisure from gainful pursuits) can participate in honors and offices. What this situation of legal equality and factual inequality tells us is that the distinction between the classes in aristocratic Persia rested upon a basis which the aristocrats themselves were not willing to defend openly as such: namely, inherited wealth. As for the commoners, we can be sure that they regarded their exclusion from political equality, and their hard lot generally, as undeserved.[41] Cyrus therefore spoke to them as follows:

> Men of Persia, you were both born and raised in the same country as we [peers] were; you have bodies no worse than ours, and it befits you to have souls no worse than ours. Yet, though you are men of this sort, in the fatherland you did not share equally with us, excluded not by us but by the necessity of providing your daily provisions. Now, on the other hand, it will be my concern, with the gods, that you have those; but you, if you want, can take up arms such as we have, undertake with us the same risks, and, if something noble and good comes of that, be deemed worthy of the like rewards.[42]

In this way, thirty thousand new peers were created, regarding their elevation as due to Cyrus alone or above all, with all that that meant both for Cyrus' relations with the (newly endangered) old peers within the army and for the prospect of the army's ever being reabsorbed into old Persia.

The reform of the army was then completed by two further steps. First, by a general consent (orchestrated by Cyrus) the principle was adopted to give rewards (including promotions of course) according to merit, with Cyrus to be the judge of that merit.[43] This was necessary not only for the sake of invigorating the army through incentives but also to provide a new basis for distinction and hierarchy in place of the old discredited one. Hierarchy would be as necessary in the new order as in the old. In addition, on his own authority Cyrus ordered that those expelled from the ranks as unworthy be replaced by the best human beings available, whether or not these were fellow citizens, "just as in

---

41. Consider ibid., II 1.19; compare VII 5.67.

42. Ibid., II 1.15 ff.

43. Ibid., II 2.17–21, 3.1–16.

the case of horses you seek those which are best in preference to those of the fatherland."[44]

Needless to say, Cyrus turned to the tasks of enlarging his army with allies and of preparing the subordination of the allies to the Persians and to him personally, as well as to the military tasks proper, with the same energy and ability he revealed in reorganizing his army. Moreover, he was greatly aided in drawing human beings to him by his manifest decency and considerateness, fairness and generosity, loyalty and dependability.[45] These qualities, joined with his great military skill (which brought him an immediate reputation once he had a chance to display it in action), made a powerfully attractive combination. But we will pass by all of this activity, enjoyable as it is to read of it in Xenophon's account, to continue our consideration of the political seeds planted by Cyrus in his reorganization of the Persian army and the fruit they bore in the Persian empire he founded.

His efforts can be seen by now to have rested on a profound understanding or, at least, a remarkable intuitive grasp of the limitations of "Persia," that is, of classical aristocracy. He knew, for example, that the loyalty it demanded, like that for any particular, nonuniversal society, rested on an arbitrary division of mankind into fellow citizens (friends) and strangers (enemies actual or potential). (Compare Plato's analysis in the *Republic* of the defects of justice understood as helping friends and harming enemies.) He knew likewise that the class hierarchy without which, in the premodern condition of material scarcity, the unique Persian system of public education could not have been supported, rested not on merit or natural capacity but on the indefensible criterion of inherited wealth. (In the *Republic*, Plato was able to remove this stain from classical aristocracy only by the extreme expedient of abolishing the family.) These defects of the old order were to be removed in the new by the creation of a universal (and therefore all-inclusive) empire

---

44. Ibid., II 2.26; compare I 6.27–34.

45. In speaking of Cyrus' manifest qualities, we do not mean to deny what Machiavelli delights to point out, that the judicious use of qualities of a different sort was almost equally necessary to Cyrus' success. (See note 19 above.) Xenophon, too, of course, lets us see those other qualities and their importance to Cyrus, though only in a manner consistent with the principle he enunciates in the *Anabasis* (V 8.26), that "it is noble as well as just and pious, and more pleasant, to remember (or mention) the good things rather than the bad." That is, he did not entirely forgo the pleasure of mentioning the bad things.

and by making positions of wealth, honor, and responsibility within it depend upon merit alone.

Above all, Cyrus knew or sensed the weakness of that attachment to virtue and virtuous deeds as ends in themselves which the old Persian education prided itself on producing, an attachment on which the preference for old Persia and its way of life depended. To speak now only of the attachment itself and not of the virtue that was its object, it was not truly the result of education in the strict sense of the word. Rather, it had been beaten into the Persian peers both literally[46] and figuratively (through praise and blame).[47] And an attachment so produced is vulnerable to temptation. (Compare what Plato suggests, in the myth of Er which concludes the *Republic*, by his tale of the choice of lives.) Still, in providing that temptation, in suggesting to the peers that they no longer pursue what they take to be virtue for its own sake but rather for its rewards, Cyrus would appear to be more of a corrupter than a reformer. (We note in passing that this may be the only way in which he resembles Xenophon's other hero, the alleged corrupter of the young.) And by presenting Cyrus' revolution favorably, Xenophon seems to extend his sympathy to the peers' corruption. The question of how Xenophon did view that corruption is a part, if the most important part, of the question of his final judgment on Cyrus' new order as a whole.

In what amounts to a preface to the work,[48] Xenophon tells us that he turned his attention to Cyrus after reflecting on the frequency with which democracies, monarchies, oligarchies, and above all tyrannies are overthrown and reaching the conclusion that it is exceedingly difficult, not to say impossible, for human beings to rule successfully over other human beings. This conclusion seemed to be refuted by the career of Cyrus, which demonstrated that it is neither difficult nor impossible to rule over human beings, provided that one knows how to do it. Cyrus appeared to have solved the political problem. Yet in his conclusion to the *Cyropaedia*,[49] Xenophon admits and even stresses that Cyrus' empire began to fall prey to strife and decay immediately upon his death. The reason is not merely that Cyrus' successors, lacking his great qualities,

---

46. *Cyropaedia* I 2.6–7, 3.16–17.

47. Ibid., I 2.12, 6.20.

48. Ibid., I 1.

49. Ibid., VIII 8.

were unable to maintain the institutions he had established.[50] It is also to be found in flaws in those institutions themselves.

We will leave aside the facts that Cyrus' new founding was to a considerable extent merely a "reshuffling of the deck," with the formerly ruling tribes now reduced to slavery in service to the new masters; that the resultant ill will made necessary the maintenance of an immense military establishment and a large personal guard for Cyrus,[51] a virtually omnipresent, if informal, internal spying network,[52] and the use in addition of various "bewitching" techniques to hold the ruled in awe as well as fear;[53] that the individual "merit" rewarded so lavishly by Cyrus was sometimes difficult to distinguish from loyalty to him and willingness to serve his merely personal aims;[54] and that the rewards thus received were revocable at any time at Cyrus' pleasure.[55] It is more important for our present purpose to note that the greatest danger to his throne Cyrus judged to come from the very friends he had most rewarded.[56] The significance of this may be seen from the fact that these friends were for the most part the same peers whose acquisitiveness (in all its aspects) Cyrus had emancipated by his suggestion that they replace the pursuit of virtue for its own sake with pursuit of it for its rewards. More generally, the combination that Cyrus tried to effect between the Persian education and continence on the one hand and Median dress and luxury on the other,[57] while temporarily invigorating, was in the long run and even in the short run destructive of the law-bred qualities, the habits of mind, on which not only Cyrus' military enterprise depended but the capacity of any country to defend itself must in part depend.[58] Hence the progressive deterioration in quality of Cyrus' army even as its size and overall military capacity increased.[59]

---

50. Ibid., VIII 1.6–8.

51. Ibid., VII 5.58–70.

52. Ibid., VIII 2.10–12.

53. Ibid., VIII 1.40–42, 3.1–24.

54. Ibid., VIII 4.3–5, 4.9–12.

55. Ibid., VIII 1.16–20 and 2.15–19.

56. Ibid., VIII 1.45–48, 2.26–28, 4.3; compare V 2.7–12.

57. Ibid., VIII 8.15.

58. Compare ibid., III 3.51–55 with I 5.7–10.

59. This is revealed especially in the increased reliance on technical innovations and in the changing role of the rearguard officers. Compare III 3.41–42 with VI 3.27; and see VI 1.27–30, 1.50–55, and VII 1.33–35.

Nor could the education of the new nobility, instituted by Cyrus at the gates of his palace, supply the missing heart, dedication to virtue for its own sake, which Cyrus had excised from the old Persian education—for all of its superficial similarity to the latter and for all of its success in producing a surface orderliness and mutual respect.[60]

On the basis of these and other similar considerations, we can hardly avoid the conclusion that Xenophon thought the thesis about Cyrus put forward in his preface was refuted rather than sustained by his elaboration of Cyrus' career. He must after all have regarded the *Cyropaedia* as a whole as an endorsement of the old "Persian" laws and regime rather than of their transformation by Cyrus, if an endorsement suitably qualified in light of the defects of the old order brought out in the work. But why, in that case, did he present Cyrus' transformation in such a way as to make it attractive to us, at least on a first and even on a second impression? Did he merely wish to purge us of a dangerous temptation after first eliciting our affinity for it? Or are we now running the risk of repeating our error, this time by moving too far in the opposite direction from our earlier erroneous view? Does the truth about Cyrus, does Xenophon's own view of Cyrus, lie somewhere between these extremes? We are assisted in answering this question, or at least in coming to appreciate the point of view from which Xenophon made his final assessment, by considering two conversations that he presents between the young Cyrus and his parents.

Cyrus never consulted his parents about his larger project, and it is fairly safe to say that neither of them would have approved of it if asked in advance—which is not the same thing as yielding gracefully after the fact or making the best of a fait accompli.[61] But, to judge at least from the conversations referred to, the grounds of disapproval would have been different in the two cases. Cyrus' mother spoke with Cyrus in Media, when he was still a boy, about the difference between Median and Persian justice.[62] She speaks in tones that made unmistakably clear her opinion as to the superiority of the latter, a preference Cyrus would prove not to share.[63] Cyrus' father spoke with Cyrus as he set out again for Media, this time to

---

60. Ibid., VII 5.85–86; VIII 1.10–12, 1.16–33. Of the products of this education, Xenophon says, "Seeing them there [at the palace gates] you would have thought that they really lived with a view to what is noble."

61. *Cyropaedia* VIII 5.22–28; compare VI 1.4.

62. Ibid., I 3.18 and context.

63. Compare ibid., VIII 5.24.

assume his fateful command. He speaks of Cyrus' own situation, raising the question of what it means to undertake to rule other human beings:

> Have you forgotten, son, the conclusions reached in the reckoning you and I once made: that it is a sufficient and noble deed for a man if he is able to exercise such care that he himself attains a tested nobility and goodness and that he has, for himself and his household, the daily requisite provisions? But, this being a big [enough] task, to know how to lead other human beings so that they will have all the daily provisions in abundance and so that they will all be such as they should be, that appeared to us then to be an astonishing thing. Yes, by Zeus, father, I remember your saying this; and to me too it seemed a monstrously big task to rule nobly. And even now I am of the same opinion when I consider the matter by examining ruling itself. But whenever, looking at other human beings, I recognize what sort [are able to] continue in rule and what sort of competitors we will have, it seems to me to be very shameful to cower before beings of that sort and not be willing to enter the competition against them. . . . But mark you, son, there are some things where the competition is not with human beings but with the tasks themselves, over which it is not easy to establish a sure superiority.[64]

Cyrus, as opposed to his father, apparently did not regard becoming noble and good oneself, as distinct from ruling others, as a great task. His eagerness to rule others, too, implies his belief that he had already accomplished that much or, at least, already knew quite well what it means to be noble and good. His father, whose remarks throughout the conversation remind us of Socrates, was clearly not so sure. Therefore the father was on Cyrus' *own* behalf more hesitant than Cyrus himself about the advisability of Cyrus' assuming political (or military) responsibility. And it is open to us to wonder whether some later indications of Xenophon as to the inner poverty—against a background of unlimited external splendor and success—of the life of Cyrus as king are not meant to suggest the consequences of his ignoring his father's advice.[65] Surely Xenophon never

---

64. Ibid., I 6.7–9 and context.

65. Xenophon has little to say about the life of Cyrus once his conquests are completed: see VIII 6.19–7.2. One might compare here the sort of dinner parties that formed around

says of his Cyrus, as he said once of Socrates, "He seemed to me to be himself blessedly happy."[66]

We can now return once more to the question of Xenophon's view of Cyrus' corruption of the peers. We have already remarked, if only by way of a joke, that the fact that Cyrus was a corrupter gives him something in common with Socrates. We are now in a position to see that there was a germ of truth to that remark. For the implicit criticism that his father makes of Cyrus could have been made of virtually any one of the peers educated in old Persia. The peers were convinced that their education was sufficient to make them good;[67] and, in that conviction, they would turn their attention at the "proper" age from their own development to the conduct of public affairs, just as Cyrus was to do. In fact, they were even inferior to Cyrus insofar as he was somewhat more aware than they that what they regarded as virtue was insufficient. Viewed in this light, Cyrus' corruption of the peers, his calling their virtue into question, can be seen as a liberation. And, given the prohibition in old Persia of teaching in the Socratic manner,[68] it may have been the only sort of liberation possible there. Nevertheless, it was surely an incomplete, even an abortive liberation, as such a public effort was bound to be. It earns such sympathy as it receives only by being a dim reflection of the Socratic "corruption" of a few Athenian and foreign youths. That is, it serves to remind us of the question of what a Socratic education consists in.

Xenophon has led us to suspect that Cyrus himself lacked an education of this highest kind. But if, contrary to our earlier expectation, what is most important to know about Cyrus is not the education he received but the one he lacked, what did Xenophon mean to suggest by his title "Cyropaedia" (Education of Cyrus)? Or is it no more than a fit companion to "Cyroanabasis" (Ascent of Cyrus), which refers to the "ascent" or journey up-country that the younger Cyrus did not complete? "Cyropaedia" would thus refer to the education the elder Cyrus did not complete, or call attention to the point at which his education stopped.

Cyrus (VIII 4) with the sort that formed around Socrates (Xenophon's *Symposium* as a whole). One might also consider the prominence the *Cyropaedia* gives to eros and the "two souls" theme, that is, to the question of what constitutes the harmony or health of the soul: see V 1.2–18; VI 1.31–51, 3.34–37, 4.2–11; VII 1.15–18, 1.29–32, and 3.2–16; compare VIII 2.20–21 and 7.6.

66. *Memorabilia* I 6.14.

67. *Cyropaedia* I 2.15; compare 2.5

68. Ibid., I 6.31–33; compare *Memorabilia* IV 2.11–20.

Memorabilia

As has already been mentioned, there are a number of pointers in the *Cyropaedia* to Socrates, as well as to Xenophon's Socratic writings. The conversation between Cyrus and his father—which among other things includes mention of a teacher who taught justice in the Socratic manner—is one of these. Later on, mention is made of the killing by the Armenian king of his son's teacher, a "sophist" whom the father accused of corrupting the son, that is, of alienating his affection or admiration for his father.[69] We hear also of the dealings of Croesus with the Delphic oracle and Apollo, a god whose displeasure Croesus earned by doubting his veracity.[70] We are perhaps most clearly invited or instructed to compare Cyrus and Socrates by the parallel stories of Panthea and Theodote. When Cyrus was urged by the friend to whom he had entrusted her care to have a look at Panthea, an extremely beautiful captive queen, Cyrus refused out of fear that her beauty would make him so desirous of continuing to look at her that he would neglect what he had to do.[71] When Socrates, on the other hand, was informed of the presence in town of Theodote, a woman whose beauty, according to Socrates' informant, was too great for words to describe, Socrates replied, "Then we must go have a look, for it is not possible for those who [merely] hear to learn what is too great for words to describe."[72] There was no danger of Socrates' being kept from his daily activity by desire to continue to look at Theodote.

The most obvious difference between Cyrus and Socrates is that Socrates never sought or held high political office. At first glance, this difference might not appear to be a very significant one. The reason is that Socrates, as he admitted and even claimed, was a teacher of politics. (To mention only a few pieces of evidence: it was as a teacher of politics, according to the *Memorabilia*, that his two most notorious students, Critias and Alcibiades, sought Socrates out and consorted with him,[73] and that he presented himself to the individual whose education at his hands is given

---

69. *Cyropaedia* III 1.14 and 1.38–40; compare *Memorabilia* I 2.49–55.

70. *Cyropaedia* VII 2.15–29; compare *Apology of Socrates* 14–15 as well as Plato, *Apology of Socrates* 21b3–c2.

71. *Cyropaedia* V 1.2–8 ff.

72. *Memorabilia* III 11.1 ff.

73. Ibid., I 2.12–48.

the most attention in the book;[74] in addition, another considerable portion of the book is devoted to Socrates' conversations with actual or would-be political or military leaders.)[75] A critic or rival of Socrates, who wished to steal away his students, once asked him whether his presumed belief that he made others capable of engaging in politics was not discredited by his own abstaining from politics, an abstention hardly in accord with the claim to understanding or knowledge. In his response, Socrates refused to admit that he abstained from politics: "Would I engage in politics more by doing so myself or by taking care that as many as possible be capable of doing so?"[76] Perhaps then he merely pursued by other means the same sort of goal Cyrus pursued, that is, an equally public goal. But did Socrates share the assumption of his critic that anyone who understands politics would want to put that knowledge to use by engaging in politics? And did the education by which he may have made some others more capable of engaging in politics also lead them to wish (or allow them to continue to wish) to do so?

According to Xenophon, Socrates wanted his companions to come to accept what he approved of[77]—which would have been fully possible only in the case of his best students. One of the signs by which he thought he could recognize the youths with the best natures, the ones he most wished to consort with, was their desire to learn everything required for nobly directing a political community.[78] (It is only in the section of the *Memorabilia* devoted to Socrates' conversations with actual or would-be political or military leaders that Xenophon mentions Plato, whom he implicitly but clearly identifies in the context as the student Socrates was most interested in.)[79] Xenophon tells us also that Socrates approached different sorts of youths in different ways, that he adapted his approach to the sort of nature he was dealing with.[80] Presumably then his approach to those with the best natures took into account their noble ambition; and this by itself would have been reason enough for Socratic education

---

74. Ibid., IV 2.1–7.

75. Ibid., III 1–7.

76. Ibid., I 6.15, 6.1.

77. Ibid., I 2.8.

78. Ibid., IV 1.2.

79. Ibid., III 6.1.

80. Ibid., IV 1.3.

to introduce itself to them as an education to politics. The question of where they were led from the political starting point is still a pertinent one, therefore. What is the consequence of Socratic education—the education he acquired himself and that he supplied to some others or prepared them to acquire?

Xenophon presents the Socratic education most fully in the last book of the *Memorabilia*. It is true that he presents it as Socrates had adapted it for the sake of Euthydemus, a youth of an extremely unpromising nature.[81] But by allowing for this, while considering what even the best students have in common with Euthydemus, we may learn something from this presentation of Socrates' teaching, and perhaps especially from the presentation of its beginning. The best students have in common with Euthydemus in the first place a longing for that virtue "through which human beings become capable of engaging in politics . . . and able to rule," that is, for "the noblest virtue and the greatest art," which is called the "royal art." In the second place, since their ambition is a noble one, they share with him a conviction that one cannot become good in these things without being just.[82] Socrates would apparently begin his serious instruction by appealing to that ambition or longing and that conviction. It follows that a knowledge of justice is a prerequisite of fundamental importance to political understanding and political action. But does the youth being addressed possess this knowledge? It is unlikely that the better natures will share Euthydemus' easygoing assumption that it is a simple matter to know what justice is, or, therefore, have anything approaching his naïve confidence that he does know it. But will they be entirely free of the belief that they know what justice is? And will their opinions as to what justice is be any more able to withstand Socrates' criticism than Euthydemus' were?[83]

Once this point in a conversation with Socrates has been reached, it is clear to Socrates' better students that nothing could be more important than to investigate what justice is, and to do so with the help of the one who has already performed the invaluable service of revealing the always present, but hitherto unrecognized, need for such an investigation. All thought of engaging in political activity must be postponed until that task is accomplished. But will it be accomplished in any finite period of

---

81. He belongs to the most foolish of the classes described in IV 1.

82. *Memorabilia* IV 2.11; compare IV 1.2.

83. Consider ibid., IV 2.12–20.

time? It almost goes without saying that the account of justice given by Socrates in the context of the education of Euthydemus is not fully satisfactory.[84] But is any other Socratic account in Xenophon (or in Plato) fully satisfactory either? Xenophon's Socrates[85] as well as Plato's[86] was notorious for never ceasing, that is, never finishing his investigation of what justice is. The consequence is that the activity of investigation, which was to be merely preliminary to that of engaging in politics, replaces it instead. What pretended to be an education to politics, a means, becomes the end.

The account just sketched of what might have led Socrates or some of his students to turn from a political life to the philosophic life admittedly raises more questions than it answers. One might even find that it constitutes as much a case against philosophy as one for it. For if philosophic investigation is unable to supply an answer to the question of what justice is, why would anyone who feels in his bones the deep and even urgent need for an answer be willing to spend his life in that investigation? But perhaps the Socratic answer to the question is available but not openly expressed, and perhaps in that answer, and in the answers to the apparently related questions of self-knowledge and the good,[87] lies a fuller account of the reasons for the superiority—if such it be—of the philosophic life to the political life. For the sake of Euthydemus, who never objected to an inadequate or defective argument, Socrates saw fit to provide a suitably simplified version or approximation of his views;[88] we are not told by Xenophon what Socrates did at this stage in the case of the best natures. We do not know therefore whether it was not part of his treatment to awaken them to certain fundamental dilemmas which he refused to solve on their behalf, to pose certain questions which he left it to them to answer.[89] What we do know, the rock we have to fall back on in our perplexity, is only this: that an obstacle, which can be called the problem of justice, stands in the way of a reasonable or noble satisfaction with the political life, at least temporarily; and that in seeking

---

84. Ibid., IV 4; compare especially I 2.40–46.

85. *Symposium* 4.1; compare *Memorabilia* I 1.16; IV 4.5, 8.4.

86. See the *Clitophon* as a whole; also *Republic* 354b–c and 368b4–c3, 435c8–d5 (and context) and 611a10–612a6.

87. *Memorabilia* IV 2.21–36; compare the topics taken up in III 9.

88. Ibid., IV 2.40 ff; compare IV 6.13–15.

89. Compare ibid., III 11.14 (and context) and II 6.28.

to remove it, as we must, we almost inevitably come in contact with another life, which claims to be superior to the political life. As a result, our task becomes not only to find out what justice is but to find out what philosophy is and to look into its claim to constitute the best answer to the question of how to live.

The *Memorabilia* ("Recollections") as a whole is Xenophon's account of his exposure to that other way of life in the person of Socrates. The recollections were written and brought out under something of a cloud. Their hero had been put to death by his fellow Athenians after being convicted on the dual charge of impiety and corrupting the young. In order to begin to see how this fact might have affected Xenophon's manner of writing them, we must make an effort to free ourselves, at least for a moment, from the situation today, when almost no one regards Socrates as having been guilty of a capital crime. Socrates, it is now widely believed, was innocent of the things he was charged with, or, even if he was not entirely innocent, the things he was charged with are not and should not have been treated as crimes.

We must make this effort despite the fact that Xenophon himself, insofar as he was a defender of Socrates' innocence of the charges, is partly responsible for our situation. When Xenophon wrote, general opinion on the question of Socrates' innocence or guilt must still have been mixed. If most of the immediate addressees of his work, those most interested in Socrates, were likely to have been convinced of his innocence, they almost surely had friends or relatives who were not. Nor were the primary addressees necessarily in possession of arguments by which they could have satisfied the doubters—and thus defended the respectability of their own interest in Socrates. It was for Xenophon, therefore, to supply such arguments, not only for his own sake but also for others, actual or potential Socratics. It was necessary for his recollections, as for Plato's dialogues, to take the form of a defense of Socrates. Now there have always been some for whom Xenophon's evidence carries more weight than Plato's: according to Thomas Jefferson, for example, "Of Socrates we have nothing genuine but in the Memorabilia of Xenophon."[90] Xenophon must accordingly share with Plato the credit or responsibility for the great success such defenses have had, a success which has helped to form the current view.

------

90. Letter to William Short in *The Life and Selected Writings of Thomas Jefferson* (New York: Modern Library, 1944), 694.

Unless we make the effort referred to, we approach his work under the influence of that view, hence in a particular way. We take for granted its thesis of Socrates' innocence and thus take no special notice of the arrangement and use of arguments and examples by which Xenophon endeavors to support that thesis. We are blind to the artfulness underlying his apparently straightforward discussion because we are no longer aware, as even Socrates' partisans would have been in Xenophon's time, of the strength of the case against Socrates. As a result, we are not sufficiently attentive to the indications Xenophon gives of the sacrifices he had to make in combating that case, of the distortions he had to admit into his account of Socrates in order to make the view that is currently accepted as true prevail.

For example, in the lengthy second chapter of the work, where Xenophon takes up the corruption charge, he quotes a number of specific allegations made against Socrates by his accuser.[91] In each case, the attack is followed by Xenophon's defense of Socrates on the matter in question. Since the defense is clearly meant to dispose of the attack, the impression is given that the specific allegations were entirely unfounded. But, as Xenophon surely knew, his responses did not always meet the attacks head-on or vanquish them in their entirety.

According to the first of these allegations, Socrates made his companions look down upon the established laws and the established (democratic) regime by remarks such as his criticism of the lot as a method of choosing officeholders; and he made his companions violent. To the twofold attack, Xenophon responds that Socrates certainly did not make his companions violent. Even this assertion seems to be cast in doubt by the fact mentioned next by the accuser, that the notoriously violent Critias and Alcibiades had been among those associating with Socrates. Xenophon does not seek to defend the actions of Critias and Alcibiades; nor does he deny their association with Socrates. He simply says that Socrates, with some success, did what he could to make them moderate, while they were under his influence; and that if they turned out badly later on, Socrates is no more to be blamed for this than, say, a decent father whose child turns out badly after leaving home. This is all very well, but it fails to answer the crucial question of whether—given precisely his limited influence on their characters, whose future tendencies were not invisible—Socrates should have supplied Critias and Alcibiades with tools in the form of a political education.

---

91. *Memorabilia* I 2.9, 2.12, 2.49, 2.51–52, 2.56 and 2.58.

According to the third allegation of the accuser, Socrates taught disrespect for fathers both by persuading his companions that he would make them wiser than their fathers and by an argument to the effect that it was lawful for the more ignorant person to be placed in confinement by the wiser one. Xenophon's denial touches only the point regarding confinement. The fourth allegation therefore repeats the accusation as to Socrates' effect on respect for fathers and extends it to relatives in general and to friends. Here even Xenophon admits, in the course of his response, that Socrates said the things he is alleged to have said about fathers and other relatives as well as friends: some loss of respect for relatives and even friends, as such, seems to be the unavoidable consequence of heightened respect for those who know the needful things and are able to explain them. The final allegation of the accuser states that Socrates made a mischievous use of certain passages in the most highly reputed poets, interpreting, for example, a line from Hesiod to mean that one should abstain from no unjust or shameful deed but do even such things for the sake of gain. Xenophon's response speaks of Socrates' standard as the beneficial or the good; it says nothing about his views on the noble and just.[92]

Once we have become aware of the way in which the *Memorabilia* is written, we are forced to wonder how that manner of writing might have affected the picture of Socratic philosophizing as a whole which it presents. At first glance, Xenophon seems to deny that Socrates ever engaged in what we can call natural philosophy: "Nor did he converse, in the way most of the others did, about the nature of all things, investigating the state of what is called by the sophists the cosmos and by what necessities each of the heavenly things comes into being."[93] Rather, he "was always conversing about the human things, investigating what is pious, what impious, what is noble, what base, what is just, what unjust, what is moderation, what madness, what is courage, what cowardice, what is a state, what a statesman, what is rule of human beings, what a fit ruler of human beings, and about the other things as to which he considered those who knew them to be noble and good, and those ignorant of them to be justly called slavish."[94] But there are other indications, both in the *Memorabilia* itself and in other of the Socratic writings, that Socrates

---

92. Compare Plato, *Hipparchus*, as well as *Memorabilia* I 2.54.

93. *Memorabilia* I 1.11; for the use of the term "natural philosophy" compare "inquiry concerning nature," Plato, *Phaedo* 96a8.

94. *Memorabilia* I 1.16.

did engage in natural philosophy. On one occasion, Socrates refers to his reputation as a natural philosopher, without objecting to it.[95] He seems to have identified wisdom (which he called the greatest good) with the science of *all* the beings.[96] And he never ceased investigating what *each* of the beings is, perhaps in part through reading and studying the writings of the wise men of old.[97] There is nothing to suggest that the beings in question did not include the heavenly beings, or the writings the works of the so-called pre-Socratic philosophers. In fact, Xenophon indicates quite clearly that Socrates was familiar with the doctrines of those philosophers, mentioning Anaxagoras in particular by name.[98] Even the passages that formed our first impression prove on reexamination to be more qualified than they appeared to be at first. Socrates did not converse about the nature of all things "in the way most of the others did": he may have done so in a different way. He was always conversing about the human things "and about the other things" the knowledge of which he considered to be essential to nobility and goodness (gentlemanship): knowledge of things other than the human things is evidently essential to gentlemanship in the Socratic sense. These two passages occur in the first chapter of the *Memorabilia*, the chapter in which Xenophon takes up the impiety charge. Perhaps his defense of Socrates on that charge *required* a denial of some sort that Socrates engaged in natural philosophy.[99]

To see as clearly as possible why this might have been the case, we must consider what it meant to engage in natural philosophy—both for Socrates himself and for the pre-Socratics whose manner of engaging in it he departed from and criticized. Xenophon guides us toward this consideration by his account of Socrates' criticism of his predecessors.

Socrates criticized his predecessors' doctrines about the nature of all things for their implausibility: "some of them are of the opinion that being is one alone, others that beings are unlimited in multitude; some that everything is always in motion, others that nothing is ever moved; some that everything comes into being and perishes, others that nothing

---

95. *Oeconomicus* 11.3; compare *Symposium* 6.6–7.4.

96. *Memorabilia* IV 5.6, 6.7.

97. Ibid., IV 6.1; I 6.14.

98. Ibid., I 1.14; IV 7.5–7.

99. Consider ibid., IV 7.6 and *Symposium* 6.6–8 as well as Plato, *Laws* 966e4–967a8 and *Apology of Socrates* 18b6–c3.

ever comes into being or perishes."[100] Beyond that, he regarded the matters they attempted to elucidate as undiscoverable for human beings.[101] He cannot have meant by this that reason is unable to cast any light at all on the matters in question—the implausible doctrines themselves point to plausible ones (the means between the opposed extremes). He must rather have had in mind that to be in possession even of very plausible doctrines is not yet to have knowledge of those matters. Socrates' own philosophic activity would then have been distinguished from that of at least many of his predecessors by being guided by a greater awareness of its limits.

This is already implied in Xenophon's description of that activity as the attempt to discover what each of the beings is. The aspect of nature we have most access to is the "what," the perceptible character of each of the beings, rather than their unchanging causes (causes which neither come into being nor perish). The perceptible character of each being is always the character of a group or class of beings.[102] As such, it is most visible in speech. In fact, classification, the separating of things into classes or kinds,[103] underlies our speech, our capacity to speak. According to Socrates, "conversing" (*to dialegesthai*) was given its name from the practice of those who come together to deliberate in common by separating (*to dialegein*) matters according to their kinds.[104] We might be tempted to think that knowledge of unchanging classes or kinds or species could simply take the place of knowledge of the unchanging causes. But this would be to ignore the manifest dependence of classes of beings on the existence of those (individual) beings. Xenophon's Socrates never speaks of separately existing "ideas": the classes or kinds are not separate from their members; the characters are always characters of the things possessing them. It is true that the characters are causes of those things, setting limits to them. They share this responsibility, however, with something other than them, something for which they are not responsible and whose existence and nature are guaranteed neither by them nor by anything else we know of. (Socrates may point to this shared responsibility when he calls attention to the dissimilar behavior of things possessing the same perceptible

---

100. *Memorabilia* I 1.14; compare IV 7.6–7.

101. Ibid., I 1.13 and IV 7.6.

102. Ibid., IV 6.

103. Ibid., IV 5.11 and *Oeconomicus* 9.6 ff.

104. *Memorabilia* IV 5.12.

character.)[105] As a result, we cannot know, though we may suspect, that some classes are permanent.

The deepest implication of Socrates' criticism of his philosophic predecessors becomes clear only when we consider more precisely what it was the pre-Socratics were trying to do. They had attempted to discover not merely the state of the cosmos but "the necessities" by which each of the heavenly things comes into being or "the way the god contrives each of the heavenly things" understood as the way he *must* contrive them.[106] Needless to say, they understood the reign of necessity to extend to earthly matters as well. Human prudence and folly, as well as chance, derive from the fundamental necessity and are limited by it. Their most basic contention, the inspiration of the doctrines by which they sought to elaborate and vindicate that contention, was that not just anything can come into being or come to pass but only what accords with or is permitted by the nature of the fundamental cause or causes. But if the fundamental causes are undiscoverable, must one not regard this contention as merely plausible? Yet could Socrates, either as a philosopher or as a human being, leave it an open question whether "just anything" can come to pass?

To spell this out a bit, Socrates may have known of no evidence that would support such a position, that would challenge the philosophers' basic contention. On the contrary, that contention may have been supported by all of the evidence available to him. But while he might reasonably have placed considerable weight on this fact, he would still have had to take into account the assertions of those who do claim to be aware of contrary evidence. The use of divination, for example, implies the claim that a meaningful connection may exist between two events (a sneeze and the future salvation of an army, to take one example from among many in Xenophon's *Anabasis*) that does not stem from the events themselves, the deliberate action of human beings, or chance.[107] Or, to refer to divine punishment for certain misdeeds, as Xenophon does very emphatically in the midst of his *Hellenica*, is to suggest that those deeds had consequences not stemming naturally, so to speak, from the deeds themselves.[108] In particular, it is to deny the validity of the suggestion which seems to be

---

105. *Symposium* 7.4.

106. *Memorabilia* I 1.11 and IV 7.6.

107. *Anabasis* III 2.9; compare *Memorabilia* I 1.3–4; IV 7.10; I 1.6–9,1.19.

108. *Hellenica* V 4.1; compare *Anabasis* II 6.21–29.

conveyed by the beginning and the ending of the *Hellenica*: that human affairs are drawn out of their usual confusion only when, and so long as, they are directed by human prudence in the form of a competent leader at the helm.[109] Whatever his own view on this question, Xenophon was surely aware of the difficulty confronting his Socrates. To repeat, Socrates may have known of no evidence casting doubt on the basic contention or premise (as distinct from particular doctrines) of his philosophic predecessors. He would have been unable, therefore, to *accept* claims that such evidence exists, claims contradicting what he could see and feel. But neither could he *prove* such claims to be false.

How then did Socrates proceed in this situation? The foregoing may hope to have shown why it was necessary for Xenophon to address this question. Yet his answer to it remains elusive. It is perhaps the most deeply hidden part of his account in the Socratic writings of the philosophic life represented by Socrates.

Anabasis

We have already mentioned the fact that it was Socrates and not Cyrus whom Xenophon called supremely happy. His account of the Socratic life, in the *Memorabilia* and the other Socratic writings, is thus an account of the actualization of the highest human possibility known to him. Nevertheless, as we have also seen, Xenophon himself did not follow the example of Socrates, at least not in every respect. He left Socrates to join the expedition being organized by the younger Cyrus. And, as he makes clear and even stresses, he did this against Socrates' advice. But this departure from Socrates and the Socratic path does not necessarily signify a profound disagreement. It may signify no more than that Xenophon did not feel himself fully able to follow Socrates' example to the letter. Rather than attempt the impossible and thus be forced to settle for a spuriously exact and therefore somewhat ridiculous imitation,[110] he may have chosen to follow or imitate Socrates more freely, in a manner suited to his own inclinations and abilities. As becomes clear from a reading of his deeds and speeches in the *Anabasis*, Xenophon's inclinations were largely toward politics, and his political ability was of a very high order.

---

109. *Hellenica* I 1.1–15; VII 5.26–27.

110. Consider Xenophon's portrait of Antisthenes in the *Symposium*.

But would this not imply an acceptance on Xenophon's part of a way of life that—in the form in which it had been pursued by its representative par excellence, the elder Cyrus—he clearly rejected? It is tempting to seek to avoid this difficulty by suggesting that Xenophon came to his criticism of the elder Cyrus only after, and perhaps as a result of, his association with the younger one and his own experience of political life. But this suggestion is disposed of by the consideration that his decisive criticism of Cyrus (the one brought out in Cyrus' conversation with his father) was supplied to Xenophon in advance, not by his reflections on Cyrus or politics proper, but by the Socratic education he had already received prior to his entry into politics. We are forced to wonder, therefore, whether Xenophon did not understand and pursue the political life in a somewhat different manner than the elder Cyrus had, or whether there is not a middle course between Socrates and Cyrus which is an eminently fit one to travel. The *Anabasis* seems to have been given the task of demonstrating that this is the case. The foil it furnishes for understanding the differences between Xenophon and the elder Cyrus is the younger Cyrus.

Xenophon calls attention to the similarity, amounting almost to identity, of the two Cyruses by having his Socrates once playfully treat them as the same person.[111] According to both the *Anabasis* and the *Oeconomicus*, the younger Cyrus was the most able political figure to emerge in Persia since the elder Cyrus.[112] Nevertheless, there were several respects in which they were dissimilar. First, the younger Cyrus was an erotic man. At any rate, he had two mistresses, one of whom is said to have been both wise and beautiful, and he is said on a certain occasion to have had sexual relations with a visiting queen.[113] Nothing of this sort is ever mentioned with regard to the elder Cyrus, who was willing to forgo the sight of the beautiful Panthea, made an eminently sensible political marriage (perhaps to an elderly aunt), and was described by his closest Persian associate as a cold king.[114] There may be a connection between this difference and another. Whereas the elder Cyrus, once he reached maturity, never took risks that were not more or less required by his pursuit of empire, the younger Cyrus, catching sight of his brother the

---

111. *Oeconomicus* 4.16–18.

112. *Anabasis* I 9.1; *Oeconomicus* 4.18.

113. *Anabasis* I 10.2–3, 2.12.

114. *Cyropaedia* V 1.2–18; VIII 5.28, 4.22.

king in the midst of their decisive battle, let himself go and immediately attacked him although his own guard was then dispersed—an act which cost him at the same time his life and his all but achieved victory.[115] One might compare this particularly with the elder Cyrus' coolness and caution in connection with the capture of Babylon and the killing of his chief enemy, the king of Assyria.[116] It is true that unlike some of his principal allies the elder Cyrus had not personally suffered any injustice at the hands of the Assyrian, while the younger Cyrus had been grievously wronged by his brother.[117] But this observation does not so much remove the difference between the two that we are discussing as point to what may be its underlying cause. Just as he was more erotic than the elder Cyrus, the younger one may also have been more moved by considerations of justice. It took a wrong to make him act in accord with the ambition he undoubtedly shared with the elder (which is a different matter from finding a justification or pretext for acts one already intended to take for entirely different reasons).[118]

Since the younger Cyrus was known to Xenophon partly from the latter's personal experience,[119] one can say that he was the material out of which Xenophon created *his* Cyrus, the Cyrus of the *Cyropaedia*. The elder Cyrus is an idealized or perfected version of the younger one. In accord with this, the differences between the two first come to sight as defects in the younger, at least from a political point of view. Whether even from this point of view they are always defects can be finally determined only by considering the alternative represented by Xenophon.

Xenophon shared the traits that distinguished the younger Cyrus from his more illustrious predecessor. Like him (and also like his Socrates), he was an erotic man.[120] And he was, to judge at least from the attention his writings give to the problem of justice, no less concerned with justice. But he lacked the younger Cyrus' rashness or defects of judgment. In particular, he never let zeal to avenge a wrong overcome his prudence,

---

115. *Anabasis* I 8.21–29.

116. *Cyropaedia* VII 5.20–34.

117. *Anabasis* I 1.1–4; compare *Cyropaedia* IV 6.2 ff.; V 2.27 f., 4.35 f.

118. Compare *Cyropaedia* I 5.7–13, VII 5.72–73 and 5.76–77.

119. *Anabasis* III 1.8–9; I 9.1.

120. *Anabasis* VII 3.20; V 3.10; *Memorabilia* I 3.8–15; compare *Symposium* 8.2 as well as *Memorabilia* II 6.28.

even for a moment. To state this point in a manner more Thucydidean than Xenophontic, he knew that the existence of an injustice does not guarantee that the attempt to provide due retribution will meet with success; that our situation may be such as to require us simply to bear an unavenged wrong.[121] At the time of his leading the Greek force that had belonged to the younger Cyrus back to Greece, and indeed for the larger part of Xenophon's adult life, such wrongs were more likely than not to have been committed by Spartan hands. For Sparta's defeat of Athens in the twenty-seven-year Peloponnesian War had replaced the balance of power between the two great powers, which had prevailed in Greece for upwards of seventy-five years, with undisputed Spartan ascendancy.[122] And as Xenophon shows in both the *Anabasis* and the *Hellenica*—without departing from his customary restraint but with perfect clarity—the Spartan rule was in general distinguished by neither wisdom nor gentleness. As a political leader, Xenophon was forced to adapt himself to this situation and to induce those he led to do so. Among the most impressive passages in the *Anabasis* are the speeches in which he instructs his fellow Greeks on the necessity of compliance with certain Spartan demands that are far from just or reasonable and, in general, on the necessity of accommodating themselves to "those who now rule Greece."[123] Readers who are at all sensitive to how harsh political necessity can occasionally be may also find in Xenophon the writer, in his treatment of the Spartans, a model of how to proceed under like circumstances. He applauded and thus encouraged what was good, while pointing out without rancor or bitterness what was bad, to the extent that it was prudent and useful to do so. To return to what distinguished him from the elder and younger Cyruses, the high qualities which in the case of the two Persians (that is, barbarians) could be prevented from doing political harm only by being suppressed, or excised from the soul, could safely thrive in Xenophon,

---

121. Thucydides, *The Peloponnesian War* IV 62.4; compare *Anabasis* V 1.15 and II 6.21–29 in light of V 8.26; compare *Cyropaedia* V 4.35.

122. Sparta had supposedly fought the war to free the Greek cities from actual or impending "enslavement" by the Athenian empire. (See, for example, Thucydides, *The Peloponnesian War*, II 8.4.) Toward the beginning of his *Hellenica*, Xenophon tells us that after Athens's final defeat, her "long walls" were torn down to the music of flute girls and with the general expectation that that day would be the beginning of freedom for Greece (II 2.23). The rest of the *Hellenica* shows how mistaken that expectation was.

123. *Anabasis* VI 6.8–16 and VII 1.25–31; compare III 2.37 and VI 1.26–28.

who had had the benefit of a Socratic education, an education that those qualities among others fitted him to receive.

The result was not only his ability to match the elder Cyrus on the plane of cool political calculation, hindered neither by the eros he had nor by the misguided zeal he lacked, but also the grace and dignity his whole stance toward politics derived from an inner freedom not shared by Cyrus. Xenophon too was "ambitious": he was tempted by the prospect of becoming sole commander of Cyrus' Greek army, and he aspired to become founder of a new Greek city on the shores of the Black Sea.[124] But whereas Cyrus wanted his praises to be sung by all human beings, Xenophon was concerned primarily with honor from his friends.[125] Unlike Cyrus, he was not as eager for praise from incompetent judges as from competent ones. This difference helps us to understand his equanimity in the face of the most varied political fortunes: for example, the dignity and wit with which he defended himself when confronted with ingratitude and baseless hostility on the part of the very men whose lives he had saved.[126] It helps us also to understand his ability to leave political life to return to a private life. When there was some good to be done by his leadership both for himself and for others, or some pressing need, he acted with supreme determination and ingenuity to accomplish the task or meet the need. When no more could be done, at least by him—that is, when there was nothing useful to accomplish—he stepped aside. But then his education had not left him entirely unequipped for leading a private life. Country retirement, while lacking the immediate challenges to heart and mind presented by politics at their peak, would have appealed to him as allowing more leisure for contemplation and writing—especially since that contemplation might embrace, as we know from the *Anabasis* that it did, his own political experiences among other things. For a man like Xenophon, the contemplative reliving of experiences was sure to be a deepening of them. It could thus have been looked forward to as promising a more profound enjoyment than the original experiences themselves, and one less mixed with pain.

---

124. Ibid., VI 1.19–21; V 6.15–16 (compare VI 4.1–8).

125. *Cyropaedia* III 2.31; *Anabasis* VI 1.20.

126. *Anabasis* VII 6.11 ff.; compare V 7.5 ff. and 8.2 ff.

13

On Plato's Political Philosophy

Plato's political philosophy is accessible to us primarily through the three great works whose very titles point to their political themes: the *Republic*, the *Laws*, and the *Statesman*. The *Republic* and the *Laws*, which happen to be his longest works by far, are devoted chiefly to developing very thoroughgoing schemes of political reform; the *Statesman* is devoted to the search for the rare qualities or qualifications that would make a man worthy of that name. Plato's political philosophy first comes to sight then as both critical and reformist: it establishes immediately its distance from actual politics and looks to the true politics, which Plato's own educational efforts are presumably intended to help bring about. It can thus have an apparently contrary effect, however. Even as it raises its readers' political hopes, it may lower their willingness to participate in the only politics available to them; for the small good that might be done there seems smaller still when it is compared with the good they have been led to expect from the schemes of radical reform that they have become acquainted with in Plato.

We may take as a typical example of such readers Raphael Hythloday, the would-be Platonist to whom Thomas More ascribes his *Utopia*. Raphael refuses to give advice to kings and princes on the ground that—unless they were to become philosophers themselves—they would be unwilling to accept the full measure of Platonic reform, nothing short of which will suffice to remedy their countries' ills. Now, Raphael's refusal does not meet with the approval of More. More rebukes Raphael for adopting a "school philosophy . . . which thinketh all things meet for every place," and he offers him the following counsel: "there is another philosophy more civil, which knoweth . . . her own stage, and thereafter ordering and behaving herself in the play that she hath in hand, playeth her part accordingly with comeliness, uttering nothing out of due order and fashion. And this is the philosophy that you must use. . . . So the case standeth in a commonwealth, and so it is in the consultations of kings and princes. If evil opinions and naughty persuasions cannot be utterly and quite plucked out of their hearts, if you cannot, even as you would, remedy vices which use and custom hath confirmed: yet for this cause you must not leave and forsake the commonwealth . . . . For it is not possible for all things to be well, unless all men were good. Which," More concludes, "I think will not be yet these good many years."[1] Now there may well be some advantage to keeping zealots like Raphael out of politics, and it may therefore be doubted that More expected or desired to encourage Raphael or his like to take an active political role. But there can be little doubt that the graceful and witty More, not Raphael, was the genuine Platonist—nor that, by contrasting himself with the character he had created, More was attempting to put his own readers on the path to a more adequate appreciation of the master's intention. But precisely if, following More's lead, we hesitate to accept the opinion that Plato put forward his radical schemes either to discourage political men from attempting to accomplish the good within their reach or to have the schemes themselves taken as practical proposals (one should consult here More's criticisms of communism at the end of each book of the *Utopia*), then we are compelled to raise, as if from the beginning and with a combination of puzzlement and wonder, the elementary question of why he did put them forward.

We will attempt to begin to answer that question by looking at Plato's three great political works—first and most extensively at the *Republic*, which is more fundamental than the *Laws* and easier of access than the *Statesman*. The *Statesman*, as the third member of a trilogy, must be approached by way of the *Theaetetus* and the *Sophist*, two formidable works that apparently have little to do with politics; and the *Laws*'s elaboration of a "second-best" regime explicitly relaxes the more severe demands on political life made in the *Republic* (see *Laws* 739a–e)[2] and thus presupposes familiarity with the *Republic* as with a prior work.

---

1. Sir Thomas More, *Utopia* (New York: A. L. Burt Company, n.d.), pp. 208–09.

2. All citations to Plato are to the standard Greek edition of Burnet (Oxford University Press). Unless otherwise noted, the passages cited in the text are to be found in the dialogue under discussion where the citation is made.

But we must, in addition, not neglect entirely Plato's other dialogues, which (along with the *Republic*) are mostly devoted to memorializing the conversations or refutations of Socrates. As it was the task of conducting those refutations that kept Socrates himself from engaging in politics—to judge, at least, from his own statement in his *Apology* (23b7–9; cf. 31c4–e1)—we might be inclined to pay them little or no attention in an examination of Plato's political philosophy. But to yield to that inclination would be to overlook the fact that, quasi-public as at least some of the refutations were (21d1, 23c2, 33b9–c4) and devoted to moral improvement—especially the moral improvement of Socrates' fellow citizens—as all of them apparently were (29d5–30a4 and 31b1–5; cf. 20d6–21d7 and 33a6–7), they might well be described as political themselves, indeed as constituting the true political activity. Indeed, this is the way in which they are described by that same Socrates in the *Gorgias*, where he claims that he alone of his fellow Athenians engages in politics (521d6–8). There are then two versions of the true politics presented to us by Plato's political philosophy: the one elaborated in various ways in his schemes of political reform and the one actually practiced by Socrates. As for the relation between the two versions, it is not free from perplexity. To mention only the most massive point, the regimes of both the *Republic* and the *Laws* would place rather severe restrictions on the sort of refuting activity that Socrates carried out virtually unhindered in Athens—in particular, on the philosophers' access to the young.[3] Just as we were compelled to wonder, then, about Plato's intention in putting forward his schemes of political reform, we must wonder also about his intention in memorializing the Socratic refutations. In other words, why must his political philosophy articulate two versions of the true politics, and how do those versions complement one another so as to stand together as parts of one whole?

∾

The *Republic* presents itself as a consideration of justice. The first general question to be raised in the work is the question, "What is justice?" It is raised and pursued, by a man named Polemarchus, among others, not as

---

3. *Republic* 497d8–498d1 and 537c9–540b7; *Laws* 634d4–635a5, 952c5–d2 and context, and the regulations regarding the composition and conduct of the Nocturnal Council more generally: 951d4ff. and 961a1ff. One might consider in this light Socrates' eulogy of democracy, of *life* in a democracy in *Republic* 557c4ff., especially 557d1–2.

a merely theoretical question but as a question of vital import to all who wish their lives to be governed by justice and who are, or become, aware of the inadequacy of their understanding of justice and hence of what it demands of us (cf. 334b7–9 with 335e–336a and 336e). The pursuit of the question, "What is justice?" is interrupted at a certain point by a man named Thrasymachus, who has no desire to join in the search for justice and whose intervention could well be seen as an attempt to put an end to that search. His reasons are not the same as those which motivate similar attempts closer to home. Thrasymachus is not a so-called relativist, one of those who combine the belief that one cannot answer by reasoned argument the question of what justice is (since, as they insist, there is no true answer to it) with the fear that to allow even the search for such an answer, to leave open the bare possibility that, for all we know, there *might* be an answer to it, is to open the door to dogmatism and intolerance (which they take to be injustice pure and simple). Thrasymachus differs from our contemporary would-be relativists both in his awareness that he believes he knows what justice is and in a belief that sets him apart not only from them but also from Socrates' other interlocutors in the *Republic*. This is his belief (which he is willing also to state in plain terms) that justice is bad for the just person himself while being good for others, especially his rulers, who profit from his justice. Thrasymachus contends, in short, that a life of injustice is superior to a just life (347e2–4). Those who cannot accept his contention naturally look to Socrates for a defense of justice (cf. 367d8–e1, 358d2–3); and, in his eagerness to provide such a defense, Socrates abandons or defers the pursuit of his original question as to what justice is (cf. 345b9–c1 with 347e2); but this very deferral renders his first defense of justice (in the latter part of book 1) inadequate (354c1–3): how can the goodness or badness of something be established before one knows what the thing in question is? Since Socrates' first defense of justice is admittedly inadequate, the demand can reasonably be made that he undertake a second defense. And that demand is made, and made with considerable force and eloquence, by the two brothers Glaucon and Adeimantus (at the beginning of book 2). Glaucon and Adeimantus properly insist that this new defense begin from an adequate explanation of what justice is. More precisely, what they want to know is not so much what justice is (or the definition of justice) as what power it has when it is present in our souls, what power it has all by itself, whether or not its presence is noted by others (358b4–6, 367b3–5, d2–4, e3–5). Their request is a reflection of their belief (as to which they may be hardly conscious) that they are not entirely ignorant as to what justice is; they believe that they know of it at least this much: that it involves the willingness to subordinate one's own good to something else (to a higher cause, as we would say); and they want Socrates to convince or to reassure them that such subordination is compatible with, nay demanded by, one's own truest good. Their request is thus not entirely coherent; but, for that very reason, it gives testimony to their love of justice. And the strength of their love of justice makes significant, in turn, precisely their acknowledgment of the fundamental fact. That fact had been acknowledged, it is true, even prior to the intervention of Thrasymachus (331c1–d1, 332a11–b4, b9–c4, 335c1–5), but only implicitly; it is given its most exalted expression in the teaching (in which the most important part of the *Republic* culminates) of the supremacy of the Idea of the Good (504d2–6, 505a2–4, d5–e1, 508e1–509c4).

Socrates outlines the very radical scheme of political reform for which the *Republic* is justly famous by way of response to the brothers' request. That is, he responds to their request by constructing a city in speech together with them and by observing with them its coming-into-being. His procedure is apparently based on the following consideration: while there is justice of a man as well as justice of a city or country, the justice in the larger being—where there is presumably more of it—will be easier to discern; after they have discovered it there, they can look in the smaller being, in man, for its likeness (368e–369a). But, even if we grant that justice has the same form in an individual as it has in a community, the consideration referred to would not explain why they turn to constructing a city in speech. The reason is apparently based on the further consideration (though this is not made clear until the construction is well on its way to completion) that justice is to be found especially in a good city; and, as we can well suppose, none of the actually existing cities was sufficiently good for their purpose (434d6–e2, 420b5–c1; cf. 427d3–5 as well as 369a6–7, 371e12, 372e2–6). We must assume, then, that the city to be constructed in speech is intended by Socrates from the beginning to be a good one. This still does not explain, however, why we must observe its coming-into-being; nor does it suffice to explain the particular sequence of measures and stages by which it does come into being. For some of those stages are puzzling in themselves (I have in mind, for example, the first stage of the city's development, which is based on Socrates' suggestion that political life in general, and hence their city in particular, has its origin in our lack of economic self-sufficiency, in our economic need alone, a suggestion that ignores among other things the desire for procreation and the role of the family)[4]; and, in other cases, what appear to be measures designed to serve certain ends are puzzling insofar as they prove to serve more important ends than those they are suggested to serve when they are introduced or even to be such ends themselves (the most obvious examples are the education of the ruling class, as that is first described, and the institution of the philosopher-kings)[5]. As we will see, the latter difficulty, especially, can be traced in large part to the role that the two brothers play in the construction of the city, whose development is affected both by what they insist upon and by what they resist (372c2–e6, for example, as well as 473e6ff. and 487b1ff.). But this only raises the further question of why the brothers are allowed, and even encouraged, to play such a role.

The necessary assumption, then, that the city is intended by Socrates from the beginning to be a good one, is the expression of an enigma rather than itself a solution. At the minimum, it compels us to wonder what Socrates takes the goodness of a city to consist in: by what understanding of a city's goodness does he take his bearings in initiating the steps which he takes on his own and in turning to his use the steps which are forced upon him by others? To put this another way, from which point of view is the goodness of the city to be judged? The adequacy of the judgment will depend on the adequacy of the point of view from which it is made. Now, according to Plato and his Socrates, no point of view is more adequate or more worthy of respect than that of philosophy, of the philosophers. But the philosophers' standard is reason. What conceivable ends, then, of a political community are reasonable ones? And what would the political community have to be, if it is to pursue reasonable ends alone? In setting out, together with the brothers, to construct his city, Socrates is setting out after such a political community: as the best commentator on the *Republic* has said, "In the *Republic*, reason or intellect guides the foundation of the city from the beginning, and eventually rules the city in broad daylight without any dilution or disguise."[6] And, in observing the coming-into-being of that city in speech, we are meant to come to

---

4. Cf. 369b5–e1 with Aristotle, *Politics*, bk 1, chap. 2.

5. Cf. 376c7–8 (in light of 373d4–374a2 and 375b9–c5) with 399e5–7; cf. 473b4–e2, toward the beginning of a section which runs through 502c5–9, with 543a1–6 and d1f. as well as with 496c5–497d6, which stands 473b4–e2 on its head.

6. Leo Strauss, *The Argument and the Action of Plato's Laws* (Chicago: University of Chicago Press, 1975), p. 38.

understand its character, at the same time as we come to understand (and largely by virtue of our coming to understand) the obstacles which its coming-into-being must confront.

This suggestion as to the understanding of goodness which guides Socrates in his construction of the city in speech is admittedly an hypothesis, but it has the advantage of permitting a resolution of most, if not all, of the perplexities connected with that construction which we were compelled to note. The presence of the brothers, for example, as participants in the construction is required if the character of Socrates' city is determined as much by the obstacles it must confront and the means it must use to overcome them as by the ends it seeks to serve—as much by its efforts to remove the resistance to the rule of reason as by the rule of reason itself. The participation of the brothers is required, that is, if the resistance to the rule of reason is to be treated not just thematically but also through the action or drama of the dialogue, if it is to be brought to life before our eyes and ears in the form of the reactions of Glaucon and Adeimantus (and the others) to Socrates' proposals. For these two outstanding young men—for all their admirable qualities and for all their goodwill toward Socrates—are certainly not philosophers and probably not potential philosophers, either, not even Glaucon: the only interlocutor of Socrates in the *Republic* of whom Plato informs us that he turned later on to philosophy is Polemarchus.[7] Their participation is thus meant to impose upon Socrates constraints in the discussion of the good city that are similar, if not identical, to those that any attempt to implement such a project would encounter. In name, cofounders of the city with Socrates (for example, 378e7f., 458c6, 534d8–e1), the brothers are in fact stand-ins for its future citizens; and they are meant to be affected by the discussion of the measures to be applied to its citizens in ways similar—to the extent possible—to those in which the citizens would be affected by the measures themselves. The difficulty has to do with both ends and means: steps desirable in themselves but not seen as desirable by the brothers must be introduced as serving purposes that the brothers already accept; while the same is true for measures needed for overcoming their resistance to future steps: measures which must already be in place if those future steps are to win eventual acceptance cannot, for that very reason, be introduced as serving the purposes they are truly meant to serve. Thus, to return to the examples already mentioned, the education

---

7. *Phaedrus* 257b3–4; see also *Parmenides* 126a–c and *Symposium* 172c3–173a3.

of the ruling class, as that is first described, is introduced in the context of a consideration of how to make the soldiers of the city's newly-formed army gentle to one another and to their fellow citizens; and the education surely promotes that end (for example, 378c1–8 and context). The army itself had been formed when it became clear that the city's pursuit of the luxuries which Glaucon, in particular, had insisted upon would force it to attempt to seize land from its neighbors. The education in question thus appears to be introduced as a means to facilitate the city's aggression by (among other things) helping to prevent the army formed for that purpose from destroying its fellow citizens or itself by internecine warfare. Only after the discussion of the education has had on Glaucon an effect akin to that which the education itself is intended to have on the soldiers, can Socrates reveal to him that it has rather, "without their noticing this," purged the city of those very desires which had made expansion appear to be necessary. The purging which Glaucon is at that point ready to accept is the very one that he has to some extent already undergone (see the passages cited in the first part of note five). Similarly, the rule of philosopher-kings is introduced as merely the necessary means to the coming-into-being in deed of the good city and not as an integral part of the city, without which the city's goodness would be incomplete. (In imitation of this feature of the *Republic*, Socrates' discussion of the same regime in the *Timaeus* omits mention of the philosopher-kings from the summary proper, as distinct from his subsequent remarks.)[8] Only after the considerable opposition which its introduction meets with even then has been assuaged, can the rule of philosopher-kings be revealed to be also (or rather) part of the peak, not to say the peak itself (see the passages cited in the second part of note five).

As for the suggestion that political life in general, and hence their city in particular, has its origin in our lack of economic self-sufficiency, in our economic need alone, Socrates makes it because he regards that need as a true need and the contribution made to fulfilling it by cooperation among fellow citizens as a genuine, and perhaps even necessary (369e2–370c6), contribution. He goes so far as to call the city which limits itself to pursuit of so genuine a good the true (or truthful) city (372e6–7). But, as is shown by his ready acceptance of Glaucon's revolt against that city (the revolt which expresses itself in a demand for luxuries). Socrates does not really expect the political community to be able to restrict itself to the pursuit

---

8. Cf. *Timaeus* 17c1–19b1 with 19e5.

of this limited, if rational, end (372e2–4). Moreover, Glaucon's insistence on luxuries, along with the attempt to expand the city's territory which it entails, makes necessary and hence possible the introduction into the city of education, in the sense of formation of character (376c7ff.). Now, Socrates uses that education, as we have seen, to purge the city of the very desires which his acceptance of Glaucon's demand had allowed to grow strong in it; and, as he indicates, this is in a way to take the city "back" to its pre-corrupted state (cf. 399e5–6 with 372e7). But only in a way: the position to which the city returns is different from that which Glaucon forced it to leave. Its self-restraint, which was formerly the unconscious child of innocence, has been reestablished on the basis of a frank confrontation with desire and a taming of it. Innocence has been replaced by virtue.[9] We have reached, then, another stage in the good city's development—apparently a higher one. The city that offered us no more than to provide efficiently for our bodily well-being has been transformed into one that promotes virtue. And virtue is an end which, as the brothers believe or wish to believe (cf. 359b6–7 with 358c6 and 366c6–d1), is dearer to them not only than bodily well-being but even than life itself—deservedly so, as they hope that Socrates will confirm (see especially, in Glaucon's speech, 361b5–d3). The philosophers, who judge from what they know of themselves and observe of others, not least of such noble youths as Glaucon and Adeimantus, agree to this extent: the dissatisfaction with the limit that nature sets to our life and therefore also with the pursuit merely of the well-being of our mortal bodies, the dissatisfaction which the claim made on behalf of virtue and the hopes connected with that claim so nobly bespeak, is not only apparently inescapable for us, who call ourselves human, but also reasonable (but consider *Statesman* 272b1–d2). The only question is whether our situation leaves us any genuine recourse other than resignation and the life of serene freedom that such resignation opens to us. In the *Phaedo*, which is set on the day of his own death, Socrates equates philosophizing with the practice of nothing else but to die and be dead.[10] In the *Republic*, he limits himself to indicating that the "Isles of the Blessed," to which the other citizens of the good city are to believe their philosopher-rulers depart when they die, are believed by the philosophers themselves to be their ordinary dwelling-place while they are alive (cf. 540b5–c2 with 519c5–6). We should not be very surprised,

---

9. Cf. *Laws* 679b7–e5 in the light of 678b1–4.

10. *Phaedo* 64a4–6.

then, to find of this second stage in the good city's development that it, too, will have to be surpassed. It is, in fact, a transitional stage. The virtues which the city has now undertaken to promote link it with both the first stage and with the third or final one. On the one hand, as Socrates will explain later on, those virtues are somehow close to bodily virtues (518d9–e2): this is so not merely because of the sort of education by which they are inculcated, an education which relies on habit and exercise, but also (as we can add on the basis of our earlier consideration of that education—pages 337–38 above) because the virtues in question are necessary to the bodily well-being of the citizens. Indeed, they are hardly less necessary to that end than is the economic exchange that was introduced in the first stage. On the other hand, insofar as their rank appears to us to transcend that of means to such an end, those virtues point to a third stage (cf. 543d1f.), a stage in which the city is not only ruled by philosophers but also takes as its purpose, above all, the fostering of the capacity for philosophizing in the natures suitable for it (540b5–6 and the education scheme of book 7). Thus it is only there that we finally arrive, as it would seem, at the city good without qualification, a city ruled by reason and devoted to reasonable ends.

The good city was to be constructed, we recall, and we were to observe its coming-into-being ostensibly because it was thought that by discerning first the justice of the larger being, and then looking for its likeness in man, we might more easily discover what justice is. But the consideration of the good city continues through book 7, long after, that is, it has served its alleged purpose of leading us to the discovery of justice, which it does in book 4. Moreover, what we learn from it about justice is ambiguous: if we take our bearings by the good city itself, we are led to conclude that justice requires of us nothing so much as that we fulfill our own task (that for which we are most naturally suited) within the political community (433a1–b4); whereas, if we take our bearings by the likeness of this justice in the individual, we are led to conclude that justice requires of us nothing so much as that we tend to the health of our own souls (441d5–e3, 443b7–d3). Socrates does call our attention to the need to remove any apparent divergence between the justice that we find in the city and that which we find in the individual (by rubbing the divergent understandings together until the flame of the true justice bursts out [434d2–435a3])[11]; but no attempt is made in the dialogue, in

---

11. Cf. *Seventh Letter* 341c5–d2.

any obvious way, to carry out such a comparative examination. It remains unclear, therefore, how or whether the consideration of the good city leads us to an adequate understanding of what justice is.

The difficulty posed by the divergence between the two understandings of justice may serve to remind us of the somewhat similar difficulty buried within the request made of Socrates by the brothers that set the consideration of the good city in motion. Since that request was not entirely coherent, no response to it could reasonably have hoped to satisfy it in every respect. This fact may perhaps make us open to the suggestion that the consideration of the good city must be understood as part of an implicit response of Socrates to the brothers' request, a response which takes as its starting point the opinion that justice demands of us devotion to the common good, together with the opinion that the common good is, for most practical purposes, identical with the good of the city, of the political community. That is the meaning of justice according to the central of the three definitions offered in Book One (helping friends and harming enemies), as becomes clear when one considers the fact that the sort of help originally envisaged by the man who offered that definition, the appropriately names Polemarchus, is especially that provided to fellow citizens in war (332e2–5; cf. 334c1ff. and 335b2ff.).[12] And it is consistent with the understanding of justice by which the brothers are moved. This is confirmed not only by their passionate interest in political reform, to which Socrates is able to appeal in enlisting their participation in the construction of the city, an interest fueled in part by their concern for Athens in her decay (563d2–3 and context); it is confirmed also by the approval they give to Socrates' suggestion that the happiness of citizens or parts of the new city is to be subordinated to the happiness (the well-being or cohesion) of the whole (421c7 and 520a5), as well as by their willingness to judge philosophy by the standard of its usefulness to the political community (487d5 and context; but cf. 519d8–9).[13] If justice consists, for most practical purposes, in service to the political community, the question of the goodness of justice can almost be reduced to the question of the goodness of such service. For the reason already indicated (see page 336 above), that question can then be restated in this more precise form: in which case or cases do the philosophers regard service to the

---

12. Cf. *Clitophon* 410a7–b1.

13. My summary does not always take sufficient note of the very significant differences between the two brothers.

political community as something more than a necessity—that is, as a positive good? The case or cases in question are presumably to be sought among those in which the ends pursued by the political community are reasonable ones. Hence the search for a political community that would pursue reasonable ends and reasonable ends alone. But this suggestion as to the meaning or purpose of Socrates' construction of the good city would render his response to the brothers' request somewhat playful; and playfulness may well appear to be out of place in connection with a matter of such gravity.

It is impossible and impermissible to doubt that Socrates wished to respond to the brothers' request or that he did respond to it in some fashion; but it is equally impossible, as it seems to me, to make the consideration of the good city fit neatly into any conceivable plan of a response, to conclude that the meaning and purpose of considering it are exhausted by whatever contribution that consideration may make to such a plan. But if they are not exhausted by this, then we are compelled to wonder whether the construction of the good city and the observation of its coming-into-being in speech were not of interest to Plato and his Socrates in their own right. We thus return to the question from which we began as to the character of Plato's interest in the scheme of reform that is outlined in the *Republic*. What we believe to have seen in the meantime is something of the character of the reform itself and something of what is to be learned about that character from observing the good city as it comes into being in speech. For the aim of the reform is nothing less than a truly rational politics. And such a politics, for Plato as well as for his Socrates, would require nothing less than the rule of fully rational human beings—that is, philosophers, who rule moreover not in the manner that More recommended to Raphael but rather *as philosophers*, responsible to no other authority than themselves. To observe the coming-into-being in speech of the good city is, therefore, to become aware of the obstacles to philosophic rule. Those obstacles would in all probability, to say the least, prevent philosophic rule from ever coming into being also in deed; and, as we noted earlier (page 337 above) they place their stamp even on the city in speech in the form of the measures which are required for over-coming them. As we also noted earlier (pages 337–38 above), regarding measures which are required for overcoming obstacles to proposals that would be unacceptable if the measures in question were not already in place, those measures cannot be introduced as serving the purposes they are truly meant to serve. What we are now in a position to add is that the most important measures introduced in the course of the *Republic*, whatever they may be said to be introduced for, must be understood to be required rather for the purpose of overcoming obstacles of one sort or another to philosophic rule. More precisely, they must be understood to be required for overcoming the obstacles which prevent non-philosophers, or the most politically significant class of non-philosophers, from accepting philosophic rule, with all that such rule entails. But the most important measure introduced in the *Republic*, a measure which has a greater effect than anything apart from philosophic rule itself on the character of the city or which goes further in transforming political life as it has always been known (as the reaction to it of Socrates' interlocutors confirms), is the notorious communism of women and children, together with the sexual equality which paves the way for it (see the transition at 458c6–e2). There is a link, then, according to Plato, between the implementation of such a communism as would deprive a man of any spouse or children of his own and the capacity of the best kind of non-philosophers to accept philosophic rule and all that it entails.

In order to understand the nature of that link, we would probably have to study Plato's erotic works, the *Symposium* and the *Phaedrus*, in addition to his political ones; but we can confirm that Plato does indeed point to its existence by glancing at the *Timaeus* and *Critias*, which form together a sort of appendix to the *Republic*, and at the *Laws*. The *Timaeus* and *Critias* take place on the day after Socrates has provided (to a group including Timaeus, Critias and Hermocrates) a discussion of a political regime which, from the summary he gives of the discussion at the beginning of the *Timaeus*, sounds very much like the regime outlined in the *Republic*. Socrates' summary is a prelude to his repetition of a request that he has made of his listeners of the day before: that they show him his city in motion, that is, at war, by ascribing to it such actions and speeches as would be appropriate to it in those circumstances (17b5–c1 and 19b3–20b7). His companions propose to fulfill Socrates' request by describing a war once fought by an ancient Athenian regime of which Critias has heard through some family tradition and which bears a number of resemblances to Socrates' city. Critias himself will undertake that description, but his speech will be preceded by a speech of Timaeus on another subject. As a result of these explanations and arrangements, there are three distinct accounts (in the *Timaeus-Critias*) of the regime whose conduct in war is to be described. Socrates' sketch of his city at the beginning of the *Timaeus* is followed by Critias' first account of the old Athenian regime; then, after Timaeus' speech, Critias gives a second account, in the early part of the *Critias*, of the same Athenian regime. Now, as we noted earlier in another connection, Socrates' summary does not refer to philosophic rulers, but he refers to such rulers just a bit later, in the course of the repetition of his request (19e5–6; cf. 18a5); the summary proper refers to both sexual equality and communism regarding marriages and children (18c1–4; 18c6–d5). In Critias' first account of the old Athenian regime, on the other hand, a regime whose resemblance to Socrates' city is sufficiently great, as he claims, to allow him to use it in fulfilling Socrates' request, both sexual equality and communism regarding marriages and children are conspicuous by their absence (24a2–d6); and, in accord with this, the philosophic rulers, too, are gone (but cf. 24c7–d3): the military class (from which the philosophic rulers were drawn in the *Republic*) is to limit its concern to matters connected with war (24b1–3), and there is added, alongside or above it, a class of priests (24a4–5). Moreover, the interconnectedness of these changes is underlined by the fact that, in his second account of the old Athenian regime, Critias has a change of heart (apparently brought on in some way by the intervening speech of Timaeus). In the second account, sexual equality (110b5–c2) and communism regarding "everything" (110c5–d2) are back for the military class, which is also said to practice "everything" which the comparable class in Socrates' city had the day before been said by him to practice (110d3–4); finally, the military class is now said to live by itself on the acropolis, with accommodations appropriate to its domestic and political communism (112b3–c7): there is no longer any mention of a class of priests. Similarly in the *Laws*, where the regime it sets forth differs most obviously from that of the *Republic* in the absence of philosophic rulers—the so-called Nocturnal Council introduced in the latter stages of the work is but a dim reflection of them—the only passage which explicitly compares the two regimes traces the inferiority of the one being set forth in the *Laws* to the absence of communism, especially communism of women and children (739a1–740a2). To conclude, then, our discussion of the *Republic*, we suggest that the consideration of the good city is meant to reveal how political life would have to be transformed in order to admit of philosophic rule and why it is unreasonable to expect, perhaps even to desire, such a transformation.

We turn now to a brief discussion of the *Laws* and the *Statesman*. If the regime outlined in the *Republic* is meant to show how the political community would have to be transformed in order to admit of a truly rational politics, the regime elaborated in the *Laws* may be said to be meant to show how far a reform moving the same direction can proceed in a political community which does not undergo the transformation effected or called for in the *Republic*.[14] As we have already seen, there is no communism in the regime of the *Laws*—in particular, no communism of women and children—and hence no philosophic rule. The *Laws* is thus a more practical work than the *Republic*, and this difference is reflected in the difference in conversational settings. An old philosopher—not Socrates but another Athenian[15]—converses not with inexperienced youths (not to mention a foreign rhetorician) but with two old citizens of highly regarded law-abiding regimes, experienced political men, one of whom has been entrusted with a grave political responsibility, for the carrying out of which he seeks guidance from the conversation. But the more practical character of the *Laws* does not mean that the work is devoid of theoretical interest or intent. To the contrary, for what is difficult to see from an examination of the good city of the *Republic* alone and can be better seen by contrasting the city of the *Republic* with precisely that city which is elaborated in the *Laws*, is what the absence of communism and philosophic rule *means* for the political community. We must limit our consideration to the most important point. If the *Republic* culminates (in books 5 through 7) in a discussion of philosophy and of the so-called Ideas or Forms (which are supposed to supply the Platonic answer to the question of the highest causes), the *Laws* may be said to culminate (in book 10) in a demonstration of the existence of a providential god or gods: the more important of the Athenian's interlocutors regards such a demonstration—in particular, a demonstration of the existence of punishing gods—as the noblest and best introduction to their law code as a whole (887b5–c2). We may grant that the connection between the god or gods whose existence is demonstrated in the *Laws* and the Olympian gods worshipped by ordinary Greeks remains dark (cf. 898c1–899c1 with 904a9–b1 and e4).[16] Still, the theological teaching of the *Laws* is far closer to the ordinary understanding than is the theological teaching of

---

14. Cf. Aristotle *Politics* 1265a2–6.

15. But cf. Aristotle *Politics*, bk 2, chap. 5, as well as Strauss, *Plato's Laws*, pp. 1–2.

16. Cf. *Timaeus* 40d6–41a5 with 39e3–40d5.

book 2 of the *Republic*, whose gods do not harm anyone and are, in their exemption from all change, prefigurations of the Forms or Ideas introduced later on (379a5–b10 and 380a5–c3; 380d1–381c10 and 381d1–4).[17] Now, the theology of book 2 may be diluted in other passages (427b1–c5, for example, as well as 540b7–c2); but it is not altogether misleading to say that the regime of the *Republic* stands or falls by the success or failure of the attempt to form a citizen body that can accept it.[18] In the regime of the *Laws*—and this is its significance for us—the attempt to introduce such a "theology" is not even made. That is, even in the regime that is meant to come as close as is practicable (739e3–4) to that of the *Republic*, it is impossible, in Plato's view, to go so far.

In order to make them receptive to the reform he intends to propose, the Athenian of the *Laws* must induce the two old citizens with whom he speaks to admit that the law codes of their own countries (Crete and Sparta) are flawed and thus capable of being improved upon. The chief barrier to such an admission is their claim or contention that the codes are of divine origin (cf. 624a1–b4 with 628c9–e5 and 630d2–3) and hence perfect. In this situation, the Athenian proceeds by granting their premise and even insisting upon its implication (630d4–631a8); he only requests in return—and this is a request which the defenders of the codes prove to be unable to refuse him—that they consider what the perfection, which divinely inspired laws of course possess, must consist in (631a8–632d1). He then suggests that the law codes of Crete and Sparta be examined to see how they pursue the goods which a perfect code has been agreed to procure (632d1–633a3). Not surprisingly, their pursuit of those goods manifestly falls short of the standard which their defenders have accepted (634b7–c9). By proceeding in this way, the Athenian succeeds in making it clear to the old men themselves (or clearer than it had been) that the claims of divine origin had been made to protect their codes from unwise criticism, especially on the part of the young (634d4–635a2). This development of the early part of the *Laws* links the *Laws* with the *Statesman*. The counterpart in the *Statesman* to the critique of the two particular divine codes carried out in the *Laws* is a critique of law, of the rule of law, as such. That critique, too, is the work not of Socrates (who merely

---

17. Cf. *Sophist* 248e6–249b1 regarding the theological—or anti-theological—implications of the Ideas.

18. For an indication as to where the chief obstacle lies, compare *Republic* 603d9–604a9 with 387d1–e10.

listens to it) but of another philosopher. Rule of law or according to law is compared in it with rule of a man who possesses the kingly art together with prudence (294a7–8). Such a man would be able to take into account what no law can, however wisely it was framed: the countless differences that distinguish from one another the cases as to which a disposition has to be made, in particular, the differences among the human beings involved and their activities (294a10–c9; cf. 296e1–297a5 and 301c6–d6). Rule of law is compared also, implicitly, via a mythical account of the Age of Cronos presented earlier in the dialogue, with direct divine rule over human beings (271e4–272a1 and context). Now, as the philosopher points out, laws, which in their generality disregard the differences referred to, are nevertheless necessary (294c10–d1). No one would be capable of sitting beside each human being throughout his life in order to prescribe what is fitting for him (294d3–295b2). Or, if someone were capable of this (the philosopher must be thinking here of the rule belonging to the Age of Cronos), he would never put obstacles in the way of the exercise of his discretion by laying down laws which are supposed to be incapable of being improved upon (295b2–6; cf. 295b7–296a3 and 300c9–d3 with 297d4–e14 and 299b2–d1). The critique in the *Statesman* thus seems to go further than that in the *Laws* by calling into question the very possibility of divine law; but, while it exceeds the critique of the *Laws* in its reach, it may fall short of that critique in its grasp. Its persuasiveness is limited by the fact that the philosopher who carries it out appears to rest his argument on a premise not necessarily shared or granted by the adherents of the view opposed to his own.

We have already called attention to the fact that the *Statesman* is the third member of a trilogy consisting also of the *Theaetetus* and the *Sophist*. In the *Theaetetus*, Socrates has a conversation with several mathematicians which attempts to answer the question, "What is knowledge?" Much of that conversation, however, is taken up by a consideration of a position of Protagoras that would seem to deny the very possibility of knowledge (151e8–183c4). The attempt of the interlocutors to answer the question to which the *Theaetetus* is ostensibly devoted ends in failure (210a9–d1); and the same can be said of their attempt to vindicate the possibility of knowledge in the face of the Protagorean challenge (183b7–c1).[19] When

---

19. On this passage, and what is at stake more generally in the Protagorean challenge, see David Bolotin, "The *Theaetetus* and the Possibility of False Opinion," *Interpretation, A Journal of Political Philosophy* 15 (1987): 179–93.

the group reassembles, as they had agreed to do, the next day, the mathematicians bring along with them a philosopher from Elea, a member of the Parmenidean circle there. Socrates asks this man whether, according to the Parmenideans, the three names "sophist," "statesman," and "philosopher," are properly applied all to the same individual or to two or three individuals. The philosopher's elaboration of his initial or provisional answer (*Sophist* 217b1–3) constitutes the bulk of the *Sophist* and the *Statesman*. According to our Platonic commentator, "It could seem that the question regarding the identity or nonidentity of the sophist, the statesman, and the philosopher takes the place of the question, or is a more articulate version of the question, What is knowledge?"[20] Since the question "What is knowledge?" is shown in the *Theaetetus* to include or imply the question "Is knowledge possible?" we take this suggestion to mean that in order to answer the question of the possibility of knowledge, we must ask whether sophist, statesman, and philosopher are the same or not the same. Surely a part of the question which Socrates asks of the philosopher from Elea, and not its least important part, is the question whether a genuine philosopher is necessarily also a statesman, in the sense that he necessarily knows also what the statesman as statesman knows. And in raising and addressing this latter question, the *Sophist* and *Statesman* approach political matters from a direction opposite to that from which they were approached in the works we have already discussed. There, a philosopher addressed men who took the importance of politics for granted, and he tried to lead the conversation to, or at any rate towards, philosophy.[21] In the *Sophist* and *Statesman*, a philosopher converses with mathematicians, who take the importance of theory for granted, and he explores with them the question whether—precisely on theoretical grounds—a philosopher must turn his attention to politics. The philosopher's answer to that question must be gathered from the elaboration of his initial response to Socrates, rather than from the initial response itself; and the high point of that elaboration, as far as the *Statesman* is concerned, is the critique of law which we have already considered. Could the philosopher who carries out that critique have thought it necessary to his theoretical enterprise that he be able to do so? We recall, in this connection, that he is an Eleatic, that is, a follower (of sorts) of the philosopher whose thought seems to have ushered in or borne witness to

---

20. Leo Strauss, "Plato," in *History of Political Philosophy*, ed. Leo Strauss and Joseph Cropsey, 3rd ed. (Chicago: University of Chicago Press, 1987), p. 68.

21. Regarding the *Laws*, see especially 963a10–965c8.

the first great crisis of philosophic self-doubt or self-criticism. Moreover he himself, in the *Sophist*, gives an account of the difficulties attending all pre-Socratic philosophic positions (242b6–250e7).[22] It was in response to such difficulties that Socrates had turned from the direct examination of the beings to the speeches about them, as he tells us in the *Phaedo* (95e7–100a7), and eventually to his refutations of his fellow Athenians and others. The philosopher of the *Sophist* and *Statesman* does not seem to have gone this far: to what we have already observed (pages 346–47 above), we can add that the mathematician who introduces him to Socrates remarks that he is of too measured a manner to take verbal disputes (eristics) seriously, and that he himself (in the *Sophist*) is highly critical of eristics (224e6–226a5, 232a1–235a7, 267e4–268d5; cf. 229e1–231b8). On the other hand, or for this very reason, he is able to call attention (in the *Statesman*) to a most important political-rhetorical task which only a philosopher can accomplish but which, as one can see from the *Clitophon* as a whole, a philosopher engaging in Socratic refutations might find it especially difficult even to take up (306a1–310b1). The task is that of reconciling the naturally moderate human beings (for example, the young addressee of the *Theaetetus* and the *Sophist*)[23] and the naturally manly ones (for example, the young addressee of the *Statesman*)[24] and thus benefiting both the political community and philosophy by producing harmony among their (potential) adherents. And it is accomplished by teaching the right opinions about the noble, just, and good things and their opposites (309c5–6, d10–e1, e5–6). Plato's political philosophy, which shows us—in the *Republic* and the *Laws*—what is at stake in the quarrel between philosophy and politics and—in its memorials to the Socratic refutations—presents the activity by which Socrates tried to vindicate the philosophers' side of the quarrel, seems also to have taken up and accomplished the political-rhetorical task that his spokesman in the *Sophist* and *Statesman* calls to our attention.

It is difficult for us to appreciate today the magnitude of Plato's rhetorical accomplishment. This is due, at least in part, to the fact that we in

---

22. The "Theory of Ideas" in the form in which it was presented by the young Socrates to Parmenides himself for criticism is properly included among the pre-Socratic positions (*Parmenides* 128e5–135d6).

23. *Sophist* 265c1–e2.

24. *Statesman* 261e8–262b7, 263c3–e1: in order to appreciate properly the Stranger's vehemence, one must ask oneself whether the hypothetical case he has in mind is truly that of thinking cranes.

the modern West live under forms of government which owe their origin to philosophy, to modern political philosophy, and which appear to have accomplished the goal of the philosophic politics that Plato experimented with in the *Republic*, especially, and in the *Laws*, without asking of us the sacrifices which he felt compelled to demand. At the same time, however, we apparently become, day-by-day, ever more indifferent to the problem that both united and divided the two pre-modern camps (it united them in mutual acknowledgment of its supreme importance and divided them by virtue of the diametrically opposed character of their responses to it). As a result, we become ever more blind even to the meaning of the political victory that modern political philosophy achieved. This indifference would probably be understood by modern political philosophy itself as a confirmation of its view that the natural concerns of human beings do not look beyond such goods as human beings can themselves procure (prevention of *violent* death, for example, or "recognition"). As we have seen (page 339 above), this view of the natural human concerns is not Plato's view. From his perspective, the indifference referred to is merely apparent indifference and its root is not nature but rather the modern teaching about nature. If he is correct, the political achievement of modern political philosophy, so far from being without cost, may have come at the price of our estrangement from our fundamental concern through loss of self-awareness. To test whether this is the case is perhaps the most urgent reason for studying Plato's works.

14

Aristotle on Theory and Practice

Modernity all but begins with a forceful attack on Aristotle. In the words of Hobbes, "scarce anything can be more absurdly said in natural philosophy, than that which now is called *Aristotle's Metaphysics*; nor more repugnant to government, than much of that he hath said in his *Politics*; nor more ignorantly, than a great part of his *Ethics*" (*Leviathan* Ch. 46, 439 [Blackwell edition]). It is not altogether surprising therefore that recent years have seen the rise of something called "neo-Aristotelianism," in other words, a revival of interest in Aristotle, especially in what he has to say about moral and political matters. For the heirs of the rationalism inaugurated by Hobbes and his fellow moderns no longer believe that reason can supply the guidance that we need in politics and life; and so, if reason remains (in the words of Locke's *First Treatise* §58) our "only Star and compass," as the founders of modernity assumed, it makes sense to wonder whether the older rationalism which they rejected might not have possessed resources that they overlooked, while remaining perhaps invulnerable to the sort of critique from within that has sapped the strength and, in the end, silenced the voice of the movement that they themselves launched. And the older rationalism, in its Aristotelian form, does indeed seem to possess such resources.

Aristotle's "philosophy of human matters" ascends in his *Nicomachean Ethics* to an account of prudence, which it presents as one of two intellectual virtues (i.e., as the perfection of a part of the rational part of the soul) and one of five dispositions, each of which, in a different way and with regard to different matters, guides a soul possessing it infallibly to truth (1138b35–1139a17, 1139b12–13, 1140b25–26, 1143b14–17, 1144a1–6,

1139b14–18). The matters that are the particular province of prudence are the things that are good or beneficial for human beings—not in a partial sense, as for instance for health or strength, but with a view to living well altogether (1140a25–31, b4–10). Since human beings are by nature political animals, and still more coupling or domestic ones, there are both domestic and political forms of prudence, the political form being divided further into a legislative or architectonic form and the political form proper, which itself consists of a deliberative and a judicial part (1097b8–11, 1162a17–19, 1169b18–19, 1142a9–10, 1141b22–33). And the *Politics*, which follows upon the *Ethics* and completes the "philosophy of human matters," appears to be largely directed to the legislative prudence, or even to be an expression of it (1180a32–34 and context, 1180b28–29, 1181b12–15; *Politics* 1289a11–13 and context; cf. 1258b9–11 as well as 1279b11–15). Finally, since a prudent human being is one who deliberates, and deliberates well, about the matters with which prudence is concerned, and deliberation is a sort of search—for means to an end already grasped—Aristotle makes a further stipulation to prevent a possible misunderstanding: to deliberate well in the unqualified sense is to locate the means, not to just any end, but to what is, for us human beings, unqualifiedly the end, an end of which prudence is (or has) a true grasp (1142b28–33 and context).

Prudence, then, "right reason" itself regarding moral-political matters according to Aristotle (1144b27–28), appears to be the answer to the need that we experience as we do in the wake of the collapse of modern rationalism. As Franco Volpi has observed, the knowledge that it provides "is rehabilitated by the neo-Aristotelians in the general context of an attempt to respond to the crisis of the modern notion of reason, deprived of any substantiality and incapable of indicating in a compelling manner ultimate ends for human action."[1] Volpi himself, indeed, has some doubts as to whether prudence alone can accomplish the task thus assigned to it;[2] and

1. Franco Volpi, "The Rehabilitation of Practical Philosophy and Neo-Aristotelianism," in *Action and Contemplation*, ed. Robert C. Bartlett and Susan D. Collins (Albany, NY: State University of New York Press, 1999), 18. The article of Volpi was translated from the French version, which appeared in *Aristote politique: études sur la Politique d'Aristote*, ed. Pierre Aubenque (Paris: Presses Universitaires de France, 1993). The volume in which the translation appeared took as its first task, according to its editors, to confront "directly . . . the most fundamental and controversial question of concern to students of Aristotle today, namely the possibility of grounding moral and political action in some version of Aristotelian rationalism" (xi).

2. *Action and Contemplation*, 18.

caution, if not doubt, does appear to be warranted to this extent: we would like to *know* that the end or ends to which prudence will direct us, and direct us in the right way, are the best ends, that the knowledge of their goodness, which it presumably supplies as well, is *genuine* knowledge. We turn back to Aristotle, then, eager to see how he will show this to us and prepared to consider with an open mind the case that he will make on behalf of prudence. Here, however, we are in for a surprise: he has made no such case!

The reason is ready to hand. Prudence is an intellectual virtue, but one that is inseparably linked to moral virtue (1178a16–17): it performs its function together with moral virtue (1144a6–7, b30–32); and it does not accrue to the soul without moral virtue (1144a29–31). For this and perhaps also other reasons, Aristotle addresses his moral-political works to readers who have been brought up properly, that is, to those who have acquired the habits of virtue (1095b4–6, 1098b3–4). But readers such as this already have a firm, if insufficiently precise, grasp of the "ultimate ends for human action" that they will bring with them to the books. And as Aristotle himself puts it, if the "what" or the character of noble and just things is acceptably clear, there will be no need of the "why" ("on account of what") or the cause (1095b4–7, 1098a33–b4). Such readers will want, not an explanation of what makes noble or just and good things noble or just, not a validation of their grasp of them as such, but rather knowledge, sufficiently precise to be a reliable guide to action, of what justice or nobility may require in a particular set of circumstances. And this is the knowledge Aristotle suggests to them that prudence supplies: a knowledge that endows one's grasp of the "ultimate ends for human action" with a precision that is commensurate to the demands of action (1106b36–1107a2, 1143b14–21, 1144a6–9, b4–14, 30–32). Nor does he leave matters at merely suggesting this: he attempts to show them how prudence goes about its task (1138b18–34ff.). If one wishes, one can say that this is the case for prudence that Aristotle makes; but its persuasiveness rests upon a prior acceptance of the very principles that we wished him to show us that prudence can establish.

But could Aristotle himself have left it at this? In adapting himself, as we have seen that he does, to the outlook that his readers bring with them to his books, he endorses that outlook in deed, just as he also does frequently in speech—most simply by calling the dispositions of character that it praises "virtues" and those that it censures "vices" (1103a3–10; cf. 1106b24–27, retaining "psegetai" with the manuscripts at b26). To this extent

Aristotle, too, accepts the principles we are concerned with. But at the same time, he corrects or amends his readers' outlook by excluding from the list of virtues qualities that his readers would probably have included (1108a30–b6, 1128b10–33; cf. Plato *Charmides* 160e2–8, *Laws* 730d2–7) and by adding others that they omit, as is indicated by the fact that the dispositions in question lack names (1107b29–30, 1108a5–6, 16–19). Now, such additions and subtractions are evidence of an exercise of judgment on Aristotle's part that must have governed not only his rejection of those opinions of his readers that he did not accept, but also his endorsement of those opinions of theirs that he approved of. And an exercise of judgment on the part of a man such as Aristotle presupposes reasons that ground the judgment. Would he not have left traces of those reasons in his books, if only for the sake of a certain subclass of his readers that he alludes to from time to time (1113a22–25, 1095b10; consider in this light 1095a30–b8 and compare Plato *Seventh Letter* 341e2–3)? But where are such traces to be found?

Our difficulty is connected with the fact that Aristotle does not offer to make a case that most of his readers do not demand of him on behalf of the moral-political life, the life to which prudence belongs and which in a way it governs. For what is essentially the same reason, he does in the last stages of the *Nicomachean Ethics* make a case for a life that in his view stands still higher than the moral-political or practical life: the life devoted to theory or contemplation (1177a12–1179a32; cf. 1095b17–19 as well as 1096a4–5). Here then, we have the expression not merely of a judgment of Aristotle's but also of the reasons on which it is based. Could not these reasons supply a clue to the reasons that ground his moral-political judgments? Might they not even constitute, themselves, a not insignificant part of his reasoning on those matters? A positive answer to the latter question would admittedly amount to the paradoxical suggestion that the foundation for Aristotle's practical or prudential science is to be found, in whole or in part, in the case that he has made for the theoretical life. Nevertheless, I will try to show in the balance of my talk that a positive answer to the question would be justified. The difficulty of doing so would appear to be increased by the fact that the explicit case for the theoretical life that Aristotle spells out toward the end of the *Ethics* is incomplete. It must therefore be supplemented, as we will see, by an implicit argument, developed gradually in the course of both the *Ethics* and the *Politics*; and the implicit argument of these works deepens the critique of the practical life that was already a fundamental part of the explicit case for theory. To suggest as much—is this not to add paradox to paradox? For it is, first, to seek to ground a favorable judgment on practice, to ground moral-political judgments altogether, in a *critique* of practice and, second, to claim to find that critique in works that are manifestly devoted to the portrayal of the practical life in its highest possibilities. But perhaps this claim, at least, is not quite so strange as it may look to be: to portray something in its highest possibilities is inevitably to delineate at the same time its limits or limitations.

The explicit case for theory is spelled out by Aristotle in the next to last part of the last book of the *Nicomachean Ethics*, where he returns to the theme to which he had devoted its first book, happiness. The discussion of happiness in the first book had postponed to an unspecified sequel a consideration of the claim of the theoretical life in that regard (1096a4–5). Connected with this postponement is the fact that while the earlier discussion had indeed called attention to the link between happiness and some activity—the point from which the later discussion can be said to begin—it had failed to identify the activity in question (1097b22–1098a20, 1177a12–19, 1176a32–b2). Given the intrinsic priority of activity to virtue, that is, the priority of knowledge of the preeminently human activity or function (1097b24–25) to knowledge of the virtue that equips one to perform that function well or to engage in that activity properly (1098a12–15, 1139a15–17), this meant that the earlier discussion had failed also to identify the preeminently human virtue. It had thus made possible a procedure that is suggested toward the end of the first book and that sets the tone for the greater part of the work, according to which an understanding of virtue is allowed to affect or even determine our understanding of happiness and of the activity or activities that constitute it (1102a5–7); for that procedure entailed Aristotle's acceptance of the portrait of virtue drawn by respectable opinion, only "retouched" more or less lightly by him. However that may be, the difference between the two discussions of happiness—that with which the work begins and that with which it all but ends—can be put in this way: the second attempts to fill the lacuna or lacunae that had been left by the first (cf., e.g., 1177a12–17ff. with 1098a16–18ff.).

Yet Aristotle could hardly have undertaken at the end of the *Ethics* to revise as radically as he does the conclusion regarding happiness that the greater part of the work conveys—less by express statements, it is true, than by pointing to it (as at 1117b9–11, for example)—if he had not remained faithful to the spirit that prevails throughout. What enabled him to do so, or the link that he found between the old spirit and the new conclusion, is suggested by a remark he makes in the *Politics* about a certain dispute:

> It is disputed by those themselves who agree that the life with virtue is most choiceworthy, whether it is the political and practical life that is to be chosen or rather the one set loose from all external matters, as some theoretical [life is] which some [people] assert to be the only philosophic one. For it is these two lives, just about, that the human beings, both formerly and now, most ambitious as to virtue manifestly choose: I am speaking of the political [life] and the philosophic [life] as two. (1324a25–32)

The explicit case that Aristotle makes at the end of the *Ethics* undertakes to settle the dispute in favor of that theoretical life. In order to do so, he must appeal to standards that are recognized at least in principle by both sides. And among the arguments on behalf of theory that he offers there, the most important in the context are those therefore which purport to establish that it is superior to the moral-political life even as regards virtue and nobility. As to virtue, he accordingly suggests at the outset that the virtue that theoretical activity requires is the highest virtue, since it is the virtue of the best or highest part of us, namely, intellect. And by way of forestalling a possible objection, he adds later on, if with some hesitation, that we are (each of us) not the composite being that we might seem to be, but just this highest and best part (1177a12–21, 1177b31–1178a7; cf. 1177b26–31 as well as 1178a9–22). As to nobility, he reveals now that the political and military actions, which surpass all other virtuous actions in nobility and greatness, are not chosen on their own account but for their consequences. He had insisted throughout, and reiterated in the very chapter that introduces the second discussion of happiness, that noble or serious actions are choiceworthy on their own account. Theoretical activity, which *is* chosen on its own account and is, therefore, truly leisured, thus comes to sight as the only virtuous activity to which this habitual and just-reiterated description of noble action strictly applies (1177b6–18, 1176b8–9, 1177b1–6, 19–22).

Now arguments such as these cannot be said to have settled the matter. To begin with, Aristotle had declared earlier in the *Ethics*, in a memorable passage, that man as originator (or origin [*archē*]) of choice is not intellect alone but "appetitive intellect" or "reasoning appetite" (1139b4–5). And if the earlier suggestion is the sounder one, the question would have to be raised of whether or how the virtue of the "highest part of us" can still be *the* virtue of the whole being that each of us is. As for nobility, if being chosen on its own account were sufficient to render an activity noble, then the pleasures of play, too, would be noble—something that Aristotle had made clear, in the chapter introducing the second discussion of happiness, that they are not (1176b9–11 and context; cf. 1176b33–1177a1). The claim of theoretical activity to nobility must rest then on other grounds: for example, on the nobility of the objects of its contemplation (1177a15; cf. 1141a18–20, b2–3). Within the human realm, to judge from other remarks made earlier in the *Ethics*, the highest object is the human good, in the form of the happiness of a city or nation; but it is here a question of procuring and preserving that happiness, rather than merely reflecting on it (1094b6–10; cf. 1129b17–19, 25–29). The superiority as to nobility of the theory in question at the end of the *Ethics* could not have been so confidently maintained therefore, if the eligibility of the whole human realm as an object of contemplation had not in the meantime been discounted (1141a20–b2, 1143b18–20). Still, those earlier remarks will have made it difficult to accept that the nobility of virtuous political or military actions is diminished by the fact that they have such an extrinsic end as, for example, the happiness of their author together with that of his fellow citizens (1177b12–15). And, besides, such actions could well appear to be more in accord with our composite nature than contemplation alone would be.

The explicit case for theory with which the *Ethics* all but concludes, with its perplexing critique of practice, will hardly then have done more at first than to prompt a return to the manifestly positive account of practice that the body of the *Ethics*, together with the *Politics* as a whole, presents. Motivating the return is likely to be the search for material with which to correct the concluding critique. But any such return runs the risk of discovering also evidence that may sustain it.

From among the many passages whose reconsideration might yield such evidence, I will take up briefly two that have some bearing on the points already raised, as well as a significant, if somewhat concealed, relation to one another: the treatment of the just ordering of the political community in Book III of the *Politics* and the attempt in Book VI of the *Nicomachean Ethics* to explain how prudence goes about its task. Let me preface my consideration of the two passages by repeating that *the* objective of the practical life or of practice—insofar as the description of that objective is not exhausted by saying that it is noble or virtuous action itself—may be said to be the happiness of the political community of which one is a part. That is to say, the virtue to which practice is devoted, or whose exercise practice consists in, finds for its efforts no higher recipient than the political community. Yet for that community to be an appropriate recipient, for its happiness to be an appropriate objective of moral endeavor, it and its happiness must themselves be conceived of in moral terms. And this means, among other things, that the good served must be the good of the community as a whole, not just a part of it. Now, in ordinary circumstances, this requires that the community itself be properly organized, that it have a just regime. Thus practice at its peak, or the virtuous action in which it consists, has of itself a tendency toward the service of the political community, and in particular toward serving it through preserving in it, or founding, a just regime. And Aristotle expects readers to approach his *Politics* with a keen interest in this matter. Among many indications that he gives of this expectation, the most telling perhaps is this: he announces without any "fanfare" an examination of the question of the best regime (as, e.g., at the beginning of Book II, where he also devotes extensive discussions to Plato's *Republic* and *Laws*, as if they were intended to present practical proposals for political reform), whereas he prefaces his examination of regimes that fall short of the highest standards (in Books IV through VI) with a lengthy explanation of the necessity for such an examination.

However that may be, the most searching treatment of what one may call the *problem* of the just regime is to be found in the central chapters of Book III. It is hardly possible in a brief review to convey any sense of the suppleness and delicacy of this discussion, the main substantive points of which are as follows. Aristotle's question is of the political arrangements that would satisfy the requirements of justice. He approaches it *via* the dispute on that score between the oligarchs and the democrats, which he proposes to arbitrate. The presence of these two groups, the rich and the poor—the irreducible components of any political community (1291b2–8)—is thus presupposed from the outset: even their oaths can be heard (1281a16, b18). Oligarchy and democracy had been identified in the immediately preceding section of the text as unjust regimes, insofar as they look not to the common benefit but to that of the rulers themselves (1279a17–31, b4–10). Aristotle now acknowledges that the partisans of these regimes lay claim, on each side, to their own notion of justice (1280a7–9ff.). Moreover, the notions in question prove to be partial (and therefore distorted) versions of the principle that properly governs in these matters, which he had explained in the *Ethics* (to which he refers in this context [1280a17–18, referring to 1131a25–29 and the discussion to which that passage belongs]). The principle discernible in the appeals of the two sides, and to that extent acknowledged by them, holds that equal people deserve equal things and unequal people, unequal things. It is their acknowledgment of this principle that offers hope of a resolution of their dispute. They disagree only as to what constitutes the relevant equality or inequality or as to how that equality or inequality is to be measured. And that disagreement Aristotle proposes to remove by calling attention to what both sides omit to mention (1280a25ff.). If the true end of the political community is neither wealth nor even freedom or security but rather, as Aristotle himself contends, noble action, then those who contribute most to a community of that sort deserve to have a greater share in the city than either the oligarchs or the democrats (1280b39–1281a8).

Aristotle's arbitration of the dispute between the two chief parts of the city thus points to aristocracy as the only just regime (1279a34–37, 1278a18–20). Yet he refrains from drawing this conclusion; instead he brings the first portion of the discussion to a close by remarking that it has made clear that "all those disputing about the regimes say only a part of what is just" (1281a8–10). The immediate sequel confirms—what the remark itself leaves somewhat in the dark—that it was his intention to include among the "all" any possible disputants on behalf of aristocracy (1281a11–14, 28–34; see also 1283a26–40, b13–23; cf. 1301a39–b1). He thus forces us to ask what reason he had for including them. And, as it seems to me, we will not understand his verdict on the question of the just regime before we have uncovered that reason.

Is it that a truly aristocratic arrangement would deprive the many poor of a voice in the affairs of the city that cannot safely be denied them (1281b28–30)—a hard political fact that is not without moral significance, since "virtue does not destroy what possesses it, nor is what is just destructive of a city" (1281a19–20)? Or is it that, since offices are considered to be among the goods that are at the disposal of the political community, to deprive the many of all share in them, that is, of all share in such honors, would be an injustice comparable to depriving them of their possessions? (cf. 1281a28–32 with 24–28) Of course monarchy, by this argument, even in the form of the rule of the one best, would be still more unjust (1281a32–34). But if it is to be a valid argument, must there not be a positive ground on which the many can base the justice of their claim to a share of rule? Surely when, in the wake of his inclusion of aristocracy among the flawed regimes, Aristotle elaborates a strikingly democratic arrangement, explicitly as an alternative to aristocracy (1281a39–42ff.), he himself attempts to provide such a basis. This is where he speaks of the collective superiority of the many to the few in virtue (1281a42–b21). And when, dissatisfied with the democratic arrangement, too—less perhaps for its practical flaws, which prove to be rather amenable to practical correctives (1281b31–34, 1282b1–6), than for the flaw that he is compelled to note in the basis he had found for the justice of the many's claim (1281b24–25, 34–38)—he reopens the fundamental question (1282b14–23ff.), he is still or again on the lookout for that elusive basis. Whether or not the many are superior in their collective virtue to the few, it cannot be denied that they make a necessary contribution to the political community or to its work (1283a1, 10–19). But can a just claim to a share in the direction of that work be entirely divorced from pretention to capacity to direct it (1282b30–1283a3), and is the pretention warranted in this case (1291b5–6)?

The situation that Aristotle has adumbrated in this way can be summed up as follows: the many present a claim that cannot safely be denied because its ultimate ground is the strength that lies in numbers (1283b23–25), although this fact is somewhat concealed by their pretention to something higher (1291b5–6). But cannot and must not the same be said of the aristocrats? Is it not in this way, rather than along the line we have been pursuing until now, that the flaw on the level of principle of aristocratic justice is to be understood? Aristotle indicates as much immediately after reformulating the question of the regime in such a way as to make clear that it is on the level of principle that he is now considering it (1283a42–b9). He first calls attention, as a question, to the bearing on their claim of the aristocrats' numbers (1283b9–13). Then he raises, first as a general problem, which "perhaps" pertains also to aristocracy, the case of an individual who is outstanding precisely in that quality to which the higher claim of the partisans of each regime appeals (1283b13–23; in b23–27 strength, too, is perhaps treated as such a higher claim, as in the "right of the stronger"; cf. Plato *Laws* 690a–c). The injustice that mars a regime—even or precisely aristocracy—in relation to such an individual can be avoided in only two ways. Aristotle takes them up in turn, after restating the problem with exclusive reference to the situation in aristocracy (1284a3–17; see also 1283b35–1284a3). The first of these ways, ostracism or the forced removal from the city of the individual in question (1284a17ff.), is obviously incompatible with the understanding of justice on which aristocracy understands itself to rest (1284b25–30). This leaves, as the only alternative compatible with that understanding, that such individuals become permanent kings of their cities (1284b30–34).

With this conclusion, Aristotle's treatment of the problem of the just regime comes to an end—unless, that is, one considers the examination of kingship, which follows immediately in the text, to be a part of that treatment. But perhaps it is necessary to consider the examination of kingship in this light (1284b35–36). Aristotle raises there the question whether kingship is beneficial to the cities (1284b35–40); and the kingship he is most interested in has a remarkable resemblance to the permanent kingship of which he has just spoken (1285b33–1286a7, 1287a1–3). When his dissatisfaction with the democratic alternative to aristocracy had induced him to reopen the fundamental question, he had indicated that justice in political matters has two components: that each be given his due and that the common benefit be secured. The expectation of decent people is that the common benefit is secured by giving to each his due (1282b14–21). The examination of kingship, especially when it is read in the light of the discussion that immediately precedes it (1284b35–36), explores the question whether this is true in the highest or most demanding case. Aristotle's answer is disclosed in its concluding portion to those who pay sufficient attention to his use and nonuse of the term "beneficial" (*sumpheron*) (1287b35–1288a32).

If the happiness of the political community of which one is a part is *the* objective of the practical life or of practice, a virtuous human being is bound to be moved by what is uncovered in a thoroughgoing reflection on the essential nature of such a community. And this, despite the fact that the happiness of one's political community is not *de jure* the end of the virtuous life. For as Aristotle shows in his account of prudence in the sixth book of the *Ethics*, it is impossible to give a noncircular explanation of how prudence goes about its task, if one limits oneself to that *de jure* end: virtuous action itself (1144a6–1145a2). And this means—since prudence does go about its task, which it accomplishes moreover with remarkable precision (1106b14–16)—that other ends are present to it *de facto*, and present in a certain ordering.

Book VI opens with a clearly articulated statement of the nature of that task, together with a frank acknowledgment of the insufficiency of what has been said hitherto for explaining how it is carried out (1138b18–34;

cf. 1103b31–34). The expectation is thus raised that an explanation of the required sort will now be forthcoming. Yet, if we leave aside, as we should, a number of more or less unthematic remarks that prepare the second discussion of happiness (1145a6–9, 1144a3–6), we will search Book VI in vain for such an explanation. The reason, as it seems to me, is that Aristotle refuses there to go beyond the explanation that might be given by the prudent themselves. And they are apparently reluctant to acknowledge, even to themselves, the extent to which their actions are directed by concern for (among other things) the happiness of the political community to which they belong (1141b29–30 and context). This is why Aristotle's disclosure of this to them, in the course of his second discussion of happiness, is a revelation (1177b12–18). Book VI as a whole may thus be said to point to the question of the cause of this reluctance on the part of the morally virtuous. It is not likely to be divination of the disappointment to which we have alluded, which they may fear that they will expose themselves to by acknowledging the extent of their deference in deed to the concern in question, since the reluctance to do so does not appear to be limited to those who give indication of anticipating that disappointment. Let us leave this question unanswered then, as Aristotle himself has done. By pointing to it as a question, he has made us aware that the practical life is a life marked by a specific recalcitrance to self-knowledge. Is it as evident, then, as we have assumed it to be, that that life is more in accord with our composite nature than the life that is free from such recalcitrance?

Of course, even if this and similar questions, to which a second look at the *Ethics* and *Politics* might lead, should induce us to consider with greater sympathy than before the case that Aristotle makes at the end of the *Ethics* on behalf of the theoretical life (including those aspects of the case that we have not discussed), this would not yet establish the thesis that I have promised to defend. Let me say, then, a few words in conclusion as to how that case helps to provide the foundation for a practical or prudential science. And here I will just mention several points that would merit further consideration.

The first and most fundamental is this: a reasoning that establishes the superiority of one way of life to another is, by the very fact of doing so, practical. It leads to a valid conclusion concerning the question that comprises all other practical questions: how should one live? Its demonstration of the limitations of prudence will have done nothing therefore to cast doubt on the possibility of a practical science—to the contrary!

Second, the critique of prudence which that reasoning was compelled to carry out, the critique of the self-understanding of the prudent human beings, began from the recognition of the precision with which they accomplish their task—that is, from a very good reason for leaving them to that task. And in its completed form, the critique is an antidote to any temptation to add to the task requirements that would exceed the limits of prudence as it has itself uncovered them.

Third, as the same critique has made clear, the precision with which the prudent are able to accomplish their task presupposes an adequate grasp on their part of a broad range of human ends, in their proper ordering. Here, however, their view can be enlarged, and by just such an appreciation of theory as, prepared in part by modifications introduced by Aristotle into the catalogue of the virtues, is conveyed by the presentation of theory at the end of the *Ethics*. The role that such an enlargement of view might play in taming the savagery of political life is indicated by Aristotle in the last two books of the *Politics*.

Fourth and finally, the rhetoric of the passage at the end of the *Ethics* has as its aim to present the theoretical life as a sort of parallel to the practical life, but on a still higher level. The critique of practice to which we were led by that passage shows practice, on the contrary, to be the matrix of theory. Still, this fact confers on the practical life an authentic dignity to which Aristotle's *Ethics* and *Politics* bear noble witness.

Part V

Death and Happiness

15

Death in the Perspective of Philosophy

I.

If my surmise is correct, the aim of this collection, to which I have been asked to contribute an essay, is analogous to that of the collection on which it is modeled. *Über die Liebe* directed attention to and invited reflection on something that we are in danger of losing sight of today and thus losing altogether, something without which we cannot live well. *Der Tod im Leben* calls our attention to what we cannot indeed lose—since it visits even where it is least expected or sought after—but what we can lose sight of and perhaps, today more than ever, have lost sight of. As this implies, men have always, to some degree, already lost sight of death; life, as it is ordinarily lived, is constituted by this loss of awareness,[1] and perhaps necessarily so. How then can we even ask, as the theme of the series would seem to bid us to do, whether the loss of awareness of death—either in its usual or in its (extreme) contemporary form—is conducive to our living well or an obstacle to it, a sign of health or of disease, something to be accepted gratefully or combated with all of the grim determination we can muster? To ask this question would require that we have before us, equally laid open for our inspection, both the awareness (of death) and its absence, or it would require at least that the former be readily accessible to us. But, as we have surmised at any rate, it is the very doubt, a reasonable doubt, that this is the case that has inspired this series and thus given occasion to my talk. We can, of course, pronounce the words

---

1. Consider Xenophon, *Apology of Socrates*, 27.

indicative of such awareness: so could Shakespeare's Glendower "call spirits from the vasty deep." But, as Hotspur replies, "Why, so can I, or so can any man; But will they come when you do call for them?"[2] At the least, it must be said that the spirit we would have to seek is likely to respond only to those who know how to call it; and we, for better or worse, lack such knowledge.

It is in these straits that we seek guidance from a class of men who made it their business, so to speak, to confront and reflect on the matter: from the philosophers of our Western tradition, or from some of them. What stance toward death do they recommend to us? We seek them out "in these straits," because of the predicament in which we find ourselves, even though this very predicament is likely to limit the use we are able to make of their advice. For that advice, if sound, will draw upon an experience which they have had and we have not had. Nor can we come significantly closer to their experience merely by reflecting on words that take their bearings by it. We would have, rather, to begin where philosophy itself necessarily begins, with the question which is truly primary and which concerns not our ultimate fate but our present duty: what must we do to comply with the demands of justice or (to begin even more from the beginning) in what, precisely, do those demands consist?[3] Nonetheless, I believe it can do no harm—if we neglect for now the truly primary question—to consider the question that has been put to us by turning to the remarks that I propose to take up. And, to begin with, that in the *Phaedo*, where Plato's Socrates shows also by deed that he knew how to die. Socrates makes there the memorable pronouncement that, though this escapes the others, those who correctly lay hold of philosophy (that is, the best way of life) practice nothing other, themselves, than to die and be dead.[4] We find, incidentally, an echo of his words in those which the philosophic poet puts into the mouth of his wise hero at or about the close of the *Tempest*: Prospero there resolves to "retire me to my Milan, where Every third thought shall be my grave."[5] However that may be, we hear counsel of a very different tenor from no less a figure than Spinoza (among others): "A free man" (by which he means "one who lives according

---

2. *Henry IV Part I*, Act III, 1.53–55.

3. Consider Plato, *Republic*, Book I.

4. 64a4–6.

5. Act V, 1.310–11.

to the dictate of reason alone") "thinks of nothing less than of death, and his wisdom is a meditation on life, not on death."[6] Our authorities, then, apparently disagree. But perhaps we can learn something even from their disagreement. And, in the expectation that this will prove to be the case, I will take that disagreement itself as the more particular theme of my essay.

II.

Socrates' words in the *Phaedo* were uttered on the last day of his life, in the prison in which he had been confined since his trial. They are spoken to the followers or companions who regularly gathered there to spend with him his last days. His execution had been delayed owing to an Athenian law which prohibited public killing during the voyage of a certain vessel. This was the vessel conveying the delegation that the Athenians had promised Apollo to send each year to Delos in return for the safe return from Crete of Theseus and the "twice seven" youths whom Theseus saved together with himself. Among the younger people present with Socrates on his last day, those who are named by Plato are also fourteen. During at least part of the additional time which the god's festival had given him, and in light of his trial and conviction, Socrates had turned, in obedience to a dream, from the practice of the "greatest music" (that is, philosophy) to what he calls himself "the vulgar music." As the vulgar music is distinguished from the other by its use of myths, and Socrates is not skilled in myths, he makes use of those (Aesop's) which were ready to hand and he already knew.—It is striking, after this prelude, that Plato gives us in the body of the *Phaedo* no example of Socrates' practice of the vulgar music, but rather what the young eponymous narrator calls a philosophic discussion.[7]

The words of Socrates that particularly concern us belong to a part of the discussion that he himself calls an "apology"[8] that he addresses to his young friends, as we may call them. The pain which these youths are

---

6. *Ethics*, Part IV, proposition 67 (edited and translated by Edwin Curley, Princeton, 1985).

7. 59a3–5; compare 61e2 and 70b6, as well as 91a1–3 and David Bolotin, "The Life of Philosophy and the Immortality of the Soul: An Introduction to Plato's *Phaedo*," *Ancient Philosophy*, 7, pp. 39–56.

8. 63b1–5, e8–9, 69d7–e4.

experiencing in the presence of his impending death has not been entirely vanquished, though it has no doubt been lessened, by the fearless and noble demeanor that he has displayed throughout his ordeal.[9] This is due in part to the fact that they fail to understand the ground of his conduct.[10] As a result, they cannot be altogether confident that the fear he apparently lacks is truly unwarranted; and they are, for the same reason, puzzled (if not also somewhat hurt) by the ease with which he bears his impending separation from them.[11] As to the latter point, Socrates limits himself to saying that he expects, in death, to join human beings among the dead who are better than those here.[12] But in response to their fear, he tries to persuade the youths that someone who has spent his life in the practice of philosophy—as he has done and they, too, aspire to do—has plausible grounds for approaching death with confidence.[13] It is to the attempt to persuade them of this that his "apology" here is chiefly devoted.[14] The words with which we are concerned articulate its thesis or theme; and it, in turn, serves to explicate them.

According to that explication, death is nothing but the release or separation of the soul from the body[15] and—this being the case—philosophizing consists either in approximating death (in one manner or another) or in preparing for it. For example, a man who is a philosopher and who, as such, has turned his attention to the soul, deprecates the so-called pleasures of the body.[16] And, for the acquisition of wisdom, he places his reliance not on the cooperation of body and soul which yields the evidence of the senses, but rather on reasoning that the soul carries out, so far as this is possible, on its own.[17] Moreover, there are beings which are not accessible to the eyes or any other bodily organ of sense,[18] but only to the mind: beings such as "justice itself" as well as nobility and

---

9. 58e–59a.

10. 61b8–c5, 62a, 64a4–b1.

11. 63a7–b1.

12. 63b5–c2 as well as 67a6–8 and 69d7–e3; compare 60a.

13. 63e8–64a3.

14. 63b4–5, 69e3–4.

15. 64c2–9, 67d4–6.

16. 64c10–65a3.

17. 65a9–d3.

18. 65d9–12 and e7–66a1; compare 65b3–4, c6, 66a4.

goodness, together with magnitude, health, strength and, in a word, the very being of each thing or class of things; and, so far from assisting the philosopher's endeavor to attain the purity of mind requisite for coming together with these beings, which are themselves of the utmost purity, the body and its senses even disturb that endeavor. It thus becomes a question to the philosophers (or philomaths, as Socrates also calls them in this context) whether they can acquire what they desire while they are alive—that is, so long as their soul remains inextricably confounded with the body—or whether their only hope for the pure knowledge they believe they long for[19] does not lie in death. And, as they are in no small measure bolstered in that hope by recalling the efforts that they have made throughout their life to purify their mind by separating the soul as much as possible from the body, those efforts now come to sight also as the best preparation for death.[20]

So far as we can judge from their reactions to this "apology," however, the youths are not altogether convinced that such approximations or preparations on the part of the philosophers amount to a practice of dying and being dead.[21] They are not yet confident, therefore, that it would be absurd or ridiculous in a man who had throughout his life eagerly pursued them, if he were—even so—to be grieved at the approach of death.[22] The stumbling block proves to be their doubt that the soul survives what we can call its true separation from the body.[23] That it does survive this separation had been the all-but-tacit[24] presupposition of the "apology" as a whole and thus, in particular, of its explication of the words which chiefly concern us, the words in which Socrates finds the best life to consist in a certain anticipation of death. The questioning of that presupposition forces Socrates to turn, in the greater part of the *Phaedo*, to a series of arguments that are meant to convince especially the younger part of his audience[25] of the immortality of the soul. It remains

---

19. Compare 67a8–b1 with 66b7 and d7; consider 66e2–3, 68a1–2 and 7–8.

20. 65d4–67d11.

21. 65a3, d3, 67d11; compare 81a3.

22. 64a6–b1 and 67d12–e4, assigning the repetitious *ou geloion* to Socrates with the manuscripts.

23. 69e5–70b4.

24. 64c7–8.

25. Compare 115c3–d6.

unclear at the conclusion of the dialogue whether they have succeeded in doing so, not to raise now the question of whether they are deserving of success. We are all the more struck, in reading those arguments today, by the eagerness to be convinced by them which is evinced by these quite intelligent and even well-educated youths;[26] we are struck, that is, by what we are tempted to call the youths' naiveté. We will have to consider later on whether that eagerness, together with certain other facts to which the dialogue unobtrusively directs our attention—for example, the silence of Socrates after his return from bathing[27]—does not provide a more solid foundation for understanding Socrates' pronouncement on philosophy and death than that underlying the explication of it that we have tried to follow. But it is necessary first to consider an early modern alternative to the Socratic view, which is also the classical view more generally.

III.

The contours of the modern alternative to the classical view that I have in mind can be discerned by attending to a series of characteristic remarks to be found in thinkers ranging from Francis Bacon at least to Hume. It is possible, as we will see, that one or another of the figures under consideration would not have accepted—in one or another of its aspects *did not accept*—the position that I shall ascribe to them as a group: it remains true that that position has an integrity and coherence of its own, which rests finally, moreover, on a premise that they all give evidence of having held. In order to see that this is the case, however, we must confront at the outset a very striking disagreement in the passages to be considered that seems to mark them as anything other than expressions of a single and consistent view.

Already in *The Elements of Law*, Hobbes speaks of death as "that terrible enemy of nature . . . from whom we expect both the loss of all power, and also the greatest of bodily pains in the losing."[28] But Bacon had claimed in the *Essays* ("Of Death") that "many times death passeth with less pain than the torture of a limb, for the most vital parts are not the quickest of sense" and, further, that "It is as natural to die as to be

---

26. Consider especially 88c and context.

27. 116b6–8.

28. Part I, chapter 14, paragraph 6; see also *De Cive*, chapter 1, paragraph 7.

born; and to a little infant, perhaps, the one is as painful as the other." The contrast between these remarks may suffice for indicating the difficulty. Its solution is suggested by an observation ventured by Lessing toward the end of his essay, "Wie die Alten den Tod gebildet": "Likewise is it certain that that religion, which first disclosed to man that even natural death is the fruit and wages of sin, must have augmented infinitely the terror of death." For when we return to Bacon's essay to examine it in the light cast by this observation, we find there—just after the assertion that "Men fear Death as children fear to go in the dark; and as that natural fear in children is increased with tales, so is the other"—mention of "the contemplation of death, as the wages of sin and passage to another world." We find also praise of one who, speaking "only as a philosopher and natural man," found "the circumstances surrounding death" to be "more terrifying than death itself." To the same effect is Hume, who in an essay which he left unpublished in his lifetime ("Of the Immortality of the Soul") refers to "some unaccountable terrors with regard to futurity" which "would quickly vanish, were they not artificially fostered by precept and education." The all-but-explicit intention of such remarks as that of Bacon, then, is not to deny to death its terrors—we have only to recall in this connection the interest that he took in the prolongation of life—but rather to reduce those terrors to what he and other early moderns regarded as their natural proportions. And this is an intention that is fully consistent with the movement of Hobbes' own thought.[29]

But what are these natural proportions and how are they to be gauged? It is here that the true difficulty in the position under discussion begins to show itself. For the degree of terror that death may or may not hold for us is relative to the order of our fundamental concerns. Now, Hobbes—for whom death is "that terrible enemy of nature," for whom, therefore, rationality can be reduced to drawing the full consequences from this alleged fact—had found "preservation" to be "the end that everyone by nature aimeth at" or what "we intend always."[30] But Spinoza, too—according to whom death is of so little concern to "one who lives according to the dictate of reason alone" that "he thinks of nothing less than of" it—holds self-preservation to be our fundamental concern: "The

---

29. Compare, for example, *The Elements of Law*, Part II, chapter 6, paragraph 5 and chapter 9, paragraph 2 with chapter 9, paragraph 8 and chapter 5, paragraph 1 as well as Part I, chapter 14, paragraph 6.

30. Ibid. Part I, chapter 17, paragraph 14; chapter 14, paragraph 13.

striving by which each thing strives to persevere in its being is nothing but the actual essence of the thing";[31] moreover, that striving "involves no finite time but an indefinite time";[32] and "Since reason demands nothing contrary to nature, it demands . . . that everyone should strive to preserve his own being so far as he can"; indeed, "the foundation of virtue is this very striving to preserve one's own being."[33] Thus Spinoza and Hobbes—whose disagreement as to death and its alleged terrors we are not in a position to question—prove to agree as to the fundamental concern by which the measure of those terrors must be taken. Their disagreement must be traced, then, to some ambiguity in the concern that both thinkers have identified as our fundamental one, an ambiguity which cannot fail to have left its traces also within the thought of each.

This seems to have been the case at least with Hobbes, as can already be seen from the question we are forced to put to him whether it is death, simply, that we are so anxious, in his view, to avoid, or rather violent death. (At least on one occasion, the *Leviathan* speaks simply of "fear of death" where what is meant, as is confirmed by the Latin version, is "fear of violent death."[34]) The ambiguity in question comes to sight most clearly in a remark in *De Homine* according to which "it is necessary" for us "to desire life, health, and further, insofar as it can be done, security of future time."[35] For what is the force of this "insofar as it can be done," which qualifies the natural necessity we are said to be under to desire "security of future time"? The answer to this question will determine also the interpretation that must be given to what Hobbes, in the *Leviathan*, puts "for a general inclination of all mankind," namely, "a perpetual and restless desire of power after power, that ceaseth only in death." He traces the restlessness of this desire above all to the fact that a man "cannot assure the power and means to live well, which he hath present"—that is to say, assure these *for the future*—"without the acquisition of more."[36] What, if any, are the limits to our concern for the future? Is it only one who is "over-provident" or "looks too far before him, in the care of future time"—as Hobbes seems to wish to suggest in the immediately following

---

31. *Ethics*, Part III, proposition 7.

32. Ibid. Part III, proposition 8.

33. Ibid. Part IV, proposition 18 scholium.

34. Page 58, note added by the editor, Edwin Curley (Indianapolis, 1994*)*.

35. Chapter 11, paragraph 6 (edited by Bernard Gert, Garden City, 1972).

36. Chapter 11, paragraph 2.

chapter ("Of Religion")—who "hath his heart all the day long gnawed on by fear of death" (among other things)?[37] Does this "perpetual fear," which (according to Hobbes' suggestion in the same place) always accompanies "mankind in the ignorance of causes,"[38] accompany us *only* so long as we are in the grip of ignorance? If that is the case, then a contentment of which Locke speaks in his *Essay* (and a certain version of which Spinoza, too, may have had in mind as belonging to his "free man") would appear to be within the reach of any healthy and sufficiently well-informed man. According to Locke, "All *uneasiness* . . . being removed, a moderate portion of good serves at present to content Men; and some few degrees of Pleasure in a succession of ordinary Enjoyments make up a happiness, wherein they can be satisfied" since, as he had already claimed, "all absent good does not at any time make a necessary part of our present *happiness*, nor the absence of it make a part of our *misery*."[39] Hobbes, however, seems to have had his doubts. He does say that "*Continual success* in obtaining those things which a man from time to time desireth, that is to say, continual prospering, is that men call FELICITY"; but he adds at once, "I mean the felicity of this life. For there is no such thing as perpetual tranquility of mind, while we live here."[40] Or, as he also puts it, "the felicity of this life consisteth not in the repose of a mind satisfied. For there is no such *Finis ultimus* (utmost aim) nor *Summum Bonum* (greatest good) as is spoken of in the books of the old moral philosophers," a situation whose cause he finds in the fact "that the object of man's desire is not to enjoy once only, and for one instant of time, but to assure forever the way of his future desire."[41]

Still, one would have to say that even Hobbes was tempted by the thought that what (as he was convinced) we cannot have[42] is also of no fundamental concern to us—which is to say that he, too, was tempted

---

37. Paragraph 5; compare Spinoza, *op. cit.*, Part IV, proposition 63 corollary scholium.

38. Paragraph 6.

39. *An Essay Concerning Human Understanding*, chapter 21, paragraph 44; compare Spinoza, *op. cit.*, Part IV, proposition 18 scholium: "happiness consists in man's being able to preserve his being" and proposition 68 scholium, where he seems to separate "desiring to live" from fearing death, as well as proposition 64 and corollary and Part V, proposition 4 corollary scholium; see also Part IV, Appendix XXXII and Part V, proposition 6 scholium.

40. *Leviathan*, chapter 6, paragraph 58: the Latin version omits "here."

41. Ibid., chapter 11, paragraph 1.

42. Compare ibid., chapter 6, paragraph 58: "What kind of felicity God hath ordained to them that devoutly honour Him, a man shall no sooner know than enjoy . . ."

to think that our true concern does not look beyond such goods as we can by ourselves provide: protection against *violent* death, for example, or "recognition." By way of explanation, one might wish to have recourse to the common inclination of human beings to deny that we want or need what we regard as being beyond our hopes. And it is true that an awareness of that inclination can help us properly to appreciate the naiveté of Socrates' young interlocutors in the *Phaedo*, under the protection of which they give unfeigned expression to what they believe they long for. But to have recourse to it in the case of Hobbes and the other moderns we are considering is to forget that they were philosophers, men as to whom the term "sophistication" must have an entirely different meaning than it has when applied to us. "Sophistication," then, can be no answer to the question of what conferred on a position so problematic in itself a plausibility sufficient to make it a temptation that at least some of them appear to have succumbed to: the question, in other words, of what made it plausible to them that nature *both* inspires us "with an aversion towards" death *and* confines nonetheless "all our concern . . . to the present life." (The formulations are Hume's in various parts of the short essay from which we have already quoted.) Or is there one respect in which even *their* sophistication might have been excessive? I have in mind the premise, which they all give evidence of having shared, that (as Hobbes put it) nature "dissociates" men.[43] For this amounts to the assumption that justice has no natural hold on our heart or to an acceptance—to which these thinkers appear to have come very quickly—of the natural primacy of selfishness: "why should I be angry with a man for loving himself better than me?" as Bacon slyly remarked in his *Essays* ("Of Revenge").[44] Yet, what if justice, so far from being without a hold on our heart, is precisely the form in which our most fundamental concern finds a first, if somewhat enigmatical, expression? This much, at least, is clear: the view that

---

43. Ibid. chapter 13, "Of the Natural Condition of Mankind," paragraph 10; Hume, *A Treatise of Human Nature*, Book III, Part II, section 1, "Justice, whether a natural or artificial virtue?" and section 2, "Of the origin of justice and property"; Spinoza, *op. cit.*, Part IV, proposition 37, scholium 2; Bacon, *On the Dignity and Advancement of Learning*, Book VII, chapter II, pp. 275f., as well as Book VIII, chapter III, aphorism II (edited by Joseph Devey, London, 1911).

44. Compare Hume, *op. cit.*, Book III, Part II, section 2: "Now, it appears, that in the original frame of our mind, our strongest attention is confin'd to ourselves"; Spinoza, *op. cit.*, Part IV, proposition 22 and corollary, as well as *Tractatus Theologico-Politicus* chapter 16, paragraph 1, Bruder number 4.

nature dissociates men is in direct and occasionally explicit opposition to the classical teaching that man is a political animal.[45] We thus find on the one side, in the classical position, recognition of a fundamental concern with immortality or eternity, going together with an assertion of our natural sociality, and on the other side, on the part of these early moderns, a frank denial of natural sociality, going together with a tendency to deny that our true concerns reach beyond this life.[46] In the meantime, this tendency has—thanks in no small part to their efforts—extended its influence over the entire Western world. In the process, it has led not altogether surprisingly to a forgetting of death itself, a forgetting against which Heidegger, for one, raised his powerful voice in protest. Before returning to the *Phaedo* for a final word, let us briefly consider, therefore, the question whether the Heideggerian protest against this intended or unintended consequence of the modern alternative constitutes a return to the older, classical or Socratic, view.

IV.

It may suffice for this purpose to touch on a number of points that must strike someone who is familiar with that older view on a reading of *Sein und Zeit*. Heidegger's protest is directed against "das alltägliche Sein zum Tod" which is "als verfallendes eine ständige *Flucht vor ihm.*"[47] He detects such flight not only in the way in which, in everyday speech about it, we seek to reassure ourselves and one another of death's unthreatening character,[48] but also in our allowing ourselves to be absorbed in the matters of concern that lie immediately before us—not to say our frantic pursuit of such absorption.[49] And he uncompromisingly and insistently calls us back, one and all, from that reassurance and absorption. I know

---

45. Hobbes, *De Cive*, chapter 1, paragraph 2; compare Aristotle, *Politics*, Book I, chapter 2, 1253a1–18.

46. Bacon is, at least in the latter respect, apparently an exception: *The Wisdom of the Ancients*, "Orpheus or Philosophy," as well as *The Dignity and Advancement of Learning*, conclusion to Book I (see Book VIII, chapter III, p. 345); but compare also Book VII, chapter II, pp. 277f.

47. P. 254, paragraph 3.

48. P. 253, paragraph 2.

49. P. 258, paragraph 2.

of nothing like this call on the part of the ancients. It is true that they were not confronted with a forgetting of death that had, partly for the reason we have indicated, become so extreme and so entrenched in its extreme position, as that which dismayed Heidegger; and it is *perhaps* for this reason that they refrained from issuing such a call as he did. For Socrates' remark in the *Phaedo*, to the effect that philosophy consists in the practice of dying and being dead, can hardly be considered in this light. Even apart from the fact that the remark was addressed only to philosophers or potential philosophers or to philomaths of a certain sort, its legitimate interpretation must begin from the explication of its meaning that Socrates himself gives in the context; and that explication, as we have seen, outstrips in its reassurances as to death even the everyday speech about it that Heidegger bemoans.[50]

To this one might reply that even Heidegger—though he explicitly rejects any possibility of "overcoming" the death that he calls upon us to face up to[51]—is, for all of that, not simply a prophet of doom. For the second point that must strike someone familiar with the older view is the promise that *Sein und Zeit* holds out of a "Daseinsganzheit"[52] or "*Ganzsein des Seienden . . . das existiert*":[53] the possibility "als *ganzes Seinkönnen* zu existieren" through the proper stance (das Vorlaufen) towards death.[54] In this case, Heidegger himself invites comparison with the classical view, by having recourse (in clarifying what he has in mind) to the distinction drawn by Plato and Aristotle between the terms *holon* and *pan*.[55] Yet, in the very portion of the *Phaedo* that we have considered, Socrates lends his voice to the plainest of denials that even the best human beings can gain, while living, what they particularly desire.[56] The satisfaction of our deepest concern is of course *not* what Heidegger had in mind in speaking

---

50. Compare also Plato, *Apology of Socrates* 39e1–41d6. The close of Book III of Lucretius, which may perhaps be said to approach Heidegger's call, nevertheless differs from it in many ways, not least in intent.

51. P. 310, paragraph 2; consider there also the references to freedom from illusion and to sober Angst.

52. P. 245, paragraph 6.

53. P. 242, paragraph 2.

54. P. 264, paragraph 2.

55. P. 244, note 1.

56. 68a1–b4, 66d7–67a1.

of a possible "Daseinsganzheit"; but, as the *Republic*[57] and especially the *Symposium*[58] make plain, it is the only sort of wholeness that would have been acknowledged by Socrates to be a genuine one. And if we are tempted to discount his denials in the *Phaedo* as merely exoteric, we can turn to Aristotle's treatment of the character and possibility of happiness in the first book of the *Nicomachean Ethics*. Read with the necessary care and discernment, that treatment confirms that a doubt (to put it this way) that human life can attain to wholeness was a most important component of the classical view. In this respect, the remark of Hobbes in disparagement of a *Summum Bonum*, which we quoted earlier,[59] anti-classical in intent as it was, is closer in spirit to the classics than the Heideggerian treatment of wholeness, which (as we can add) is not intended to be merely theoretical-methodological, but to lay bare a "*faktisch-existenzielle*" possibility.[60]

Here, too, in the case of this departure of Heidegger's from the classics—as in the intra-modern divergence of which we were just reminded by mention of Hobbes' remark on a *Summum Bonum*—the disagreement may have to be traced to a difference over the character of our most fundamental concern.[61] For Heidegger is so far from conceding any legitimacy to a concern with immortality,[62] that he traces the very "Vorstellung" of an unending time,[63] as also the wish to bring time to a halt,[64] to the outlook of "verfallendes Dasein"; to show, moreover, that the same holds for "the traditional concept of eternity" needs, as he contends, "keiner ausfürlichen Erörterung."[65] This, then, is a third point that must strike a reader of *Sein und Zeit* who is familiar with the classical view. And, as it seems to me at least, its source may have to be sought in a fourth point of difference. According to Heidegger, death individualizes us (vereinzeln). And this, not only in the sense that it claims us as individuals[66] or that death is in

---

57. 505d11–e4.

58. 204e2–205a8, 205d10–206a13.

59. See note 41 above.

60. P. 309, paragraph 3.

61. Compare p. 259, paragraph 3: "Das Sein zum Tode gründet in der Sorge."

62. Compare pp. 247–248.

63. P. 424, paragraph 3; p. 426, paragraph 2.

64. P. 425, paragraph 2.

65. P. 427, note 1.

66. P. 263, paragraph 3.

the case of each of us only one's own[67] or that, since no one else can die in one's place, each of us must die for himself,[68] but also in the sense that, standing before one's own death or its prospect, one is entirely cast back upon his own possibilities so that "alle Bezüge zu anderem Dasein" are in such a one "gelöst."[69] Yet, even if this were the case (which may well be doubted), since "Das Sein zum Tode gründet in der Sorge,"[70] death itself could do this only to the extent that, by the order of our fundamental concerns, we were already "individualized."[71] To ascribe individualization to death, then, as Heidegger seems to do, would be—even if he were correct as to the fact—to miss the available evidence of its authentic cause, and therefore to misconstrue the fact as well. And, if I am not mistaken, there are remarks of his in the very portion of his text that we are considering which suggest that he has indeed misunderstood, or failed to think through to its end, the alleged fact that he proclaims with such abandon.[72]

These striking departures from classical thought and practice lead us, in turn, to a final point of difference, which (from the perspective of philosophy) is in a way the most important. Although Heidegger distinguishes, with all of the clarity one could desire, between a merely empirical certainty of death (which we already possess) and an apodictic certainty of it (which we apparently lack), he shows little or no interest in attempting to acquire the latter.[73] The certainty of death on which he is intent discloses itself to us not in theoretical knowledge but "ursprünglicher und eindringlicher in der Befindlichkeit der Angst."[74] In the *Phaedo*, on the

---

67. P. 265, paragraph 2

68. P. 240, paragraph 2.

69. P. 250, paragraph 6.

70. See note 61 above.

71. Compare p. 263, paragraph 3: "Diese Vereinzelung . . . *macht offenbar*, dass alles Sein bei dem Besorgten und jedes Mitsein mit Anderen versagt, wenn es um das eigenste Seinkönnen geht"—my emphasis—as well as p. 307, paragraph 2.

72. P. 263, paragraph 3; p. 264, paragraph 2. This is to say nothing of pp. 384, paragraph 3–385 top.

73. Pp. 257–258; compare p. 383, paragraph 1: "das Vorlaufen in die Möglichkeit [of death] keine Speculation über sie . . . bedeudet"; compare also pp. 247–248. Compare Aristotle's criticism of Democritus: *Parva Naturalia* 472a16–20.

74. P. 251, paragraph 2; compare p. 258, paragraph 1: "eine 'höhere' als nur empirische Gewissheit"; compare also p. 265, paragraph 1 on this certainty: "*es gehört überhaupt nicht in die Abstufungsordnung der Evidenzen über Vorhandenes*" [all emphasized by Heidegger]; and consider pp. 264–265 more generally.

other hand, the discussion of death and immortality is eventually—and perhaps even from the beginning—placed by Socrates in the context of a consideration of the (necessary and necessitating) causes of generation and corruption generally;[75] and it is surely no mere coincidence that this dialogue contains the most complete, as well as the most frank, account of his lifelong scientific endeavor.[76]

V.

From what we have been able to observe, we draw the conclusion that it is in the *Phaedo*, rather than its modern or anti-modern alternatives, that we find the exemplary case of what we were seeking all along: a philosopher speaking to others about death. Yet, for all of that, the *Phaedo* no longer speaks to us directly. A philosopher is a man who, as such, has come to terms with death to the extent that it is possible for a human being to do so[77]—something that cannot be presumed to be true of those to whom he speaks, though it may come to be true of some of them. Very much may depend on how the philosopher approaches them. His task is complicated by the fact that his audience (even if he speaks to one alone, who may after all report what he hears to some dear friend or friends) consists of human beings of diverse natures and therefore of diverse prospects. It is further complicated if he wishes his words on death, together with his speeches more generally, to survive him;[78] for their survival may depend in part on how they are received by those who are not and cannot be brought into the best condition.[79] And the *Phaedo* is, not incidentally—as the setting and the circumstances surrounding its narration already indicate—also the dialogue which treats of the transmission of the Socratic teaching. Now, the genuine survival of that teaching would consist in the continuation of an intellectual endeavor that is philosophic-scientific in the original sense of these terms. And it may at least be questioned whether we still find that endeavor today, though there is no reason why it could not be recovered. Yet for its recovery to be more than a strictly private

---

75. 95e9–96a1; compare 70d7–e2.

76. 96a1ff.

77. *Phaedo* 84e2–3 and 91b6; compare note 27 above.

78. 89b9–c1.

79. *Republic*, 380e3–381a4.

occurrence (which it must also be, in part), someone would have to make the endeavor broadly compelling, as Socrates was able to do both for his own and for many succeeding generations. For it is in this connection that we are obliged to note that his words in the *Phaedo* no longer speak directly to us. There Socrates was able to presume and, indeed, had to presume in his audience—even or precisely the best part of it—the presence of beliefs which we no longer hold and of a disposition to believe that we have abandoned or suppressed: we referred earlier to what strikes *us* as the naiveté of his young interlocutors. In order to address us directly, someone would have to take due account of the dispositions and beliefs that have taken the place of those which shaped Socrates' audience. He would have to approach us in the manner that our present condition, with its own weaknesses and strengths, demands. This would require that he have carried out a comprehensive analysis of that condition. And that analysis, in turn, would have to be guided by an adequate understanding of the simply good condition of the soul. Since some philosophers of the past have worthily dealt with this theme, and the efforts of others have helped to shape our present condition, it may be that merely historical studies, like the present essay, will prove to be useful to the one or ones who, as we may hope, will take up this worthwhile task.

16

Happiness in the Perspective of Philosophy

A remarkable passage from one of Stendhal's novels, *La Chartreuse de Parme*, may perhaps be allowed to serve as prelude to my discussion of a theme whose proper handling would require song, rather than the prose to which I am limited. The young hero of the novel, troubled by an affair of the heart, is making a journey to seek counsel from an older friend. Pausing at midnight by the shore of Lake Maggiore and moved by the sublime beauty of his surroundings, he resolves never to pronounce the word "love" in the presence of the woman for whom he cares more, by far, than any being in the world. He has become aware a short while before, that she is in love with him; but he swears to himself that he will never tell her that he loves her, for the simple but sufficient reason that, as he believes, he does not love her—not at least in the way that she loves him. Rather, he takes the resolution to tell her at the first opportunity that his heart has never known love. From this height of generosity and virtue, whose proximity to happiness is noted at this point by the author, the young man's thoughts came gradually, as he resumed his journey, to take another course. Not surprisingly, perhaps, they turned to a number of abuses on the part of authority, of which he happened to be aware and for which he expressed to himself a becoming contempt. But it suddenly occurred to him, to his profound unease, that he was himself the indirect beneficiary of abuses of the same sort. The inner struggle, the turmoil that ensued, led him to a decision which left him discontented with himself: he would not be such a fool as to refuse the profit that fell to him by birth as his part from such arrangements, but he would avoid the hypocrisy of denouncing them in public. Stendhal adds here the following comment:

"Ces raisonnements ne manquaient pas de justesse; mais Fabrice était bien tombé de cette élévation de bonheur sublime où il s'était trouvé transporté une heure auparavant. La pensée du privilège avait desséché cette plante toujours si délicate qu'on nomme le Bonheur."[1]

~

Happiness is a term that is used in both a stricter and a looser sense. Today it is used mostly in the looser sense, as one can everywhere observe: on radio and television; in movies, newspapers and magazines; not least among the young. I will use it throughout my paper in the stricter sense that it had throughout our tradition of philosophic reflection on the matter; but, in tracing the course of that reflection by considering several important stages in its history, I will never lose sight of the question of the origin of our own looser usage and of its significance for life.

In that stricter sense, then, happiness is said by no less an authority than Aristotle to be that for the sake of which all of us do all of the things that we do.[2] This is of course by no means a self-evident proposition—it can be denied without obvious absurdity—but it is in at least rough accord with what we may still be able to sense of ourselves. For while, as serious human beings, we regard it as incumbent on us to take in each case the just course rather than that which is most immediately advantageous to ourselves or to our own, we sense—even if we do not see it with perfect clarity—that the just course is the path on which happiness, too, is to be found. Otherwise, as Plato on occasion pointed out, we could hardly urge that course with such confidence as we do urge it upon our children and others for whom we care deeply.[3]

The happiness in question is obviously not a petty thing, consisting merely in a sum of small gains, a positive balance sheet, so to speak, in the daily give and take of life. It is better understood, as Aristotle himself had already indicated when he made the remark to which we have referred, as *the* good at which all human efforts, if not also all things simply, seem to aim.[4] In other words, the happiness in question is that

---

1. Stendhal: *La Chartreuse de Parme* (Paris: Éditions Garnier Frères, 1961), pp. 145–48.

2. *Nicomachean Ethics* 1101b35–1102a4; compare 1097a34–b5.

3. *Laws* 662c5–663a2.

4. *Nicomachean Ethics* 1094a1–3.

highest end which, through conferring order on the objects of our choice or will, brings it about that human striving is not, or need not be, empty or futile.[5] Moreover, it could not do this, or not to the same extent, if it were not also, as Aristotle indicates as well, a self-sufficient good, making (by itself alone) life choiceworthy and deficient in nothing.[6] The point from which we began is closely related to this one, if it does not indeed follow from it, as our authority indicates by mentioning it next: while being most choiceworthy, happiness is not a sum of goods—which, as such, could always be rendered more choiceworthy still by the addition to it of the least significant member of the class.[7] Rather, "it comes to sight as something complete and self-sufficient, being the end of all our doings."[8]

It is of course a tall order to give content to this vision; and Aristotle more than once acknowledges and even stresses as much in the course of the discussion we have been following.[9] As Plato had said before him of the highest good, which is at the same time the highest objective of any learning deserving of the name, it is "what every soul pursues and that for the sake of which it does all of the things that it does, divining that something (of the sort) exists but being at a loss, able neither to grasp adequately what it is nor to have recourse to (some opinion of it on which to place) a lasting reliance, as in other cases."[10] Yet in making, in having his Socrates make this remark, Plato seeks nothing so much as to encourage at least some of his readers to make it their utmost endeavor to acquire a most precise knowledge of this elusive good—if this were not evident in itself, it would have been made sufficiently clear by the context of the remark.[11] And Aristotle's *Nicomachean Ethics* as a whole, framed as it is by the two discussions that it devotes explicitly to happiness, is an attempt to supply content to what, according to Plato's formulation and his own indications, we all somehow "divine" to exist.[12]

---

5. Ibid. 1094a18–22 and 1095a14–20.

6. Ibid. 1097b14–16.

7. Ibid. 1097b16–20.

8. Ibid. 1097b20–21.

9. For example, *Nicomachean Ethics* 1095a14–22, 1095b14–1096a10, 1097b22–24 and 1098a20–22, 1102a5–7.

10. *Republic* 505e1–4.

11. Ibid. 504a2 and following.

12. See again *Nicomachean Ethics* 1102a5–7 as well as 1117b9–15.

Or do we? Departing from Plato, if only tentatively, I referred a few moments ago to "what we *may* still be able to sense of ourselves." In doing so, I had in mind a long, centuries-long discussion that may have brought it about in the meantime that *we* pause just here—and that, whether we have heard anything ourselves of that discussion or not.

It seems to have been initiated by Hobbes. Traces of the fundamental change in perspective that we have now to consider may indeed be found in such earlier authors as Machiavelli and Bacon. But it was Hobbes with his customary candor and bluntness, and his incomparable power of vivid and forceful expression, who addressed the question head-on. What "men call FELICITY," he said, is nothing more than "*Continual success* in obtaining those things which a man from time to time desireth, that is to say, continual prospering . . . . For there is no such thing as perpetual tranquility of mind, while we live here; because life is but motion, and can never be without desire, nor without fear, no more than without sense." He had taken care to underline the qualification already contained in these remarks from the sixth chapter of his *Leviathan* by adding, "I mean the felicity of this life"; but the worth of the qualification would have to be judged by reference to another remark which he did not refrain from making there: "What kind of felicity God hath ordained to them that devoutly honour Him, a man shall no sooner know, than enjoy; being joys, that now are as incomprehensible, as the word of Schoolmen *beatifical vision* is unintelligible."

The position was of sufficient importance to Hobbes, to bear repeating, with even greater emphasis, in the eleventh chapter of the same work, where he treats of "those qualities of mankind, that concern their living together in peace, and unity":

> To which end [he continues] we are to consider, that the felicity of this life, consisteth not in the repose of a mind satisfied. For there is no such *finis ultimus*, utmost aim, nor *summum bonum*, greatest good, as is spoken of in the books of the old moral philosophers. Nor can a man any more live, whose desires are at an end, than he, whose senses and imaginations are at a stand. Felicity is a continual progress of the desire, from one object to another; the attaining of the former, being still but the way to the latter.

But he adds now a reason for the view of felicity or happiness that he has come to, a further reason. The passage that we have been listening to continues as follows: "The cause whereof"—that is, the cause of the alleged fact that our attaining of one object of desire is "but the way" to another—"is, that the object of man's desire, is not to enjoy once only, and for one instant of time; but to assure for ever, the way of his future desire. And therefore the voluntary actions, and inclinations of all men, tend, not only to procuring, but also to the assuring of a contented life . . . ." And it is only in the light cast by this further reason that the full dimensions of Hobbes' position regarding happiness become clear. For he was tough enough, or complacent enough, to leave matters in this state—without, that is, suggesting how what he was still able to discern as a fundamental concern of "man" as such, of "all men,"[13] might be satisfied. And the discussion was continued after him by men who followed in his footsteps so far as the rejection of the classical view of happiness was concerned, but assessed differently (one must assume) than he had apparently done the consequences for human life of the position that he was able or content to accept. They therefore took up again the problem that, in the remark last quoted, he had exposed to light. If they could not solve that problem—any more than Hobbes had solved it—they could attempt, at any rate, to get around it. The first such attempt that I am aware of was made by Rousseau, the second by Nietzsche.

A way around the problem would perhaps have been found, if one were able to avoid speaking and thinking of happiness altogether. And there is evidence that both Rousseau and Nietzsche were tempted by this path. In a fragment called to my attention by my colleague Christopher Kelly, editor of the American edition of Rousseau's "Collected Writings," Rousseau speaks characteristically of the necessity, in seeking "the source of our passions," to go back to man's natural state. What "one imagines," namely that the "first" of them is "the desire to be happy," is thus revealed to be a mistake: "The idea of happiness is very composite, happiness is a permanent state the appetite for which depends on the extent of our knowledge, whereas our passions are born from a present feeling independent of our intelligence. The development is accomplished with the aid of reason, but the principle existed before it." This might suggest to us that it is less the principle itself, than the state of our passions as they are affected by intelligence—the state which they have reached through a development "accomplished with the aid of reason"—that ought to be of concern to us, as the beings we now are. But Rousseau seems to hesitate. Identifying the principle he seeks, "the source of all our passions," with

---

13. Compare Plato, *Symposium* 204e1–205a8.

"the desire to exist," he adds that, "Everything that seems to extend or consolidate our existence gratifies us, everything that seems to destroy or restrict it afflicts us"; and he denies that even "understanding" can affect or modify the "feeling" or "sentiment" in question "except by its relation with our existence" or via our "judgment" of it.[14]

Nietzsche, of whom this fragment from Rousseau could well of itself put one in mind, goes even further in the same general direction: "Der Mensch strebt nicht nach Glück";[15] "der Satz 'der Mensch strebt nach Glück'" is "psychologischer Widersinn";[16] or as Zarathustra says almost at the end of the fourth part of the work devoted to him, "Trachte ich denn nach *Glücke*? Ich trachte nach meinem *Werke*."[17] He is only repeating there what he had said at the beginning of the fourth part in answer to the question whether he looks out for his happiness: "Was liegt am Glücke! . . . ich trachte lange nicht mehr nach Glücke, ich trachte nach meinem Werke." But as the same passage shows, Zarathustra cannot, at any rate does not avoid speaking of happiness, including his own—of which he says here that it is "schwer."[18] As for Nietzsche himself, he says, speaking in the foreword to *Die Fröhliche Wissenschaft* of what he has gained from some experiences he mentions there, "Wir kennen ein neues Glück," a remark which two pairs of aphorisms later on in the work may be intended to elaborate on further;[19] and in the first aphorism of *Der Antichrist*, he speaks of "our happiness" and of its "formula." Nietzsche too, then, cannot or does not avoid speaking of what he takes genuine happiness to be; and the same must of course be said of Rousseau. But this is precisely our question: what sort of happiness is that?

Rousseau has given a memorable answer to this question in the Fifth Promenade of his *Les Rêveries du promeneur solitaire*. The theme of this Promenade is the happiness that Rousseau enjoyed during the "two

---

14. Christopher Kelly, ed., *The Collected Writings of Rousseau* (Hanover: Dartmouth College Press, 2007), vol. 12, p. 279; compare vol. 5, pp. 577–580 (Letter to Malesherbes of January 26, 1762) as well as *Les Rêveries du promeneur solitaire*, VI paragraph 14.

15. *Götzen-Dämmerung*, "Sprüche und Pfeile," 12; compare *Werke In Fünf Bänden*, Karl Schlechta, ed. (Frankfurt: Ullstein, 1984), vol. IV, p. 273 as well as pp. 335–336.

16. *Ecce Homo*, "Warum ich so gute Bücher schreibe," 5.

17. Schlechta, vol. II, p. 835.

18. Ibid., p. 751. Compare p. 692 as well as p. 788.

19. *Die Fröhliche Wissenschaft* (Schlechta vol. II pp. 287, 451–453, 471–475) [Aphorisms 3, 302–303, 337–338].

months" that he lived on the island of St. Pierre, a period that he counts for the most happy time of his life. He poses the question, "Quel était donc ce bonheur et en quoi consistait sa jouissance?" And he suggests that he will provide the material for answering it by describing the life that he led there.[20] But his description includes or is accompanied by a general reflection on happiness as such, on the problem of happiness. And it is to this that we will confine our attention.

We may begin with a remark that recalls Rousseau's characterization of happiness in the fragment at which we have already glanced, where he calls it a "permanent state." He says now, of "le bonheur que mon coeur regrette," that it is not composed of fleeting moments but is "un état simple et permanent."[21] But "sur la terre," as he continues in the paragraph that follows, "Tout est dans un flux continuel"; insofar, then, as our affections attach themselves to the ever-changing things exterior to us, they necessarily change along with those things: "Toujours en avant ou en arrière de nous, elles rappellent le passé qui n'est plus ou préviennent l'avenir qui souvent ne doit point être: il n'y a rien là de solide à quoi le coeur se puisse attacher. Aussi n'a-t-on guère ici bas que du plaisir qui passe . . ."[22]

As he indicates by the inclusion of this little "guère," Rousseau allows for the possibility of a pleasure, at least, which is not a merely passing one. He can do so because he has not ruled out the attachment of our affections to an object other than exterior things. But does this remove entirely the difficulty which is constituted not only by the past which is recalled but also by the future which we anticipate? Continuing on in the same paragraph, he restates the problem: "A peine est-il dans nos plus vives jouissances un instant où le coeur puisse véritablement nous dire: *Je voudrais que cet instant durât toujours;* et comment peut-on appeler bonheur un état fugitif qui nous laisse encore le coeur inquiet et vide, qui nous fait regretter quelque chose avant, ou désirer encore quelque chose après?"[23]

We see, I believe, the advance that this formulation makes on its predecessor, when we reflect that even a pleasure lasting as long as life itself endures must appear fleeting when measured against the notion of

---

20. *Les Rêveries du promeneur solitaire,* V paragraph 6.

21. Ibid., V paragraph 12.

22. Ibid., V paragraph 13.

23. Ibid., V paragraph 13.

happiness as a "permanent state." For Rousseau finds no stronger expression for such pleasure as he has in mind than to say that it so fills and calms our heart as to make the heart able truly to say to us that it would wish the (pleasurable) moment to last forever: in saying this, in entertaining this wish, the heart opens the door once again to its disquiet—nay, disquiet has already been welcomed back within it.

That this was, at any rate, Rousseau's view of the matter is shown by the step that he takes next in the argument:

> Mais [he continues at the start of the next paragraph] s'il est un état où l'âme trouve une assiette assez solide pour s'y reposer tout entière et rassembler là tout son être, sans avoir besoin de rappeler le passé ni d'enjamber sur l'avenir; où le temps ne soit rien pour elle, où le présent dure toujours sans néanmoins marquer sa durée et sans aucune trace de succession, sans aucun autre sentiment de privation ni de jouissance, de plaisir ni de peine, de désir ni de crainte que celui seul de notre existence, et que ce sentiment seul puisse la remplir tout entière; tant que cet état dure [he concludes] celui qui s'y trouve peut s'appeler heureux . . . d'un bonheur suffisant, parfait et plein, qui ne laisse dans l'âme aucun vide qu'elle sente le besoin de remplir.[24]

He had already spoken of the "sentiment of existence"—and that, most beautifully—earlier in the Fifth Promenade,[25] and it will fully occupy him in what remains of it.[26] The specific function of the present passage, as its context shows, is to indicate the part that this "sentiment" may play in supplying an answer to the question that was posed at the outset. Rousseau clearly wished to find such an answer as would be equal to the requirements or demands of a genuine happiness, as he had spelled them out in the meantime. And in the "sentiment of existence" we have at last a state which disquiet as to the future cannot taint, since the wish that it would last forever forms no part of it.

The difficulty that remains is indicated by what he adds immediately: "Tel est l'état où je me suis trouvé *souvent* à l'île de Saint-Pierre . . ."[27] I

---

24. Ibid., V paragraph 14; compare *Discours sur l'inégalité*, Heinrich Meier, ed. (München: Ferdinand Schöningh, 1984), p. 110 and p. 106.

25. *Les Rêveries du promeneur solitaire*, V paragraph 9.

26. Ibid., V paragraphs 15–17.

27. Ibid., V paragraph 14.

have underscored "souvent": it is unnecessary to insist on the information supplied by the editor to the effect that Rousseau had first written "quelquefois";[28] "souvent" by itself suffices to show that there must be a transition (repeatedly effected) to the state in which the future is of no concern to us. But a transition from what? Presumably from a state or states in which the future is one, not to say the chief, of our concerns. It is reasonable to wonder, then, whether a specific forgetting is not necessary for that transition to occur and whether forgetting does not thus become an integral part of the sense of sufficiency or perfection of the "sentiment of existence"—which is to say an integral part of the "sentiment" itself. And in this connection, we cannot help noting the role that dream-like reverie plays in the experience, as Rousseau describes it:[29] reverie, to which uniform and moderate motion is conducive, since motion which is unequal or too strong awakens, whereas absolute silence offers an image of death;[30] reverie, to be released from which is to be brought back not only to what surrounds one, but to oneself.[31] But can a happiness that presupposes a fundamental forgetting be the happiness worthy of our concern?

This question is starkly posed by a passage in Nietzsche's "Vom Nutzen und Nachteil der Historie für das Leben." In the passage in question, toward the beginning of that early essay, Nietzsche speaks first—in a manner that could well remind one of Rousseau's discussion in the Fifth Promenade[32]—of the superiority of the smallest happiness, "wenn es nur ununterbrochen da ist," to the greatest which is only episodic. In this context, he then acknowledges, more frankly than Rousseau himself had done, the contribution that forgetting appears to make to any happiness that is available to us: "Bei dem kleinsten aber und bei dem grössten Glücke ist es immer eins, wodurch Glück zum Glücke wird: das Vergessenkönnen . . . ." And he adds that a man who lacked the power of forgetting would be condemned to see everywhere "becoming," would lose himself in "this torrent of becoming."[33] Now Nietzsche, the teacher of "the eternal return,"[34]

---

28. Henri Roddier, ed., *Les Rêveries du promeneur solitaire* (Paris: Éditions Garnier Frères, 1960), p. 151.

29. *Les Rêveries du promeneur solitaire*, V paragraphs 9 and 16.

30. Ibid., V paragraph 16; compare V paragraph 9.

31. Ibid., V paragraph 17.

32. Ibid., V paragraph 12.

33. Schlechta, vol. I, pp. 212–213.

34. *Götzen-Dämmerung*, "Was ich den Alten verdanke," 5.

that is, of the highest possible affirmation of "becoming,"[35] can hardly have been—at any rate, can hardly have remained content with a solution to the problem of happiness that is dependent upon a forgetting of "becoming."

Indeed, may it not have been his discontent with such a solution that induced him to explore a more radical course than the one that had been suggested by Rousseau? In a remarkable passage in *Menschliches, Allzumenschliches*[36] that he repeats almost word for word in *Ecce Homo* as evidence of the sureness with which he had, already at the time of that earlier work, grasped his task and its "world-historical" importance,[37] he refers to a thought which, properly developed, can perhaps serve one day as the ax that is applied to the root of man's " 'metaphysischen Bedürfniss.' " What this need may be is not spelled out in the passage—still less therefore whether or not Nietzsche regards it as a genuine need.[38] But some change in us, in our most basic make-up, would seem to be required if we are to become capable of such an affirmation as Nietzsche demands. That affirmation is a "Jasagen ohne Vorbehalt, zum Leiden selbst" among other things, a "Ja zum Leben" from which nothing that is, is excluded or dispensable; it demands that we would have nothing otherwise than as it is, "vorwärts nicht, rückwärts nicht, in alle Ewigkeit nicht," that we not merely bear what necessity imposes upon us, but even love it.[39] But all of us affirm some things in life and deplore others, even when we understand and accept the necessity of them.[40] And it is difficult to see how we could cease to do this, so long as we remain in contact with life as it is lived, rather than merely observed.[41] We are compelled to conclude that this demand of Nietzsche's, as a basis for any happiness he should

---

35. *Ecce Homo*, "Also sprach Zarathustra," 1, "Die Geburt der Tragödie," 3.

36. Schlechta vol. I, pp. 477–478 [aphorism 37].

37. *Ecce Homo*, "Menschliches, Allzumenschliches," 6.

38. Compare "die Übersetzung der Moral in's Metaphysische" in *Ecce Homo*, "Warum ich ein Schicksal bin," 3 with "Warum ich so klug bin," 10, as well as *Menschliches, Allzumenschliches* (Schlechta vol. I, pp. 686–687) [aphorism 476].

39. *Ecce Homo*, "Die Geburt der Tragödie," 2, "Warum ich so klug bin," 10.

40. Contrast *Ecce Homo*, "Also sprach Zarathustra," 6.

41. Compare *Ecce Homo*, "Die Geburt der Tragödie," 3: "Das Jasagen zum Leben . . . als Brücke zur Psychologie des *tragischen* Dichters"; compare also *Jenseits von Gut und Böse*, 56.

wish to hold out to us,[42] is no more possible than the basis that had been suggested by Rousseau is satisfactory.

Yet, so far as I am able to observe, a change has taken place in us, if not in our basic make-up—and that, at least in part, through the very "discussion" regarding happiness whose course I have tried to sketch. I have in mind the looseness, to which I referred at the outset, with which we are now wont to use the term "happiness." What is the meaning of this change? What has happened when a term hitherto applied solely to objects of the highest sort—let us take "love" as an example—comes to be applied regularly to objects—or, in our example, to passions and experiences—of a much lower sort? To say that the meaning of the term has then changed is true, but not simply true; and it is altogether insufficient for capturing the phenomenon. For the meaning of a term is determined not merely by the objects to which it is applied, but also by the way in which we identify those objects as members of a class, that is, by the associations that we attach to them or by the place that we give them in the economy of human life or of the whole. The application of an old term to new objects amounts therefore to the claim that these objects meet the old criteria, that they are not unworthy occupants, as associates or successors, of the place that their predecessors had occupied. Moreover, so long as this claim remains implicit, as it usually does, a mere implication of the altered usage, the user of the term in the new way feels himself under no obligation to confront the new with the old objects in order to determine whether the claim is justified. In other words, an innovation is made whose significance is at the same time denied. And in this way we conceal from ourselves a loss, the acknowledgment of which would pain us, indeed, but for that very reason prompt, perhaps, an effort sufficient for recovery. This, then, is what I wish to suggest regarding the looseness of the contemporary use of the term "happiness": that we conceal from ourselves, by that usage, the fact that we have lowered our sights from a high and demanding—but perhaps sufficient—goal to the many lesser goals that we now pursue under this banner, goals that cannot possibly satisfy any human being worthy of the name; that, by the retention of the high term, we conceal from ourselves the insufficiency of these successor goals and therewith the deepest cause of our dissatisfaction with ourselves and with life; and that by concealing this cause, we do away in advance with any effort to remove it.

____

42. See as well *Also sprach Zarathustra,* "Zarathustras Vorrede," 3.

But even if all of this is so, what has any of it to do with such great figures as Hobbes, Rousseau and Nietzsche and their rather complicated relation to the teaching on happiness developed by Plato and Aristotle, the classical teaching? It is to this question that I wish now to turn in the last part of my paper.

The simple answer, I believe, is that Hobbes—in denying the possibility of happiness as the classics had conceived of it—and Rousseau and Nietzsche—in seeking and in failing to provide demanding alternatives to the classical conception—all worked together, in effect, to undermine our faith in any high notion of happiness. And the very common weakness just alluded to, which leads us to accept a hard conclusion that we regard as unavoidable, while at the same time denying that we accept it, did the rest. This suggestion would mean, then, that even Nietzsche contributed to a result that he warned us against more passionately and eloquently than anyone before or since.[43]

But the suggestion itself, this simple answer, is in need of some elaboration. The classical teaching had been meant to articulate what we all somehow already know or at least sense. This has already been mentioned; but what has not yet been sufficiently stressed is what—given that there is no greater power on earth than good and evil ("Von tausend und einem Ziele")—follows from it. Insofar as it merely articulates what we ourselves already somehow know, the classical teaching brings to light what is known within a moral horizon or intelligible within such a horizon. Aristotle makes this clear in his *Nicomachean Ethics* by indicating that he addresses that work as a whole, and therewith its teaching on happiness in particular, primarily to those who have had a decent upbringing, that is, to those who can be expected to be preeminently moral human beings.[44] And Plato shows us in the *Republic* the difference between such auditors or readers and others, whose moral foundation is less sound, the difference between them regarding happiness in particular, by letting us see and hear how the cynical rhetorician Thrasymachus, on the one hand, and the noble youth Glaucon, on the other, conceive of happiness.[45] We should also note in this connection that the only philosopher

---

43. Ibid., 5.

44. *Nicomachean Ethics* 1095b3–13; compare 1095a2–13 as well as 1098a33–b8.

45. Compare *Republic* 344a4–c4 with what is implied by 358b4–7 and 361e4–362a2 about what Glaucon wishes to be shown; compare further, on this difference between the two types of men, *Theaetetus* 177b1–7 and context.

to attempt, so far as I am aware, in the modern centuries to restore the classical teaching on happiness in its integrity, is primarily known for his efforts to reestablish the credibility of classical natural right, that is, of the classical moral teaching. For, as Aristotle had suggested, if there is a good greater and more perfect than the individual good, it is also more noble and more divine to bring it about.[46] Such a good—he is thinking in particular of the good of the political community—would be one not subject to the vagaries of individual good or ill fortune.[47] And as Strauss says, going still further in the same direction, "The insecurity of man and everything human is not an absolutely terrifying abyss if the highest of which a man knows is absolutely secure."[48]

Hobbes, too, was of course a teacher of natural right. But he built his teaching on an individualistic and even hedonistic foundation. The state of nature as he conceives of it is a state in which human beings are "without all kind of engagement to each other,"[49] and the passions are all self-regarding.[50] Rousseau took over this foundation. The state of nature is for him one in which men appear to have "entre eux aucune sorte de relation morale";[51] and while he modifies Hobbes' account of the passions by the introduction of pity,[52] the very injunction that he attributes to pity—"*Fais ton bien avec le moindre mal d'autrui qu'il est possible*"[53]—shows that this modification leaves the Hobbesian basis untouched in its essential point. On just this point, Nietzsche, who insists in *Ecce Homo* "Es giebt *weder* egoistische, *noch* unegoistische Handlungen,"[54] is less clear than the two earlier thinkers; but this did not prevent him from declaring more loudly than they had done his break with traditional morality. Now, Hobbes apparently saw immediately that the break with the classical moral teaching entailed necessarily that one break also with the classical

---

46. *Nicomachean Ethics* 1094b7–10; 1129b17–19 and 25–29.

47. Compare Ibid., 1100b12–13 and following.

48. Leo Strauss, *Spinoza's Critique of Religion* (New York: Schocken Books, 1965) p. 11.

49. *De Cive* VIII 1.

50. See, for example, *The Elements of Law,* Part I, chapters 7–9.

51. *Discours sur l'inégalité,* Meier, ed., p. 134.

52. Ibid., p. 140.

53. Ibid., p. 150.

54. *Ecce Homo* "Warum ich so gute Bücher schreibe," 5; compare "Warum ich ein Schicksal bin," 7 on the term "Selbstsucht": "das Wort schon ist verleumderisch!"

teaching on happiness;[55] whereas his successors attempted, in the ways that have been suggested, to discover or construct satisfactory alternatives on the new Hobbesian basis—their efforts falling short of the goal. Indeed Hobbes, who took up the classical teaching in the terms in which it had been put forth, remained in a manner closer to that teaching, even in flatly rejecting it, than they did. One could still learn from him what happiness originally meant.

My argument has attempted to establish such a link between the classical teaching on happiness and the classical moral teaching as amounts to the dependence of the former on the latter. On the chance that someone may regard this result as true but trivial—a judgment with which I would not agree—I will conclude by pointing to a clearly non-trivial implication of it. I alluded earlier to the difficulty of the task of supplying content to the classical vision of happiness. Perhaps the most impressive effort to do so culminates in the treatment of the theoretical life as the happiest one in chapters seven and eight of the tenth and last book of the *Nicomachean Ethics*. Now, Aristotle does indeed present the theoretical life there as a life in accord with virtue; but this virtue, while it is said to be the highest one, is no longer moral virtue.[56] As a sensible human being living among human beings, the theoretical man will of course choose to act also in accord with moral virtue.[57] But the question could still be raised of the point of view from which he complies with the moral demands. One of the advantages of the theoretical life over the moral or political life that Aristotle mentions is that it is less in need of equipment or external goods for the exercise of its proper activity: "for the generous man will need money for performing the generous actions and the just man for repayments," for example, and in general the greater and nobler the actions, the more goods of this sort they require; but for the one engaging in theoretical activity, such goods are not only of no use but are even impediments.[58] In other words, the question can be raised whether theory or philosophy

---

55. *The Elements of Law*, Part I, chapter 7.6.

56. Compare *Nicomachean Ethics* 1177a12–18 with 1178a9 and following.

57. Ibid., 1178b5–6.

58. Ibid., 1178a23–b5.

is not "the actualization of a human possibility which, at least according to its own interpretation, is trans-historical, trans-social, trans-moral, and trans-religious."[59] But if one should be compelled to accept this characterization of the theoretical life, with what right could one still speak of the happiness of that life?

As I began with a story, so I would like to end with one. Xenophon tells us of a number of remarks made by Socrates in responding to the sophist Antiphon, who had raised the question whether Socrates is not a teacher of misery rather than happiness. After Socrates' first remark, Antiphon had renewed his attack by drawing an unflattering inference from the fact that Socrates does not charge those associating with him a fee. Socrates' response therefore pointed out to him that, according to the Athenians, what nobility demands of one in teaching is similar to what it demands in love—and these are of course demands with which the conduct criticized by Antiphon complies. But Socrates also added a postscript to this remark:

> But I myself, Antiphon—as another is pleased by a good horse or dog or bird—so am I pleased, and still more, by good friends; and if I have something good, I teach it, and I put them together with others from whom I believe they will be helped in some respect towards virtue; and the treasures which the wise men of old left behind in the books they wrote I go through, reading them in common with these friends. And if we see something good, we take it out, and we hold it a great gain if we become friends to one another.

At this point in his text, Xenophon makes a comment of his own which we may render as follows: "To me, hearing (the speech that concludes in this way), he seemed to be himself happy and to lead the hearers (of it) to moral virtue."[60]

---

59. Leo Strauss, *Natural Right and History* (Chicago: The University of Chicago Press, 1953), p. 89.

60. *Memorabilia* 1.6.2–14.

17

What Xenophon Learned from Socrates about Philosophy and the Philosophic Life

My intention is to summarize—for you and for myself—the results of a recent re-reading of the four writings which Xenophon devotes wholly to his presentation of Socrates: the *Memorabilia*, the *Oeconomicus*, the *Symposium*, and the *Apology of Socrates to the Jury*. Since Socrates was for Xenophon, as he was for Plato, *the* philosopher, Xenophon's presentation of Socrates is at the same time his presentation of philosophy as such. And therefore a lecture on this subject would ordinarily start—or would seem properly to start—from a consideration of why we should be concerned with philosophy (and hence with anyone's presentation of it) to begin with. And even the circumstance, which may well be the present circumstance, that all of the parties to the discussion are already interested in philosophy would not exempt the speaker from the obligation to attend to this primary task. For the circumstance, as it may be, that we are already interested in philosophy does not relieve us of the necessity to make clear to ourselves the grounds of our interest—so that we can address the question of their soundness. Yet we cannot even pose that question adequately, if we lack a clear and otherwise adequate grasp of what philosophy is. And here the fact that we, for the most part, pursue our interest in it by studying writings left behind by thinkers of the past might give us pause. In my own field of political science, for example, we study not so much philosophy (political philosophy, in this case) as the *history* of political philosophy, as if the thing itself were a matter not of present experience but, at best, of recollection. And, in light of the possibility that this may prove to be true today more generally—since, as

399

Plato assures us, the august name retains its allure even in the absence or decay of the thing (*Republic* 495b8–d7)—we perhaps do well to put off the primary task until, having done our best to activate our recollection by the appropriate historical studies, we are in a better position to take it up. The question could still be raised of the suitability of Xenophon's Socratic writings for inclusion in a course of historical studies intended to activate a recollection of philosophy. Why not, for example, go directly to his contemporary Plato, a fellow student of Socrates, whose unique place in the esteem of their master was very graciously and delicately acknowledged by Xenophon himself? (*Memorabilia* III 6 beginning; compare III 7 and III 8.) The beginning, at least, of an answer may perhaps be found in the very aspect of Plato's superiority that must strike every reader of the two authors at first glance: his superior power to *move* us. For everyone who turns to the Socratic writings of Xenophon, on the basis of some familiarity with Plato, is bound to experience a degree of disappointment on this score. And yet this same Plato has insisted that genuine philosophy, genuine attachment to philosophy, presupposes a "conversion of the soul" (*Republic* 521c5–8, 532b6–d1), which is most difficult and even painful to undergo (515e1–4). Is that conversion not likely to be, in the same degree, rare? And, in that case, what makes philosophy so broadly moving, so attractive to us in Plato's writings is hardly likely to be simply a straightforward depiction of it, a depiction of it as it is in itself, as it must be presumed to present itself to those who have already undergone the conversion in question. Is it not possible, then, that the reason that Xenophon's presentation of philosophy moves us less than Plato's does is not so much lack of rhetorical power on Xenophon's part as that he has been more scrupulous or fastidious, less willing to compromise, to deck out his mistress in spurious adornments, than Plato was? Yet he might have been scrupulous and fastidious to the highest degree in this regard, and not altogether lacking in rhetorical power either, and still be found wanting in the decisive respect: that is, he may have *wished* (within the limits of the possible) to give a straightforward and unadorned depiction of philosophy, as it is in itself, but have been *unable* to do so. By way of a provisional response, let me have recourse to a story that he tells in one of his non-Socratic writings. A large boy with a small coat accosts a small boy with a large coat and compels the latter to exchange coats with him. The question was then put to a third boy by his teacher, who wished to test the boy's knowledge of justice, as to whether the bigger boy should be allowed to keep the coat that fit him. To the teacher it was clear that the culprit should not be allowed to profit from his illegal and coercive act; but his precocious pupil, at least, was aware of the difficulty of leaving the matter in such a state that neither boy had a coat that fit him (*Education of Cyrus* I 3.16–18). In other words, the boy to whom the teacher put his question was impressed, as Xenophon himself must have been, by the tension between the just, in the sense of the legal, and the fitting. And I would submit that an author who has grasped the basic elements of this grave problem—and who is, moreover, able to convey some of them to his readers with the simplicity and force, not to mention charm, that we witness here—is not likely to be any more deficient in the other qualifications required in the guide we need. But perhaps all of this—whether he was equipped, that is, to be our guide or not—will become more visible as we proceed.

I must begin with a qualification, or rather with somewhat of a clarification. I suggested that Xenophon may have wished to give a depiction of philosophy as it is in itself, "within the limits of the possible." Those limits, insofar at least as they were established by the laws of Athens—a rather easy-going country by the older standards—or by the laws of any other Greek or non-Greek country of the time, were narrow by our standards. For such laws forbid not only actions but also certain thoughts. Socrates, in particular, had been tried, convicted, and put to death by the Athenians on a charge whose more important part alleged that he did not believe in the gods that the city believed in. And, as Xenophon indicates, the Athenians were more broadly convinced of his guilt on this part of the charge against him—the part to which this allegation belongs—than on the other part, which accused him of corrupting the young (compare *Memorabilia* I 1.20 with I 2.1). Xenophon accordingly devotes the very first chapter of his longest and most comprehensive Socratic writing, the *Memorabilia*, to refuting the allegation that Socrates did not believe in god or gods (see I 1.5). Now the heart and soul of that refutation is a passage in which he attempts to draw a line between what Socrates was conversing about and investigating, and what his predecessors (and contemporaries) in philosophy conversed about and investigated (I 1.11–16; compare *Oeconomicus* 11.3 and *Symposium* 6.6–8). In other words, Xenophon implies that his readers—if not also his fellow Greeks, more generally (compare Plato *Apology of Socrates* 18b1–c3 and *Laws* 966e2–967a5 with *Memorabilia* I 2.31 and *Symposium* 6.6)—could be expected to equate philosophic activity as such with the holding of thoughts that were forbidden by law. Did Socrates, *the* philosopher, share the thoughts in question? Xenophon's answer is necessarily somewhat guarded. If we give ourselves up entirely to the drift of his argument in the first chapter of the *Memorabilia,* we receive the impression that its exoneration of his master leaves nothing to be desired. Yet to say, as Xenophon does toward the end of the chapter, that he wonders how the Athenians could have been persuaded of Socrates' immoderation regarding the gods (I 1.20) or to ask, as he does towards its beginning, what proof could have been used to show that he did not believe in the gods that the city believed in (I 1.2), is not yet to deny outright that there might have been such proof or that reasonable grounds of persuasion might have existed.

Since Xenophon attempts to draw a line between Socrates and the other philosophers, we cannot understand Socrates, as Xenophon presents him to us, without coming to some understanding of what the others were doing. According to Xenophon's indication, they were conversing about the nature of all things (or beings), investigating the state (or origin) of what the sophists call the "cosmos" and the particular necessities by which each of the heavenly things (or beings) comes into being—while Socrates apparently did not do this (I 1.11). No wonder, then, that the Athenians and others suspected them of atheism: as Xenophon informs us later on in the *Memorabilia,* Socrates discouraged those who associated with him in order to become perfect gentlemen (compare IV 7.1 with I 2.48) from becoming thinkers about the heavenly things (or beings), about the way in which the god contrives each of those things (or beings); and among his reasons for doing so was his belief that one does not please gods by looking into what they were unwilling to make clear (IV 7.6; compare IV 3.14). It would be wrong, however, to infer from this that the philosophers from whom Xenophon attempts to distance Socrates were so heedless or reckless as to disregard the danger that their investigations of the heavenly things (or beings) might be displeasing to the god or gods who contrive them. Rather, those philosophers assumed—what they tried also to show—that divine contrivance has had nothing to do with the coming-into-being of the world or with its actual state; these were to be traced instead to necessity, in one form or another, if not also to chance (compare I 4.4 with Plato *Laws* 889c1–2). Socrates, on the other hand, as Xenophon indicates more than once, tried to show those of his companions who needed to be shown it—for example, because they were not regularly performing the legally required worship (I 4.2)—that the whole cosmos is the product of divine forethought and agency, as one may infer from the signs of benevolent design manifest in the world around us (I

4.4–6ff., 4.13, 4.17; IV 3.3–4ff., 3.13). But this means that Socrates, too, gave some thought to the state and origin of what the sophists call the "cosmos": indeed, had he not done so, he could hardly have made the criticisms of those who were investigating these matters that Xenophon, both in the first chapter of the *Memorabilia* and elsewhere, asserts that he did make (I 1.11–16, IV 7.6–7; compare *Symposium* 7.4 as well as *Memorabilia* I 6.14 and IV 7.5). Nor, to come back now to that chapter, is it clear that Xenophon denies there that Socrates conversed about and investigated what the other philosophers were conversing about and investigating: what he says is that Socrates did not do this "as" or "in the way that" most of the others did (I 1.11). It is true that he insists at the end of the passage with which we are particularly concerned that Socrates was always conversing about and investigating (merely) the human things, like What is just? What is unjust? (I 1.16); but in a later restatement, at the beginning of a chapter devoted to explaining the Socratic instruction in dialectics, he admits that Socrates never ceased investigating what *each* of the beings is (IV 6.1).

Evidently, we must take a closer look at what the other philosophers were doing, if we are to reach a point from which we may be able to understand what Socrates had and did not have in common with them. Being or the beings, for example, were concerns also of the other philosophers. According to a criticism that Socrates made of them, their opinions in this regard contradicted one another: to some of them it seemed that being is only one, that nothing ever moves (or changes), and that nothing ever comes into being or perishes; while to others it seemed that the beings are unlimited in multitude, that they are all always in motion (or changing), and that they all come into being and perish (I 1.14). Now, Socrates took the reason for this divergence of opinion among those with the greatest pretensions to speak on these matters—those who concern themselves with, who investigate, the nature of all things or beings (I 1.11, 1.14)—to be that the discovery of the particular necessities by which each of the (heavenly [on the ambiguity of "heaven," see Aristotle *On the Heaven* 278b9–21]) things or beings comes into being is beyond human capacity (I 1.13; IV 7.6). And, as this implies, he understood the philosophers to have sought those necessities in the very beings under investigation: they had presumed that they would find them in being or in some beings or in some aspect or relation of beings. The necessities which they sought were "the causes" (IV 7.5; compare Plato *Phaedo* 96a6–10), the causes responsible for the coming-into-being of things and for their being the way they are: they sought these causes in the beings themselves—in being or some beings or some aspect or relation of beings. Moreover, by calling the causes "necessities," the philosophers implied that they could not be otherwise than what and how they were. The being or beings which are responsible for the coming-into-being of things, and for their being the way they are, are thus at the same time the fundamental facts or fact. But if they are, in addition, to be *knowable* as such, they must be more than mere facts, mere givens: both their responsibility (for the changing things) and their own unalterability must be intelligible in them. And it was on the extravagant, not to say mad (I 1.13f., IV 7.6f.), effort to discover this much in being or the beings that the first philosophers expended their prodigious powers. (Compare Aristotle *On Generation and Corruption* 317b29–31, *On the Heaven* 298b12–25, especially 22–23.)

It was an effort which, as we have seen, Socrates judged to have failed. And since he traced the failure not to any accidental shortcomings on the part of the philosophers, but to the impossibility of their goal, he cannot reasonably be supposed to have pursued that goal himself, even if he regarded it as in principle a desirable one. (Compare Maimonides on the intention of Aristotle: *The Guide of the Perplexed* II 19.) Yet, as we have also seen or been led to suspect, Socrates too was concerned with the nature of all things (or beings): even if his conversation concerned chiefly the human things, at any rate, he never ceased investigating what each of the beings is. And we inferred from this that his activity constituted not simply a break with what the philosophers were doing but also a continuation of it. In what, then, did the continuity consist? Since Socrates seems to have regarded wisdom as science or knowledge of the beings (IV 6.7), we can perhaps formulate our question more adequately as follows: what was it that he thought could be known of the beings, and in what point or points, if any, was what he sought to learn about them the same as what the philosophers sought to learn? According to Xenophon, Socrates associated knowledge of the beings with "dialectics," in the twofold sense of this term. For knowledge of what each of the beings is, was in his view what makes one able to explain the beings to others, or the foundation of dialectics as the art of friendly conversation (IV 6.1); while, as he also thought, such knowledge itself presupposes dialectics, in the more elementary form of separating the beings into classes or kinds—and he accordingly suggested that the very term for conversing (*dialegesthai*) had derived its meaning from a separating activity (*dialegein*) of this sort (IV 5.11–12). In investigating what each of the beings is, Socrates was investigating, then, not each individual being—each dog, for example—but each class of beings, in both its similarities with and its differences from the other classes. As Xenophon indicates with regard to his investigation of the human things, he was asking, for example, "What is just?"—which is to say: what is it, what characteristics or what character is it, that binds together all just things and makes them just, while at the same time distinguishing them not only from the unjust things but also from the pious things, the noble things, and so on? (I 1.16) And to ask this about "the just" is to ask what characteristics or what character just things must have, must necessarily have, if they are to be regarded as just. Moreover, the presence of (any given) characteristics, or elements of the characters of things, entails the presence of certain other characteristics or elements—just as their presence excludes the presence of certain others. And it does so, in some cases, with a necessity as intelligible as the necessity with which, to take this example, the squareness of a square excludes the commensurability of its diagonal with its side. Now, when they sought to discover the causes of all things, understanding those causes in terms of necessity, the philosophers were seeking to understand the limits of all things, what determines of anything whether it can come into being or not and how it can be. And as we have now begun to see, Socrates' investigations, too, led toward or to the discovery of necessities. Was the discovery of them not also the intention of his investigations, just as the discovery of the necessities they sought was the intention of theirs? Is it not here, in this point, that we find the continuity that constitutes their enterprise as one enterprise—here, in the concern, not to say preoccupation, with the necessary, the possible, and the impossible? To suggest as much is not to deny that the necessities sought by the first philosophers were of a more fundamental kind than those sought by Socrates. Nor is it to deny that, insofar as he confined his attention, as he apparently did, to necessities that are more or less fully intelligible to us (Aristotle *Metaphysics* 996b13–14), he unavoidably left open alternatives that they sought to foreclose. This is the reason, for example, that he could plausibly argue, as they could not, that the whole cosmos is the product of divine forethought and agency. But even when he made the case for such an origin of the world, and therewith for the role of choice in its design, Socrates did not forget the results of the investigations that both distinguished him from and linked him to his predecessors (compare Aristotle *On the Parts of Animals* 642a24–29). As one can perhaps say, his awareness of the limits inherent in the characters of things made him appreciate all the more the wisdom of the divine contrivances that made the best use of the possibilities which those limits circumscribe (consider, for example, I 4.6).

It is not entirely misleading to call such appreciation Socrates' piety (compare the use of "daimonion" in IV 3.14–15 and I 4.2 and 4.10 with that of "daimonia" in I 1.12: the "daimonic" things are the natural things; compare Aristotle *On Generation and Corruption* 333b20–22). Was it that same appreciation that made the wisdom which fostered it, his own wisdom, attractive to him? (IV 5.6 beginning) Or was this wisdom—the core of which is a knowledge of limits, of what is necessary, possible, and impossible—attractive to him chiefly or exclusively on some other ground? It is obviously not sufficient to say, in answer to this question, that knowledge or science is as such knowledge of necessity, since any alleged knowledge of the merely changeable must be as transitory as its object (Aristotle *Posterior Analytics* 71b9–16, *On Generation and Corruption* 337b35–338a2); for the question could then be directed to knowledge or science itself: what is it that makes knowledge as knowledge, as it is and must be, even apart from any utility that might be derived from it (I 1.15), attractive—attractive to man as man or, at any rate, to some men? That Socrates was one of these men seems to have been clear beyond any shadow or possibility of doubt, as we can see from the very fact that his investigation of the beings was an unceasing one. What was it, then, that rendered the knowledge which he pursued in this investigation so attractive to him as to have called forth his extraordinary effort?

To ask this question is the same, almost the same, as to ask what (in addition to the strength of his nature) prepared Socrates to lead a life of unceasing investigation of each of the beings. And, according to a hint of his that Xenophon conveys to us, what prepares one for the philosophic life is a certain investigation of the human things (I 1.12). It was no doubt partly for this reason that Socrates was apparently always conversing about the human things: always asking, for example, What is just?—so that it appeared that he never got to the bottom of the matter (IV 4.5–6 and I 2.37 as well as *Symposium* 4.1; but compare *Memorabilia* I 2.36). Now Xenophon is rather sparing in what he lets us see directly of this preliminary Socratic investigation (I 4.1, compare IV 2.11–21 as well as I 2.39–46); but, just as he has given us a rather straightforward (unadorned) depiction of philosophy (including Socratic philosophy) or of its core, he gives us also a rather straightforward (unadorned) portrayal of the Socrates who, having completed the necessary preliminary, engaged in the philosophy so depicted. And perhaps it was the restraint referred to that permitted Xenophon to be so comparatively bold or generous in these other respects. However that may be, in the last part of my talk I will try to say something about his portrayal of this Socrates.

For this purpose, it will be necessary to turn from the *Memorabilia*, on which I have largely been relying hitherto, to his three other Socratic writings. The reason has been very beautifully explained by Xenophon's greatest commentator: the *Memorabilia* is devoted to the defense of Socrates rather than to portraying him *tout court* (Leo Strauss, *Xenophon's Socratic Discourse*, pp. 85–86)—in the first place to proving that he was not guilty of the charge on which he was condemned to death. (This is why, incidentally, it had to consider, as comprehensively as it did, his thought: he had been condemned, as we saw, not least on account of his thought.) In the second place, the *Memorabilia* tries to show that Socrates was exceedingly helpful to his companions. Now one cannot help another, in any profound respect, without being of a certain quality oneself. And if the *Memorabilia* has been given by Xenophon the task of showing us Socrates as helper, it is not unreasonable to suppose that it has been left largely to the three other works to show us the man himself.

The largest and most important of these is the *Oeconomicus*, which purports, as its title indicates, to present to us a model economist. And what must surprise us about the work—as the suspicion more or less gradually gains hold of us that this is the case—is that Socrates himself is the model economist to whom the title points. For what this proves to mean is not just that Socrates had reduced his needs to a minimum, so that he could get by on a very little income (*Oeconomicus* 2.2–4, *Memorabilia* I 3.5), nor that he had managed to find the most convenient source of the income that he did need (*Oeconomicus* 2.8 and 1.14), but also and above all that his whole outlook was somehow or in some respect an "economic" one. There had been hints of this fact already in the *Memorabilia*: in a conversation that Xenophon reports him there as having had with an old war veteran, for example, whom the Athenians had passed over in their election of generals in favor of an outstandingly successful businessman. Socrates' attempt to reconcile the veteran to his electoral loss or to soften, at least, his anger against his fellow citizens, takes the form of a defense of their choice that culminates in the admonition not to despise economic men: "for taking care of private matters differs only quantitatively from taking care of public ones" (III 4.12; see also II 10.4 and 5.2–5 as well as III 9.4; compare *Oeconomicus* 13.4–5 with 21.2–5 and 21.11–12). In the *Oeconomicus* itself, after leading his first interlocutor to define property as whatever is beneficial to oneself (1.7), Socrates goes on to make clear that what renders anything beneficial is the knowledge of how to use it (1.8 and following), with the result that all things become the property of the knower. (The furthest consequence of this line of reasoning is indicated, if not reached, at 1.15.) And speaking in his own name, later on, to another interlocutor, whom he has asked to instruct him in the art of farming, he explains in the following manner where he wishes the instruction to begin: "What I think I would be pleased to learn first—since it is particularly appropriate for a man who is a philosopher—is how, if I should wish it, I might by working the earth get most barley and most wheat" (16.8–9 and 15.3; compare Plato *Hipparchus*). Are we not forced to conclude, then, that Socrates himself associates the economic outlook, of which Xenophon's *Oeconomicus* makes him the model representative, with the outlook of the philosopher as philosopher, or of philosophy as such?

To this the objection might be made that the model economist to whom the title of the *Oeconomicus* points is not Socrates but rather his instructor there—in both farming and other matters—the perfect gentleman, Ischomachus. And, if this is the case, we have misinterpreted as well the character or nature of the economic model that the work holds up to us. For there are significant differences, not least in economic outlook, between the two men, as can be seen from an exchange which they have concerning wealth. When Socrates asked Ischomachus, who was quite wealthy, whether it bothers him that his efforts to increase his wealth increase also the troubles that he has in attending to it, the latter replied (in effect) that he welcomes them: "for I think it pleasant Socrates," he continued, "to honor the gods magnificently and to aid friends, should they need anything, and that the city, for my part, should lack no adornment for (want of) money" (11.9; compare *Memorabilia* I 3.3 as well as IV 3.16–17). Moreover, Socrates himself acknowledged Ischomachus' superiority—and that could appear to include the superiority of his economic outlook (7.15)—in advance. He presented himself to Ischomachus, at any rate, as indeed poor but possessed of a good nature and therefore capable of becoming a good man: once he has learned what he can from the account of Ischomachus' life that he requests of him, Socrates will attempt—starting tomorrow, a good day for making a start toward virtue—to imitate him (11.3–6; see also 11.10–11 and 11.19–20). Yet, as the very structure of the *Oeconomicus* shows, no such attempt was ever made. Socrates narrates to his first interlocutor, a young man named Critoboulus, the conversation which he had had at some time in the past with Ischomachus (6.12–17);

and he reveals enough of himself in the preliminary conversation with Critoboulus to let us see that the Socrates who speaks there is no different from the Socrates who had presented himself, as in need of improvement, at some time in the past to Ischomachus. (Consider again, in this connection, especially 2.2–8, and compare 20.14–15.)

But I must correct myself at once: there is one respect, and that not an insignificant one, in which the Socrates who speaks to Critoboulus differs from the one who had approached Ischomachus. The older Socrates knows, as he could not have known prior to his earlier conversation, that he is superior to Ischomachus. (See in particular 20.29 together with 11.22–25; 20.29 supplies in advance Socrates' commentary on the claim that Ischomachus makes at 21.5 and 21.11–12: Socrates is superior to Ischomachus in self-knowledge.) It was, as one can say, the discovery of his superiority in the course of that earlier conversation that accounts for the fact that he has made no subsequent effort to imitate the perfect gentleman. This might seem to raise the question of why it was necessary for Socrates to establish or to confirm his superiority to Ischomachus in the first place. But this question presupposes—what Socrates himself did not presuppose—that everything, or almost everything, is permitted. The older perspective, which Socrates shared, was given powerful expression by a passing remark in the *Nicomachean Ethics* which modern translators of the work, almost without exception, cannot bring themselves to render literally. "The law does not command it," Aristotle says there of an action he is in the course of discussing, "and the things that the law does not command, it forbids" (1138a6–7). Socrates could not know, then, prior to a most thorough examination not only of the law itself (compare *Memorabilia* I 2.33–34 and context with I 2.39–46), but also of what its spokesmen say on its behalf (*Oeconomicus* 7.16 and 7.29–31 together with 6.14–17), whether his own activity was not a forbidden one. And it was no doubt for this reason, too, that he was always, so to speak, conversing about the human things.

But I have allowed myself to stray for a moment from the difficulty which is still, or now more than ever, before us—now that we no longer have any basis for dismissing out of hand Xenophon's indication that Socrates associated the economic outlook that he is made to represent in the *Oeconomicus* (among other places: compare *Symposium* 3.10 with *Memorabilia* I 2.56) with the outlook of philosophy as such. The difficulty, or the challenge, is to come to grips with what we cannot dismiss: to see what, if anything, can justify the view ascribed to Socrates, and to consider what consequences his holding it may have entailed. It is with respect to the latter of these questions that the two Socratic writings of Xenophon which remain to be looked at, the *Symposium* and the *Apology of Socrates to the Jury*, may be of some help.

Xenophon's *Symposium* is undoubtedly the most charming of his Socratic writings, if not also the most charming work simply that Greek antiquity has bequeathed to us. And this is due in no small part to the fact that the atmosphere in which the speeches and deeds of its characters take place—for the *Symposium* is concerned with the deeds of its characters still more than with their speeches (1.1)—is a thoroughly erotic one. The occasion portrayed is a dinner party given by a wealthy man, whose credentials as a gentleman are not above suspicion (consider 8.12 in light of 8.3), for his favorite, a young athlete (who is accompanied to the feast by his father). The presence of the boy, together with that of some of the other guests as well as of a pair of young dancers, engaged for the evening's entertainment by the host, guarantees that beauty is always before the eyes of the participants, to claim the homage that is so universally accorded it (1.8–9, 5.9–10, 9.5). A high point, if not necessarily *the* high point, of the evening is a speech which Socrates addresses to the host in order to persuade him—with a view to his passion for that boy—that love of the soul is far superior to love of the body (8.12 and context). And the party—and the work—concludes with a performance by the two dancers which portrays the love for one another of a young married couple, and does this in so graceful and alluring a manner that it sends all of the husbands at the party, with the exception of Socrates, home to their wives (9.7 and context; compare 2.10). Now as this exception might help to confirm, the question of Socrates and love or of Socrates as lover has been at issue in the work all along (consider, for example, 4.27–28 and 1.3 as well as 4.23–25 and *Oeconomicus* 3.7). And, in this connection, we are forced to remind ourselves of Xenophon's statement at the outset that he has devoted his *Symposium* to the portrayal of *playful* deeds (of Socrates and others). Socrates says of himself in its course that he is unable to tell of a time in which he did not continue to be in love with someone (8.2): he fails to indicate that the object of his passion was always the same—to the contrary. And, if only for this reason, we may find it difficult to rid ourselves of the suspicion that his passions were not altogether serious ones. (Compare *Memorabilia* IV 1.1–2.) It is also worth considering here that the lesson conveyed by the beautiful and moving scene which brings the *Symposium* to a close is not in any simple harmony with the lesson conveyed by the speech of Socrates to which we have referred and which immediately precedes it: responsibility for that final scene is ascribed by Xenophon to a character who had attacked Socrates at an earlier stage of the proceedings (6.6–8—see also 4.52–54; compare 7.2–5 and Leo Strauss, *Xenophon's Socrates*, pp. 169–170 and 177–78). None of this is meant to deny, of course, that Socrates had a most erotic nature, nor that he knew a great deal about love (compare 8.1 and 1.10; *Memorabilia* II 6.28, III 11.16–17 and context).

The *Apology of Socrates to the Jury* is devoted to the task of explaining how, when he was summoned to trial, Socrates deliberated about his speech of defense and the end of his life (1). According to Xenophon, all of those who had written of the trial had remarked on the fact that Socrates spoke proudly or arrogantly there (literally, "talked big")—a course of behavior that had undoubtedly provoked many jurors and thus contributed to his conviction and condemnation to death (1; compare 14–15 and context). Xenophon's explanation of Socrates' pre-trial deliberation will therefore serve the purpose of showing that Socrates' "talking big" in his speech was appropriate to his thought or intent in its regard (2): that is, it will serve the purpose of explaining also Socrates' behavior at the trial, which would otherwise appear rather thoughtless (1). And the explanation of that behavior is apparently to be found in a belief of Socrates that death was then (he was about seventy years old at the time) more choiceworthy for him than life (1, 5–9, 23, 27, 33). Now, the particular task that Xenophon has assigned to his *Apology of Socrates to the Jury* did not require him to include in it—what Plato purports to give the reader of his *Apology of Socrates*—Socrates' entire speech of defense: it was enough for Xenophon to provide as much of the speech as will serve to make clear the thought or intention of the speaker (10 beginning) or his overriding concern (22). But the concern which Xenophon eventually claims to have shown in this way to have been Socrates' overriding one, is the concern neither to be impious toward gods nor to come to sight as unjust toward human beings (22). It may be, then, that Socrates was somewhat less eager to die than Xenophon had apparently taken him to be—or than Xenophon's authority, so to speak, in his *Apology*, a man named Hermogenes, did take Socrates to be. (Consider the "perhaps" which is added at *Memorabilia* IV 8.8 to its version of *Apology* 6.) It may be that death is a sufficiently grave matter to give one pause in its regard even at Socrates' relatively advanced age. He was certainly willing to die then—otherwise he could not have determined to behave at the trial as he did (23); yet that willingness is truly impressive precisely as (an) outcome and expression of an unusually active awareness of mortality on his part, of its significance to him. The *Apology of Socrates to the Jury*, at any rate, this shortest and least imposing of Xenophon's Socratic writings, is unusually rich in Socratic sayings which give evidence of the awareness in question (23, 27, 28; compare 33).

In the last part of my talk, especially, I have hardly done more than attempt to lay down some markers that may be of use in finding one's bearings in a difficult and largely unknown terrain. To do this, to do what I have attempted to do, is inevitably to stress some aspects of the works under discussion, while neglecting many others, and thus to present even those aspects which are touched upon in a distorting light. I hope that this difficulty will be no more than an additional incentive for you to have a look at Xenophon's Socratic writings for yourselves.

Part VI

An Undelivered Lecture

18

Theses Bearing on the Understanding of Aristotle's Natural Science

A Lecture prepared for delivery at the
Carl Friedrich von Siemens Foundation, Munich, Germany,
October 18, 2021.

Abstract

Hegel and Aristotle, for all of their differences, have this in common, that each attempted to restore to philosophy its original breadth of scope: the one in the face of the limitations imposed upon it by Kant, the other as against that which appeared to have been suggested by the practice of Socrates (*Parts of Animals* 642a28–31). Less visible, but perhaps at the root of those more or less parallel attempts, is their shared appreciation of the enigmatic character of our unreflective grasp of the world. By considering their similarities and differences as to this ordinary grasp of the world, the necessary starting point for a philosophic science, the lecture aims to bring to light an insufficiently appreciated aspect of Aristotle's natural science, as summarized in the six "Theses" of the title.

∼

The Theses which I wish to discuss with you this evening were compiled for my private use, as I began a third or fourth reading of Aristotle's *Meteorologica*. The *Meteorologica* is an important work. This is so not only because, in introducing it, Aristotle divulged the plan of his natural science as a whole, or the order of the works comprising it, but also because of the place which he gave the *Meteorologica* within that plan. It stands between the works (already written) "on the first causes of nature and on all natural motion, as well as [those] on the stars [that is, on the so-called fixed stars and the planets] whose order follows the upper [heavenly] movement and on the bodily elements, how many and of what sort [they are], and their changing into one another and on generation and corruption in general"—the *Meteorologica*, to repeat, stands between these works and those which Aristotle intends to write "in the manner indicated" on animals and plants. It is left open whether this is the manner that has already been indicated in those earlier works or rather one that will have been indicated in the *Meteorologica* itself (cf. 370b4). This question can be answered only on the basis of an adequate understanding of the work, and the *Meteorologica* is even more difficult to understand than is usually the case with works of Aristotle. Its announced theme is "what happens indeed by nature, but by a nature that is more disorderly than that of the first element of the bodies" (that is, than the nature ascribed to what is alleged to be the element of the heavenly bodies). Its implicit theme, if my suspicion is correct, is the true nature of body, or of what we take to be bodies, whether animate or inanimate. However that may be, it is surely striking that Aristotle makes a work of this character the gateway to his biological writings.

It was this work, then, which led me to compile these Theses—in an effort to find a standpoint from which one might approach the work and begin at least to understand it. But when they stood before me in their completed state, I began to wonder whether they might not be of more general interest. And so I am particularly grateful to Heinrich Meier for providing this forum for my own public introduction of them, a forum, moreover, which obliges me to accompany them with some such commentary as their introduction here requires. At the same time, in undertaking the attempt to fulfill this obligation, I am conscious of a weight of no common responsibility. For, as it seems to me, the Theses point to a ground for considering Aristotle's natural science to be the true natural science—not in every respect, of course, but not merely in its general approach, either: rather in his unparalleled grasp of a problem intrinsic to any such science. And it is no light matter, therefore, to say something worthy of them. I'll begin by reading the Theses, simply as they stand.

Theses bearing on the understanding of Aristotle's natural science

1. The largest part of the science about nature is about bodies and magnitudes and what concerns them (*On Heaven* 268a1–6).

2. We encounter bodies as the particular or individual beings that they are (cf. *Metaphysics* M10, *Posterior Analytics* B19).

3. We know them, each of them, by the qualities or attributes or "differentiae" (*On Soul* 423b27–29) that belong to it as the particular body that it is:

    > these attributes are the principles of (the sublunar) bodies (*Meteorologica* 339a13–14); there is no "common body" (*On Generation and Corruption* 320b22–23; cf. *Physics* 194b8–9), that is, no body that is simply "body," body as such.

4. —The attributes, however, belong to the particular body to which they belong, not merely as the individual that it also is but insofar as it is one among a number of bodies—

    > to which it is similar as well as different;
    > by which it is affected and which it in turn affects.

    In other words, it has these attributes not as it is one alone but as it is a part, in contact with other parts (bodies), a fact that makes each individual body, in a manner, also many (*On Heaven* 268b5–8).

    > (n.b. This remark applies not merely to the obviously relative attributes—large and small, heavy and light, etc.—but to those "essential" qualities that belong to the body as the being that it is, or to its form: cf. *Philebus* 14c1–15c3.)

5. Since to encounter any one body is therefore to encounter the multiplicity that is at once both internal and external to it, it follows that the sense perception by which we know its particular qualities or attributes is a discriminating or dividing faculty (*Posterior Analytics* 99b35).

> And if, as this suggests, body as body is a correlate of sense perception (consider *Meteorologica* 341a12–15 as well as *On Soul* 423b27), it would follow that no body as body can be *the* substratum (*On Generation and Corruption* 319b14–21; compare *On Soul* 422b32–33 and context with 423b27).

6. It follows more generally that the stability of the being or form of any particular body or class of bodies depends upon the stability of the whole of which they are parts, its perfection, one can say (*On Heaven* 268b8–10 and context).

> Aristotle devoted his *Meteorologica* to the consideration of what occurs in the sublunar sphere according to a nature that is admittedly more disorderly than that of "the first element of the bodies" (338a25–339a5: consider, for example, 351a19–25, 356b4–5). We are to believe, however, that the changes he is compelled to discuss come about in accord with some order or regularity (351a25–26) or within a whole that is permanent, whose time will never fail (353a14–18; compare *Physics* 223a16–29). And the great efforts that he made to argue that this is the case are a lasting testimony to the importance he placed on this doctrine about which questions, as he well knew (*Topics* 104b7–8, 14–16, 105b24–25; compare *Physics* 252b27–28, *Motion of Animals* 699b21–31, 700a20–21, and 29–35, *Generation of Animals* 778a2–4), could be raised.

I.

The problem that Aristotle adumbrates in this way—I'm thinking now particularly of Theses 1–4—was lost sight of after him, so far as I know, until it was in a manner rediscovered by Hegel. And the Hegelian treatment of it, which differs in characteristic and revealing ways from that of Aristotle, is perhaps the best way for us to approach the latter. But the Hegelian treatment itself is best seen against the background of his stance on another problem, which indeed he does not confront directly—no doubt because he thought he had the solution to it already in hand—but which is, none the less, most relevant to his thought. To appreciate that "solution" with the necessary sympathy, as we must do if we are to take Hegel seriously, we must first consider the problem to which in its way it responds, on our own: the full gravity of that problem.

It is the problem posed by the Cartesian doubt, particularly as it bears on the question of sense perception: the doubt, or rather the outright denial (*Meditations*, "Response of the Author" to the 5th set of "Objections," to what is objected to the Second Meditation, #1 pp. 350f.) that what the senses give us as the world, as the world in which we live and breathe as ourselves part of it, is the world as it is truly, in itself so to speak. Now this denial is a very old story among those who concern themselves with knowledge or science. In a Platonic dialogue devoted to the question "What is science?" Socrates suggests to Theaetetus, the young mathematician after whom the dialogue is named, that all of the thinkers prior to himself, with the sole exception of Parmenides, held some such view as the following with regard to sense perception: that the color we call "white" for example—in other words, the "white" of anything we think of as white—is not anything outside of our eyes, nor even in our eyes, nor anywhere else such that one could assign to it a place; nor is it anything that has any stability, any independence of the momentary collision of we know not what, which produces, for that moment, what we regard as a perception (of white) via the senses (151e6ff.). So the denial of the truthfulness of the renderings of the senses is, to repeat, an old story; yet it did not have, among the ancients at least, the impact that it came to have in the wake of Descartes—neither upon ordinary life, which was altogether more removed from theory than it came to be later on, nor upon theory (the pursuit of knowledge) itself, which was taken in a different direction by Plato and Aristotle. But as to understanding its impact on the times with which we are concerned in speaking of Hegel (times which are in the decisive respect still our own), I believe we do not go wrong in starting from the admittedly somewhat later testimony of Nietzsche in *Jenseits*: "Auf welchen Standpunkt der Philosophie man sich heute auch stellen mag: von jeder Stelle aus gesehen ist die *Irrtümlichkeit der Welt*, in der wir zu leben glauben, das Sicherste und Festeste, dessen unser Auge noch habhaft werden kann . . ." (#34).

Now that this is a problem for life (cf. #10), one can judge, if one needs to, from the prominence that Nietzsche gives in the same work to the questioning of the value of truth and of the will to truth (#'s 1 and 4, e.g.). But whether this path leads to a genuine solution to *this* problem—for after all, as Plato had pointed out in the *Republic*, with regard to the good, at least, we want the real thing (505d5–9)—and whether even Nietzsche himself thought that it did—as already the Vorrede to *Jenseits* could lead one to doubt—the problem for science itself would remain.

But what precisely is the problem for science? Or, if the problem itself is evident, what is science to do in the face of the fact—what is taken to be the fact—that the world that it sets out to explain, that even Descartes set out to explain, this whole perceptible world, "totum hunc mundum aspectabilem" (*Principles of Philosophy* Pt. 4 #188 p. 315) is not the true world? Is it, simply, to admit, and to content itself with the admission that it concerns itself only with appearances, that its findings, the laws it develops, have bearing and validity only for appearances?—Hegel, for one, protested vigorously against this (Kantian) reinterpretation of science, which would reduce it to an allegedly true knowledge of untruth.—Or is science to seek with Descartes, who was after all less radical than his pre-Socratic precursors, to explain the appearances themselves (in other words, the perceptual manifold) by recourse to bodily causes that are taken to be real (*not* mere appearances) and that are seen or hypothesized to act on our bodily organs, also taken to be real, so as to produce the appearances, whose sole home as such is the brain (*Principles*, Pt. 4 #'s 188–199 pp. 315–323; cf. #'s 201 and 203–204 pp. 324f. and 325–327)?—Whatever else is to be said about this approach (to the problem he had raised, or raised again) suggested and pursued by Descartes himself and others—about its adequacy as an account of sense perception, about the feasibility of the task that it would impose upon a science that is to remain a science of "this whole perceptible world"—it, too, was not the path taken by Hegel.

The difference between Descartes and Hegel on this score can be illustrated by two quotations. The first is taken from Descartes' *Principles of Philosophy*, from the very section of it that we have been considering. The second is from Hegel's *Phenomenology*.

> Nihil enim inter naturae phaenomena est recensendum, nisi quod sensu deprehenditur. Atqui exceptis magnitudine, figurâ & motu . . . nihil extra nos positum sentitur, nisi lumen, color, odor, sapor, sonus, & tactiles qualitates; quae nihil aliud esse, vel saltem à nobis non deprehendi quicquam aliud esse in objectis, quàm dispositiones quasdam in magnitudine, figurâ & motu consistentes, hactenus est demonstratum. (*Principles*, Pt. 4 #199 p. 323)

> Es ist hiebei wesentlich, dies zu betrachten, dass die *reine Materie* nur das ist, was *übrig* bleibt, wenn wir vom Sehen, Fühlen, Schmecken usf. *abstrahieren*, d.h. sie ist nicht das Gesehene, Geschmeckte, Gefühlte usf.; es ist nicht die *Materie*, die gesehen, gefühlt, geschmeckt wird, sondern die Farbe, ein Stein, ein Salz usf. . . . (*Phenomenology*, ed. Hoffmeister p. 409)

It is a curious fact, to me at least, that Hegel does not seem to have looked upon his relation to Descartes as the contrast between these two passages suggests that he should have done: that, to judge from various remarks of his on Descartes, those in the Vorbegriff to the 1830 *Encyclopedia Logic*, for example, it was not the Cartesian *doubt* that impressed him in this regard. The reason is probably that he understood Descartes in the light of Spinoza: "Spinozism is related to Cartesianism simply as a consistent carrying out or execution of Descartes' principle" (*Lectures on the History of Philosophy 1825–1826* Vol. III p. 151). And it was Spinoza who had pointed to the solution to the doubt which Hegel adopted. For, as I intimated earlier, it is only by attributing to him the conviction that he had a solution to it ready to hand that we can understand his failure to stress a problem that hangs over us still today, however much we may try to ignore it or for the very reason that we try to ignore it. And how else, moreover, can we understand his insistence in the passage quoted, from rather late in the *Phenomenology*, that what we see, for example, when we see, are "the colors"—that is, the colors *in* the things of which they are the colors—an insistence that is so far from being called into question by the critical treatment of sense perception in the first two chapters of the work that it is, rather, already presupposed by that earlier treatment?

What Spinoza had suggested, then, is that a "mode of extension"—let's say, some extended thing—and the "idea" of that mode "are one and the same thing, but expressed in two ways" (*Ethics* Pt. II Prop. VII Scholium; cf. Hegel's *Logic* ed. Lasson Vol. I p. 100 and, for his association of Descartes with the Spinozistic principle that he adopts, *Encyclopedia Logic* #64, last paragraph, as well as the first item in #76). Now, to see the significance of this suggestion, we should consider the fact that Descartes himself had admitted, in confining the extension of the doubt that he was truly serious about to the limits within which we have been considering it, that no one "of sound mind" had ever doubted the existence of "some world" or of what we can call *some* external reality (*Meditations* pp. 15–16). And this is just what Spinoza in effect, and after him Hegel, did call into doubt (cf., in the *Encyclopedia Logic* #50, the response to the reproach to Spinozism that it is atheistic). The whole burden of the *Phenomenology*, as we can confirm from a number of Hegel's own references to the work in the *Logic*, is to show how consciousness (Bewusstsein), which is mind (Geist) as a knowing entangled in externality, frees itself from this entanglement: in plain terms, from the belief that its object is something external to it (Vol. I pp. 7, 35)—this freeing of consciousness from its contradistinction (Gegensatz) to its object (p. 29) being what pure science must presuppose (pp. 30, 32). But if the objects of consciousness, which include the objects of the senses (*Phenomenology* p. 398), are reduced to thought, or are thoughts, they are at once freed from that dangerous dependence on anything outside of and underlying them that could serve to render them suspect. And thus, however severe the critique they may be subjected to, they can be restored—and with them the world, the very world in which we believe we live—as a *stage* of thought, in accord with Hegel's promise early on in the *Logic* (Vol. I pp. 55–56) whose fulfillment is meant to be shown in its third and last part (Vol. II pp. 229, 231).

So far so good. But since the objects of consciousness are in fact subjected to a severe critique precisely by Hegel—I'll read here a comment that he makes on the claim that our consciousness of such objects constitutes a form "des unmittelbaren Wissens":

> Was das gleichfalls unmittelbare Bewusstsein von der Existenz *äusserer* Dinge betrifft, so heisst dasselbe nichts anderes als das *sinnliche* Bewusstsein; dass wir ein solches haben, ist die geringste der Erkenntnisse; es hat allein Interesse zu wissen, dass dies unmittelbare Wissen von dem *Sein* der äusserlichen Dinge Täuschung und Irrtum, und in dem Sinnlichen als solchem keine Wahrheit ist, das *Sein* dieser äusserlichen Dinge vielmehr ein zufälliges, vorübergehendes, ein *Schein* ist . . . (*Encyclopedia Logic* #76.3; cf. #51 toward the end, as well as *Phenomenology* p. 110).—

since, to repeat, this is the case, the question must arise of the basis of the *Hegelian* critique of the objects of the consciousness. That that basis can't be a critique of the senses as such, to which in part we owe them, we have already seen; and the passage just read in a back-handed way itself confirms this. Nor is it solely or even chiefly, as the passage could indeed seem to suggest, the claim to externality made on behalf of those objects—if not already by the objects themselves—that is at issue. Hegel sharply distinguishes his approach from that of a merely "subjective idealism" which, satisfied to reject the *external* reality of the objects or contents of our sensation and observation, our conceiving or thinking, fails to consider—that is, to consider critically—that content as it is in itself, a content which, unsubjected to critical examination, is thus left intact (*Logic* Vol. I p. 146). It is the content, then, of our consciousness or, more precisely, the categories by which we grasp it (cf. pp. 183–184 on the "richtigerer Weg") that are the preeminent focus of Hegel's analysis. And it was this focus which brought him back to or towards what Aristotle had already seen.

II.

What Hegel too saw, then, is that what is customarily distinguished as content from form is, in every case, already formed: that it is, in itself, as he says in the Vorrede to the second edition of the *Logic* (Lasson, Vol. I p. 18), "nicht formlos, nicht bestimmungslos." He saw, to turn now to his treatment of perception (Wahrnehmung) in the *Phenomenology*, that the objects of our perception are the things with their properties (Eigenschaften) or with what I called in the Theses their "attributes." But—and this is a second point, one emphasized by Hegel—these properties or attributes must themselves, if they are to be what they are, be of a determinate character, and this they could not be, if they were, each of them, entirely self-contained, if each had reference only to itself. Each of them has then the character that it has or is only insofar as it is "set against" what is other than it (p. 91). And, further, since it is with or by their properties or attributes that we perceive the things, the things that constitute our world, what is true of the former is true also of the latter: each of the things is not what it is by itself alone; it stands, precisely as the thing that it is, in a relation to what is other than it (pp. 98f.). But this means, further, that that other is, somehow, also immediately "on" or even "in" it, to borrow the formulations employed by Hegel later on in a somewhat different though related context (p. 124). This relation in which a thing stands to its other or others is the negation of its "Selbständigkeit" (p. 99; cf. *Logic* Vol. I pp. 100f.).

Hegel now drew the conclusion—we can call this the third point—that the thing "geht . . . durch seine wesentliche Eigenschaft zugrunde" (p. 99);

in other words, the very determination (by properties or attributes) that distinguishes it from others, or the self-contradiction that such determination according to him entails (p. 93), brings the thing to ruin. And, therefore, from the point of view of the thought, the understanding, that sees this, the sensibly perceived things are "Erscheinung" or "ein Ganzes des Scheins" (p. 110), a *world* of appearance, one can say.—But, however that may be, and whether or not this world, *our* world, could ever be restored to us as the world we take it to be (cf. p. 563), with this third point Hegel is no longer standing on ground that he shares with Aristotle.

For Aristotle, the thing remains—for all of the difficulty or obscurity involved in our apprehension of it, and even when we become aware of the difficulty—the particular or individual thing that we encounter among the sensibly perceived beings that constitute our world (cf. *Logic* Vol. II pp. 61f.). He would never have said, with Hegel, that "der Begriff als Begriff des Verstandes dasselbe ist, was das Innre der Dinge" (*Phenomenology* p. 120; cf. pp. 128–129). In this respect, he is closer to Kant, for whom, as Hegel more than once reminds us, the "existence" or "being" of a thing is "no real predicate," no Begriff that adds to our Begriff of the thing, but rather that through which, in the context of our "gesamten Erfahrung," we receive an object of perception (*Logic* Vol. I pp. 71 and 73, referring to *Kritik der reinen Vernunft* pp. B628–629): in other words, Aristotle does not deny the being of an external world. But for him, unlike Kant, the beings that we encounter in the way Kant indicates are not appearances, but rather the things themselves.

As this summary statement already indicates, this summary of his difference from Hegel with regard to what I called the third point or the conclusion that Hegel drew from the first two points, Aristotle must have differed from him also regarding the interpretation, at least, of those two earlier points where they share substantially the same ground. For Aristotle, one can say, the relativity of the properties or attributes of the things and of the things themselves—to one another as well as to us—does not detract from what one can call, if one wishes, their "Selbständigkeit" (that of the things, the attributes being mere aspects of the things); for the Selbständigkeit of each of them is that of something whose very being is *also* to be a part (Thesis 4). For this reason, too, then the problem rediscovered by Hegel does not bear for Aristotle on the existence of the things as the things that they are. It bears on their transparency. It is the problem of the resistance that they offer to our desire or wish to know them through and through. If we would know any thing as it is, we must know it as it is determined by its relation to what is other than it; but when we therefore ask what *it* is, the particular or individual thing, such that it enters into the relation that so determines it, we find it already determined by the relation in question.

Now if the particular or individual beings are the true beings, as Aristotle says not only in the *Categories* (2a11–19, 35–b6, 3b10–18) but also elsewhere (e.g., *Metaphysics* 1087a2, 21–24; cf. *On Soul* 432a3–5), and if it is these true beings that must be the ultimate first principles of demonstration and therefore of demonstrative science (*Posterior Analytics* 81a38–b2), then what Aristotle says toward the beginning of the *Posterior Analytics* about the indemonstrable first principles of demonstration is consistent, at least, with what we have seen of the resistance that these beings oppose to our attempt to know them. He says there, roughly, the following: that if it is through "the first things" that we know, and trust in what we know, then we must know and trust more in our knowledge of them, the first things themselves, than in our knowledge of what we know through them; but we cannot trust in them more than in what we know, unless we happen either to know them, too, *or* to be so disposed toward them as to be better off in their regard than if we knew them (72a30–34). For from what we have seen of the recalcitrance of the true beings to being known, we would have to grant that we *don't* truly know "the first things"; but, on the other hand, we are in a very real sense better off in their regard than if we did know them: they are the things we encounter every day in our least contestable experience, that of ourselves in the world that they, together with us, comprise (*Physics* 254a23–33; cf. *Phenomenology* p. 398).

As this implies, then, and as Aristotle's remark in the *Posterior Analytics* must have been intended to indicate, we do in a way know them. We know them by their properties or attributes, through which (all or some of them) they group themselves into the kinds or classes which are the most important of what we can call the proximate first principles of demonstration: the universals (see again *Posterior Analytics* 81a38–b2). The kinds or classes become visible to us in our speech, which they make possible, even or especially in our ordinary everyday speech. Hence the connection that Aristotle drew between the investigation that he conducted in the *Topics* into the "endoxa"—how to meet them in argument—and the treatment of the first principles of the sciences (101a25–b4). But the kinds or classes, too, are what they are by the relation in which they stand to one another and therefore to the whole of which they are parts. I am not concerned now with what this means for their knowability, for in that regard they have a source that is not available to the particular or individual beings from which, ultimately, they derive. I am concerned rather with their stability as the kinds or classes that they are, which is put in question by their dependence upon a whole whose stability is itself, as Aristotle indicates precisely in the *Topics* (among other places), not without question. In other words, Aristotle's insistence on the permanence of that whole is perhaps better understood as an indication of a problem, as was suggested in Thesis 6, than as an absolutely firm doctrine.

III.

Thesis 5 is less closely related to the other Theses than they are to one another. It raises a question about their theme, however, as they do in connection with its. The question that they raise is this: would not the problem that they adumbrate regarding the knowability of the (perceptible) bodies, the particular or individual things we have been speaking about—would not the same problem arise on the level of the substratum, the underlying natural cause or causes of the bodies, if they too are taken to be bodies or body-like? But this is a question that must be left, by me at least, unanswered. The question that Thesis 5 puts to the others is the following: if Aristotle distinguishes the bodies, as correlates of sense perception, from their underlying cause or causes, how can he continue to regard them as the true and truly external beings, as we have assumed throughout that he does? The answer to this question would require, in addition to a return to some points already made, a most thorough study of his infinitely rich and subtle treatment of sense perception in *On Soul* (*De Anima*) and its sequel, the *Parva Naturalia*. But that he *did* regard the bodies in this way—in other words, that our assumption as to his position was correct—can be seen from a summary comparison of his treatment with two well-known alternatives to it. And since our discussion of the Theses began from a consideration of the *problem* of sense perception, it is perhaps appropriate to conclude it with such a comparison.

The first alternative is the one we have already come across: the Cartesian attempt to explain our perception of the manifold sensible attributes or qualities of the bodies by recourse to their dispositions, or those of their insensible parts, in magnitude, figure and motion. The latter, only, are taken to be truly in the bodies and to be what produce in us what we experience as perception of the sensible manifold. In this approach, then, the perceptible world—which it remains, however, the aim of Cartesian science to explain—is no longer the true external world. It has also the defect pointed out by Locke in his *Essay Concerning Human Understanding*. With his distinction between the primary qualities of the bodies—again "bulk, figure, and motion"—and the "*Ideas* of sensible secondary qualities," which the primary qualities are taken to produce in us, Locke is himself a Cartesian regarding sense perception. But he had the candor to admit that those "Ideas" can in "no way [be] deduced from [the] bodily Causes" that are taken to produce them, "there being no conceivable connexion between any impulse of any sort of body, and any perception of a Colour, or Smell, which we find in our Minds" (pp. 558–559; cf. p. 545). To put this another way, to establish, however confidently, that there is such a connection is not yet to explain it, and therefore to fail to explain what it is meant to account for: perception as we in fact experience it.

The second alternative can be found in Heidegger's work *Die Frage nach dem Ding*. Heidegger poses there the question raised by Eddington's famous distinction between the two tables, that of our ordinary experience and the one as understood by modern physics: the question, Which is the true table? (p. 10) And he says, in what amounts to a response to it, "Wir nehmen den Standort in der alltägliche Erfahrung"—but with the "Vorbehalt," as he adds, "dass auch ihre Wahrheit einmal eine Begründung fordert" (p. 11; also p. 9). Now whatever that "Begründung" may be, what it is *not* emerges from remarks later on in the work, in a context that recalls the Eddington dilemma (pp. 163f.), remarks about the color of a thing as belonging to the thing: "findet sich da nicht das mindeste von einer Ursache, die eine Wirkung in uns auslöst" (p. 163) or, again, the color "gibt sich uns auch nicht als Ursache eines Zustandes in uns" (p. 164). For this will not suffice as a vindication of the color, or the colored thing, as *external* to us. As external to us, it is of course experienced as the cause of a "Zustand" in us, namely, that of our seeing it. But to fail to insist on the externality of the objects of our ordinary experience is to fail to take one's stand within the horizon of that experience.

It was here, then, that Aristotle did take his stand—but with full awareness of the obstacles to doing so, obstacles that led thinkers of the power of those we have been considering to dismiss, in whole or in part, the evidence of our most ordinary experience and to abandon the horizon constituted by it, departing in one direction or another, openly or in silence. And it is the manner in which he confronts those obstacles that confers on his treatment of sense perception its richness and subtlety. For in its most obvious outlines or contentions his treatment is straightforward enough. But even in beginning with these, as we must if we are to understand him, it is important to note what he does or suggests and what he does not even attempt to do. To conclude with an example that is perhaps more than an example, in accepting unambiguously the existence of an external world while, at the same time, ascribing to the things that constitute it the attributes or qualities that we are aware of through the senses, Aristotle puts himself under the obligation to say something of how the qualities of these (external) things are conveyed to us, such that we become aware of them. His general answer is that a motion originating in the qualities themselves affects the medium separating us from them, which medium in turn conveys the motion to the sense organ in question. But he doesn't attempt to determine much further the character of the motion itself, how it is produced, or the way in which it works on the sense organ. When he asks therefore in *De Sensu*, the first treatise of the *Parva Naturalia*, what each of the objects of the senses is, such that it produces in us the perception that it does (439a16–17), he speaks by way of answer not of what those objects do, but of what they are, what precisely the color is, for example, that we see. It is, in other words, the color—precisely as what it is—that is responsible for our perception of it. But this, the manner of its responsibility, must of course be properly understood.

I want to say, finally, only this: that one of the many things I love about Hegel is his appreciation of the greatness of Aristotle and that it was in that same spirit that this talk was conceived.

Bibliographical Note

Editions used that were not identified in the text are the following: for Descartes, those edited by Adam and Tannery; for Spinoza, by Gebhardt; for Locke, by Nidditch; for Nietzsche, by Schlechta; for Hegel's *Encyclopedia*, the Suhrkamp edition; for the *Lectures on the History of Philosophy*, the translation edited by Robert F. Brown and published by the University of California Press.

First Appendix: Hegel

Wir kommen eigentlich jetzt erst zur Philosophie der neuen Welt und fangen diese mit Cartesius an. Mit ihm treten wir eigentlich in eine selbständige Philosophie ein, welche weiss, dass sie selbständig aus der Vernunft kommt. . . . In dieser neuen Periode ist das Prinzip das Denken, das von sich ausgehende Denken. . . .

Les modernes au-dessous des anciens? Pour beaucoup de rapports sans doute, mais pour la profondeur et l'étendue des principes, nous sommes en général sur une ligne plus élevée.

The assertion of Hegel from which we begin (taken as quoted by Heidegger in the Hegel chapter of *Holzwege*, pp. 128f.), and which we understand to state the principal ground of the superiority to the ancients that, in the letter to Victor Cousin (*Briefe von und an Hegel*, Vol. III p. 223), Hegel claims for the moderns, finds a complement in a passage (in the Vorrede to the *Phenomenology*, pp. 48–54, ed. Hoffmeister) that he devotes to a critique of the form of sentence that we ordinarily use in the effort to express our thought. In a sentence of this form, predicates (one or more) are ascribed to a subject that as "ruhendes" (remaining what it is) is taken to be "der feste Boden" for those predicates—which, however, as "general" may of course be ascribed also to other subjects. But the critical point, both for Hegel and for us, concerns the subject itself. For in such a sentence the subject goes beyond (geht hinaus über) its predicates, those therein ascribed to it as well as any that might be added to them. In other words, the being or meaning of the subject, or its nature, is not exhausted (erschöpft) by its predicates, whether these are considered individually or collectively. Since it is preeminently a name, as (common) name, that designates the subject, the same point could also be put in this way: our awareness of the being or class of beings that we designate by some name—what we "see" somehow in our encounter with the beings that make up the class—is not exhausted by anything we may be able to say about them. And this is what Hegel does not want to grant. It is the ordinary sentence, precisely as thus understood, that is the target of his critique.

What he would replace it with—in philosophic use—is the "speculative sentence": a sentence in which the being, meaning, or nature of the subject *is* exhausted by its predicate, which thus becomes itself the subject.

More precisely, it is the dialectical movement of the predicate in which that "ruhende" subject "geht . . . selbst zugrunde"; and the "Darstellung" of that movement is to include nothing except "insofern es begriffen wird und der Begriff ist." But that "Darstellung" or, in other words, the dialectical movement itself has sentences—*ordinary* sentences—as its "parts or elements." Hegel seems to grant that there is a difficulty here that seems to be a difficulty of the "Sache selbst." He likens it to that which is met with in the customary form of proof, where the grounds on which the proof is based are themselves in need of proof, a proof which requires in its turn other grounds—and so on, without end. And he suggests that that difficulty arises because dialectics has been excluded from the form of proof in question: as a result, the understanding of what it is to prove something in philosophy is lost. Philosophic proof is then possible, according to Hegel. The reason is given in the context. In philosophic proof, the element of the proof is "der reine Begriff" (p. 48, ed. Wessel und Clairmont, correcting what is apparently a printing error in Hoffmeister). The proof has therefore a content that is through and through its own subject. There is no content that would stand as predicate in relation to a "zum Grunde liegenden Subject"—a predicate that, as we recall, would not exhaust the subject, so that something in or of the latter would remain without its reach. And it is by excluding this possibility (that proof must rely ultimately on something unproved) that Hegel is able to say that with the moderns—in the wake of Descartes, as Hegel understands him—the principle has become thinking itself, "das von sich ausgehende Denken."

But has he truly excluded it? Since the "dialectical movement," which is inseparable from or constitutes philosophic proof, has itself (ordinary) sentences as its "parts or elements," Hegel is obliged to add here the remark that "the sentence is . . . a merely empty form." But he has given us no reason in the context as to why we must accept that this is the case. We are free to wonder therefore whether it is not the ordinary sentence, rather than the "speculative" one, that is the cornerstone even of any genuinely philosophic or scientific understanding.

To see what this would mean, we must recall once more that in an ordinary sentence the subject, as designated by a (common) name, "goes beyond" any and all of its predicates. Yet it is by virtue of what we "see" somehow in or of the subject, even or precisely as it goes beyond its predicates, that we are able to ascribe to it predicates in the first place—and ultimately to form some "Begriff" of it, to define it. This amounts admittedly to the paradoxical suggestion that speech and intellectual grasp more generally rely on something in beings and their inter-relations that eludes speech and that we grasp with an awareness that doesn't rise to the level of intellectual grasp. But it can perhaps be rendered sufficiently plausible to be admitted as worth considering, by one or two examples. Socrates' first definition (in the *Meno*) of shape or figure, the definition he himself prefers, is that shape is that alone of the beings which happens to be always accompanying color (75b8–11). As we can see, the "definition" does not say what shape is but rather points to where we see or are aware of it, such awareness being, as we claim, the ultimate source of any definition that is truly such. Or when Hegel says in the *Phenomenology* that "Die *Zeit* is der *Begriff* selbst," whether or not the statement is true, its very intelligibility is dependent upon some prior awareness, however rudimentary, of what we call "time." (One might equally well have referred here to the *Logic* Vol. I p. 182, ed. Lasson, or the *Encyclopedia Natural Philosophy* #'s 257–258.) The first question to be asked therefore (as Socrates had indicated with his statement on shape in the *Meno*) is "Where do we 'see' it?" Is it as what there is more of in a slower motion than a faster one over the same distance, for example, that we are primarily aware of time or must we look elsewhere to find what we somehow already see of it? Whatever the answer to this question, the question itself in its general application points to the necessity of a very different beginning for science than that laid out by Hegel in his *Logic*. But however far we may be forced to depart from him, we will always be grateful for the clarity with which he lays out the problems, a practice and gift in which he is surpassed, if at all, only by Aristotle himself.

Second Appendix: Aristotle

A Free Rendering of *On Soul* Book III Chapter 5

Since it is necessary—just as in all of nature there is something that is the matter for each genus (this is what is all of those things potentially) but something different that is the cause and responsible for their making (having, in making them all, the relation to the matter in question which an art has to the matter it requires)—that there be, also in the soul, what correspond to these distinctions . . . [The sentence has not been completed: see the Bolotin translation, p. 119 n. 72. Moreover, the sentence which immediately follows it could give the impression of being its awkward, not to say ungrammatical, completion: see, for example, the Corcilius translation, p. 185. In this way, the author both conceals and points to what he has refrained from stating outright, namely, that the distinction to be drawn in the new sentence is not the one that its incomplete predecessor had ascribed to soul insofar as soul is a part, as it *is* also a part, of the "all" that is nature.] And the one intellect is such (that is, intellect) by becoming all things, the other by making all things—as some state of being like light, for in a manner light, too, makes what are potentially colors, actually colors. And this latter intellect [or, according to the first hand of two mss. as reported by Förster, "And in this way, the intellect"] is separable and free of affection and of admixture, as being, in its very being, actuality. For what makes or affects is always more honorable than what is affected, as is also the ruling principle [*archē*] than its matter. Knowledge in actuality is the same as the thing; what is potentially knowledge is prior in time in the particular individual, but not wholly prior in time; but it, what is potentially knowledge, is not sometimes perceiving, sometimes not perceiving. Only as separated is this intellect just what it is, and only as having been, or become, separated is it deathless and everlasting. We don't remember it, however, as it was before we were what we are—and as it is in itself—because in this state it is free of affection; and the intellect which is subject to affection, and without which there is no intellectual perception strictly speaking, is perishable (430 a10–25).

Third Appendix (With regard to the Abstract)

In reflecting on the results of a study, extending over several decades, of Aristotle's writings on natural science, it occurred to me to ask who the intended audience of those writings might have been. The answer that comes of course immediately to mind is "those who desire to know"; and Aristotle was for many centuries "the master of those who [wish to] know"—just as today, now that what are taken to be his scientific views have been discredited, serious people turn to other sources of knowledge. But is the desire or wish to know to be so readily taken for granted as this answer would seem to imply? At the very least, must one not ask what we wish to know, and how much, and why? Hegel, for example, is said to have remarked that we fully reconcile ourselves (beruhigen uns vollständig) to the conflicts between peoples of differing manners and beliefs, which we see in almost all great epochs, by the victory that we discern in them of the higher over the lower principle, a victory won by a courage that admittedly leaves nothing to those who have been vanquished (*Vorlesungen über die Ästhetik*, Vol. III, p. 353 [Suhrkamp]). But whatever other reservations we may have about the remark thus attributed to him by Hotho, what if the course of world history, "where for the ordinary eye only darkness, chance and confusion seem to prevail," fails to reveal itself even to the most penetrating as "the actual self-fulfilling of what is in and for itself rational" (ibid. p. 481)? What if there should be heard, precisely at the moment of history's achieved or anticipated completion, a wrong or false note? (Cf. *Vorlesungen über die Philosophie der Religion*, Vol. II, p. 342 [Suhrkamp]: "Allein, was hilft es? Dieser Misston ist in der Wirklichkeit vorhanden.") Would we, in that case, be so eager to follow its course, so eager for knowledge thereof?

Now, must not this same question, in suitably altered form, be put with regard to the pursuit of knowledge more generally? And this could well mean that a specific education was required, a moral-political education, to prepare for their task those very few who, in fulfillment of their nature, sought the truth with the unfettered openness of mind that stems from a certain inner freedom. Now Aristotle could assume that some of his readers would have undergone that education, the Socratic education, as he himself had done (*Rhetoric* 1399a28–32 together with 1366b36–1367a1; cf. 1371a33–34)—but not all of them. Nor could he afford to ignore the many who had not.

How then, in writings compelled to accommodate them, did he manage to speak to the very few who must have been closest to his heart? I won't try to answer this question here. To begin to do so, one would have to pay the closest attention to questions that he raises without supplying them with explicit answers, as well as to explicit "answers" that fail to resolve problems he had raised in developing the questions to which they claim to be the answers, and to other things of this sort. One would also have to make clear to oneself to which class of readers, as a rule, the scholars who mediate between us and the Aristotelian text belong; for while we owe them indispensable benefits, they can also be responsible for egregious errors, like the removal by both the Oxford and Budé editors of "gennōmenon" (generating) from the text of *On Heaven* 305a17, where its presence is attested by the best manuscript.

Instead, I want to raise in conclusion a not entirely unrelated question. Given the limitations which, as he has intimated, circumscribe any genuine scientific endeavor, including of course his own, how could Aristotle even have anticipated for the latter any sort of completion? (Cf.

Meteorologica 339a8–9.) Or is it those very limitations that may make this in a way possible? For if the cause of consciousness, as of the context in which it arises, is ultimately unknowable, and if it is consciousness itself, as sense perception to begin with, which makes of that context a world, a world of things (ourselves included), then perhaps it is only in this way that there can be a world—and therewith any intelligibility—at all. The world, as it is primarily given to us, would thus be the sum of what is truly real. And Aristotle's natural science, which is first and last a science of the phenomena (*On Heaven* 306a9–17), would be so with the understanding that the "phenomena" are the "substance."

Index